# Sexualities
# and
# Society

# Sexualities and Society

## A Reader

*Edited by*

# Jeffrey Weeks,
# Janet Holland,
*and*
# Matthew Waites

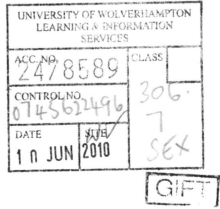

polity

Copyright © editorial matter and organization Jeffrey Weeks, Janet Holland and Matthew Waites 2003

First published in 2003 by Polity Press in association with Blackwell Publishing Ltd

*Editorial office*:
Polity Press
65 Bridge Street
Cambridge CB2 1UR, UK

*Marketing and production*:
Blackwell Publishing Ltd
108 Cowley Road
Oxford OX4 1JF, UK

*Distributed in the USA by*
Blackwell Publishing Inc.
350 Main Street
Malden, MA 02148, USA

ISBN 0-7456-2248-8
ISBN 0-7456-2249-6 (pbk)

A catalogue record for this book is available from the British Library and has been applied for from the Library of Congress.

Typeset in 10.5 on 12 pt Times New Roman
by Kolam Information Services Pvt Ltd., Pondicherry, India
Printed in Great Britain by TJ International, Padstow, Cornwall.

This book is printed on acid-free paper.

# Contents

# The Contributors

**M. Jacqui Alexander** is Fuller-Maathai Associate Professor of Gender and Women's Studies in the Department of Gender and Women's Studies at Connecticut College, Connecticut, USA. Her research interests include transnational feminism, post-coloniality and the state, particularly in relation to the history and political economy of the Caribbean.

**Dennis Altman** is Professor of Politics in the School of Social Sciences at La Trobe University, Melbourne, Australia. His current research interests centre on the relationships between globalization, sexuality and AIDS, and he is currently President of the AIDS Society of Asia and the Pacific.

**Henning Bech** is Associate Professor in the Department of Sociology at the University of Copenhagen in Denmark. His research interests are in urban life, gender, sexuality, media, history and social and cultural theory.

**Chetan Bhatt** is Senior Lecturer in the Department of Sociology at Goldsmiths' College, University of London, UK. His research interests are in the areas of ethnicity, nationalism, social theory and philosophy.

**R. W. Connell** is Professor of Education at the University of Sydney, Australia. His current research concerns intellectuals and globalization, gender equity, class in secondary education, and business masculinities.

**Gillian A. Dunne** is Senior Lecturer in the Department of Sociology at the University of Plymouth, UK. Her research interests are in non-heterosexual experiences of gender, work and family life. Her recent work includes a study of gay fatherhood, and a study on young lesbian, gay and bisexual people.

**Harriet Evans** is Reader in Asian Studies in the Centre for the Study of Democracy at the University of Westminster, London, UK. Her current work is on the formation of gender subjectivities through mother–daughter relationships in rural and urban China, and on HIV / AIDS in China.

**Anthony Giddens** is Director of the London School of Economics and Political Science in London, UK. Among his recent books is *The Third Way* (Polity, 1998).

**Janet Holland** is Professor of Social Research and Director of the Social Sciences Research Centre in the Faculty of Humanities and Social Science at South Bank University, London, UK. Her research interests include sexuality, young people, gender, education and feminist theory and methodology.

**Stevi Jackson** is Professor of Women's Studies and Director of the Centre for Women's Studies at the University of York, UK. Her research interests are in feminist theory, especially theories of gender and sexuality; the sociology of the body; and the sociology of childhood.

**Lynn Jamieson** is Co-Director of the Centre for Research on Families and Relationships and Reader in the Department of Sociology, University of Edinburgh, UK. Among her research interests are personal relationships and social change, intimacy, commitment, identity, sexual offences, childhood, youth and oral history.

**Mark Johnson** is Senior Lecturer in Social Anthropology at the University of Hull, UK. His research interests include gender and sexual diversity, the body, landscape and heritage.

**Lois McNay** is Reader in Politics and Fellow of Somerville College at the University of Oxford, UK. Her current work is on the idea of intersubjectivity in feminist and social theory.

**Julia O'Connell Davidson** is Professor of Sociology in the School of Sociology and Social Policy at the University of Nottingham, UK. Her current research interests are in prostitution, 'trafficking' and migration, and the commercial and sexual exploitation of children.

**Rosalind Petchesky** is Distinguished Professor in the Department of Political Science at Hunter College of the City University of New York, USA. Her current research and writing focuses on the disjunctions between global capitalism and health, human rights and gender equality.

**Oliver Phillips** is Senior Lecturer in the School of Law at the University of Westminster, London, UK. His current research focuses on the contingency of rights on status (defined in relation to sexuality, health and identity), and hence the tensions between intellectual property rights and the right of access to healthcare.

**Ken Plummer** is Professor of Sociology at the University of Essex, UK. He has been editor of the journal *Sexualities* (published by Sage) since its launch in 1998.

**Caroline Ramazanoglu** was formerly Reader in Sociology at Goldsmiths' College, University of London, UK. Her research interests include gender, sexuality, ethnicity, feminist theory and methodology.

**Lynne Segal** is Professor of Psychology and Gender Studies at Birkbeck College, London University, UK. She has written widely on gender issues and feminist theory.

**Tom Shakespeare** is Senior Research Associate of the Department of Sociology at the University of Newcastle, UK. He has continuing research interests in disability and sexuality, and has also increasingly become involved in promoting research and debate on the social and ethical aspects of genetics.

**Sue Sharpe** is Research Fellow in the Social Science Research Unit, Institute of Education, University of London, UK. Her main interests are young people and gender, family life and relationships, and social aspects of men's health.

**William Simon** (1930–2000) was one of the most influential sociologists of sexuality of the twentieth century. His work with John Gagnon at the Kinsey Institute for Sex Research in the late 1960s, culminating in the publication of their book *Sexual Conduct* (1973), made him one of the first social scientists to question the biologism and naturalism that pervaded much existing sex research. He was Professor of Sociology at the University of Houston, Texas, USA, until he died of cancer on 21 July 2000.

**Arlene Stein** is Associate Professor in the Department of Sociology, Rutgers University, New Jersey, USA. Her current research interests are in the clash between fundamentalism and pluralism, particularly in relation to sexuality, in the American and international contexts.

**Merl Storr** is Senior Lecturer in Sociology in the School of Social Sciences at the University of East London, UK. Her current research project is an ethnographic study of Ann Summers parties – exploring a concrete example of the relationship between the sexual and the economic.

**Rachel Thomson** is Senior Research Fellow in the Social Sciences Research Centre in the Faculty of Humanities and Social Science, South Bank University, London, UK. Her current research interests are in young people, values and identities, gender and sexuality.

**Randolph Trumbach** is Professor of History at Baruch College and the Graduate Center, City University of New York, USA. He is currently working on the history of love in the modern world – love domesticated and libertine, heterosexual and homosexual, human and divine.

**Matthew Waites** is Lecturer in Sociology in the School of Social Science and Law at Sheffield Hallam University, UK. He has published book chapters and journal articles on historical and contemporary debates over age of consent legislation in the UK and on lesbian, gay and bisexual struggles in British politics. His current research is examining the Home Office Review of Sex Offences in the UK, focusing on the legal framework regulating young people's sexual behaviour.

**Jeffrey Weeks** is Professor of Sociology and Dean of the Faculty of Humanities and Social Science at South Bank University, London, UK. He is the author of numerous articles and books on the history and social organization of sexuality and intimate relationships.

# Preface and Acknowledgements

To understand society we need to understand sexuality. Growing recognition of this has led to the development of a new, rich literature on the relationship between sexualities and society.

In this volume we offer some of the best of recent scholarship on human sexualities, from a range of disciplines. Whatever their starting point, all the articles published here focus on the complex and rapidly changing implications of the dense interconnections between the social and the sexual. Contemporary sexualities, we argue, are made in and through societies. In order to understand the force of the erotic in the contemporary imagination, we need to explore the historical, political, economic and cultural factors that shape it. We believe that the selection of articles in this book will provide a valuable and thought-provoking overview of what has become one of the key debates in contemporary social science.

In editing this book we have incurred many debts. We would like to thank all our colleagues at South Bank University and beyond who have provided intellectual, moral or practical support.

In particular we would like to thank past and present members of the Sexualities, Identities and Values research grouping in the Faculty of Humanities and Social Science, for their engagement with us in debates over sexualities, and for their assistance in suggesting possible authors and/or articles and chapters for inclusion in the book: Pam Alldred, Clare Farquhar, Rayah Feldman, Philip Gatter, Brian Heaphy, Paula Reavey and Rachel Thomson. We would also like to thank participants in the Sexualities, Identities and Values monthly seminar series, which has provided us with a regular forum for engagement with new research on sexualities.

We owe many thanks, as ever, to Donna Thompson, who provided key administrative support at a crucial time. We would also like to thank our editors at Polity for commissioning the book in the first place, and then for their patience and support in waiting for it. Thanks are also due to the anonymous reviewers who gave valuable supportive advice about the shape of the book. We absolve them of course from any responsibility for the final product.

Our warmest thanks must go to all the contributors to this volume, who have patiently endured our editorial queries and have given solid support for the project. We must also thank the original publishers for their kind permission to publish the material here.

We owe a number of personal debts:

Jeffrey Weeks gives particular thanks to Micky Burbidge for his continuing friendship; and to Mark McNestry for his endless patience and love as yet more weekends were consumed by writing.

Janet Holland thanks all her friends and colleagues in the Social Sciences Research Centre and, as ever, Robert Albury.

Matthew Waites thanks his parents, Neville and Lilian Waites, for providing him with inspiring examples of commitment to education and academic integrity, equality and social justice. Thanks also to friends and colleagues at South Bank University, particularly those in the Social Sciences Research Centre. Special thanks to Brian Heaphy for academic and political engagement throughout the period of the book's development.

Jeffrey Weeks, Janet Holland and Matthew Waites

# Copyright Acknowledgements

The editors and Polity gratefully acknowledge the authors and publishers concerned for granting permission to reprint edited excerpts from the following copyright material:

## Part I   Social and Historical Approaches to Sexualities

Randolph Trumbach, Extramarital relations and gender history, chapter 1 in *Sex and the Gender Revolution, Volume One: Heterosexuality and the Third Gender in Enlightenment London* (University of Chicago Press, Chicago and London, 1998), pp. 3–22, 431–4. Reprinted by permission of the University of Chicago.

William Simon, The postmodernization of sex, chapter 1 in *Postmodern Sexualities* (Routledge, London and New York, 1996), pp. 18–39. Reprinted by permission of Routledge.

Ken Plummer, Intimate citizenship and the culture of sexual story telling, in *Sexual Cultures: Communities, Values and Intimacy*, ed. J. Weeks and J. Holland (Macmillan, London, 1996), pp. 34–52. Reprinted by permission of Palgrave Publishers Ltd.

## Part II   The Gender of Sexuality

R. W. Connell, The big picture: masculinities in recent world history, *Theory and Society*, 22 (1993), pp. 597–623. Reprinted by permission of Kluwer Academic Publishers.

Gillian A. Dunne, A passion for 'sameness'? sexuality and gender accountability, chapter 5 in *The New Family?*, ed. Elizabeth B. Silva and Carol Smart (Sage, London, 1999), pp. 66–82. Reprinted by permission of Sage Publications Ltd.

Stevi Jackson, Heterosexuality, heteronormativity and gender hierarchy: some reflections on recent debates, chapter 12 in *Heterosexuality in Question* (Sage, London, 1999), pp. 159–85. Reprinted by permission of Sage Publications Ltd.

Janet Holland, Caroline Ramazanoglu, Sue Sharpe and Rachel Thomson, When bodies come together: power, control and desire, chapter 6 in *The Male in the Head* (Tufnell Press, London, 1998), pp. 106–28. Reprinted by permission of the Tufnell Press (<www.tufnellpress.co.uk>).

Lynne Segal, Only the literal: the contradictions of anti-pornography feminism, *Sexualities*, 1(1), (1998), pp. 43–62. Reprinted by permission of Sage Publications Ltd.

Mark Johnson, Anomalous bodies: transgenderings and cultural transformations, chapter 7 in *Beauty and Power: Transgendering and Cultural Transformation in the Southern Philippines* (Berg, Oxford and New York, 1997), pp. 215–39. Reprinted by permission of Berg Publishers.

## Part III  Sexual Identities

Jeffrey Weeks, Necessary fictions: sexual identities and the politics of diversity, chapter 3 in *Invented Moralities: Sexual Values in an Age of Uncertainty* (Cambridge, Polity, 1995), pp. 82–101. Reprinted by permission of Polity Press (UK rights) and Columbia University Press (world rights).

Arlene Stein, Becoming lesbian: identity work and the performance of sexuality, chapter 3 in *Sex and Sensibility: Stories of a Lesbian Generation* (University of California Press, London, 1997), pp. 65–90, 220–2. Reprinted by permission of the Regents of the University of California and the University of California Press.

Tom Shakespeare, 'I haven't seen that in the Kama Sutra': the sexual stories of disabled people. Commissioned article, printed by permission of Tom Shakespeare.

Merl Storr, Postmodern bisexuality, *Sexualities*, 2(3), (1999), pp. 309–25. Reprinted by permission of Sage Publications Ltd.

Oliver Phillips, Zimbabwean law and the production of a white man's disease, *Social and Legal Studies*, 6 (1997), pp. 471–91. Reprinted by permission of Sage Publications Ltd.

M. Jacqui Alexander, Not just (any)body can be a citizen: the politics of law, sexuality and postcoloniality in Trinidad and Tobago and the Bahamas, *Feminist Review*, 48 (1994), 5–23. Reprinted by permission of M. Jacqui Alexander.

## Part IV   Globalization, Power and Resistance

Dennis Altman, Globalization, political economy, and HIV / AIDS, *Theory and Society*, 28 (1999), pp. 559–84. Reprinted by permission of Kluwer Academic Publishers.

Chetan Bhatt, The land, the blood and the passion: the Hindu far-right, chapter 6 in *Liberation and Purity: Race, New Religious Movements and the Ethics of Postmodernity* (University College London Press, London, 1997), pp. 179–231, 279. Reprinted by permission of University College London Press.

Julia O'Connell Davidson, Power, consent and freedom, chapter 1 in *Prostitution, Power and Freedom* (Polity, Cambridge, 1998), pp. 15–41. Reprinted by permission of Polity Press.

Harriet Evans, Sex and the open market, chapter 7 in *Women and Sexuality in China: Female Sexuality and Gender Since 1949* (Continuum, New York, 1997), pp. 167–88, 233–5. Reprinted by permission of the Continuum International Publishing Group (world rights) and Polity Press (UK rights).

Rosalind Petchesky, Introduction, in *Negotiating Reproductive Rights: Women's Perspectives across Countries and Cultures*, ed. Rosalind Petchesky and Karen Judd (Zed Books, London, 1998), pp. 1–30. Reprinted by permission of Zed Books Ltd.

## Part V   Sexual Values and Life Experiments

Lois McNay, Aesthetics as ethics, chapter 4 in *Foucault: A Critical Introduction*, (Polity, Cambridge, 1994), pp. 133–63, 182–5. Reprinted by permission of Polity Press (UK rights) and the Continuum International Publishing Group (world rights).

Anthony Giddens, Intimacy as democracy, chapter 10 in *The Transformation of Intimacy: Sexuality, Love and Eroticism in Modern Societies* (Polity, Cambridge, 1992), pp. 184–204. Reprinted by permission of Stanford University Press (US, Can, Phil rights) and Polity (all other territories).

Lynn Jamieson, The couple: intimate and equal?, chapter 6 in *Intimacy: Personal Relationships in Modern Societies* (Polity, Cambridge, 1998), pp. 136–57, 179–80. Reprinted by permission of Polity Press.

Henning Bech, The disappearance of the modern homosexual, chapter 6 in *When Men Meet: Homosexuality and Modernity* (Polity, Cambridge, 1997), pp. 194–217, 269–74. Reprinted by permission of Polity Press.

\*\*\*

Every effort has been made to trace all copyright holders, but if any have been inadvertently overlooked the publishers will be pleased to make the necessary arrangement at the first opportunity.

# Publisher's Note

An ellipsis [...] has been used whenever material from the original has been omitted. Where a paragraph or more has been excluded, a line space appears above and below [...].

In some cases, changes have been made to the original text by the authors, to update the articles. Otherwise, apart from the omission of material discussed above, each chapter has been presented as it was originally published. The decision to do this has necessarily entailed inconsistencies of style and spelling between the chapters.

# Introduction:
# Understanding Sexualities and Society

*Jeffrey Weeks, Janet Holland and Matthew Waites*

### *Sexualities and society*

Over the past generation there has been a revolution in our understanding of sexualities in society. From being on the periphery of historical and social scientific studies, sexuality has increasingly come to be seen as close to the heart of our understanding of contemporary societies. Since the early 1970s there has been an explosion of new sexual knowledges, including academic research, which has done more than simply explore an uncharted continent – it has reshaped the ways in which sexuality is understood. These new or enhanced knowledges of sexuality have produced challenging work from a wide range of scholars, especially those who came to maturity in the 1970s and 1980s and who were often deeply influenced by the impact of feminism, lesbian and gay politics and other sexual movements. This in turn has brought about a significant reorientation of thinking about the past and the present on the part of more established scholars in social and historical studies. These shifts have been reflected in a proliferation of university courses, concerned with gender, feminist studies, sexualities, the body, and lesbian and gay studies, as well as influencing mainstream courses in disciplines across the social sciences.

The aim of this collection is to make available some of the more exciting texts from this developing field of sexual studies. We have not attempted a comprehensive survey of the development of sexual theory. This can be found elsewhere, in other collections. What we have sought to do in this volume is to demonstrate how an understanding of sexuality helps us to have a clearer understanding of the development of contemporary societies, conceived in global perspective.

*Sexualities and Society* addresses sexualities in global perspective, conceiving 'society' in the title as referring both to global society and to multiple particular societies around the world. Since the objective is to introduce a selection of contemporary ideas and perspectives which facilitate the understanding of

sexualities, the collection does not attempt to represent different cultures propor-
tionately. Social research on sexualities has developed more extensively in Western societies, and this is reflected in the substantive focus of the research presented,
in the backgrounds of the authors, and in some of the arguments advanced.
Nevertheless, we have attempted to provide a collection which will offer a blend
of empirical and theoretical content stimulating to readers worldwide.

In this introduction we set out the context for the new emphasis on sexuality in
social scientific writing. We begin with the ways in which sexuality has been
rethought over the past few generations. We follow this with a brief overview of
how contemporary writings conceptualize the significance of sexuality in contemporary societies. Finally, we provide an overview of the five main themes of the
book.

## The historical development of sexual knowledge

Many generations of writers emerging from 'modern' Western societies, associated with the Enlightenment, reason and science, have taught that sexuality is the
most natural thing about us. Sexuality has often been seen as the essence of who
and what we are. The typical approach that follows from this has been to examine *reactions to* sexuality as a fixed natural phenomenon rather than to explore
how sexuality has been *shaped by* history and culture.

The first sustained attempt to put the understanding of sexuality on a scientific
basis, by the European sexological pioneers of the late nineteenth century, in
many ways built on 'common sense' understandings. Pioneers such as the Aus-
trian psychologist Krafft-Ebing, and Havelock Ellis in Britain, attempted to
understand the 'laws of nature', just as the first generation of sociologists such
as August Comte, Max Weber and Emile Durkheim were attempting to understand the 'laws of society' (Weeks 1985). Built into their theories were naturalistic
assumptions about the overwhelming force of the male sex drive, the subordinate
and reactive character of female sexuality, and the biologically given divide
between heterosexuality and homosexuality. They looked for the biological
roots of sexual variations with a categorizing zeal, which gave rise to a host of
taxonomic distinctions, from bisexuality and fetishism through coprophilia, uro-
lagnia, sadism and masochism, to transvestism, inversion and perversion generally. They attempted to fix sexual characteristics as if they had existed through all
eternity as fundamental natural divisions, and in the process created a whole
continent of knowledge about sexuality. Many of the sexological pioneers, in
tandem with pioneering sociologists, saw themselves as the heirs of Enlightenment thought, bringing to bear scientific knowledge to understand human behaviour.

Yet in these classifying endeavours they also subtly, and perhaps unintention-
ally, began to point to the importance of understanding historical and social
variations, and therefore the culturally specific nature of sexualities. Harry
Oosterhuis's (2000) recent study of Krafft-Ebing brings the Janus-like character
of the sexologists very clearly to the fore. Krafft-Ebing's initial interest in
sexuality came from his concern to understand the sexual behaviour of the

emotionally disturbed patients he was treating, and the unorthodox behaviour on which he was asked to advise as people came before the courts for sexual misdemeanours. Originally he assumed that there was some breakdown in the physical make-up of his patients. Gradually, Krafft-Ebing came to see the importance of psychological factors, and in so doing gave birth to the psychology of sexuality, which was to influence many of his successors, not least Freud. In a growing dialogue with his clients, he came to realize the significance of their own sexual desires, however unusual, in their lives. Central among these interlocutors were self-identified 'inverts' (a category that later became associated with and then replaced by the term 'homosexual') who had a sense of who they were, and who increasingly came to believe in the validity of their own sexual needs. The case studies that Krafft-Ebing published in a succession of editions of his landmark book *Psychopathia Sexualis* demonstrate his growing dialogue with a more and more self-conscious community. In many ways he was still anxious to explore the nature of perversions as aberrations, but his tone became more empathetic, and he came to an awareness of the importance of understanding the social factors which influenced people's behaviour, not least the weight of social prejudice and hostility.

The dialogue between the biological and the anthropological and cultural can also be seen very clearly in the writings of the pioneering British sexologist Havelock Ellis, who was extremely interested in the cultural variations of sexual behaviour. Despite his belief in a basic sexual sub-structure, his wealth of historical evidence served to open up a variety of questions about the historical and the cultural. His contemporary, the anthropologist Edward Westermarck, like many who followed Ellis, was able to show the range of patterns of, for example, marriage which had given a different meaning to the body and the erotic in different cultures.

The most influential of all of this pioneering generation of writers on sexuality was Sigmund Freud. He is often misleadingly seen as the fount and origin of the twentieth-century preoccupation with the importance of sexuality, but, as he freely acknowledged himself, his knowledge of sexuality was based on the writings of Krafft-Ebing and the first generation of sexologists. Freud was, of course, famously concerned with the relationships between sexuality and 'civilization'. Though frequently criticized throughout the century for being deterministic in his emphasis on sexuality, and for attempting to impose the preoccupations of the Viennese bourgeoisie of the early twentieth-century on all cultures, Freud was sensitive to the different patterns of sexuality on a global scale. At his most subtle, Freud did manage to suggest the hazardous nature of the journey from an initial polymorphous perversity towards adult (hetero) sexuality and fixed gendered divisions (Coward 1983).

So although the pioneering sexologists began by attempting to draw knowledge of the sexual from the natural sciences, they were driven by their researches into understanding the complex and inextricable interconnections between the biological, the psychological, the social and the cultural. The anthropological evidence accumulated in the context of colonialism demonstrated a huge variety of cross-cultural patterns of attitudes towards the family, gender divisions, reproduction, and what the sexologists called the 'perversions'. Knowledge of their own societies led the sexologists to recognize the significance of historical change. Even within their own cultures there were different attitudes towards sexual behaviour – class differences, gender differences, ethnic differences, geographical variations and the like. The sexologists' awareness of social, historical and cultural differences, and their dialogue with patients, inevitably led them to question the arbitrariness of the norms of their own societies. When people adopted new categories to label themselves as fetishists, bisexuals, transvestites or homosexuals, forcefully expressing the normality of their own desires, it became difficult for sympathetic scientists to ignore the passion of people's commitment to their own sexual needs and desires. Many of the pioneers in fact became committed to progressive liberalization of the ancient taboos and laws against 'deviant' sexual behaviours. Krafft-Ebing, Ellis, Freud and, above all, Magnus Hirschfeld in Germany became committed to more liberal attitudes, often as active campaigners for 'sex reform'.

The most influential of the next generation of sexologists, the American Alfred Kinsey, exemplified the characteristic Enlightenment commitment of modern sexual science to progressive liberalization apparently founded upon objective scientific methods (Kinsey et al., 1948; 1953). He had made his reputation as an expert on the gall wasp, and ostensibly brought the same objective, detached scientific zeal he needed for the study of insect behaviour to the study of human sexual behaviour. But as recent biographers have made clear, and as was indeed apparent to his contemporaries, his writings had an inevitable political and cultural impact. His exploration of the huge variety of sexual patterns in the United States of the 1940s served to challenge the moral codes of the time. His demonstration, for example, of the widespread nature of 'homosexual' behaviours provided a stark challenge to the notion that homosexuality was the preserve of a tiny, diseased minority. If 37 per cent of Kinsey's male research sample reported some form of homosexual experience to the point of orgasm, then such assumptions surely became untenable. Furthermore, by documenting the diversity of sexual behaviours, and suggesting that 'perverse' forms existed on a continuum with 'normal' behaviour, Kinsey's work opened the door to fuller social explanations – and to cultural and political responses.

What the pioneers of sexology succeeded in doing was to put into some sort of relief the taken for granted assumptions of the Western societies from which they came. The 'social book-keeping' approach (Plummer 1975) of researchers such as Kinsey effectively demonstrated that, despite law, public opinion and rigid norms, people tended to follow their desires rather than what society told them they ought to do – even as they suffered the often painful consequences. In parallel with the new sexual science, anthropologists such as Margaret Mead, working in the 1930s and 1940s (Weeks 1985), were also able to challenge the rigidity of Western perspectives by suggesting that evidence from other cultures demonstrated other ways of organizing sexuality. In the context of increasing globalization, the colonial encounters of anthropology, and also of Western sexual science more broadly, produced new sexual categories but also contributed to destabilizing Western norms. By the mid-twentieth century, the way was prepared for more radical, social scientific understanding of the relationship between sexualities and society.

Implicit in the early sexological writings was the assumption of a tension between the domain of sexuality, which was assumed to be essentially natural, and the demands of society. The critical breakthrough in rethinking this dichotomy came with work of two social scientists who had worked with Alfred Kinsey, John Gagnon and William Simon. In a series of papers, and their book *Sexual Conduct* (1973), they posed challenging questions which contributed in turn to a radical rethinking of the significance of the sexual. They suggested that, far from being the most natural phenomenon, sexuality might actually be the most socially malleable. Instead of taking for granted an enduring tension between sex and society, they suggested that at a certain stage of its evolution society had 'invented' the significance of the sexual. Sexual conduct, they proposed, was shaped in culture, and sexual meanings arose from socio-sexual scripts, which inevitably varied in any particular culture and changed through history. Instead of society being shaped by sexuality, they argued that society shaped sexuality. These insights can in retrospect be seen as crucial to the subsequent work of Michel Foucault, whose *History of Sexuality, Volume One* (1979) is often seen misleadingly as the origin of such approaches to sexuality.

Foucault's work did indeed have a huge impact on our thinking about the sexual. His suggestion that the whole contemporary apparatus of sexuality was a historical invention had a profoundly important impact on subsequent writings, which can be seen in many of the contributions to this book. But it should now also be clear that he was building on new forms of sexual knowledge already in development. These were being heavily influenced by radical social movements, including second-wave feminism and the gay liberation movement which emerged from the late 1960s. The work of young scholars inspired by these movements began to develop critical social scientific approaches to sexuality. Already by the mid-1970s feminists were questioning the basic categories of sexuality (Radicalesbians 1970; Firestone 1971; Millett 1971), and a number of pioneering lesbian and gay historians were interrogating the fixity of the heterosexual – homosexual dichotomy to show that this dichotomy had a relatively recent history (Altman 1971; Smith-Rosenberg 1985; Katz 1976; Trumbach 1977; Weeks 1977). If the homosexual identities we took for granted were indeed a historical construction, then so could the norm of heterosexuality be seen as something that was invented (Katz 1995). In a similar way, the sharp distinction that some of the pioneering sexologist writers on sexuality had drawn between 'civilized' and 'uncivilized' patterns of behaviour could also be challenged. Racialized Western assumptions about the closer to nature, 'primitive' aspects of other societies could now be seen in the burgeoning post-colonial literature as reflecting the way in which both Western and non-Western behaviours had been constructed in the imperial encounters of the nineteenth and twentieth centuries.

In other words, sexuality, far from being the domain of the given, the natural, the biological, was pre-eminently social, and moreover shaped in relations of power. Traditional male power over women constructed female sexuality as subordinate. The power of the heterosexual norm, which itself was historically specific, was central to the construction of the sexual 'other', of homosexuality. The racist and orientalist ideologies which emerged in the context of Western imperialism and colonialism had constructed non-Western peoples and sexualities as fundamentally inferior and lower down the evolutionary scale. In his introductory volume to *The History of Sexuality*, Foucault (1979) hinted at all these elements, and provided a research agenda, which has been enormously creative. But work was already going on, and many other influences were already at play, from the post-Kinsey traditions of sexological research, and the new history influenced by the new social movements, to a radical sociology, and subsequently new critical and post-structuralist approaches within cultural studies and the humanities.

## The social significance of sexuality

The most significant effect of the new thinking about sexuality is the displacement of the assumed conflict between the 'sexual instinct' and society. Gagnon and Simon (1973) called this the 'drive reduction' model, and it is still embedded in common sense thinking about sexuality. The emphasis on the social and historical shaping of sexuality, however, puts the emphasis on the significance of complex social forces. This is revealed in a significant shift in the metaphorical discussion of sexuality. The drive reduction model assumes a pattern of 'repression'/'release' in relationship to sexual desires. The new approaches give rise to metaphors suggesting the 'invention', the 'making', or the 'construction' of sexualities.

This in turn underlines an emphasis on understanding the distinctive characteristics of different sexual cultures, shaped by history, by relations of power, and by differentiated traditions even within one particular society. It has to be recognized, especially, that discussion of the significance of sexuality in non-Western societies still carries with it problematic assumptions about what sexuality is which were born deep in the heartlands of the colonizing Western powers. To understand sexual cultures one has to distinguish between the erotic possibilities of the body, which are fairly constant across cultures, and the importance given, for example, to reproduction, interpersonal relationships, or the relationships between men and women. To understand sexuality today we need to understand the diverse contexts in which meanings are attributed to intimacy and eroticism, and the complex social interactions which shape the erotic cultures of different societies.

But recognition of the diversity of sexual forms should not give rise to an easy pluralism, which assumes their happy coexistence. Sexualities are hierarchically organized, with some forms being dominant while others are subordinate and marginalized, and are shaped by complex relations of power. The most familiar of these relate to gender, class, age, race and ethnicity. In recent years there has also been an increasing recognition that sexualities have been organized into institutionalized forms of heterosexuality, leading to critiques of heteronormativity. These formations intersect with a host of other factors, high among which are religion and the traditional patterns of life that shape cultures.

Sexualities are organized and institutionalized in different ways, including the systematic patterning of forms of subjectivity. A crucial aspect of this is the way we organize our sense of self around our sexual desires. The extent to which sexuality is central to people's sense of self is itself historically specific, as the first volume of Michel Foucault's *The History of Sexuality* powerfully suggested (Foucault 1979). Foucault argued that sex became increasingly central to under-standings of the self and the construction of a sense of being in modern Western societies from the seventeenth century onwards. The most clear-cut example of this is in the emergence of distinctive homosexual identities, beginning from the seventeenth century but developing into recognizably modern forms from the late nineteenth and early twentieth centuries (Weeks 2000).

In a culture in which a particular form of sexuality was either denied or punished, it was inevitable that people organized their sense of self around their sexuality in various forms of resistance – through what Foucault described as a 'reverse discourse'. Historians have increasingly sought to understand the dynamics of push and pull, definition and self-definition, which have shaped the emergence of non-orthodox sexual identities. It is significant that, in the sexo-logical writings of the late nineteenth century, the terms referring to same-sex behaviour emerged before the language of heterosexuality. It was those with sexual desires which were socially stigmatized and regarded as deviant who needed to assert their sense of self in relation to sexuality by claiming as their own the perverse sexological categories made available to them (Oosterhuis 2000). Of course, as societies have developed complex responses to sexual diver-sity and nonconformity over the last hundred years, these identities have them-selves become complex and overlapping, and in some instances have become focal points for challenges to the very notion of fixed sexual identity.

The final point to emphasize is that the recognition of the role of the social in constituting what we regard as the sexual provides a focus for political and cultural confrontations. The emergence of an explicit and increasingly main-stream political discourse around sexuality since the 1960s is no accident. It is a product of the disruption of settled patterns of sexual life under the impact of profound social change on a global scale. Traditionalists aspire in vain to a restoration of stability. New voices articulate the aspiration for recognition of new identities and new ways of being. A cacophany of sexual narratives, of old and new 'sexual stories' (Plummer 1995), compete to be heard. And an apparent paradox emerges. New sexual subjects seek ever more the right to privacy in their sexual choices, and yet engage in a proliferating public discussion of their needs and desires, their rights and responsibilities. The growing 'sequestration' or privatization of sexual life that Giddens (1991) noted as a characteristic of modern Western erotic experience has been balanced by an explosion of dis-courses about sexuality, which have profoundly redefined what we understand as sexuality on a global scale.

## Outline of the book

The *social* understanding of sexualities we have outlined above has shaped our selection of texts, which have been chosen to illustrate the best of recent scholar-ship. The book is organized into five sections, the titles of which are intended to be suggestive and promote reflection on important shared themes among the articles.

The opening section, 'Social and Historical Approaches to Sexualities', is intended to introduce sexualities in historical and sociological perspective, and to raise questions about how we gain knowledge about sexualities. 'The Gender of Sexuality' places the analytical category of gender centre-stage, because we believe it has been so central to the social organization of sexualities – which is not to argue that other categories do not also play a vital role. 'Sexual Identities' brings to the foreground the idea of 'identity' which has been so important in many recent debates over sexuality. 'Globalization, Power and Resistance' explores the impact of transnational social forces and processes of globalization, examining various economic and cultural dynamics. Finally, 'Sexual Values and Life Experiments' concludes the volume by exploring recent debates over the extent to which new forms of subjectivity and agency associated with late modernity are emerging to transform intimate life. Each of the sections, and the articles they contain, are described in greater detail in the introductions to each section.

We are aware that the selections could have been organized in a variety of other ways. Readers should approach the text in the knowledge that most of the articles touch upon the themes of several sections, and that there are several important cross-cutting themes. For example, while we have chosen to highlight the issue of gender in section 2, we could also have devoted sections to other themes closely related to social divisions and inequalities, such as class or race and ethnicity. Our decision reflects a particular desire to highlight the ways in which gender and sexualities are intertwined, especially in dominant forms of heterosexuality. But articles throughout the reader, such as those by Johnson, Phillips, Alexander and Bhatt, demonstrate the ways in which race and ethnicity, and the related issue of the impact of colonialism, also systematically structure sexual hierarchies. Similarly, a variety of authors draw attention to the impact of economic forces, the effects of capitalism, the division of labour and the consequences of poverty. These include Dunne, Phillips, Alexander, Altman, O'Connell Davidson, Evans, Petchesky and Jamieson.

The significance of debates over postmodernism, and the concepts of modernity and postmodernity, are foregrounded in our introduction, and are central in the first and last sections of the book. They are a particular concern of articles by Simon, Plummer, Storr, Giddens and Bech. The body is another cross-cutting issue, discussed in articles such as those by Holland et al., Johnson, Shakespeare, Phillips, Alexander, Bhatt and Petchesky.

One important theme which does not appear in the title of any article is the idea of 'queer', and the concepts of 'queer theory' and 'queer politics'. However, these concepts and associated bodies of theoretical work are clearly introduced and discussed at the beginning of the essay by Stevi Jackson. They are subsequently referred to and discussed in a number of articles throughout the volume. In particular, Merl Storr's essay explicitly engages with queer theory and its relationship to postmodernism, postmodernity and bisexuality. Henning Bech's final chapter situates his analysis of sexual transformations in late modernity in relation to the distinctive character of American queer theory, thus leaving the volume as a whole engaged in an ongoing dialogue with queer ideas. Our decision not to include an article addressing queer theory as its central theme reflects our sympathy with Jackson's desire to problematize the category and question queer theory's distinctiveness from earlier theoretical positions. But an explicit or implicit engagement with contemporary work claiming the label 'queer theory' is evident in many of the articles which comprise the book's five sections.

In conclusion: we realize that in a vast and ever-growing literature our specific choices of articles for inclusion in this reader may cause debate. But we believe that the articles presented here represent a strong selection of current writings on sexuality, well-suited to the task of introducing key themes, concepts and controversies. We trust that they will engage the reader fully. Above all, we hope and expect that they will stimulate further reading and research, in order to generate clearer understandings of the complex and ever-changing interactions between sexualities and society.

## References

Altman, D. 1971: *Homosexual: Oppression and Liberation*. London: Allen Lane.

Coward, R. 1983: *Patriarchal Precedence: Sexuality and Social Relations*. London, Boston, Melbourne and Henley: Routledge & Kegan Paul.

Firestone, S. 1971: *The Dialectic of Sex*. London: Cape.

Foucault, M. 1979: *The History of Sexuality, Volume 1: An Introduction*. London: Allen Lane.

Gagnon, J. H. and Simon, W. 1973: *Sexual Conduct: the Social Sources of Human Sexuality*. London: Hutchinson.

Giddens, A. 1991: *Modernity and Self-Identity: Self and Society in the Late Modern Age*. Cambridge: Polity.

Katz, J. 1976: *Gay American History: Lesbians and Gay Men in the USA*. New York: Thomas Y. Crowell.

Katz, J. 1995: *The Invention of Heterosexuality*. New York: NAL / Dutton.

Kinsey, A., Pomeroy, W. B. and Martin, C. 1948: *Sexual Behaviour in the Human Male*. Philadelphia: W. B. Saunders.

Kinsey, A., Pomeroy, W. B., Martin, C. and Gebhard, P. 1953: *Sexual Behaviour in the Human Female*. Philadelphia and London: W. B. Saunders.

Millett, K. 1971: *Sexual Politics*. London: Hart-Davis.

Oosterhuis, H. 2000: *Step Children of Nature: Krafft-Ebing, Psychiatry, and the Making of Sexual Identity*. Chicago and London: University of Chicago Press.

Plummer, K. 1975: *Sexual Stigma: An Interactionist Account*. London: Routledge & Kegan Paul.

Plummer, K. 1995: *Telling Sexual Stories: Power, Change and Social Worlds*. London: Routledge.

Radicalesbians 1970: The woman-identified woman. In M. Blasius and S. Phelan (eds) 1997: *We are Everywhere: A Historical Sourcebook of Gay and Lesbian Politics*, London: Routledge.

Smith-Rosenberg, C. 1985: The female world of love and ritual. In C. Smith-Rosenberg, *Disorderly Conduct: Visions of Gender in Victorian America*, New York and Oxford: Oxford University Press.

Trumbach, R. 1977: London's sodomites: homosexual behaviour and Western culture in the 18th century. *Journal of Social History*, fall.

Weeks, J. 1977: *Coming Out: Homosexual Politics in Britain, from the 19th Century to the Present.* London: Quartet Books.
Weeks, J. 1985: *Sexuality and its Discontents: Myths, Meanings and Modern Sexualities.* London: Routledge & Kegan Paul.
Weeks, J. 2000: *Making Sexual History.* Cambridge: Polity.

# Part I

# Social and Historical Approaches to Sexualities

A historical perspective is vital in allowing us to perceive the development of attitudes to sexuality, in particular social contexts. The first section of the book provides this perspective in order to situate the articles in subsequent sections, and contains three articles which examine successive historical periods. But the articles can simultaneously be seen as raising three central questions in the study of sexualities which underlie the concerns of this book: How is sexuality socially organized? How do we research sexuality? And how do the ways in which sexuality is narrated and represented shape the ways in which it is experienced?

One central theme raised by these three articles is the relationship of transformations in sexual life to broader social transformations associated with the concept of modernity. Understandings of modernity are highly contested, and an over-reliance on the concept can be associated with teleological understandings of social progress, which assume a linear pattern of social development. Nevertheless it remains a crucial concept for understanding sexual transformations, and the articles here suggest how sexualities have been affected by the emergence of specifically modern forms of society, as well as by tendencies associated with more recent shifts giving rise to notions of late or postmodernity. The concepts of late modernity and postmodernity are subject to continuing debate (Giddens 1991; Bauman 1992), but there are significant commonalities between the ways in which these concepts characterize contemporary societies, and many social theorists now endorse the view that modernity either has been transcended or has shifted significantly in character.

The first article, by Randolph Trumbach, dramatically introduces the idea that understandings of gender and sexual identity are socially and historically specific. Employing comparisons between cultures worldwide, Trumbach describes the emergence since the eighteenth century of a 'new sexual system' in specifically modern and Western societies, which has subsequently come to have a profound influence on many other sexual cultures. He argues that the early eighteenth century in Europe saw the appearance of a third gender, and henceforth there were men, women and sodomites, the last of these representing the emergence of a distinctive minority, later labelled homosexual. This was associated with the emergence of new heterosexual roles, which gave rise to patterns of extra-marital sex that endured until the middle of the twentieth century. Distinctive forms of prostitution, illegitimacy and violence in marriage were associated with these developments. For much of the period, female sexual lives were organized through forms of family life, which varied by social class. Trumbach argues that working-class life focused on extended families based on patriarchal dominance, while among the upper classes less oppressive patterns of relationships, organized around romantic courtship and tender care of children, began to emerge. This organization of gender and sexuality continued until fundamentally disrupted by the changes that gathered pace after the mid-twentieth century. From this period, with shifts towards less hierarchical relationships between men and women across the class divides, it became possible for the gender order to be radically challenged.

William Simon, one of the founders of what became known as the social constructionist approach to sexuality, chronicles the development of sex research in the twentieth century. In doing so he examines the ways sexual knowledges were formulated. A number of conceptual questions are raised about how sexuality is researched, ranging from questions of methods and methodology to issues of politics, ethics and the philosophy of social science. These are issues which are vital to consider when interpreting articles throughout *Sexualities and Society*.

Simon organizes his article around the notions of the modernization and postmodernization of sexuality. His concern is less with the broad sweep of modernity, and more with the effects of the modernism of the twentieth century upon sex research. He argues that the social nature of the sexual order was disguised for most of the period of modernization by the naturalizing zeal of the theorists of sexuality, as sexual science made strenuous efforts to dehistoricize the erotic. It dissolved the multiple meanings of sexuality into universal identities, which reaffirmed pre-given distinctions. As a result, the controversial and implicitly challenging work of the modernizers of sex could be presented as objective and factual, presenting the 'truth' of sexualities. Postmodernization, on the other hand, can be seen as denaturalization, recognizing the plurality of sexualities and the role of human beings in producing sexual categories. Meanings change over time as the socio-cultural context changes. Today it becomes not only possible but also necessary to talk of *homosexualities* or *heterosexualities*, and the sexual is seen not as a given but as problematic. Sexual forms are not the realization of a 'biological mandate'. Instead sexualities have to been seen as the result of a process of construction and negotiation, shifting over time and within the life cycle.

Ken Plummer's article is concerned with the way we tell stories about sexuality and live within specific sexual narratives (see also Plummer 1995). Plummer's article can be seen as representing a growth of interest in the constitutive role of culture in recent work on sexuality, and more particularly growing attention to the role of narratives and/or discourses in shaping understandings and experiences of sexuality. Much of this work has been influenced by post-structuralism, though Plummer's work itself develops from the symbolic interactionist tradition.

Plummer is also concerned with modernity, but now concentrating on the important role of modernist and 'late modern' stories or narratives in constructing the forms and patterns of sexual life. Humans are story-telling beings, and through stories we create our world. There has been a proliferation of sexual stories since the eighteenth century, but only in the late twentieth century have these stories gained a mass audience. The sexual stories we tell are deeply implicated in moral and political change, and shifting stories of self and identity carry the potential for radical transformations of the social order. Over the past generation we have seen a change in the forms and organization of the stories we tell each other, and late modern stories reveal and create a multiplicity of new projects, new constituencies, new possibilities for the future. These are stories of human life chances, of emotional and sexual democracy, of pluralistic forms of sexual life, opening the way for a new culture of intimacy and what Plummer describes as 'intimate citizenship'.

## References

Bauman, Z. 1992: *Intimations of Postmodernity*. London: Routledge.

Giddens, A. 1991: *Modernity and Self-Identity: Self and Society in the Late Modern Age*. Cambridge: Polity.

Plummer, K. 1995: *Telling Sexual Stories: Power, Change and Social Worlds*. London: Routledge.

# 1

# Sex and the Gender Revolution

*Randolph Trumbach*

Around 1700 in northwestern Europe, in England, France, and the Dutch Republic, there appeared a minority of adult men whose sexual desires were directed exclusively toward adult and adolescent males. These men could be identified by what seemed to their contemporaries to be effeminate behavior in speech, movement, and dress. They had not, however, entirely transformed themselves into women but instead combined into a third gender selected aspects of the behavior of the majority of men and women. Since a comparable minority of masculinized women who exclusively desired other women did not appear until the 1770s, it is therefore the case that for most of the eighteenth century there existed in northern Europe what might be described as a system of three genders composed of men, women, and sodomites.

[...]

In the eighteenth century these new meanings and the reorganization of long-standing forms of sexual behavior produced among men (but not among women) what the late nineteenth century described as a heterosexual majority and a homosexual minority. The terms *heterosexual* and *homosexual* were nineteenth-century inventions. But the behavioral patterns they described came into existence among men in the first generation of the eighteenth century. It is difficult to understand that homosexuality and heterosexuality are conditions that were socially constructed first for men at a specific moment in time and then for women because the development of the late-nineteenth-century descriptions over the last hundred years has tended to leave most Westerners with the conviction that a heterosexual majority and a homosexual minority are biological constants that must have been present in all times and places. The heterosexuality of the majority is usually taken for granted – how can the human race otherwise have continued to exist? The homosexuality of the minority has been more difficult to understand or to accept. For this very reason, a brief analysis of the differences in Western homosexual behavior before and after 1700 will clarify what it means to say that an exclusive male heterosexual majority first appeared in Western societies in the early eighteenth century.

To understand the nature of homosexual acts in European society before 1700, one begins from the presumption increasingly made by historians, sociologists, and anthropologists that homosexual behavior in all human societies has been organized by differences either in age or in gender. From this it is apparent that the postmodernist presumption that sexual forms are unlimited cannot be true. In some societies like ancient Greece or Renaissance Italy sexual behavior was structured by differences in age, and adult men had sexual relations both with women and with adolescent males who were sexually passive. In other societies like those of traditional South Asia the majority of both adult and adolescent males had relations both with women and with a minority of passive adult men who had been socialized into a lifelong third-gender role that combined elements of male and female behavior. This fundamental distinction is sometimes difficult for modern Western scholars to see since in their society any experience of homosexual desire assigns an individual to a decided minority without reference to the age or gender of the person desired. From this practice of their own societies Western scholars presume the presence in all times and places of an effeminate minority of males exclusively interested in other males and use this presumption to misinterpret the evidence for homosexual behavior in the ancient Mediterranean world and in European societies before 1700.[1]

This distinction between homosexual behavior organized by differences in either age or gender therefore reorients the historical quest into a more fruitful path and makes it possible to understand the nature of the change that occurred in Europe around 1700. In European society before 1700 probably most males felt desire for both males and females. Adult men expressed this by having sexual relations with adolescent males and with women. This pattern of behavior was of very long standing in Western societies. It had appeared in ancient Greece and Rome, in early Christian Europe, and in Europe of the later Middle Ages. This is sometimes doubted by modern readers because the sources are fragmentary and literary, and a historian like John Boswell was always determined to find an exclusive homosexual minority and to deny the plain presumption of his sources that homosexual activity occurred between most men and boys. But the brilliant work of Michael Rocke on the exceptional sources from Renaissance Florence allows the pattern to be displayed with statistical certainty. By the age of thirty, one of every two Florentine youths had been implicated in sodomy, and by the age of forty, two of every three men had been incriminated. Sodomy was therefore so widespread as to be universal. But it was always structured by age. Between fifteen and nineteen, boys were always passive. Individuals between nineteen and twenty-three were in a transitional phase in which they were either active or passive but with the older partner always active. After twenty-three men were always active. During this third period young men sometimes also went to female prostitutes. At thirty they married. Sodomy was illegal, and the church taught that it was immoral. But male opinion largely approved of it as long as adult men were always active. There were, in other words, two competing systems of morality in Christian societies, but the actual sexual behavior of men had changed very little from what it had been in the ancient pagan Mediterranean world.[2]

[...]

But in the 1690s opinion changed after a new way of organizing homosexual desire appeared throughout the modernizing societies of northwestern Europe, in England, France, and the Netherlands. No longer did differences in age justify sexual relations with males in the libertine's mind. Instead adult men with homosexual desires were presumed to be members of an effeminate minority. They were given a status similar to that of the hijra in Indian society or the berdache among the North American tribal peoples, who had passive sexual relations with the majority of males in their societies. European society had begun to move from one to the other of the two worldwide systems for organizing homosexual behavior: from a system in which subordination was achieved by differences in age to one whose focus was a third-gender role for a minority of men. In the old system all males had passed through a period of sexual passivity in adolescence. In the new system, the majority of males could not conceive of themselves as passive at any moment; passivity was instead for the minority, the homosexuals (as they have been called since the late nineteenth century), who from childhood were socialized into their deviant role. European societies in the early eighteenth century gave such sodomites a status equivalent to that of the most abandoned women. The majority of men were supposed to avoid any sexual contact with them. But such contact nonetheless occurred, and when it did, it caused profound anxiety to adolescents and adult men – but also perhaps profound excitement.[3]

The new effeminate adult sodomites can be documented among the London poor because of the attacks against them made by the Societies for the Reformation of Manners. These sodomites constructed around themselves a protective subculture of meeting places and ritual behavior. A few who seem to have been involved in prostitution played out a largely feminine identity. They took women's names, spent nearly all their time in women's clothes, and were referred to as 'she' and 'her' by their male and female acquaintances. Their male customers in some cases must have known that these prostitutes were genital males, but in other cases perhaps they did not, since some sodomites worked the streets as members of a group of female prostitutes. The gender identity of these transvestite males was not entirely feminine because they sometimes wore men's clothes and were prepared to take the active or inserter's role in sexual intercourse. They were neither male nor female but a third gender that combined some characteristics from each of what society regarded as the two legitimate genders. A few such men may have existed before 1700, when they were likely to have been confused with biological hermaphrodites who sometimes changed (though illegally) from the male or female gender to which they had been assigned at birth. After 1700, however, transvestite adult men who clearly possessed male genitalia and whose bodies showed no ambiguity were classified as part of a larger group of effeminate men who were supposed to desire sexual relations only with other males, who might be either adult or adolescent.

These men, for whom the formal term was *sodomite*, were in the slang of the streets known as *mollies*, a term that had first been applied to female prostitutes. Many of them could not be identified as sodomites outside the context of the molly-house, or tavern. Some of them were married with children, and others provided themselves with female companions so that they could pass with their neighbors. Once inside the molly-house, they displayed many of the feminine characteristics of the male transvestite prostitute: they took women's names and adopted the speech and bodily movements of women. On some occasions, especially at dances, some of them dressed entirely as women. Some sodomites in the molly-houses played men to match the role of female prostitute that others took. But all of these men were obliged to play two roles, one in the public world in which they worked and spent most of their time and another in the molly-house. Some men, of course, could not disguise their effeminacy in public and as a consequence were abused or blackmailed. This suggests that they had internalized their gender role to such a degree that they could not hide it, even though that would have been very much to their advantage in the public world. But in the public mind, all the men in the molly-houses – as well as those who used the public latrines, the parks, the cruising streets, or the arcades to find sexual partners – belonged to the same category no matter what their behavior in the public sphere. All were members of a third gender who deserved to be treated with contempt. Some were hanged in the few cases where anal penetration and seminal emission could be proven. And others were fined, imprisoned, and sentenced to stand in the public pillory, where a few were stoned to death.

Sexual relations between women, on the other hand, were not prosecuted. When they occurred, the women were not described as masculinized until the last generation of the century, when some women were categorized as sapphists or tommies, as the effeminate male minority had been called sodomites or mollies since the beginning of the century. Throughout the century there were some women who cross-dressed, and they were sometimes prosecuted for it; but their cross-dressing was undertaken so that they could pass safely in a male occupation rather than to sexually attract women. It was essential that their disguise be fully convincing; any ambiguity that might arise from the mixing of gender traits (as male sodomites mixed them) would have led to their discovery and the failure of their purpose. Among some of these cross-dressing women, there were a few who eventually married women and perhaps even engaged in intercourse with an artificial penis. These women had crossed the gender boundary and were condemned for it, but other women who lived as husbands to women for many years – but against whom no sexual charges were leveled – seem to have passed unscathed. After 1770 there were occasional examples of aristocratic women (sometimes singly, sometimes as part of a female couple) who were either romantically or sexually attracted to women and who cross-dressed in the ambiguous way that effeminate sodomites did. They were accepted when the romance was stressed and the sex vigorously denied, and condemned and ostracized when it was otherwise. It was, however, always much more possible to be unaware that sexual relations between women existed in any form than it was to be ignorant of the existence of effeminate male sodomites.[4]

For most of the eighteenth century, therefore, sexual relations between women still occurred in the context that had applied to sexual relations between males in the seventeenth century, when persons who engaged in sexual relations with their own gender were presumed to be attracted to the other gender as well, and when sexual acts with one's own gender did not compromise an individual's standing as masculine or feminine. Only sexual passivity in an adult male or sexual activity by a woman who used an artificial penis or a supposedly enlarged clitoris had endangered an individual's gender standing. Such individuals, along with bio-logical hermaphrodites, were likely to be viewed as dangerous, since they passed back and forth from active to passive rather than remaining in the passive female or active male conditions to which they had been assigned at birth. Only the temporary passivity of adolescent males whose bodies had not yet acquired secondary male characteristics did not threaten this system. Seventeenth-century society had therefore presumed that although there were three kinds of bodies (men, women, and hermaphrodites), there were only two kinds of gender (male and female).

After 1700 this system was replaced by another for men but not for women. For males, there were now two kinds of bodies (male and female) but three genders (man, woman, and sodomite) – since the sodomite was supposed to experience his desires and play his role as a result of a corrupted education and not because of his bodily condition. For women, the old system of three bodies and two genders could still be presumed. But men had entered a new gender system by changing the nature of their sexual relations with each other: men no longer had sex with boys and women – they now had sex either with females or with males. They were now supposed to be either exclusively homosexual or heterosexual. The majority of men now desired only women. This necessarily brought them into more intimate relations with women, and their intimacy could threaten the continuing male desire to establish domination. This dilemma was in part resolved by assigning those men who desired males to a third gender role that was held in great contempt. This role played its necessary part in the new relations between men and women produced by the emergence of individualism and equality in eighteenth-century society since it guaranteed that, however far equality between men and women might go, men would never become like women since they would never desire men. Only women and sodomites desired men, and this was true for males from adolescence to old age.

The new heterosexual role for the majority of men that was produced by the system of three genders that came into existence after 1700 affected men of all social classes. It resulted in a pattern of extramarital sexual behavior that endured until the middle of the twentieth century. [...] The women who engaged in these extramarital relations did not, however, have their behavior structured by a standard of exclusive female heterosexuality. Their sexual lives were organ-ized instead by the forms of family life that during the eighteenth century came to vary considerably by social class. Poor women, whether as wives, widows, or maids, were bound by the forms of the traditional patriarchal household and family in which servants, children, and wives were subordinated to the authority of older, dominant, and supposedly provident men. Women from the middle and landed classes, on the other hand, lived in families constructed by increasingly egalitarian relations that found expression in romantic courtship, the close friendship of husbands and wives, and the tender care of children. [...]

Heterosexuality, patriarchy, and romance always operated in the persistent presence of men's violence. The violence might appear as an expression of men's contempt for the prostitute or in their attempts to cure themselves of the prostitute's venereal disease by forcing themselves on prepubescent girls; or in courtship when marriage could be offered as a compensation for rape; or after marriage by the husband who to establish his sexual domination of his wife or the absolute possession of her property could treat her in ways that would certify him as mad if used against anyone else. Heterosexuality and the family were also in constant dialogue with Christian religion in its different forms. The last gasps of traditional reforming urban piety appeared early in the century in the Societies for the Reformation of Manners, which attempted to control prostitution and other forms of extramarital relations by turning to the secular magistrates after the church courts had failed. For them sexual sin was equally reprehensible in men and in women. But the Evangelicals at the end of the century were more concerned about the prostitute than about her male customer, for without realizing it, they had become affected by the presumptions of the new male heterosexuality. Women throughout the century were more likely than men to make Christianity their bulwark against the libertine's justification of his practices. But since male heterosexuality made it increasingly difficult for men to enter into intimate relations with a male God, it is likely that the tie between sex and religion was weakened even for those men who were not self-consciously libertine.

[...]

A number of the previous attempts to interpret the history of eighteenth-century sexuality have dealt with many of the forms of behaviour described here. They have not, however, organized themselves around the presumption that heterosexuality and homosexuality are not biological givens but are instead socially constructed aspects of male and female gender roles that did not appear until the early eighteenth century, when the modern Western culture system in which we still live first arose. Michel Foucault originally intended that his history of sexuality should start in the early eighteenth century, and it is with that period that his introductory volume is mainly concerned. Foucault seems to have been struck by the literature against masturbation that first appeared in that period and used it to document the origins of what were for him the repressive structures of modern society. But he did not see in that volume any connection between masturbation and homosexuality. Instead he argued in a paragraph that has had an influence out of all proportion to its importance that the modern sense of the homosexual as a distinct kind of person did not appear until the late nineteenth century. In an interview two years before his death, however, he apparently changed his mind and declared that homosexuality first became a problem in the eighteenth century. But his followers (many of whom have tied their work to his first declaration) have not so far taken up their master's later position. Foucault's account of the eighteenth century (in what admittedly was to have been merely an introduction) is also unsatisfactory because it fails to deal with the histories of adultery and prostitution.[5]

Foucault's argument that modern homosexuality was a product of the late nineteenth century – which was simultaneously made by Jeffrey Weeks on the basis of a much more serious documentation – has been used by Jonathan Ned Katz and Kevin White to argue that modern heterosexuality must therefore similarly have been a product of the late nineteenth and the early twentieth centuries. But all four of these historians make the same mistake and fail to see that the late-nineteenth-century discussions of homosexuality and heterosexuality (in which the words were first coined) did not invent the roles that they considered. By 1880 modern Western homosexuality and heterosexuality had existed for nearly two hundred years. The new names therefore only represent a new stage in the public discussion of these roles, however much the discussion may have changed the political environment in which the roles were enacted.[6]

[. . .]

There remain a series of large speculative questions that establish the need for a new kind of history. [. . .] Why did a new sexual system come into existence in all of northwestern Europe (in England, France, and the Netherlands) in the early eighteenth century? Why did the division into heterosexual and homosexual roles occur first in men, and at what point did the distinction (or some variant of it) become crucial for the gender identity of women? What connection was there between the distinction into heterosexual and homosexual roles and the development of the ideals of romantic marriage and domesticity? When did a system that first appeared in northern Europe and North America spread to the rest of the Western world, to southern, central, and eastern Europe, and to Latin America; and how did the system change during this process of diffusion? And finally, why did a system of almost three hundred years' standing begin to change considerably after 1960, and did it change sufficiently to warrant the description of being postmodern? No-fault divorce, widespread premarital sexual relations between men and women who were not engaged to marry, widespread birth control, the expectation that women should have equal pay and equal access to work and that men should share in the duties of childrearing, the decline in prostitution, the control of venereal disease, and the appearance for the first time in most Western societies of a gay and lesbian movement – all these occurred together in a single generation, and in the very same countries that first experienced around 1700 the modern sexual system that these new forms of behavior have to some extent displaced. [. . .] It is apparent that we do not have much of an idea why or how cultural systems change rapidly in the course of a single generation, whether the change occurs around 1700 or around 1960. It is as baffling as trying to explain the rise and fall of diseases – the plague, syphilis, smallpox, or AIDS. It is enough to begin the analysis of the division of the sexual world into a homosexual minority and a heterosexual majority that has been one of the most salient features of the modern Western culture that first appeared in the generation after 1700.

## Notes

1   This distinction was introduced into historical scholarship in Randolph Trumbach, 'London's Sodomites: Homosexual Behavior and Western Culture in the Eighteenth Century,' *Journal of Social History* 11 (1977): 1–33.

2   K. J. Dover, *Greek Homosexuality* (Cambridge, Mass.: Harvard University Press, 1978); Eva Cantarella, *Bisexuality in the Ancient World* (New Haven, Conn.: Yale University Press, 1992); Craig Williams, *Roman Homosexuality* (New York: Oxford University Press, 1998); John Boswell, *Christianity, Social Tolerance, and Homosexuality* (Chicago: University of Chicago Press, 1980), and *Same-Sex Unions in Pre-modern Europe* (New York: Villard Press, 1994); Michael Rocke, *Forbidden Friendships: Homosexuality and Male Culture in Renaissance Florence* (New York: Oxford University Press, 1996), and 'Male Homosexuality and Its Regulation in Late Medieval Florence,' Ph.D. diss., State University of New York at Binghamton, 1989.

3   A full discussion is forthcoming in the second volume of *Sex and the Gender Revolution, The Origins of Modern Homosexuality*. For my earlier discussions, see Trumbach, 'Gender and the Homosexual Role in Modern Western Culture: The 18th and 19th Centuries Compared,' in Dennis Altman et al., *Which Homosexuality* (London: GMP Press, 1989), pp. 149–69, and 'Sex, Gender, and Sexual Identity in Modern Culture: Male Sodomy and Female Prostitution in Enlightenment England,' in *Forbidden History: The State, Society, and the Regulation of Sexuality in Modern Europe*, ed. John C. Fout (Chicago: University of Chicago Press, 1992), pp. 89–106. For the sodomitical subculture in the Netherlands, see Theo van der Meer, *De Wesentlijke Sonde van Sodomie en Andere Vuyligheeden: Sodomieten vervolgingen in Amsterdam, 1730–1811* (Amsterdam: Tabula, 1984) (of which there is an English summary in van der Meer, 'The Persecutions of Sodomites in Eighteenth-Century Amsterdam: Changing Perceptions of Sodomy,' in *The Pursuit of Sodomy: Male Homosexuality in Renaissance and Enlightenment Europe*, ed. Kent Gerard and Gert Hekma [New York: Haworth, 1989], pp. 263–301), 'Sodomy and the Pursuit of a Third Sex in the Early Modern Period,' in *Third Sex, Third Gender*, ed. Gilbert Herdt (New York: Zone Books, 1994), pp. 137–212, and *Sodoms Zaad in Nederland* (Nijmegen: Sun, 1995). For the French subculture, see Michel Rey, 'Parisian Homosexuals Create a Lifestyle, 1700–1750: The Police Archives,' *Eighteenth-Century Life* 9 (1985): 179–91, and 'Police and Sodomy in Eighteenth-Century Paris: From Sin to Disorder,' in Gerard and Hekma, *The Pursuit of Sodomy*, pp. 128–46; and Jeffrey Merrick and Bryant T. Ragan Jr., eds., *Homosexuality in Modern France* (New York: Oxford University Press, 1996).

4   Randolph Trumbach, 'London's Sapphists: From Three Sexes to Four Genders in the Making of Modern Culture,' in Herdt, *Third Sex, Third Gender*, pp. 111–36, and 'The Origins and Development of the Modern Lesbian Role in the Western Gender System: Northwestern Europe and the United States, 1750–1990,' *Historical Reflections / Réflexions Historiques* 20 (1994): 287–320. See also Emma Donoghue, *Passions between Women: British Lesbian Culture, 1668–1801* (London: Scarlet Press, 1993).

5   Michel Foucault, *The History of Sexuality*, vol. 1, An Introduction, trans. Robert Hurley (New York: Pantheon, 1978); Didier Eribon, *Michel Foucault* (Cambridge, Mass.: Harvard University Press, 1991), p. 316.

6   Jeffrey Weeks, *Coming Out* (London: Quartet Books, 1977), and *Sex, Politics, and Society* (New York: Longman, 1981); Jonathan Ned Katz, *The Invention of Heterosexuality* (New York: Dutton, 1995); Kevin White, *The First Sexual Revolution: The Emergence of Male Heterosexuality in Modern America* (New York: New York University Press, 1993).

# 2

# The Postmodernization of Sex

*William Simon*

[...]

### Modernism as a way of life

Modernism represented a pervasive adherence to the concept of progress, to the idea of constant movement toward the achievement of ever-changing ideals. As modernism in art was to take us ever closer to the purest expressions of the sublime, modern science was charged with bringing us closer to pure truth, final truth – and if not these, then an improved version of truth, one closer to truth than any of the previous versions of the truth, as if changes in truth were synonymous with increases in truth. In more practical terms, the application of science to the realm of the sexual was expected to solve its historic mysteries, to unlock puzzles old and new, until all that was natural yielded up its lawful recipes.

Sexology was born in this modernist tradition. The modernization of sex critically involved the naturalization of sex; the sexual was to be subjected to the perspectives of natural science which, in turn, required the quest for taxonomies, structures, and mechanisms of change that paralleled the vocabulary of the natural sciences as they were applied to all other life forms. A cool detachment or impersonality and a grinding empiricism, more often in rhetoric than practice, justified the license to investigate, to observe, and commit public talk about sex.

[...]

### Modernization as naturalization

Cultural license was granted to contemplate the sexual, but in an isolation that actually reinforced the continuing exile of the sexual from the rest of social life.

The experience of sexual *conduct* was necessarily viewed as translatable into the facts of sexual *behavior* – the idea that the establishing of the physical geography of the sexual orgasm could become the foundation of sexual science at its most transcendent. The naturalization of the sexual required a view of the sexual that was increasingly ahistorical. An ahistoricism, in turn, that produced a concrete abstractness that allowed orgasm to become a thing unto itself, a 'hyperreality' with a physiology, chemistry, and neurology all its own. From Kinsey *et al.*'s (1948, 1953) 'outlet' to the Masters and Johnson's (1966) graphic representation of *the* stages of *the* orgasm, the new science of sex was complicit in producing an alienated orgasm – one fortunately alienated more in its thinking about orgasm than in most people's experience of orgasm.

This naturalization of sex encouraged, first, the adoption of a preference for taxonomic distinctions that assumed permanent basic differentiations. The Kinsey homosexual – heterosexual continuum often became in its uses discrete categories as if delineating sub-species, describing individuals by the number of their position on this continuum as if some specific position along it was reflective of some basic characterological attribute. [. . .] In effect, what was little more than an analytically convenient but shallow typology was transformed into an oppressive taxonomy; the multiple meanings of all sexualities were dissolved into global identities that obscured more than they revealed [. . .].

Involved was a conceptualization of the object of sexual desire so abstract that, when applied to behavior, the issue of sexual desire was almost totally obscured by a preoccupation with the limited issue of the gender of the sexual object. This encouraged a vulgar behaviorism that tended to render invisible the meaning of the larger part of observable behavior and virtually all of non-observable behavior, such as motivation and the intrapsychic landscapes that evoke sexual excitement. This objectification also served the politics of sexual behavior by allowing the issues of inclusion and exclusion to appear to be solidly based upon the biological substrate. Thus, ironically, what were initially attempts to reduce the significance of the homosexual – heterosexual distinction evolved into the raw material for the creation of a homosexual whose difference was inscribed in nature, appearing almost 'racial' in character (Epstein 1987; Escoffier 1985).

## Drive as truth in itself

Similarly, the naturalization of sex that accompanied its modernization tended to welcome Freud's drive theory and its corresponding invention of a sexually responsive infant and child, even when much of the other baggage of psychoanalytic theory was rejected. Viewing sexuality as a biologically ordered developmental process allowed for the introduction of a language of sexual behavior that seemed to be independent of the specific meanings necessary for its expression beyond childhood; it defined a sexuality that need not have immediate social or emotional meanings.

The surviving illusions of childhood's essential innocence allowed for scientific discourse on the sexual to occur without involving heavily charged erotic meanings. As a result, an emotional distance was created that gave credibility to the objectification of sexual behavior, which, in turn, could be described as resembling biological systems like the digestive process.

## Information please: explanation without understanding

The naturalization of sex occurred in the larger context of the application of scientific method to a wide number of human activities, not all of which could equally be subjected to this objectifying approach. A new sexual science was viewed as the accumulation of the exhaustive and precise delineation of the parts constituting the sexuality of the person. The implicit expectation was that once all the essential facts of each part were in hand, the explanation of the phenomenon would be realized, its mysteries revealed. The approach was not unlike that of the eighteenth-century anatomists who were convinced that they would find the secret of life on the dissecting table. Some analogies to this reductionist application of scientific method, frequently a caricature of scientific method, could be found in the German Sexual Hygiene Movement of the 1920s (Haeberle 1983), elements of Wilhelm Reich's concept of bio-energy (1961), as well as many of the applications of technologically fixated 'hard science' appearing in our current journals.

[. . .]

## The factuality of sex

This narrow conception of the application of scientific method found passionate adherence among sexual researchers for the obvious reason that it provided protection and legitimacy. The language of science, its postures, even its costumes, became the conceptual rubber gloves that allowed for the examination of what the larger social world predominantly viewed as 'dirty business'. Sexual activity could be described in a cool, unexcited language wondrously remote from passionate emotional conflicts or heavy breathing. It also created the illusion of distance that protected researchers from accusations of self-interest beyond the admirable quest for truth and the facilitation of individual and social health. [. . .] By describing subjects in language through which they rarely could recognize themselves, sex researchers also shrouded themselves in a protective suggestion of little direct involvement. Sex researchers, themselves, were to be seen as being beyond sexual failure and anxiety, beyond being moved by sexual fantasies involving the improbable, the unattractive, or the unacceptable. Such objectivity muted concerns about questions of motivation for initiating research [. . .].

Beyond the work of Stoller (1979, 1985) and relatively few others, the question of what creates sexual excitement, how it is rooted not in our bodies but in our lives, has only been considered in the most superficial ways. In other words, we have been encouraged to avert our attention from the creation of the erotic, the creation of sexual meanings, sexual motives, and sexual priorities. The naturalization of sex rendered such concerns unnecessary: as an expression of the natural it was alleged to be there at the very beginning – that it came as standard equipment with the body. Postures associated with reproduction, though they might also be little more than shared metaphors capable of many different uses, became a psychobiological bedrock that need be examined only when they appeared in unattractive or undesirable guises.

[…]

## Heroic research: milestones and millstones

In Paul Robinson's (1976) view, the modernization of sex was associated with the works of Havelock Ellis, Kinsey, and Masters and Johnson. To which I would add the path-breaking work of John Money for having enlarged our attentions to the fullest implications of gender. These are people we associate with works and traditions of work from which we have all been beneficiaries. However, as monumental as such labors justifiably appear, they have also proved to be curiously barren of expanding traditions of exploration or understanding. […]

The Kinsey tradition was the least ambiguous about its commitment to empiricism at its most reductionist. The very titles of the classic works, *Sexual Behavior in the Human Male* (1948) and *Sexual Behaviour in the Human Female* (1953), spoke directly to this narrow conception of 'scientific' treatment of the sexual. The basic model for the research on sexual behavior was anticipated by Kinsey's prior work on the gall wasp (Robinson 1976: 51–2). This model was the source of his aspiration to finalize his research by completing a hundred thousand sex histories; his assumption was that in doing so he would be able to sample the human experience with sufficient density to reveal all forms of human sexuality in their relative frequency. Being an individual of extraordinary gifts, he often went beyond his own empiricist model, providing us with insights that went well beyond his statistics. But he rarely questioned the model itself.

More than two decades later, Bell and Weinberg (1978) and later Bell *et al.* (1981) did little better and possibly worse. Demonstrating how little they understood the implications of the titles given to their monographs (*Homosexualities* and *Sexual Preference*), they sought the cause of object preference through a maze of quasi-simulations of reality (path models). Finding no one satisfactory social or psychological explanation of homosexual preference in men and women, from their data they concluded that its source must surely be found elsewhere. Their work culminated in finding a probable explanation of sexual preference in innate attributes that they could not describe, let alone explain or understand. Still conceptually trapped in the simplistic approach of the medical model, the possibility that sexual preference might be the outcome of a complex and highly variable process was not seriously considered. […]

More recently, Lauman and his colleagues have provided us with what will remain for the indefinite future the definitive Kinseyesque survey of patterns of sexual behavior in contemporary North America (Lauman *et al.* 1994). This study's unequaled methodological sophistication probably qualifies it as the apotheosis of the modernist project to comprehensively audit sexual behavior.

Moreover, embracing a tamed social constructionist or 'scripting approach', the authors remain comfortably within a modernist paradigm by shifting the regulation of the sexual from the laws of nature to the laws of social life. This is accomplished by the employment of 'network analysis', a questionable statistical method pretending to be a theory, and an 'economic resource approach', which provides for an emotionally eviscerated conception of the sexual actor. Assuming with remarkable naivety that *sexual behavior* is virtually synonymous with *sexuality*, the major and largely ignored finding of the research is its demonstration of how little of sexual behavior is in the direct control of sexuality, as it ignores the profound and complex role that sexuality, in the fullest sense of that word, plays in the dynamics of cultural, social, and personal life and, in particular, in the interplay between these.

The crisis of modernist perspectives seems to have come to the area of human sexuality more understandably than to most other areas: the best of a tradition of research that promised so much appears to have brought us close to a kind of disturbing pause, as if trapped in a sentence that cannot be completed. It should be obvious, except for the most myopic or naively optimistic, that the mere continuing of accumulation of more information, of more data, will not move us forward substantially. We are not dealing with an issue of information – at least, not of information alone; it is not so much a matter of *what* we think about the sexual as it is a matter of *how* we think about the sexual, not a matter of explanation, but one of understanding.

[...]

## *Postmodernization as denaturalization*

The issues setting the agenda of postmodernism, simultaneously observable within many contexts, tend to share several elements or perhaps several ways of describing the same fundamental phenomena. The most common of these is an emergent consensus about a seeming absence of consensus. And perhaps this is not so much an absence of consensus as a sense of being forced to an unexpected and often discomforting pluralism. [...]

One positive aspect of this new pluralism is the movement towards an abandonment of linear, one-dimensional concepts of intellectual progress, an abandonment of the promise of bringing a contingent and malleable reality into closer harmony with the essential (permanent) principles guiding life. This pluralism has brought with it a corresponding reappraisal of a model of incremental, incorporative progress in science, a concept of science that can be seen as having yielded little beyond coercive and latently ideological banalities when extended to consideration of human sexuality. In the postmodern debate, there is an increased acceptance of the possibility that the broad realm of human behavior creates a relativity that condemns us to what is, in some sense, permanent failure, or at least to an obligatory sense of the provisional. [...] Recent historical research too abundantly reveals that the efforts at framing the 'facts' of a specific time and place in the language of the timeless and the universal serves neither science nor society.

### The realities of the sexual revolution

What threatens the recently established, and still disputed, naturalization of the sexual is a growing awareness that not only do the meanings of the sexual change as the sociohistorical context within which it is experienced changes, but also that the very nature of the sexual may change as well. In other words, the possible need for new concepts regarding the sexual does not follow merely from the inadequacies or errors in the older concepts of sexuality but from the fact that sexual realities have undergone and are continuing to undergo substantial change.

The 'sexual revolution' may in fact have been just that: a revolution – one that created a temporal compression such that, both within and across cohorts, it becomes difficult to speak of many dominant sexual homogeneities, except at the most overly concrete levels, the level of organs and orifices. It becomes increasingly possible that individuals separated from each other only by a few years or only by small differences in their respective personal histories may experience identical sexual behaviors in vastly different ways and often with vastly different consequences. Behind the deceptive stability of language ('a kiss is just a kiss'), the meaning of experience and the experience of meaning change.

Recognizing the existence of a plurality of homosexualities has been, and remains, a slow process. There may be even greater resistance to recognition of the existence of a plurality of heterosexualities. One major source of the resistance to this recognition has been the naturalization of sex with its commitment to concepts of the sexual as a matter of organs, orifices, and phylogenetic legacies.

[. . .]

### The sexuality of a postparadigmatic society

[. . .]

What is at issue is not only that the distribution of behaviors, meanings, and institutional responses has changed but also that, with these and related changes, the very character of the human experience may be in the process of changing as well.

[. . .]

In relatively stable, largely homogeneous social settings (paradigmatic social orders) the continuity of the self is assured, indeed, mandated, by the continuities of social life. In such settings remarkably few conceive of being anything but what they are. There are abundant exemplars of the individual's past and future in her or his immediate company, and the 'community of memory' is experienced as a living presence, one that in being constantly re-enacted is constantly reconfirmed.

In contrast, in large, heterogeneous, complex, and change-prone settings (post-paradigmatic social orders), the self, its integration and cohesiveness, becomes as problematic as the meaning of a past that is constantly subject to being viewed from different contexts of experience and, thus, constantly subject to revision. [...] In such settings, the self must achieve its continuity by recourse to the reflexive, as even shared experiences often can only be preserved as personal history. The ensuing growth of the responsibilities of the psyche increases the power and claims of psychic realities.

As the behavior styles of different settings evolve different characteristics, the individual increasingly must question who she or he is by remembering where and with whom she or he is. And in contexts where vacations replace community festivals, the community of memory relies more upon the standardized idioms of a personal narration than upon collective myth. The increasing diversity of personal histories has made the sexual an increasingly unstable chemistry of social and personal meanings, making most forms of sexual conduct problematic to some degree.

[...]

What has been neglected in the naturalization of the sexual is its capacity for and reliance upon a complex text, a script of the erotic. The erotic is often viewed as the expression of sexual desire, when more appropriately it might be seen as the sexualized representation of desire – the costuming and posturing of desire often, but not always, in the culturally available idioms of the sexual.

[...]

A capacity to revise one's own history, including sexual history, is too often required by unexpected destinies; histories change even when the 'facts' do not. Further, the meaning of any sexual episode, as anticipation, as an enactment with its own immediate past and future, and as a memory, is subject to multiple uses and revisions. This raises the question, for which of these aspects of sexual behavior is a theory of sexuality responsible? Most typically, concerns have been myopically focused on the overt act itself, as if in itself it contained the explanation of all that is relevant. Such consideration, in turn, raises crucial questions of the validity or value of universal models or theories of sexual behavior, which flourish with such conceptual isolation.

## The denaturalization of sex

The denaturalization of the sexual does not require an abandonment of all we have learned about the stabilities and varieties of the biological substratum, but it does require the effort of going beyond that and examining what can only be understood in terms of individuals situated in specific points of time and social space: individuals with and within history. Moreover, the requirements and variabilities of the human organism, even as experienced at the earliest ages, must of necessity await their destiny in actual experiences; the individual does not come to social life but is created in social life.

[…]

The denaturalized approach proposes that the sexual is socially constructed, that the origins of sexual desire can only be found in social life and its variable presence in the lives of specific individuals is predominantly dependent upon their experience in social life. This is a view of sexual desire as the continuously evolving product of human culture, transmitted not through our genes but through language or through the coded behavior of others which, in turn, reflects the impact of language upon their behavior. The difficulty with this position is that it requires that we accept the relatively superficial nature of what many of us experience as emerging from our deepest and sometimes most compelling sense of our own beings.

[…]

### The sexual as problematic

[…]

The sexual becomes problematic to the degree that different aspects or senses of the self make different and possibly conflicting demands upon the sexual; it becomes even more problematic when the same situation comes to describe the others who are relevant to the sexual as either direct participants or members of the many audiences. The problem of the other or others, it must be noted, is most often not merely a problem of recruiting them to and coordinating their participation in a specific sexual event, but also a problem of establishing congruences with the actor's nonsexual identities and involvements.

This problematic finds its counterpart on the intrapsychic level, as individuals must either integrate or isolate their desired identity as a sexual actor from their nonsexual identities (Davis 1983). The issue of the other(s) is reflected in the differences in sexual behavior that frequently occur when individuals are detached from their conventional settings or 'free' from the scrutiny of a familiar audience. Similarly, the problem of the management of self-identity may find expression in the tactic of finding anonymity by hiding from oneself by the use of intoxicants or claims of intoxication.

[…]

### The oppressions of object choice

The initial task involved in the denaturalization of the sexual is a critical examination of the categories of the sexual that reinforce the illusion of compelling homogeneities. By far the most important of the categorizations must be and continue to be those based on object choice. The notion of object choice, however rich with meaning it might be, refers, almost without exception, to gender.

Perhaps it is the seeming visibility of gender and, as part of that, gender's direct reference to the reproductive aspect of sexual behavior that established claims for naturalization, for admitting to sexual theory the naive functionalism of general biologies. Even for sexual actors whose object choice and sexual practice appear to circumvent reproductive consequences, this linkage with the phylogenetic provides comfort by establishing a strong, almost independent basis for the assumed strength of sexual desire.

Clearly the powers of sexual instincts are often seen as a better explanation or apology for sexual behavior than preferences that emerge from the vagaries of individual history. Such a view is equally useful to those who would have chastity or adherence to highly restrictive sexual standards elevated to the status of exemplary behavior.

The view of object choice as the expression of a powerful biological mandate frees the observer from the embarrassments created by the plenitude of other attributes that variably and significantly enter into object choice. The seeming simplicity and obviousness of gender create a bright light effect that either obscures other dimensions of object choice or establishes the gender of the object as the encompassing distinction that renders all other attributes subordinate. However, as should be obvious, gender without further specification provides only a neutered mannequin, one with only the most limited potential for eliciting sexual interest. The most one can say about the dominance of gender in elicit-ing sexual interest or excitement is that it is a minimal precondition for most individuals most of the time, and even then not necessarily for the same reasons. The issues of age, race, physical appearance, social status, quality and history of relationship and the specifics of context, among other attributes, also play roles as compelling, if not more so, than that played by gender. Indeed, gender limited to sheer biological definition may be little more than a signifier whose larger content is totally dependent upon a history of experience and a promise of future uses.

[. . .]

Object choice viewed in its fullness of detail, viewed as a balance of permissions and exclusions, can only be understood as a process of construction and, at times, of negotiation; a process that may differ in critical details not only among individuals but also over time in the history of the same individual.

[. . .]

Object choice may properly claim its critical importance not only as an expres-sion of the sexual actor's underlying sexual identity but also because of its relationship to the actor's identity in the broadest terms: from the 'I' of personal narration to the 'me' responded to by the surrounding social world; from the subject of consciousness to the object embedded in and dependent upon social life. Sexual desire is often seen as requiring the attention of special agencies of control and repression when it should be obvious that the major agencies of control and repression are the weight of nonsexual identifications, commitments, and relationships. The sexual is simultaneously characterological and contingent: sometimes our destiny and sometimes the altering of that destiny.

[…]

The social order no longer imposes consistent coherence upon individuals as they traverse the relevant segments of social life in the course of their everyday lives; as a result, the changed requirements of self-cohesion expand the domain of psychic reality. The metaphors of the personal have a capacity to rival, and sometimes successfully contest with, the social meaning of behavior, which often appears to have lost its singularity.

The social world that once was experienced as compulsively requiring that the several aspects of individual existence make sense (all doctors are men; women who would be doctors must become like men) is experienced increasingly as indifferent. This is the essence of a postparadigmatic society as we have postulated it. The response of a self-conscious postmodernism recognizes that there is a fundamental difference between individuals who live identical or nearly identical lives and who experience that fact and those who live identical or nearly identical lives and do not experience that fact: lives may be patterned and still be experienced as invented.

This is what Barthes was responding to when he noted:

[T]he opposition of the sexes must not be a law of nature. Therefore the confrontations and the paradigms must be dissolved, both the meanings and the sexes pluralized: meaning will tend toward its multiplication, its dispersion … and sex will be taken into no typology. There will be, for example, only *homosexualities* whose plural will baffle any constituted, centered discourse.

(Barthes 1977: 69)

[…]

## The promise of postmodernism

Our approach does not necessarily imply an abandonment of the research effort or the singular importance of that effort. What it does appear to require is an abandonment of the quest for effective formulas, an abandonment of abstract causal models that are applied to specific human beings, and a profound suspicion of the minimalist categories that the actuarial approach requires and often condemns us to. What a postmodernist perspective requires and promises is the development of a conceptual apparatus that can mirror shared collective and individual experiences in what will necessarily be recognized as imperfect and temporary ways. This is a way of seeing that will move us closer, not to truth as such but to finding broadened explanations for behavior and understanding of its meaning, moving us from an arithmetic of behavior to a literacy of behavior. Promising no final goal, such a perspective provides a vision that might serve until the next difference, if you will, the next mutation, in human experience occurs and reshapes our vision of the past, of the future, and of its temporary present.

What is required more than anything else, if a promise of a postmodern sexuality is to be realized, is a self-conscious effort to free the sexual from the intellectual isolation within which the modernization of sex originally prospered. This, admittedly, is no easy task. At a minimum it requires that we place all sexual behavior in the larger context of the lives lived by those having these experiences and that our 'theories' of sexual behavior be made responsible to our sense of the human.

## References

Barthes, R. (1977) *Roland Barthes*, trans. R. Howard, New York: Hill & Wang.

Bell, A. and Weinberg, M. (1978) *Homosexualities: A Study of Diversity among Men and Women*, New York: Simon & Schuster.

Bell, A., Weinberg, M., and Hammersmith, S. K. (1981) *Sexual Preference: Its Development in Men and Women*, Bloomington, Ind.: Indiana University Press.

Davis, M. S. (1983) *Smut: Erotic Reality/Obscene Ideology*, Chicago: University of Chicago Press.

Epstein, S. (1987) 'Gay politics, ethnic identity: the limits of social construction', *Socialist Review* 93/94: 9–54.

Escoffier, J. (1985) 'Sexual revolution and the politics of gay identity', *Socialist Review* 82/83: 19–53.

Haeberle, E. (1983) 'Sexology: conception, birth, and growth of a science', paper presented at the Sixth World Congress of Sexology.

Kinsey, A. C., Pomeroy, W. P., and Martin, C. (1948) *Sexual Behavior in the Human Male*, Philadelphia: Saunders.

Kinsey, A. C., Pomeroy, W. P., Martin, C., and Gebhard, P. H. (1953) *Sexual Behavior in the Human Female*, Philadelphia: Saunders.

Lauman, E. O., Gagnon, J. H., Michael, R. T., and Michaels, S. (1994) *The Social Organization of Sexuality: Sexual Practices in the United States*, Chicago: University of Chicago Press.

Masters, W. H. and Johnson, V. E. (1966) *Human Sexual Response*, Boston: Little, Brown.

Reich, W. (1961) *The Function of the Orgasm*, New York: Farrar, Straus & Giroux.

Robinson, P. (1976) *The Modernization of Sex*, New York: Harper & Row.

Stoller, R. J. (1979) *Sexual Excitement: Dynamics of Erotic Life*, New York: Pantheon.

——(1985) *Observing the Erotic Imagination*, New Haven, Conn.: Yale University Press.

# 3

# Intimate Citizenship and the Culture of Sexual Story Telling

## *Ken Plummer*

Oppressed people resist by identifying themselves as subjects, by defining their reality, shaping their new identity, naming their history, telling their story

*bell hooks*

'Stories' have recently moved centre stage in social thought: as the pathways to understanding culture; as the bases of identity; as the tropes for making sense of the past; as 'narrative truths' (e.g. Spence, 1982; Bruner, 1987; Maines, 1993). A 'narrative moment' has now been sensed (Plummer, 1995). [...] Examples include the stories told by men and women of coming out as gay and lesbian; of women who discover they 'love too much'; of tales told by the survivors of abortion, rape and incest; or of 'New Men' rediscovering their newly masculine roots through mythical stories (e.g. Norwood, 1985; Penelope and Wolfe, 1988; Bly, 1990). For in the late twentieth century, it could seem as if every sexual story that could be told is being told. Many desires have found a voice. From the well-rehearsed tales of 'coming out', 'surviving abuse' and 'recovery' found in every book store, to the continuing babble on TV programmes such as 'Donahue' or 'Oprah', the swirling simulacrum of sexual story telling seems everywhere. [...] How have we come to this curious situation? What has led to this new culture where sexual stories are everywhere? When does a story come into its time? And what are the political implications of all this? [...]

### *Creating a culture of sexual story telling*

Sexual stories cannot always be heard. Lesbian and gay coming-out stories could hardly be heard publicly before the 1970s, although they may have been secretly said. Survivor stories of sexual abuse were largely silenced until the 1980s. These were dormant stories. But since then there has been a flood of tellings for those who would hear – in books, in therapy groups, in TV shows. [...]

Stories are best told when they can be heard. There is usually no point in telling a tale without a receptive and appreciative listener, and one who is usually part of a wider community of support. [...] Whereas once stories were largely part of a localised oral culture, told in small bounded worlds, the nineteenth century witnessed stories moving into mass print – into the tabloids, penny press and scandal sheets (cf. Bird, 1992); and the twentieth century has seen them become television docudramas, talk-show fodder and self-help manuals available for mass consumption. Modern mass media organisation has shifted access to worlds that may not have been visible, accessible or even thinkable before. Whilst in one sense it has rendered the world mass, in another it has rendered it segmented, fragmented, dispersed. Thus the new electronic media have blurred previously distinct spheres, such as those between men and women, young and old, gay and straight, black and white – making once segregated worlds more pervasively accessible (Meyrowitz, 1985).

[...]

For stories to flourish there must be social worlds waiting to hear. Social worlds are not like communities of old: no locale is required, only a sense of belonging, sharing traditions, having common memories. A key point about the 'coming out stories' is that they progressively acquired an *interpretive community of support* which enabled them to flourish. There is historical amplification and feedback at work here. For sure, people could 'come out' as gay in the 1960s and before: but then it really meant in isolation, to oneself, a solitary lover or in the disguised, furtive 'twilight' worlds of the secretive homosexual underworld. To turn this tale from a private, personal tale to one that can be told publicly and loudly is a task of immense political proportions. It requires a collective effort, creating spaces in the wider social order and the wider story telling spaces. [...]

### Back to the future: history, contingency and story telling

A full social history of the rise of these new stories and audiences awaits writing. But the fragments for assembling it already exist. Foucault, for instance, has charted the long revolution. Starting somewhere back in the eighteenth century in the Western world, he locates the paths through which the modern period brought a 'discursive explosion', an 'incitement to discourse', a desire to 'tell everything':

> Western man has been drawn for three centuries to the task of telling everything concerning his sex; that since the classical age there has been a constant optimiza-tion and an increasing valorization on the discourse on sex; and that this carefully analytical discourse was meant to yield multiple effects of displacement, intensifica-tion, reorientation and modification of desire itself. Not only were the boundaries of what one could say about sex enlarged, and men compelled to hear it said; but more important, discourse was connected to sex by a complex organisation with varying

effects, by a deployment that cannot be adequately explained merely by referring it to a law of prohibition. A censorship of sex? There was installed rather an apparatus for producing an ever greater quantity of discourse about sex, capable of functioning and taking effect in its very economy.

(Foucault, 1979, p. 23)

[. . .] Power may be ubiquitous – for Foucault, as for me. But some forms of power expand choices (coming out stories) and are empowering; whilst other forms reduce choices (pathology / victim tales), and lead to control and domination. What hence needs to be explained is why specific stories have their specific times, whilst others do not. [. . .]

A first step in this task is to avoid talking in such grand historical sweeps as Foucault, and to turn to a more specific time. Whilst the seeds of modern sexual stories are there in the nineteenth century, it is to the last four decades of the twentieth that real attention must be paid. [. . .] Most analysts of sexuality agree that something dramatic happened to sexuality during the 1960s and 1970s. This was a time which saw 'the sea-change in the sexualisation of modern capitalist societies' (Evans, 1993, p. 65), a feminization of sex and ultimately a democratisation of intimacy (Giddens, 1991, p. 65).

There are many reasons for these changes. One factor is surely the growth and proliferation of communications. Not only have the major means of mass communication become widely available to most (from mass paperbacking to records, TV, telephones, videos, etc.), but enough stories have been told publicly and circulated freely to reach a critical take off point. A string of important narrative tales around the intimate pile up in the latter part of the twentieth century, each one making it more and more plausible for others to emerge. [. . .]

Yet whilst the spread of the media and the cumulative proliferation of stories provide a context ripe for more and more sexual stories, other factors have played a part in creating a culture of sexual story telling. First is the major spread of consumerisms. The post war period is marked increasingly by the rise of a logic of consumerism, which leads to increasing advertising and marketing. 'Consumption objects' become a means to demarcate life styles and hierarchies. 'Sex' in all its forms is manifestly part of this Big Sell. [. . .] And an important part of the consumerist culture has been the rise of 'youth culture' in the post-Second-World-War period. Of course, 'youth' existed before; but not within the space of such a well organised market – of magazines, films, television programmes (the whole of MTV seems marketed for youth). An array of super pop stars sing of sex and write their sexual stories. [. . .]

Alongside the rise of both media and consumerism, a new infrastructure of 'cultural intermediaries' has developed. This large occupational culture connects to media, advertising, and 'para' intellectual information, and generates a proliferating industry concerned with the production and selling of 'symbolic goods'. [. . .]

Closely allied to this rise of new cultural intermediaries is the acceleration of the individualistic 'therapeutic / expressive culture' which fosters the telling of self narratives. There is a long history in the USA of self-help development. Reaching back to Benjamin Franklin, amplified by Freudian thought, developing through the therapies of the 1960s, symbolised momentarily by the counterculture, and drifting into the New Age, this whole modern period has been characterised negatively as the *Culture of Narcissism*, and, more positively, as the *Psychological Society*.

[...]

This, then, is the backdrop to the creation of the modern culture of sexual story telling. The growth of mass media, the expansion of consumption, the rise of new cultural intermediaries and the expansion of a therapeutic culture – all locked into conflicts which highlight stories in their warfare. It is against this backdrop that more and more stories can be told.

## Making stories happen: a formalist account

[...]

A number of themes suggest when stories can be told, what I will call *a generic process of telling sexual stories* (cf. Prus, 1987). I put them in a rough sequence which indicates necessary conditions for the full-blown 'successful' telling of a sexual story (or indeed any story): for a story 'finding its time'. These generic processes are:

1   imagining – visualising – empathising;
2   articulating – vocalising – announcing;
3   inventing identities – becoming story tellers;
4   creating social worlds / communities of support;
5   creating a culture of public problems.

[...]

Firstly, then, there are processes of imagining – visualising – empathising. Something – a feeling, a thinking, a doing – is to be envisioned. This can be a very simple task – an issue is felt, experienced, found and brought into focus as a story. *But I am thinking also of a whole world of feelings and experiences about which we may not even initially know.* They inhabit worlds where it seems that 'nothing unusual is happening' at one moment, and then some kind of 'trouble' appears at another. This 'trouble' has to be recognised – by self or other.

[...]

A myriad of little sexual stories may be imagined – stories of intrigue and romance, stories of extreme eroticism thwarted in everyday life, stories of unhappiness built up through frustrations, stories of wives leaving their partners, tales of divorce through 'bad sex'. But such stories, whilst commonplace, remain culturally insignificant as long as they fail to enter the more public domain: as long as they are silent. Hence, crucially, a second generic process – of articulating

– vocalising – announcing becomes crucial in the making of stories. To breathe life into the imagination, a language must be found for it. For what has to be seen, there may often not be words. Or if words exist, they may be the wrong words – words which place a wedge between the being and the telling. A space needs to be found where languages can be invented, words can be applied, a voice can be found, a story can be told. [...] Thus some words may become little crimped tales told in small corners whilst others become shouted expansive stories told by people aware of power dressing. Here are matters of control over space, body, face, dress, eyes and touch.

Thirdly, there are processes of inventing identities and becoming story tellers. The image I have is that bit by bit stories move out from a small space of imaginings into a language, through a few tellers and into a community ripe and ready to hear. Crucial in this process therefore must be a time when story tellers come into public view: writing books, magazines, appearing on other media, etc. [...] At this moment, the experience and a faltering language gain a voice and a personhood. The 'Gay', the 'Survivor', the 'Recoverer' becomes recognisable, an identity emerges with a sense of past, present, future: history, difference, anticipation. And the narratives of this new personhood start to enter public worlds of talk. The basis of a politics of identity is formed.

Fourthly, then, this implies creating social worlds (Strauss, 1978). The story has moved out beyond the individual story teller to a community of reception. It is being heard by others. Social worlds must be invented which will hear the story. These 'others' must in some way identify with it, feel it to be part of their 'story'. The correct audiences become crucial. Some of these social worlds may already pre-exist, whilst others may actually be formed by the stories. [...]

The critical take-off point comes when social worlds come together around the story. These interpretive communities exist in and through social worlds of power: they are hierarchically arranged, and some are marginalised whilst others are prioritised. Thus, just having a community will not be sufficient: the more power the community has, the greater the chance of the story taking hold. Hence the story needs a visible public community of alliance and allegiances which facilitate the telling of the tale.

Fifth, and finally, then, are the generic processes involved in creating a culture of public problems. Here the story moves out of a limited social world and enters an array of arenas of public discourse. [...] Stories whose time have come will be those that have entered this culture of public problems, the political spectacle. With this, there will be: (a) a large number of people willing to claim it as their own; (b) a willingness to tell the story very visibly so that others can identify with it; and (c) the presence of alliances who do not claim the story as their own, but who are keen to give it credibility and support. Indeed, it is in part a measure of political success when allies claim its legitimacy and give it support in large numbers.

### Intimate citizenship: the politics of sexual stories

Sexual story telling is a political process. Such stories play a prominent role in understanding the workings of the political and moral life of late modern societies. The stories we tell of our lives are deeply implicated in moral and political change and the shifting tales of self and identity carry potential for a radical transformation of the social order. Stories work their way into changing lives, communities and cultures. Such changes are signs of a new pattern of politics emerging: a weakening of a single-minded and often absolutist concern with the now traditional politics of emancipation (whilst still assuming it as a vast backdrop) and a suggestion of a multiplicity of new projects, new constituencies, new strategies for the future: something new is afoot. This new politics comes in a plethora of forms and labels, moving under various, often contradictory, names: a politics of difference, radical pluralism, communitarianism, a new liberalism, cultural politics, life politics. In short, *a radical, pluralistic, democratic, contingent, participatory politics of human life choices and difference is in the making* (cf. Young, 1990; Connolly, 1991; Giddens, 1991; Barber, 1992; Benhabib, 1992).

This new politics has one major axis in 'gender/sexual/erotic' politics, and is heavily dependent upon the stories invented about 'intimacy'. [...] New social movements appear and, in their wake, a whole string of smaller, less organised, and less powerful communities and claims have developed which speak to a wider range of differences. These movements have shaped new stories of identity, and new cultures of political action. 'Rape Stories' and 'Gay Stories' may be seen as emblems of many other potential stories that could be told in the future. And new forms of being have emerged alongside these new stories. Indeed, the (late) modern period has invented stories of being, identity, and community for both rape survivors and gays that has made it increasingly possible to claim 'rights' in ways that could not be done until these stories were invented. The old (and still important) communities of rights spoke of political rights, legal rights or welfare rights of citizenship: the language of women's and gay communities certainly draws upon this – such gains should not be lightly lost – but takes it further. A new set of claims around the body, the relationship and sexuality are in the making. This new field of life politics I will call 'Intimate Citizenship'.

### Stories of intimate citizenship

Citizenship has been a major concern of Western-style democracies throughout the twentieth century. In the classic formulation of T. H. Marshall, three clusters of citizen rights have emerged chronologically during the past two centuries to deal with concerns over civil, political and social rights – to justice under the law, to political representation and to basic welfare (Marshall, 1963). Despite many criticisms, it remains a useful model to sense a general and slow expansion of the idea of the citizen in modernity.

[...]

To the existing three realms of citizenship, a fourth could now be added at century's end: that of *Intimate Citizenship*. This speaks to an array of concerns too often neglected in past debates over citizenship, and which extend notions of rights and responsibilities. I call this 'Intimate Citizenship' because it is concerned with all those matters linked to our most intimate desires, pleasures and ways of being in the world. Some of this must feed back into the traditional citizenship; but equally, much of it is concerned with new spheres, new debates and new stories. For many people in the late modern world there are many decisions that can, and increasingly have to, be made about a life: making decisions around the *control (or not) over* one's body, feelings, relationships; *access (or not) to* representations, relationships, public spaces, etc; and *socially grounded choices (or not) about* identities, gender experiences, erotic experiences. [...] An array of new personal narratives that may be told around the intimate are emerging: stories which suggest new living arrangements, new families, new ways of thinking about feelings, bodies, representations and identities, and new modes of the erotic. We can see a proliferation of stories in the recent past, and there is no reason to think they will suddenly cease. Old stories will, however, remain side by side with the new. And in this lies a major source of conflict.

### The war of the intimate tales: from tribalism to difference

For with every new story, there is a rival old one. Tales of new families are countered by tales of 'family values': tales of new bodies are countered by traditional values of the 'natural'; tales of new ways of being men and women – even to the point of their dissolution – are countered by 'backlash stories' with the reassertion of traditional masculinity and femininity; and tales of the new sexualities generate intense anxiety over traditional standards of sexuality. Traditional values and absolutist moralities are evoked in the presumption of decline and relativity. Indeed, traditional and largely authoritarian stories of the past are placed severely under threat from a multiplicity of conflicting voices. Will one drown the other out? Can they co-exist, and if so how? What are the possible relationships of different stories to each other? A difficult period awaits.

[...]

The problem of conflicting and competing stories is a central political issue for the future. Can the divergent stories manage to co-exist or will certain tales triumph? There are a range of responses to the problem of competing stories – from fundamentalism and tribalism to a more pluralistic and participatory culture.

The first, and in my view the most dangerous and pessimistic response to the problem of conflicting stories, is the reassertion of *tribalism, fundamentalism* and *separatism*. Here is the affirmation of stories which are exclusive, closed, authoritarian. They prioritise one group, culture and identity over others, and provide one essential or foundational truth over and above others. In many ways it is the politics of the past, still alive in the present: it is the politics against which emancipatory models came to fruition. [...]

A more benign response may be that of *communitarianism*. This is most clearly exemplified in the philosophy of MacIntyre, and in the sociology of Bellah and Etzioni. Here is asserted the need for 'tribes' with their own 'traditions', but it is a model of the tribes at least managing to live together. The source of moral value is to be found in the community. [...]

But with such a model, how are people to live together without the conflicts becoming unbearable? The traditional liberal response to this has been to establish some sense of a *common framework*, a *minimum of ground rules* through which stories can be told. An intriguing variant on this is the necessary *constraining and limiting* of truly discordant voices. Becoming aware that some stories are so different, so at odds with each other, one suggestion is to create a silent pact: some things are best left unsaid, best left unspoken.

[...]

So what could possibly be the way ahead? The fundamentalisms on either side are now a dead end. Though they may have once been important in clarifying issues, they are now too well known to need such polarities. Conversational restraint is probably, in practice, what is taking place in many places: a tacit agreement to live together and ignore differences. Traditional communitarians – perilously close to fundamentalisms – seek out the history of their ethics through the religious or feminist community. An ideal speech situation where a communicative ethics may be established remains just that: an ideal. There is not a lot of guidance here.

Following this line, there can be no Grand Conclusion – no final story to be told. Indeed, if one analysis has come through it is surely that in the late modern period such Grand Stories are no longer possible. Indeed, such claims must be looked upon with suspicion. What we are left with are fragments of stories. What seems to be required is a sensitivity to listen to an ever-growing array of stories and to shun the all too tempting desire to place them into a coherent and totalising narrative structure.

[...]

A final word can be left, for the time being, with the prescient William James:

> No one of us ought to issue vetoes to the other, nor should we bandy words of abuse. We ought, on the contrary, delicately and profoundly to respect one another's mental freedom: then only shall we have the spirit of inner tolerance without which all our outer tolerance is soulless, and which is empiricism's glory; then only shall we live and let live, in speculative as well as practical things. (James, 1956, p. 30)

# References

Barber, B. (1992) *The Aristocracy of Everyone* (New York: Oxford University Press).

Benhabib, S. (1992) *Situating the Self* (Cambridge: Polity).

Bird, S. E. (1992) *For Inquiring Minds* (Knoxville, TN: University of Tennessee Press).

Bly, R. (1990) *Iron John* (New York: Addison Wesley).

Bruner, J. (1987) 'Life as Narrative', *Social Research*, **54**: pp. 11–32.

Connolly, W. E. (1991) *Identity / Difference* (Ithaca, NY: Cornell University Press).

Evans, D. T. (1993) *Sexual Citizenship* (London: Routledge).

Foucault, M. (1979) *The History of Sexuality*, vol. 1 (Harmondsworth, Middlesex: Penguin).

Giddens, A. (1991) *Modernity and Self-Identity* (Cambridge: Polity).

Giddens, A. (1992) *The Transformation of Intimacy* (Cambridge: Polity).

hooks, b. (1989) *Talking Back: Thinking Feminist, Thinking Black* (Boston: South End).

James, W. (1956) *The Will to Believe and Other Essays* (New York: Dover).

Maines, D. (1993) 'Narrative's Moment & Sociology's Phenomena', *Sociological Quarterly*, **34**: pp. 17–38.

Marshall, T. H. (1963) *Sociology at the Crossroads* (London: Heinemann).

Meyrowitz, J. (1985) *No Sense of Place* (Oxford: Oxford University Press).

Norwood, R. (1985) *Women Who Love too Much* (New York: Simon & Schuster).

Penelope, J. and Wolfe, S. (eds) (1988) *The Coming Out Stories* (Freedom, CA: Crossing Press).

Plummer, K. (1995) *Telling Sexual Stories* (London: Routledge).

Prus, R. (1987) 'Generic Social Process', *Journal of Contemporary Ethnography*, **16**: pp. 250–93.

Spence, D. (1982) *Narrative Truth and Historical Truth* (New York: Norton).

Strauss, A. (1978) 'A Social World Perspective', in Norman K. Denzin (ed.), *Studies in Symbolic Interaction* (London: JAI Press), vol. 1, pp. 119–28.

Young, I. (1990) *Justice and the Politics of Difference* (Princeton, NJ: Princeton University Press).

# Part II

# The Gender of Sexuality

Gender, and the ways in which its dominant forms are constructed and reinforced through the institutionalization of heterosexuality, is the theme throughout part II. The structures and meanings of gender are extremely powerful in relation to the constitution of sexuality. Some feminist theorists have suggested that gender in fact constitutes sexuality, and that female sexuality in particular is constructed through the mechanisms of male power. Others (Rubin 1984) have seen a significant distinction between the domains of sexuality and gender, regarding their relationship as more complex and contingent than is often thought. The important element to bear in mind, however, is that masculinity and femininity are always relational: one can only exist in relationship to the other. These relationships inevitably shift over time and over the life course of individuals in particular cultures. But in most societies masculinity and femininity have been organized hierarchically, with masculinity as the unspoken but assumed norm, and this has tended to shape sexual theorization.

This relationship of masculinity and femininity has also been the basis of sexual politics. The impact of feminism since the 1960s has simultaneously sharpened our awareness of the arbitrary nature of gender divisions and increased the possibility of changing them. In recent years gender has increasingly been seen not simply as lived, but as performed through the re-enactment of what are viewed as the essential characteristics of both sex (male and female) and gender (Butler 1990; Butler 1991).

There have been remarkable changes in the ecology of gender over the past thirty years. This is not simply an ideological shift; it also reflects a shift in the whole economic and social basis of gender. In most Western countries, women have increasingly been incorporated into the workforce, and legislation has formally recognized the equality of men and women. This in turn has influenced ongoing debates in non-industrialized and recently industrialized societies. But what is also increasingly clear is that, whatever the moves towards formal equality, and whatever the local successes of both long-term economic and social shifts and ideological transformations, there is considerable intransigence in the inherited assumptions about the social meanings of masculinity and femininity. This is the basis for the understanding of heterosexuality as institutionalized not only in formal structures but in our minds (Holland et al. 1998).

R. W. Connell's chapter surveys masculinities on a global scale, to show how and why 'cultural turbulence' around the themes of masculinity has grown. He suggests there has been a critical shift from studying masculinity as a single entity towards understanding men's place and practices in terms of gender relations. Connell argues that gender and sexuality have to be seen as 'social practices', and his survey demonstrates the variety of structured social practices which have defined masculinity, femininity and attitudes to sexuality. These practices give rise to dominant and subordinate forms, and challenges to dominant forms of masculinity and femininity in recent years have involved processes for many men of remaking the self. But an important question that is left open is to what degree these changes are fundamental in challenging the privileged normative status of heterosexuality.

In her chapter Gillian Dunne explores contemporary lesbian relationships as a way of understanding how we 'do gender' even in relationships which explicitly reject traditional heterosexual patterns of life. She suggests that we produce gender in the social relations of everyday life through both domestic labour and paid employment. Same-sex relationships open the possibility of doing gender in different ways, indeed of undoing 'gender' in its dominant forms. Lesbian couples, Dunne argues, have a passion for 'sameness', contesting boundaries, and dissolving traditional forms of gender. In turn Dunne suggests this undermines the rigid dichotomy of heterosexuality and homosexuality.

Stevi Jackson continues the problematization of heterosexuality, exploring critiques by feminist and queer theorists. She begins by introducing the body of work known as queer theory in order to examine whether, or in what ways, it can be distinguished from earlier forms of feminist, lesbian and gay theoretical work. She then proceeds to examine the implications of both feminist and queer perspectives for critiques of heterosexuality, stressing throughout her essay the importance of the interlinkage between sexuality and gender as both division and hierarchy. One aspect of this is how feminists' critiques of the institution of heterosexuality can co-exist with feminist heterosexual practice and pleasure. Jackson is critical of a variety of research and theoretical positions which explore this tension. She emphasizes the intransigence of the gendered order, despite recurrent challenges, because it is based on systematic inequalities. In the same way she questions the celebration of the pluralization of identities which ignore these structured inequalities. She concludes with a call to imagine social relations in ways that are radically different from those that currently exist.

Holland, Ramazanoglu, Sharpe and Thomson continue this examination of the tenacity of gendered inequalities through a study of young men and women, in a chapter which illustrates the importance of theorizing the body and embodiment to understanding sexualities. The complex inter-relationship of power and control is played out upon the gendered body in sexual relationships. Holland et al. argue that there is a continuing imperative for young women to construct a disembodied sexuality, which produces the female body as passive. This is linked to the power of masculine privilege, in a world where young men's sexuality is embodied. Women are under pressure to control their own unruly body and to subordinate it to men's desire. But male–female relationships can nevertheless be contested. Discourses of safer sex can, for example, encourage women to take control of aspects of the relationship. Negotiation between the sexes is always present, and empowerment a possibility. These can be part of a challenge to the institutionalized male power of heterosexuality.

Lynne Segal offers an exploration of the anti-pornography discourses which have been highly influential within feminism. She questions the moral conservatism of some contemporary feminists, and simultaneously rejects the reductive forms of psychology, which have been invoked to explain the factors that perpetuate women's subordination. Developing her argument in the context of a broader critique of radical feminist approaches to sexuality and heterosexuality (Segal 1994; Segal 1999), she argues for the importance of keeping open creative spaces for women as sexual agents in their own right.

Finally in this section, Mark Johnson explores the behaviour of transgendered people in the Philippines. This reveals the complex ways in which gender is performed, contested and transformed, in the context of processes of globalization which have introduced the term *gay* to the Philippines, yet allow it to be inscribed with new meanings. Johnson concludes that sexuality and gender are most usefully thought of not in terms of static boundaries, but as emergent in the telling and retelling, mapping and remapping, of forms of love and desire, identity and identification. His article provides an example of the growth of research investigating the self-understandings of transgendered people, examining the complex relationships between transgenderism, sexual behaviours and sexual identities.

## References

Butler, J. 1990: *Gender Trouble: Feminism and the Subversion of Identity*. New York and London: Routledge.

Butler, J. 1991: Imitation and gender insubordination. In D. Fuss (ed.), *Inside / Out*, New York and London: Routledge.

Holland, J., Ramazanoglu, C., Sharpe, S. and Thomson, R. 1998: *The Male in the Head: Young People, Heterosexuality and Power*. London: Tufnell Press.

Rubin, G. 1994: Thinking sex: notes for a radical theory of politics of sexuality. In C. Vance (ed.), *Pleasure and Danger: Exploring Female Sexuality*, London and Boston: Routledge & Kegan Paul.

Segal, L. 1994: *Straight Sex: The Politics of Pleasure*. London: Virago.

Segal, L. 1999: *Why Feminism?* Cambridge: Polity.

# 4

# The Big Picture: Masculinities in Recent World History

*R. W. Connell*

This article addresses the question of how we should study men in gender relations, and what view of modern world history an understanding of masculinity might give us. [...]

## Studying 'masculinity'

### Masculinity as a cultural problem

The fact that conferences about 'masculinities' are being held is significant in its own right. [...] Both the men-and-masculinity literature that has bubbled up,[1] and the debates at conferences and seminars, testify that in some part of the Western intelligentsia, masculinity has become problematic in a way it never was before.

There is no doubt what cued the discovery of this problem. It was, first, the advent of Women's Liberation at the end of the 1960s and the growth of feminist research on gender and 'sex roles' since. Second – as important intellectually though of less reach practically – it was the advent of Gay Liberation and the developing critique of heterosexuality of lesbians and gay men.

While much of the key thinking about masculinity continues to be done by radical feminists and gay activists, concern with the issue has spread much more widely. The nature and politics of masculinity have been addressed by the new right, by heterosexual socialists, and by psychotherapists of wondrous variety.[2]

[...]

To say masculinity has become 'problematic' is not necessarily to say gender relations are changing for the better. It is, rather, to say that cultural turbulence around themes of masculinity has grown. An arena has opened up. What direction gender relations move will in part be determined by the politics that happens in this arena.

[...]

## Towards a new framework: a political sociology of men in gender relations

To grasp the intellectual and political opportunity that is now open requires a shift in the strategic conception of research and in our understanding of the object of knowledge. The object of knowledge is not a reified 'masculinity' (as encapsulated, with its reified partner 'femininity,' in the psychological scales measuring M / F and androgyny). The object of knowledge is, rather, *men's places and practices in gender relations*. It is true that these places may be symbolically constructed (the subject of representation research); and that these practices are organized transactionally and in the life course (the subject of sex role and personality research). Thus the main topics of existing men-and-masculinity studies are included in this conception of the field. But these topics can only be understood in relation to a wider spectrum of issues that must now be systematically included in the field of argument.

First, masculinity as personal practice cannot be isolated from its institutional context. Most human activity is institutionally bound. Three institutions – the state, the workplace / labor market, and the family – are of particular importance in the contemporary organization of gender.

[...]

Second, masculinities as cultural forms cannot be abstracted from sexuality, which is an essential dimension of the social creation of gender. Sexuality has been leeched out of much of the literature on masculinity. This perhaps reflects an assumption that sexuality is pre-social, a natural force belonging to the realm of biology. But while sexuality addresses the body, it is itself social practice and constitutive of the social world. There is no logical gap between sexuality and organizational life. Their close interconnection has been recently documented in important studies of the workplace by J. Hearn and W. Parkin and by Pringle. The sexualization of military life is evident from work on soldier's language as well as in the more emotionally honest soldiers' autobiographies.[3]

[...]

Since gender relations produce large-scale inequalities – in most contemporary cultures, collective advantages for men and disadvantages for women – masculinity understood in this way must be understood as political. I mean 'political' in the simple, conventional sense of the struggle for scarce resources, the mobilization of power and the pursuit of tactics on behalf of a particular interest.

Interests are constituted within gender relations by the facts of inequality. They are not homogeneous, indeed are generally extremely complex, but they are powerful determinants of social action.

Different masculinities arise in relation to this structure of interests and embody different commitments and different tactics or strategies. I have suggested elsewhere that hegemonic masculinity in patriarchy can be understood as embodying a successful strategy for the subordination of women.[4] I would now add to that formula that when the historical conditions for a strategy's success have altered, the hegemonic form of masculinity is vulnerable to displacement by other forms.

To construct such an analysis requires a standpoint, and I take the most defensible one to be the commitment to human equality. The standpoint of equality is not an end-point but a starting-point for social analysis. [...]

## Masculinities in history

### Multiple cultures, multiple masculinities

Ethnographies and histories of gender have now become rich enough to give us a clear view of some culture areas at least. An important negative conclusion can be drawn immediately. The models of masculinity familiar in Euro / American discourse simply do not work for the realities of gender in other cultures, so far as these cultures can be reconstructed before colonial or commercial domination by the Euro / American world. Let me sketch, very briefly, one case.

In neo-Confucian China from the Song to the Qing dynasties (roughly, the thousand years before this century), the vast majority of the population were peasants working family farms, with administration in the hands of a tax-supported scholar-official class. The heavily patriarchal gender relations in the dominant class were regulated by an increasingly formal body of rules, an authoritarian development of Confucian moral and social philosophy. Peasant families were more egalitarian and less regulated, but the Confucian code remained hegemonic in the society as a whole.[5]

Promulgated by the state and enforced by state and clan as well as family patriarchs, the code defined conduct for men not as pursuit of a unitary ideal of masculinity, but more centrally in terms of the right or wrong performance of a network of obligations – towards emperor, parents, brothers, etc. [...]

The difference from European culture is particularly clear in two issues important to European constructions of masculinity: soldiering, and love between men. Neo-Confucian culture deprecated military life. Soldiers were regarded more as licensed thugs than as ideals of masculinity. One set of clan rules advised men of the clan not to become soldiers, remarking that this was 'another form of loafing,' i.e., not what any responsible man would do. Fighting heroes do appear in popular literature. But, in contrast to Euro / American presumptions, this kind of heroism is unconnected with active interest in sex with women.

On the other hand, early Confucian culture seems to have been far more positive about erotic relationships between men than European culture has been. There was a well-defined literary tradition within the upper class celebrating male-to-male love, with such relationships seen as exemplary rather than decadent. Over time, however, the neo-Confucian philosophers became more hostile to homosexual relationships.

[...]

Nevertheless, it is Euro / American culture that is dominant in the world now, and which must be addressed first in any reckoning with our current predicament. Imperialism was a massively important event in gender history. Some cultures' gender regimes have been virtually obliterated by imperialism. [...] Surviving cultures have attempted to reconstruct themselves in relation to Euro / American world dominance, an explosive process that is perhaps the most important dynamic of gender in the contemporary world. [...] I argue that European imperialism and contemporary world capitalism are gendered social orders with gender dynamics as powerful as their class dynamics.

[...]

### Early modern Europe

Four developments in the period 1450–1650 (the 'long 16th century' in Braudel's useful phrase) mark decisive changes in European life from which we can trace the construction of modern gender regimes.

The disruption of medieval Catholicism by the spread of Renaissance culture and by the Protestant Reformation disrupted ascetic and corporate-religious ideals of men's lives, of the kind institutionalized in monasticism. On the one hand, the way was opened for a growing emphasis on the conjugal household and on married heterosexuality as the hegemonic form of sexuality. On the other hand, the new emphases on individuality of expression and on each person's unmediated relationship with God led toward the individualism, and the concept of a transcending self, which provided the basis for the modern concept of masculinity itself.

The creation of the first overseas empires by the Atlantic seaboard states (Portugal and Spain, then Holland, England, and France) was a gendered enterprise from the start, an outgrowth of the segregated men's occupations of soldiering and sea trading. Perhaps the first group who became defined as a recognizable 'masculine' cultural type, in the modern sense, were the conquistadors. They were displaced from customary social relationships, often extremely violent, and difficult for the imperial authorities to control. An immediate consequence was a clash over the ethics of conquest and a demand for controls. Las Casas's famous denunciation of Spanish atrocities in the Indies is accordingly a very significant document in the history of masculinity.[6]

The growth of cities fuelled by commercial capitalism – Antwerp, London, Amsterdam – created a mass milieu for everyday life that was both more anonymous, and more coherently regulated, than the countryside. The changed conditions of everyday life made a more thoroughgoing individualism possible. In combination with the 'first industrial revolution' and the accumulation of wealth from trade, slaving, and colonies, an emphasis on calculative rationality began to distinguish masculinity in the entrepreneurial subculture of early capitalism. At the same time, commercial cities became the milieu (by the early eighteenth century) for the first sexual subcultures, such as the 'Molly houses' of London, institutionalizing variations on gender themes.[7] The notion that one must have a *personal identity* as a man or a woman, rather than a *location* in social relations as a man or a woman, was hardening.

The onset of large-scale European civil war – the sixteenth–seventeenth-century wars of religion, merging into the dynastic wars of the seventeenth–eighteenth centuries – disrupted established gender orders profoundly. A measure of this is the fact that revolutionary struggles saw the first radical assertions of gender equality in European history, by religious-cum-political sects like the Quakers.[8] At the same time, this warfare consolidated the strong state structure that is a distinctive feature of Euro / American society and has provided a very large-scale institutionalization of men's power. The centrality of warfare in these developments meant that armies became a crucial part of the developing state apparatus, and military performance became an unavoidable issue in the construction of masculinities.

We can speak of a gender order existing by the eighteenth century in which masculinity as a cultural form had been produced and in which we can define a hegemonic form of masculinity. This was the masculinity predominant in the lives of men of the gentry, the politically dominant class in most of Europe and North America.

[. . .]

## Transformations of hegemonic forms

The history of hegemonic forms of Euro / American masculinity in the last two hundred years is the history of the displacement, splitting, and remaking of gentry masculinity. Because I have limited space I am very summary at this point. Political revolution, industrialization, and the growth of bureaucratic state apparatuses saw the displacement of gentry masculinity by more calculative, rational, and regulated masculinities. The bureaucrat and the businessman were produced as social types. The economic base of the landed gentry declined, and with it the orientation of kinship and honor. Violence was split off from political power, in the core countries; Mr Gladstone did not fight duels, or lead armies. Rather, violence became a speciality. As mass armies were institutionalized so was the officer corps. This became the repository of much of the gentry code. [. . .] But violence was now combined with an emphasis on rationality: we see the emergence of military science. [. . .] It was bureaucratically rationalized violence as a social technique, just as much as superiority of weapons, that made European states and European settlers almost invincible in the colonial frontier expansion of the nineteenth century.[9]

But this technique risked destroying the society that sustained it. Global war led to revolutionary upheaval in 1917–1923. In much of Europe the capitalist order was only stabilized, after half a generation of further struggle, by fascist movements that glorified irrationality and the unrestrained violence of the front-line soldier. And the dynamics of fascism soon enough led to a new and even more devastating global war.

The defeat of fascism in the Second World War cut off the institutionalization of a hegemonic masculinity marked by irrationality and personal violence. But it certainly did not end the bureaucratic institutionalization of violence. The Red Army and U.S. armed forces, which triumphed in 1945, continued to grow in destructive capability. [. . .] The growth of destructive capability through the application of science to weapons development has, however, given a new significance to technical expertise.

[. . .]

Masculinity organized around *dominance* was increasingly incompatible with masculinity organized around *expertise* or technical knowledge. 'Management' split from 'professions,' and some analysts saw power increasingly in the hands of the professionals. Factional divisions opened in both capitalist ruling classes and communist elites between those pursuing coercive strategies towards workers (conservatives/hard-liners) and those depending on technological success and economic growth that allow integrative strategies (liberals/reformers). [. . .]

### Subordinated forms

[. . .] The hegemonic form of masculinity is generally not the only form, and often is not the most common form. Hegemony is a question of relations of cultural domination, not of head-counts.

[. . .]

The separation of household from workplace in the factory system, the dominance of the wage form, and the development of industrial struggle were conditions for the emergence of forms of masculinity organized around wage-earning capacity, skill and endurance in labor, domestic patriarchy, and combative solidarity among wage earners.

[. . .]

At much the same time the masculinity of the dominant class was purged in terms of identity and object choice. As gay historians have shown, the late nineteenth century was the time when 'the homosexual' as a social type was constructed, to a considerable extent through the deployment of medical and penal power. At earlier periods of history sodomy had been officially seen as an act, the potential for which existed in any man who gave way to libertin-age. From the point of view of hegemonic masculinity, this change meant that the potential for homoerotic pleasure was expelled from the masculine and located in a deviant group (symbolically assimilated to women or to beasts).

[…]

In colonies where local populations were not displaced but turned into a subordinated labor force (much of Latin America, India, East Indies) the situ-ation was more complex again. It is a familiar suggestion that Latin American 'machismo' was a product of the interplay of cultures under colonialism. The conquistadors provided both provocation and model; Spanish Catholicism pro-vided the ideology of female abnegation; and oppression blocked other claims of men to power. Pearlman shows that this pattern is also a question of women's agency.[10]

[…]

## Contemporary politics

### The present moment

[…]

The distinctive feature of the present moment in gender relations in first-world countries is the fact of open challenges to men's power, in the form of feminism, and to institutionalized heterosexuality, in the form of lesbian and gay men's movements. We must distinguish between the *presence* of these movements from the operating *power* they have won, which is often disappointingly small. What-ever the limits to their gains, and the success of the conservative backlash, the historic fact that these movements are here on the scene structures the whole politics of gender and sexuality in new ways.

These challenges are being worked out in a context of technological change and economic restructing (e.g., the decline of heavy industry in old industrial centers), globalization of market relationships and commercial mass communi-cation (e.g., the crumbling of Eastern-European command economies), widening wealth inequalities and chronic tensions in first-world/third-world relations (e.g., the Vietnam War, the debt crisis, the Gulf War). Each of these processes has its gender dimension.

### Contestation in hegemonic masculinity

Earlier in the twentieth century a split began to open in the hegemonic masculinity of the dominant classes, between a masculinity organized around interpersonal dominance and one organized around knowledge and expertise. Under the pressure of labor movements and first-wave feminism, and in the context of the growing scale of mass production, dominance and expertise ceased to be nuances within the one masculinity and became visibly different strategies for operating and defending the patriarchal capitalist order. In some settings distinct institutional bases for these two variants hardened: line management versus professions, field command versus general staff, promotion based on practical experience versus university training. Political ideologies and styles – conservatism versus liberalism, confrontation versus consensus politics – also clustered around this division.

Feminism in the 1970s and 1980s often found itself allied with the liberal/professional side in this contestation, for a variety of reasons. Notions of equal opportunity and advancement by merit appealed in a technocratic style of management. Much feminist activity was located in universities and professions. Liberal feminism (the strongest current in feminism) as an enlightenment project found itself on the same terrain, and using much the same political language, as progressive liberalism and reformist labor.

[. . .]

The reassertion of a dominance-based masculinity has been much discussed in popular culture. To my mind its most interesting form is not Rambo movies but the 1980s cult of the 'entrepreneur' in business. Here gender imagery, institutional change, and political strategy intersect. The deregulation policies of new-right governments in the 1980s dismantled Keynesian strategies for social integration via expert macro-economic regulation. The credibility of the new policies rested on the image of a generation of entrepreneurs whose wealth-creating energies were waiting to be unleashed. That this stratum was masculine is culturally unquestionable.

[. . .]

Managerialists and technocrats do not directly confront feminist programs but under-fund or shrink them in the name of efficiency and volunteerism. Equal-opportunity principles are accepted as efficient personnel management ideas, but no funds are committed for affirmative action to make equal opportunity a vehicle of social change. Research and training funds are poured into areas of men's employment (for instance the Australian government is currently pushing science and technology) because of the perceived need to make the country 'competitive in international markets.'

Speculating a little, I think we are seeing the construction of a new variant of hegemonic masculinity. It has a technocratic rather than confrontationist style, but it is misogynist as before. It characteristically operates through the indirect mechanisms of financial administration. It is legitimated by an ideology centering on an economic theory whose most distinctive feature is its blanket exclusion from discourse of women's unpaid work – which, as Waring bitterly but accurately puts it, 'counts for nothing' in economic science.[11]

### Challenges: 'alternative' masculinities

Contestation for the hegemonic position is familiar. What is novel, in Euro/
American history, is open challenge to hegemonic masculinity as such. Such
challenges were sparked by the challenge to men's power as a whole made by
contemporary feminism. Feminism may not have been adopted by many men,
but an *awareness* of feminism is very widespread indeed.

[. . .]

The challenge to hegemonic masculinity among a group of men studied in
Australia, for example, mainly takes the form of an attempt to re-make the self.
Most of them started off with a fairly conventional gender trajectory, and they
came to see a personal reconstruction as required. This turns out to be emotionally very difficult. The growth-movement techniques available to them do not
deliver the political analysis, support, or follow-through that the project actually
requires. Only a few, and those only marginally, have moved beyond this individualist framework to the search for a collective politics of gender among men.

A collective politics is precisely the basis of the challenge to hegemonic heterosexuality mounted by gay liberation. At one level this challenge was delivered
simply by the presence of an open gay milieu based on sex and friendship.
'Coming out' is experienced as entering a social network, not just as entering a
sexual practice. [. . .]

The collective work required was to construct the network and negotiate a
social presence for it. This meant dealings with the state authorities, e.g., the
police; economic mobilization, the so-called 'pink capitalism'; and organizing
political representation, the most famous representative being Harvey Milk in the
United States.[12]

[. . .]

### Deconstructions of working-class masculinity

[. . .]

With the collapse of the postwar boom, the abandonment of full employment as
a policy goal by modern states, and the shift to market discipline by business
strategists (an aspect of the contestation discussed earlier), the conditions of the
gender regime in working-class communities have changed. Significant proportions of the working class face long-term structural unemployment. Traditional
working-class masculinity is being deconstructed by impersonal forces, whether
the men concerned like it or not.

Young men respond to this situation in different ways. They may attempt to
promote themselves out of the working class, via education and training. They
may accept their poor chances of promotion and develop a slack, complicit

masculinity. Or they may fight against the powers that be, rejecting school, skirmishing with the police, getting into crime.[13]

The tattoo-and-motorcycle style of aggressive white working-class masculinity is familiar enough; Metcalfe even comments on the 'larrikin mode of class struggle.' It has generally been understood as linked with stark homophobia, misogyny, and domestic patriarchy. Our interviews with young unemployed men suggest that this pattern too is being deconstructed in a significant way. The public display of protest masculinity continues. But it can coexist with a break-down in the *domestic* gender division of labor, with an acceptance of women's economic equality, and an interest in children, which would not be expected from traditional accounts.[14]

Since structural unemployment in first-world countries is most likely to affect members of oppressed ethnic groups, such a deconstruction must interweave with race politics. American discussions of masculinity in urban black ghettos show this interplay in one dramatic form. In other parts of the world it does not necessarily follow the same course.

[. . .]

What the evidence does show unequivocally is that working-class masculinities are no more set in concrete than are ruling-class masculinities – though in a bourgeois culture they are much more liable to stereotyped representation. The conscious attempts at building a counter-sexist heterosexual masculinity have mainly occurred in middle-class milieux. Some socialist explorations did occur but are now mostly forgotten. I would argue that a progressive sexual politics cannot afford to be class-blind. It must look to the settings of working-class life, and existing forms of working-class collective action, as vital arenas of sexual politics.[15]

## Afterword

To cover the territory of this article is to skate fast over dangerously thin ice. For much of the story the evidential basis is still very slight; that is why I have called it a sketch and a historical hypothesis.

But this is the scale on which we have to think, if the major problems about men in gender relations are to get sorted out. For too long the discussion of masculinity has been bogged down in psychological readings of the issue, most often in an ego-psychology based on an extreme individualism. We need to let the breezes of politics, economics, institutional sociology, and history blow through the psychology. They may puff strategies of reform away from an individualized masculinity-therapy towards a collective politics of gender equality.

[. . .]

## Notes

1 T. Carrigan, R. W. Connell, and J. Lee, 'Toward a New Sociology of Masculinity,' *Theory and Society* 14/5: 551–604: D. Ford and J. Hearn, *Studying Men and Masculinity: A Sourcebook of Literature and Materials* (Bradford: University of Bradford Department of Applied Social Studies, 1988); J. Hearn and D. H. J. Morgan, editors, *Men, Masculinities and Social Theory* (London: Unwin Hyman, 1990).

2 G. Gilder, *Sexual Suicide* (New York: Bantam, 1975); R. W. Connell, 'Men and Socialism,' in G. Evans and J. Reeves, editors, *Labor Essays* (Melbourne: Drummond, 1982), 53–64; A. Ellis, *Sex and the Liberated Man* (Secaucus, N.J.: Lyle Stuart, 1976); R. A. Johnson, *He: Understanding Masculine Psychology* (New York: Harper and Row, 1974).

3 J. Hearn and W. Parkin, '*Sex*' at '*Work*': *The Power and Paradox of Organization Sexuality* (Brighton: Wheatsheaf Books, 1987); R. Pringle, *Secretaries Talk: Sexuality, Power and Work* (Sydney: Allen & Unwin, 1989); P. Fussell, *Wartime: Understanding and Behavior in the Second World War* (New York: Oxford University Press, 1989); S. Milligan, *Adolf Hitler: My Part in His Downfall* (Harmondsworth: Penguin, 1971).

4 R. W. Connell, 'A Whole New World: Remaking Masculinity in the Context of the Environmental Movement,' *Gender and Society* 4/4: 452–78.

5 Hui-Chen Wang Liu, *The Traditional Chinese Clan Rules* (New York: Association for Asian Studies and J. J. Augustin, 1959); W. Brugger, 'The Male (and Female) in Chinese Society,' *Impact of Science on Society* 21/1: 5–19; J. Stacey, *Patriarchy and Socialist Revolution in China* (Berkeley: University of California Press, 1983).

6 L. Hanke, *The Spanish Struggle for Justice in the Conquest of America* (Boston: Little, Brown, 1965).

7 A. Bray, *Homosexuality in Renaissance England* (London: Gay Men's Press, 1982).

8 M. H. Bacon, *Mothers of Feminism: The Story of Quaker Women in America* (San Francisco: Harper and Row, 1986), ch. 1.

9 K. von Clausewitz, *On War* (Princeton, N.J.: Princeton University Press, 1976).

10 J. B. Adolph, 'The South American Macho: Myths and Mystique,' *Impact of Science on Society* 21: 83–92; V. de la Cancela. 'A Critical Analysis of Puerto Rican Machismo: Implications for Clinical Practice.' *Psychotherapy* 23: 291–6: C. L. Pearlman. 'Machismo, Marianismo and Change in Indigenous Mexico: A Case Study from Ouxaea.' *Quarterly Journal of Ideology* 8/4: 53–9.

11 M. Waring, *Counting for Nothing: What Men Value and What Women are Worth* (Wellington: Allen and Unwin and Port Nicholson Press, 1988).

12 B. D. Adam, *The Rise of a Gay and Lesbian Movement* (Boston: Hall, 1987); D. Altman, *The Homosexualization of America, the Americanization of the Homosexual* (New York: St Martin's Press, 1982).

13 R. W. Connell, 'Live Fast and Die Young: The Construction of Masculinity Among Young Working-Class Men on the Margin of the Labour Market,' *Australian and New Zealand Journal of Sociology* 27/2: 141–71.

14 A. F. Metcalfe, *For Freedom and Dignity: Historical Agency and Class Structure in the Coalfields of NSW* (Sydney: Allen and Unwin, 1988); P. E. Willis, *Profane Culture* (London: Routledge and Kegan Paul. 1978); C. B. Hopper and J. Moore, 'Women in Outlaw Motorcycle Gangs,' *Journal of Contemporary Ethnography* 18/4: 363–87.

15 A. Tolson, *The Limits of Masculinity* (London: Tavistock, 1977).

# 5

# A Passion for 'Sameness'? Sexuality and Gender Accountability

*Gillian A. Dunne*

This chapter aims to further theoretical and empirical understandings of household divisions of labour by extending our field of vision to include the experiences of a hitherto neglected and invisible group – lesbian parents. It departs from convention by recognizing that lesbian experience has as much to contribute to debates about gender as it does to sexuality (see Dunne, 1997a, 1998b). I argue that the detailed and critical investigation of divisions of labour between partners of the same gender offers a particularly effective way of revealing those circumstances and practices which facilitate, and those which inhibit the negotiation of, more egalitarian arrangements in partnerships *per se*. Further, by moving beyond the heterosexual focus which dominates empirical research on gender, work and family life (Blumstein and Schwartz, 1985; VanEvery, 1995; for rare exceptions) we are in a position to assess the significance of heterosexuality itself in reproducing the *status quo*.

The chapter takes as its starting point findings which confirm a tendency for lesbian partners to negotiate fairly equal divisions of labour. It moves on to explore why this outcome is probable in lesbian partnerships but exceptional for heterosexual couples. [...]

### Divisions of labour in lesbian households: some evidence

When lesbians are asked to describe how their relationships with women differ from their understandings/experience of heterosexual relationships, they almost always make some reference to equality (Dunne, 1997a; Heaphy et al., 1999). [...] Findings suggest that women in lesbian relationships are much more likely than women in heterosexual relationships to describe their domestic/parenting arrangements as equal (e.g., Blumstein and Schwartz, 1985; Peace, 1993; Tasker and Golombok, 1998).

[...]

## The Lesbian Household Project

The Lesbian Household Project[1] was designed to investigate whether or to what extent lesbian partners actually manage to operationalize egalitarian ideals in relation to the organization of work. The study draws on the experience of 37 cohabiting lesbian couples with dependent children (mostly of pre-school age). [...] Methods employed included a series of two- to three-hour semi-structured interviews with both partners – joint followed several months later by individual. To explore respondents' perceptions of 'who did what', the first interview centred on the creation of a Household Portrait.[2] Data were collected on respondents' work histories and their attitudes to paid employment were explored. To avoid confining the analysis to their perceptions [...] each participant recorded her activities for seven days in a time-task diary. [...] The study differs from other work on divisions of labour in a number of ways: (1) its focus on lesbian partners with dependent children (the majority became parents via donor insemination; Dunne 2000a); (2) in the range of household dynamics explored (it extends beyond domestic and caring work to include paid employment); (3) in the diversity of methods used. [...]

*Paid employment*  A high level of flexibility and even-handedness characterized the allocation of employment responsibilities in partnerships, regardless of the age of children. Being a birth-mother [...] was a poor predictor for employment (hours, status or income) differences between partners. Views dominating accounts of employment were that each partner had a right to, and would benefit from, an identity beyond the home, and that level of pay was a poor indicator of the value of work performed. It was unusual to find one partner's 'career' taking priority over the other's (Dunne, 2000b). Their positive attitudes to employment were balanced by a strong sense that caring for a child was important, demanding and pleasurable work. Thus, it was not unusual to find both partners in half-time employment, particularly when they had pre-school children. This situation represented the ideal for many couples in the study. [...] Within reason they were prepared to experience a reduced standard of living [...] to enable what they perceived as a fairer, more sensible outcome.

*Domestic tasks*  On the basis of both how they spent their time (as recorded in their diaries), and their perceptions of who did what, the allocation of household tasks bore no relationship to the gender-segregated patterns that characterize dominant trends for heterosexual couples.[3] Except when differences in paid working hours were extreme (more than 30 hours' difference, N = 11), time spent on the performance of domestic work was fairly equally divided in partnerships (81 per cent came within a 60–40 per cent sharing threshold). As childcare was viewed as a valuable job in itself, the reduction in paid working hours to care for a child was rarely seen by either partner as justification for her performing the bulk of domestic labour (see Dunne 1998a for detailed analysis).

[...] I now want to outline and illustrate my argument that their ability to operationalize egalitarian ideals can be understood as emerging from the different configuration of gender practices that same-sex interaction facilitates.

## Gender as process

The relationship between sexuality and gender becomes particularly interesting when we conceptualize gender as an active ongoing process, rather than fixed. Gender, as formulated by West and Zimmerman (1987) and Connell (1987) and revisited by Fenstermaker, West and Zimmerman (1991) is something that is continuously achieved in our ongoing everyday interaction with others – we *do* rather than *have* gender. [...]

The fluidity (across time and space) and specificity (from context to context) of gender criteria, together with the fact that our gender identities co-exist alongside a wealth of other social identities, means that we should recognize the existence of masculin*ities* and feminin*ities* (Connell, 1987: 175–99). However, [...] to be a man or a woman rests on the idea of fundamental difference (Connell, 1987: 140; Fenstermaker et al., 1991). As such, the doing of gender must always involve the affirmation of gender difference, and failure to do this can bring censure and may expose the overlapping nature of gender and sexuality. 'Real' women and 'real' men are always heterosexual (Connell, 1987: 186).

We do gender in our mode of dress, through our occupation of and movement in space, in how we manipulate objects and so on. This kind of thinking has been useful for understanding why domestic arrangements negotiated between women and men are so resistant to change (Berk, 1985; Lewis and O'Brien, 1987; Hochschild, 1989; Morris, 1990; Fenstermaker et al., 1991). Engagement with the everyday tasks and objects of the home is not simply about getting necessary work done, it is about engaging in the production of gender (Berk, 1985). As Berk (1985) suggests, the home is a 'gender factory'. [...]

So in relation to household divisions of labour, rather than consciously participating in an exploitative process of labour appropriation, women and men are simply doing what women and men do. [...] The idea that the performance of gender-specific tasks is linked with the affirmation of gender difference is, however, somewhat dependent on this work being allocated between women and men. [...] The fact that this process of appropriation is somewhat dependent on there being a man and a woman involved illustrates the way that gendered action is mediated by sexuality. Thus, at least in this example, the interaction reproducing the social structure is the doing of gender *through* heterosexuality.

## (Hetero)sexuality and gender (difference)

Sexuality and gender are connected in a variety of powerful overlapping ways. Together they interact to (1) shape gender relations by constructing the conditions by which men and women can relate across gender boundaries, and (2) police the content of masculinities and femininities.

The full meaning of the relationship between sexuality and gender relations becomes clearer when the social origins of this core aspect of identity is recognized. [...] How we give voice to and act upon our sexual and emotional feelings is limited by social, ideological and material forces, whereby heterosexuality and heterosexual relationships are presented as *the only* 'natural', 'healthy', universally socially and morally acceptable expression of adult sexuality.[4] Given that this version of the story provides the logic for drawing women and men together out of their more usually homo-emotional worlds into relations of inequality, a key project for feminism is the understanding of how, why and with what consequences people become heterosexual.[5] This allows us to move beyond an analysis of heterosexuality as practice, to a less divisive position which conceptualizes heterosexuality as a social institution. [...] The identities 'heterosexual' and 'homosexual' can only make sense in the context of gender polarization (Connell, 1987). The likelihood that people will form heterosexual partnerships rests on the social construction of dichotomous and hierarchical gender categories and practices. As Butler observes: 'The heterosexualization of desire requires and institutes the production of discrete and asymmetrical oppositions between "feminine" and "masculine"' (1990: 17). Likewise, Rubin (1975) argues that union between women and men is assured through the suppression of similarities between them, so that a 'reciprocal state of dependency' will exist (1975: 178). (The suppression of similarities, I would stress, includes skills, competencies, employment opportunities and wages.) As these differences become translated into reciprocal needs and dependencies they become *eroticized* – heterosexuality becomes the attraction of opposites (Connell, 1987: 246) or a passion for a specific configuration of difference.

If heterosexual outcomes are assured through the suppression of similarities between women and men, [...] then we should not be too surprised to find that when men and women form heterosexual partnerships gender *difference* is being affirmed in the everyday routines of social life. The imperative link and overlap between doing gender difference and doing heterosexuality represents an important, but rarely recognized or discussed, contradiction facing the vanguard of women and men who are committed to negotiating egalitarian relationships with each other. It helps explain why relationships can be threatened when women seek equality through challenging the gender differences that structure their partnerships with men – something much greater than 'fairness' is at stake – a sense of who one is as a woman or a man. [...] Within binary thinking there can only be two genders and their existence rests on the notion of 'otherness'. Recognition of the fluidity of and overlap between gender categories threatens the logic of difference, and the *raison d'être* for compulsory heterosexual coupling.

At the same time, [...] the boundaries that separate women and men out as different from each other also provide spaces and the grounds for solidarity within gender categories (e.g., friendships, feminism). This can give rise to a passion for 'sameness' which, when acknowledged and acted upon, enables people to question the taken-for-grantedness of heterosexuality (Dunne, 1997a). Rather than escaping gender altogether, as Wittig (1992) suggests, lesbian relationships are formed and experienced in a different gender context from that of heterosexual women. If gender is mediated by sexuality, then it will have an important bearing on practice.

[...] We can take this a stage further by arguing that *the gender of the person we are doing our gender with/for and who does it to us* matters. [...] In same-sex settings the compulsion to affirm our gender difference can be less powerful and, paradoxically, we may be less aware of ourselves as gendered individuals in these circumstances. [...]

I now want to illustrate this argument by turning to respondents' accounts and exploring what can be accomplished by women who are doing gender outside heterosexuality. I will suggest that the alternative gender dynamic underpinning same-sex relationships is a key factor in enabling the negotiation of egalitarian relationships.

## Doing gender beyond heterosexuality

### Domestic arrangements between women – 'they're just jobs for us'

What is it about lesbian relationships that appears to turn upside down many of the assumptions which shape heterosexual practice and maintain the *status quo*? The answer lies in their similarities as women, together with the differences that place them outside conventionality, which provide the opportunity for (and almost require) the re-thinking of household arrangements. This position is summed up by Dolly, who has been living with her partner, Jo, for the past 19 years:

> I suppose because our relationship doesn't fit into a social norm, there are no pre-set indications about how our relationship should work. We have to work it out for ourselves. We've no role models in terms of how we divide our duties, so we've got to work it out afresh as to what suits us.... We try very hard to be just to each other and...not exploit the other person.

Many respondents had been married or had lived with male partners in the past. When reflecting on how relationships with women differed, freedom from gender assumptions around the allocation of household tasks was seen as key. While most viewed their heterosexual relationships positively, because they had usually been involved with men whom they viewed as exceptionally egalitarian, they felt greatly advantaged by the absence of 'gender scripts' to guide their relationships with women (Dunne, 1997a). They contrasted the ease with which domestic arrangements emerged in their partnerships with women. Mandy, who works half-time and is the co-parent of a two-year-old boy, describes this:

> *In comparison with heterosexual experience, is there any difference in how you approach and feel about doing housework?* Oh yes! Because it is open for negotiation in a much more real sense, and you are not fighting against anything. No matter how New Mannish or not, there is a prevailing subconscious belief that women do housework. And I think a lot of women – I mean, I did – fall into that. I did more than my fair share, or I battled not to. But I didn't negotiate on an equal footing. So yes, I think there is a big difference because it's up for grabs.

[. . .]

With persistent regularity respondents identified gender-differentiated expectations mediating the achievement of balanced relationships between men and
women. Vicky and June discuss the way their relationship differs from previous
heterosexual experience. Vicky is the birth-mother of a primary-school-
aged girl and has part-time employment which is home-based. June is the
birth-mother of two pre-school-aged children, and has a full-time paid job as a
technician:

> *Vicky*: I think it is impossible [to get balance in a heterosexual relationship]. I've had
> to do so much rebellion against the status I was expected to have in a heterosexual
> relationship. . . . It's just too complicated. I mean it's difficult for feminists anyway.

*What gets in the way?*

> *June*: Internalized sex roles and external pressure. . . . I was constantly adding it all
> up in my head (cooking, cleaning the bathroom, etc.) and thinking this isn't fair. Sex
> roles get in the way of everything. You can't forget it, you can't just let it go along,
> which I think we pretty much do really, don't we?

[. . .]

The advantages of occupying the same position in the gender order were often
stressed, particularly by respondents who had the experience of a heterosexual
relationship. In comparing their situation to past experience or that of the
heterosexual mothers in their kin / friendship networks, there was a general
sense of relief at not having to struggle with the same kind of externally derived
sources of inequality which they saw impinging on relationships between women
and men. Like Vicky, most understood that all relationships involved difficulties
and power imbalances. However, to achieve a 'good' relationship by their definition, imbalances required recognition and working through to some happier
medium. When explored in interviews, respondents appeared to understand the
term 'equality' to mean this kind of balancing of differences.

Being two women together seems to enable a relaxed approach to the performance of household work. Tasks lost their symbolic value in the disruption of the
links between 'the shoulds of gender ideals' and the 'musts of household work'
(Berk, 1985; Seymour, 1992). Anet and Mary are both birth-mothers of primary-
school-aged boys, and each has full-time employment. They reflect upon their
completed household portrait:

> *Anet*: We've put a lot of things 50/50, but within that we divide them up, like at
> different times, and it's like a fluid thing.

*Why do you think it's fluid, where does this come from?*

> *Mary*: I suppose it's like an equality on a gender basis.

*Anet*: We don't have expectations within this set-up on how we should interact ....In a heterosexual situation...there's this gender inequality which has come with just the way that you've been brought up.

*Mary*: It's just jobs to do for us, things that need doing and they don't have a value, a sort of female or male value within our set-up, they are just things that need doing and there's none of that gender thing going on.

[...]

Alternatively, some women who had struggled to achieve more egalitarian heterosexual relationships spoke of their relief from feeling that they had to perform 'male' tasks.

Importantly, respondents' similarities as women, which enabled them to put themselves in the place of the other, facilitated the construction of more balanced domestic arrangements. In discussing their approach to allocating domestic work, respondents spoke in terms of not wanting to exploit the other, or of feeling that one person should not be clearing up after the other, or of just being aware that it was their turn to do something. The balance came because the monitoring of contributions was on the basis of broadly similar criteria. This, together with the empathy experienced, enabled greater transparency in the evaluation of the fairness of contributions. This contrasts with the situation for men and women in heterosexual relationships where gender difference not only structures contributions but hinders change by shaping evaluative criteria (Hochschild, 1989; Gordon, 1990: 97). For example, a mis-match in criteria arises as a man compares his contributions favourably to other men and finds it hard to understand why he fails to satisfy his partner. The ability to be in tune with the rhythm of the household is something that women have learnt. This capacity to notice and anticipate *disadvantages* women in heterosexual partnerships because on the whole men do not do it, but it is a great source of *advantage* for women managing a home together – in the individual interviews, respondents usually spoke of both themselves and their partners as being actively involved in keeping things ticking over on the domestic front.

For two women together divisions of labour in the home were responsive to employment demands. In times of stress the balance could shift. However, there was usually a short-term / long-term distinction made. Respondents commonly challenged the idea that the pursuit of employment opportunities justified the long-term relinquishment of basic domestic and childcare responsibilities. Even in sole-earner partnerships the paid worker entered into the rhythm of the home. [...]

Routinely, respondents challenged the logic behind the statement 'surely, if one partner has a stressful job and her partner is home-based, it is only fair that she should come home to rest' with comments such as, 'the statement assumes that caring for a small child isn't stressful'. [...] Again, the capacity for one partner to place herself in the position of the other is key for understanding their views. This empathy was in turn reinforced by the experiential insights gained through lack of specialization. Thus, the performance of paid work, the domestic routine and childcare afforded no mystery. [...]

The gender dynamics underpinning lesbian relationships enabled women to operationalize their more egalitarian ideals to the extent that most felt that they had managed to achieve a satisfactory balance of power.

[...]

### Discussion: gender, sexuality and 'sameness'?

Earlier, I suggested that the boundaries drawn around gender categories create spaces for gender solidarity, and desire can be organized around 'identification and similarity rather than difference' (Connell, 1987: 182). The experience of the mothers in this study seems to bear this out. [...]

Of course the idea of a passion for 'sameness' is in many ways fallacious. First, women are different from each other in all sorts of important respects (e.g., autobiography, class, ethnicity, education, employment status, income, age, degree of able-bodiedness, looks, charisma). However, I would argue, lesbianism is about a preference for negotiating (balancing, valuing, offsetting) differences within the solidarity that comes from experiencing the world as women. A lesbian's partner is usually her best friend, or at least one of them, and the operation of power is more likely to elaborate upon the rules of friendship (equality, support, balancing the differences, reciprocity) than the rules of heterosexual romance (the eroticization of difference, 'intimate strangers' possessing different emotional vocabularies, institutional and sexual power imbalances). [...] Lesbianism is a preference for doing gender for, and being gendered by, women rather than men. [...] I am convinced that for women, moving beyond heterosexuality is deeply rooted in this gender dimension. [...] This is why so many of the lesbian women that I have interviewed have expressed views such as 'I cannot be *me* in relationships with men in the way that I can with women – or at least not the same *me*' (Dunne, 1997a: 113).

Secondly, to speak of 'a passion for sameness' is almost a contradiction in terms. As a phrase it is revealing because it exposes so clearly the deeply accepted and expected conjunction between passion and 'difference'. 'Sameness' conjures up images of blandness and dullness. [...] Aside from the reality of there being plenty of differences between partners in same-sex relationships to present exciting challenges in knowing and being known, the reality of a 'passion for difference' as it is lived in many women's everyday lives seriously throws into question the idea that eroticized difference is a very sound basis for sustaining long-standing relationships. One has to ask, what are we left with when difference loses its erotic power in a heterosexual partnership? In answering this we are offered crucial clues into why so many women are leaving relationships with men or forgoing marriage. [...] The identities available to increasing numbers of women have expanded beyond wife and mother to include a more self-conscious sense of self as perhaps mothers bringing up children alone or with a partner in a separate household, as divorced or single, as feminists, as lesbians, as breadwinners and employees. As opportunities start to open, [...] it is less likely that women will put up with disappointment in their relationships. We are in the midst of a gender revolution. [...] It may be that behind the 'crisis' of marriage and the traditional family lies a deeper problem that has yet to be consciously given voice – that the raised aspirations and expanded identities of many contemporary women may be in contradiction with the doing of gender through heterosexuality.

## Conclusion

Meanwhile, feminism moves forward in three contradictory directions. First, the more dominant, Liberal Feminist position is about enabling women to be more like men. This involves the erosion or denial of difference but retains a masculine and capitalist view of value as defined by 'public' participation. Thus, empowerment is linked with full-time employment and occupational achievement. A problem here is that new forms of inequality emerge as, for example, others (usually working-class women) are found to fill the gaps left by the 'liberated' woman (see Gregson and Lowe, 1994). This position challenges one aspect – what women (but not men) may achieve – of one dimension, *gender boundaries*, of women's disadvantage, but leaves unchallenged another central dimension, the *hierarchy of value* attached to women and men's traditional territories.

The second direction – including 'equal-but-different' and some separatist positions – recognizes and builds upon gender differences (sometimes assuming essential origins but more usually socially constructed ones). By asserting and illuminating the value of what women do, they seek to undermine the *hierarchy of value* assigned to what women and men do. Thus, women's nurturing qualities can be celebrated. The different capacities and skills of women and men may be seen to complement each other in partnerships based on equivalence. [...] The problem with this approach is that *gender boundaries* are left unchallenged. Specialization [...] simply reinforces the traditional masculine model of employment. Further, by making claims of an enduring, specifically female character, the process of socialization is reified in such a way as to leave us no further ahead than when differences have been located in nature.

A third direction is to contest both the boundaries and the hierarchies. [...] When thinking about what difference gender difference makes, it is hard to come up with any which do not relate to the very structures of inequality that feminists seek to undermine. Consequently, we have a common interest in dissolving gender as a category of both content and consequence. [...] In practical terms, this means recognizing and celebrating the value of women's traditional areas of work and influence rather than accepting a masculine and capitalist hierarchy of value. [...] In conjunction with this would be the view that this valuable work is something that male peers can and should do, the aim being to facilitate and insist upon change in men's lives – enabling them to become more like women. [...] The radicalness of this direction is that it challenges both patriarchy and capitalism. If, for example, fathers experienced parenting and domestic life in similar ways to women, then they would find the time demands of employers as unrealistic as mothers usually do. This would have serious implications for the organization of paid work and would undermine men's monopoly of economic advantage (see illustrations in Dunne, 1997b, 1998a).

[...] The erosion of gender would undermine the meanings and circumstances that give rise to the categories heterosexual and homosexual. In this way men would lose their monopoly of women. [...]

## Notes

I am grateful to the Economic and Social Research Council for funding the project (reference no.: R000234649).

1   The study was undertaken by the author and fieldwork was conducted during 1995 and 1996. For further details on methods see Dunne (1998a).
2   The Household Portrait was first developed by Andrea Doucet (1995, 1997) for illuminating the allocation strategies of egalitarian heterosexual couples. This technique involves both partners placing a broad range of task/responsibility tokens (colour-coded by themes such as routine domestic, household service work, childcare, etc.) on to a board offering a continuum ranging from 100 per cent partner A to 100 per cent partner B. This visual representation encourages respondents to reflect upon and discuss how their household is run, and participate in some initial analysis as patterns emerge.
3   While there is some evidence that men and women can form egalitarian domestic relationships (VanEvery, 1995), a distinctly asymmetrical division of unwaged labour remains the majority pattern. An unequal division of responsibilities in the home is a dominant trend in households where men are unemployed (Morris, 1995) and women are sole earners (Wheelock, 1990), among full-time dual-earner couples (Mansfield and Collard, 1988; Brannen and Moss, 1991), where both are in professional occupations (Gregson and Lowe, 1994), or the wife has a higher status job than her husband (McRae, 1986). Gendered patterns of responsibilities remain even in countries such as Sweden and Denmark, where there is a strong political commitment to promoting equality (Borchorst, 1990; Haas, 1990). Couples who perceive themselves to be sharing in the home rarely escape the impact of gendered assumptions shaping their work strategies (Doucet, 1997).
4   For feminist critiques of heterosexuality as 'natural' see the classics, Rich (1984), Rubin (1975) and Wittig (1992). Each of these positions allows us to view lesbianism as a source of empowerment.
5   See Dunne (1997a) for a case study which attempts to explore these questions and illustrates links between lesbianism and empowerment, with particular reference to work and relationships.

## References

Berk, S. F. (1985) *The Gender Factory: The Apportionment of Work in American Households*. New York: Plenum.
Blumstein, P. and Schwartz, P. (1985) *American Couples*. New York: Pocket Books.
Borchorst, A. (1990) 'Political motherhood and childcare policies: a comparative approach to Britain and Scandinavia', in C. Ungerson (ed.), *Gender and Caring: Work and Welfare in Britain and Scandinavia*. London: Harvester Wheatsheaf.

Brannen, J. and Moss, P. (1991) *Managing Mothers: Dual Earners Households after Maternity Leave*. London: Unwin Hyman.

Butler, J. (1990) *Gender Trouble: Feminism and the Subversion of Identity*. London: Routledge.

Connell, R. W. (1987) *Gender and Power*. Cambridge: Polity.

Doucet, A. (1995) 'Gender differences, gender equality and care: towards understanding gendered labour in British dual earner households'. PhD dissertation. Faculty of Social and Political Sciences, University of Cambridge.

Doucet, A. (1997) ' "You see the need perhaps more clearly than I": seeing, measuring and theorising domestic responsibility'. Paper presented to the Canadian Association of Sociology and Anthropology, Memorial University, Saint John's, Newfoundland, June.

Dunne, G. A. (1997a) *Lesbian Lifestyles: Women's Work and the Politics of Sexuality*. Basingstoke and London: Macmillan.

Dunne, G. A. (1997b) 'Why can't a man be more like a woman? In search of balanced domestic and employment lives', London School of Economics Gender Institute Discussion Paper Series, 3. London: LSE.

Dunne, G. A. (1998a) ' "Pioneers behind our own front doors": towards new models in the organization of work in partnerships', *Work, Employment and Society*, 12 (2): 273–95.

Dunne, G. A. (1998b) 'Add sexuality and stir: towards a broader understanding of the gender dynamics of work and family life', in G. A. Dunne (ed.), *Living Difference: Lesbian Perspectives on Work and Family Life*. Binghamton, NY: Harrington Park Press.

Dunne, G. A. (2000a) 'Opting into motherhood: lesbians blurring the boundaries and transforming the meaning of parenthood and kinship', *Gender and Society*, 14 (1): 11–35.

Dunne, G. A. (2000b) 'Lesbians as authentic workers? Gender, Sexuality and the status quo', *Sexualities*, 3 (2): 133–48.

Fenstermaker, S., West, C. and Zimmerman, D. H. (1991) 'Gender inequality: new conceptual terrain', in R. L. Blumberg (ed.), *Gender, Family and Economy: The Triple Overlap*. London: Sage.

Gordon, T. (1990) *Feminist Mothers*. London: Macmillan.

Gregson, N. and Lowe, M. (1994) *Servicing the Middle Classes: Class, Gender and Waged Domestic Labour*. London: Routledge.

Haas, L. (1990) 'Parental leave in Sweden', *Journal of Family Studies*, December.

Heaphy, B., Donovan, C. and Weeks, J. (1999) 'Sex, money and the kitchen sink: power in same–sex couple relationships', in J. Seymour and P. Bagguley (eds), *Relating Intimacies: Power and Resistance*. London: Macmillan, 222–45.

Hochschild, A. R. (1989) *The Second Shift*. New York: Avon Books.

Lewis, C. and O'Brien, M. (eds) (1987) *Reassessing Fatherhood: New Observations on Fathers and the Modern Family*. London: Sage.

McRae, S. (1986) *Cross-class Families: A Study of Wives' Occupational Superiority*. Oxford: Clarendon Press.

Mansfield, P. and Collard, J. (1998) *The Beginning of the Rest of Your Life: A Portrait of Newly Wed Marriage*. London: Macmillan.

Morris, L. (1990) *The Workings of the Household: A US–UK Comparison*. Cambridge: Polity.

Morris, L. (1995) *Social Divisions: Economic Decline and Social Structural Change*. London: UCL Press.

Peace, H. F. (1993) 'The pretended family – a study of the divisions of domestic labour in lesbian families', *Leicester University Discussion Papers in Sociology*, No. S93/3. Leicester: Leicester University Press.

Rich, A. (1984) 'On compulsory heterosexuality and lesbian existence', in A. Snitow, C. Stansell and S. Thompson (eds), *Desire: The Politics of Sexuality*. London: Virago.

Rubin, G. (1975) 'The traffic in women: notes on the "political economy" of sex', in R. R. Reiter (ed.), *Towards an Anthropology of Women*. London: Monthly Review Press.

Seymour, J. (1992) '"Not a manly thing to do?" Gender accountability and the division of domestic labour', in G. A. Dunne, R. M. Blackburn and J. Jarman (eds), *Inequalities in Employment, Inequalities in Home-Life*. Conference Proceedings for Cambridge Social Stratification Seminar 9–10 September 1992.

Tasker, F. L. and Golombok, S. (1998) 'The role of co-mothers in planned lesbian-led families', *The Journal of Lesbian Studies*, 12: 4.

VanEvery, J. (1995) *Heterosexual Women Changing the Family: Refusing to be a 'Wife'!* London: Taylor & Francis.

West, C. and Zimmerman, D. H. (1987) 'Doing gender', *Gender & Society*, 1: 125–51.

Wheelock, J. (1990) *Husbands at Home: The Domestic Economy in a Post-industrial Society*. London: Routledge.

Wittig, M. (1992) 'One is not born a woman', in M. Wittig (ed.), *The Straight Mind and Other Essays*. Hemel Hempstead: Harvester Wheatsheaf.

# 6

# Heterosexuality, Heteronormativity and Gender Hierarchy: Some Reflections on Recent Debates

*Stevi Jackson*

There is currently a renewed interest in problematizing heterosexuality on the part of feminists. At the same time we have witnessed the development of queer theory, which also seeks to question the normative status of heterosexuality. For the most part these interrogations of heterosexuality have been going on in two quite separate arenas, each with its own theoretical and political agendas, although some feminists are engaging with both sets of arguments. Hence, although Queer is among the perspectives which have been drawn upon in recent feminist debates on heterosexuality (Smart, 1996a, 1996b; Wilton, 1996), it has a life of its own separate from those debates and unconnected with them.

In Britain the impetus for the revival of feminist debate came, as in the past, from radical lesbian feminists. Amid fears that old wounds would be reopened, that the bitter arguments of the early 1980s would be rehearsed all over again, some commentators on the debate detected signs of the old defensiveness and guilt on the part of heterosexual feminists. Yet on the whole the response from heterosexual feminists has been more positive, with many evincing a willingness to engage in a critique of heterosexuality as institution and practice. [. . .]

Whereas feminist critiques of heterosexuality took the oppression of women as their point of departure, Queer has developed from gay political and theoretical priorities. Queer theory is not particularly easy to define; it is not a single unified perspective and most of its founding canonical texts (for instance Butler, 1990; Dollimore, 1991; Fuss 1991; Sedgwick, 1991) do not announce themselves as such by their titles. Some feel that it has had its day, or at least that the term has outlived its usefulness. One of those credited with originating the idea of queer theory, Teresa de Lauretis (1991), soon claimed that it had become 'a conceptually vacuous creature of the publishing industry' (1994: 297). The term, however, has refused to die and, if nothing else, serves as a convenient shorthand for an approach to dissident sexualities framed from deconstructionist, poststructuralist or postmodernist perspectives informed by the ideas of Lacan, Derrida and, above all, Foucault.

One area of potential confusion here is the distinction between queer politics, arising from AIDS activism, and queer theory, with its roots in the academy. In some respects they converge. Both are inclusive in scope, incorporating not only gays and lesbians, but bisexuals, transsexuals and, indeed, anyone or anything not one hundred per cent conventionally heterosexual. Both emphasize the transgression and subversion of conventional heterosexual and gender norms which, in the case of queer politics, entails an unapologetic 'in your face' activism which departs from the reformist wing of the gay rights movement. They differ in that, politically, Queer often becomes an affirmation of identity, whereas queer theory seeks to destabilize all identities. Steven Seidman, for example, sees the central tenet of queer theory as being 'its challenge to what has been the dominant foundational concept of both homophobic and affirmative homosexual theory: the assumption of a unified homosexual identity' (1997: 93). Where a queer identity is mobilized, it is for strategic purposes (see, for example, Butler, 1991) and is thus provisional and contingent, defined in relation to the heterosexual presumptions it seeks to unsettle:

> Those who knowingly occupy...a marginal location, who assume a de-essentialized identity that is purely positional in character, are properly speaking not gay but *queer*.
>
> (Halperin, 1995: 62; emphasis in the original)

Queer theory's project, then, entails disturbing and troubling heterosexuality. This, and its emphasis on interrogating the binary opposites of gay / straight, man / woman, and destabilizing the boundaries between them, suggests points of convergence with feminism. Feminist responses to Queer have, however, been mixed. Lynne Segal (1994), for example, is far more willing to embrace this form of critique than that mounted by lesbian feminists. At the other end of the spectrum are those such as Sheila Jeffreys, who have always seen heterosexuality as pivotal to women's oppression and lesbianism as a form of resistance. For Jeffreys, Queer is a means of 'disappearing' lesbians, denying both their specific oppression and their resistance to patriarchal control (1994). Others, too, suspect that it is yet another manifestation of white male dominance in radical guise (see Smyth, 1992: 31–3). Some lesbian feminists, however, see in Queer powerful analytical tools with which to explore the interconnection between the oppression of women and the maintenance of heterosexual hegemony (Wilton, 1996, 1997). Finally, some straight feminists have drawn on it to rethink heterosexual desire and practice (Smart, 1996a).

My own response to Queer – in the theoretical sense – can best be described as one of sceptical interest. Part of my scepticism arises from concerns that some of what is perceived as radical in queer theory is simply a reinvention of the sociological wheel. Moreover, queer theorizing is limited to the extent that it takes place at the level of culture and discourse, paying little attention to social structures and material social practices. I remain interested, however, because Queer does provide some new insights into the deployment of discourses around sexuality. Insofar as it is possible to accommodate the concept of discourse within a materialist frame of analysis, it may be possible to draw on Queer's strengths while avoiding its weaknesses. [...]

What both queer and feminist approaches have in common is that they call into question the inevitability and naturalness of heterosexuality, its normative status. Furthermore, feminists and queer theorists, to a greater or lesser extent, link the heterosexual/homosexual divide with gender. Whatever theoretical differences exist within and between these two diverse and overlapping constituencies, the common assumption is that neither gender boundaries nor the boundary between heterosexuality and homosexuality/lesbianism are fixed by nature. Queers and feminists both take an oppositional relationship to a social and cultural order which enshrines male dominated heterosexuality as a largely unquestioned norm. Their critique of heterosexuality is a political response to oppression and exclusion, fuelled by a belief in the possibility of resistance and the hope – at least for most feminists – of radical change. I want to reflect on some of the themes emerging from this recent work and their potential for taking the critique of heterosexuality forward.

But first I want to register a note of caution. The renewal of radical critiques of heterosexuality is in sharp contrast with some of what is going on in the world of activist gay politics, where we have seen a retreat to biological determinism accompanied by demands to be included into heterosexual privileges (see Rahman and Jackson, 1997). Meanwhile, male dominance in heterosexual relations persists. All this appears to have gone unnoticed by many of those commentating on the contemporary sexual scene, seduced by signs of trendy gender ambiguity into thinking that there has been a cultural shift towards sexual diversity (McRobbie, 1996). While some changes are occurring, we need to be aware these may be accommodated within mainstream culture without much threat to heterosexual hegemony.

[...]

The idea of being 'born that way' shapes not only narratives of self constructed by gays and lesbians, but also political strategies. This story concedes ground to the heterosexual majority, treats the majority as given and undercuts the radical potential of homosexuality (Whisman, 1996). [...] One of the contributions of Queer has been its highlighting of the ways in which the strategic deployment of homophobic discourse might be as important as its content (Halperin, 1995), since its content is often contradictory. We used to think that if we could lay bare the contradictions of ruling ideologies we could demolish them. Now it seems that the contradictions are part of their strength, enabling them to shift and be redeployed to accommodate to new political moments. [...]

### Preconditions for an effective critique of heterosexuality

[...]

An effective critique of heterosexuality – at the levels of social structure, meaning, social practice and subjectivity – must contain two key elements. The first of these is a critique of heteronormativity, of the normative status of heterosexuality which renders any alternative sexualities 'other' and marginal. The second is a critique of what some have called 'hetero-patriarchy' or 'hetero-oppression' (although I dislike both these terms), in other words heterosexuality as systematically male dominated. It follows that a critical stance on heterosexuality should pay attention to its interlinkage with gender, as both division and hierarchy. [...]

The various critiques which have so far been developed often fall short of including both elements, although there is a long feminist tradition of trying to do so, going back at least to Adrienne Rich (1980), for whom compulsory heterosexuality both kept women *in* (within its confines) and kept them *down*, subordinated. Yet feminists – myself included – have often concentrated on one side of heterosexuality at the expense of the other. We have analysed in great detail the myriad ways in which the institutions and practices associated with heterosexuality oppress women and sustain that oppression – but we have not always made it clear that heterosexuality is what we are talking about. Lesbian feminists, rarely guilty of this oversight, have addressed both male domination within heterosexuality and heteronormativity – but their analyses of the latter have been partial as a result of their wariness of male gay and queer agendas. Queer, on the other hand, is centrally concerned with destabilizing the heterosexual norm, but not with heterosexuality as patriarchal. Where Queer takes gender seriously, it is usually as division without hierarchy.

The preconditions I have outlined are applicable not only to heterosexuality as an institution, but also as an identity and as it is practised and experienced. It cannot, however, be assumed that heteronormativity and male domination always articulate with each other in predictable ways at all four levels, that it is possible to 'read off' identity, practice and experience from what is institutionalized. [...] Problems arise when heterosexuality as institution, identity, practice and experience are conflated, when heterosexuality is treated as a monolithic, unitary entity.

[...]

When talking about the system, the institution, we need a unitary concept; but when talking about identities, practices and experience we can afford to – indeed must – address diversity. Not only does this avoid the dangers of turning a critique of heterosexuality into an attack on heterosexual women, it also enables us to address intersections between different identities, social locations and patterns of dominance and subordination. Importantly, it also enables us to see heterosexuality as a site of struggle and contested meanings for those who *are* heterosexual as well as those who are not, making heterosexual feminism a tenable position rather than a contradiction in terms.

### False starts in recent feminist debates

The credit for reopening the feminist debate goes to Sue Wilkinson and Celia Kitzinger, editors of a 1992 special issue of *Feminism & Psychology* and a subsequent book (1993). [...] The way the debate was framed, however, contributed to some of the difficulties initially entailed in participating in it.

One of the problematic aspects of Wilkinson and Kitzinger's agenda was that they overemphasized the issue of political identity. Not only did this mean that other, equally crucial, aspects of heterosexuality did not at first get the attention they deserved, but the question they posed to those they invited to contribute was difficult to answer. 'How' they asked, 'does your heterosexuality contribute to your feminist politics?' (Kitzinger and Wilkinson, 1993: 5). Implicit in this question, and in much of the Editorial Introduction which explored the responses, is the assumption that heterosexuality can be a political identity and that heterosexual feminists are at fault for not making it one. Now, heterosexuality *cannot* in my view form the basis of a political identity – and certainly not an *oppositional* political identity – precisely because it represents conformity with the institutionalized norm.

[...]

The terms of the debate, as originally set, were contested and other issues emerged – especially the need to disentangle heterosexuality as an institution from the experience and practice of it and to distinguish between structural bases of male sexual power and micro-practices of power within specific (hetero)sexual encounters. [...] It was the issue of pleasure, however, which preoccupied many participants in the debate. At the same time, and sometimes unconnected with the ongoing feminist debate, issues of pleasures and practices have also featured in queer circles.

### The politics of pleasure

Can straight sex be pleasurable? Can it, perhaps, even be queer?

Even while engaging with these questions, I should make it clear that I consider debates on sexual practices to be somewhat limited in their political scope. However successful heterosexual feminists are in creating space for sexual pleasure, or for 'queer' and transgressive sexual activities, this does not necessarily challenge anything beyond our personal lives. [...]

For many women heterosexual pleasure is not easily attained, as has been demonstrated by the Women Risk and AIDS project. Not only sexual coercion but also an inability to find a language in which to discuss and assert their own pleasures serve as obstacles to the practice of safer sex among young women (Holland et al., 1990, 1991, 1998; Thomson and Scott, 1991). The young women who participated in this research disciplined their own bodies and pleasures to suit men in ways their partners were unlikely even to be aware of. In so doing they concede to men's definitions of what was pleasurable and acceptable, continuing to define sex as 'penetration for men's pleasure in which women find fulfilment primarily in the relationship, in giving pleasure' (Holland et al., 1994: 31). This attribute of femininity is not confined to erotic encounters. The ethic of service to men is integral to other aspects of heterosexuality and should alert us to the dangers of ignoring the wider context in which our sexual lives are played out.

[. . .]

Some heterosexual feminists have insisted on the pleasures, here and now, of sex with men. They have even committed the ultimate heresy in terms of past debates, of writing in praise of penetrative sex. I do not think that what is pleasurable should be beyond critique, as if erotic delights lie outside the boundaries of the social. On the other hand, it is equally unhelpful to assume that the dominant meanings of heterosexual penetration are fixed, unassailable and beyond the reach of alternative feminist reconceptualizations. To say that penetration is irredeemably patriarchal is to reduce a social relation of dominance and subordination to a physical act – an essentialist move. While I would wish to join those asserting the possibility of heterosexual pleasure, I find myself deeply dissatisfied with the ways in which others have described it.

Lynne Segal (1994, 1997) has been a staunch defender of heterosexual eroticism. She is not unaware of inequalities in heterosexual relations, of sexual coercion and violence, but she treats these less savoury aspects of heterosexuality as incidental to it. In part this is because her perspective is a psychological one, and she thus tends to individualize sexual experiences and abstract them from their social context. She is also, in my view, unduly optimistic about the degree of equality currently existing in heterosexual relations. [. . .] Segal seems to feel that sexual passion is capable of transforming, even dissolving, gender:

> In consensual sex, when bodies meet, the epiphany of that meeting – its threat and excitement – is surely that all the great dichotomies (activity / passivity, subject / object, heterosexual / homosexual) slide away. (1997: 86)

It is as if these 'bodies' are untenanted, or as if the biographies, social locations and social identities of their inhabitants have somehow been left behind. There is no history, no context. It is also a highly romanticized view of sex as magical, raising us above mundane quotidian realities.

[. . .]

Wendy Hollway, in one of the first responses to the agenda set by Wilkinson and Kitzinger, displayed, I think, enormous courage in offering a very personal account of the pleasures of sex with her lover. Like Segal's more abstract rendition, it is highly romantic. She talks of penetrative sex in terms of the 'experience of having someone you love and trust inside you', that it can 'signify as the ultimate in closeness' which 'breaches the separation from the other'. She eulogizes the virtues of feeling 'safe, protected and loved' when wrapped in her lover's 'strong arms' and speculates on the parallel significance to him of her 'cradling breasts' (1993: 413–14). What strikes me about this account, aside from the psychoanalytic framework which underpins it, is that any sense of physical pleasure is absent: there is no sensuality, no mention of the feeling of flesh on flesh. While she takes Kitzinger and Wilkinson to task for their inadequate representation of the pleasures of penetration as 'the sensation of a full vagina', she herself says almost nothing about sensation. Sexual practices are valued for what they 'signify', not for how they, physically, feel.

Two further points emerge from these attempts to articulate heterosexual pleasure, both of which may be worth exploring further. The first of these is my own sense of distance from these accounts, particularly Hollway's. [...] Yet the fact that what turns Hollway on turns me off may be significant: it is one more indicator that, at the level of practice and experience, heterosexuality is not monolithic. Those women who remain within the boundaries of heterosexuality do not necessarily experience the same forms of desire. [...]

The other feature of these accounts is their limited language of erotic pleasure, so that the only alternative to the cool and clinical seems to be a register borrowed from Mills and Boon (or potentially the vocabulary of pornography). It is not that such languages do not exist – in literary contexts they do – but what is available for both everyday and academic use seems to be restricted to very predictable conventions, to the extent that I find myself sliding into these modes in attempting to describe my own sexuality. This lack of a language of eroticism has been noted in relation to lesbian sex, particularly in Marilyn Frye's much quoted comparison with the language available to gay men. Gay men, says Frye, have at their disposal 'a huge lexicon of *words*: words for acts and sub-acts, preludes and denouements, their stylistic variations, their sequences.' Gay sex is therefore 'articulate' to a degree that 'lesbian "sex" does not remotely approach' (Frye, 1990: 310–11). This lack of articulateness may apply also to heterosexual women and is certainly evident in the WRAP research and in the safer sex advice available to heterosexual women (Wilton, 1997). [...]

Given these constraints of language it is perhaps unsurprising that discussions of pleasures and practices have largely been monopolized by those writing from within libertarian or, more recently, queer perspectives which, whether lesbian or gay, have drawn on the language of gay male sexuality. It is within this tradition, too, that we can find some of the earliest reflections on what might constitute ways of rethinking the classification of sexual desires outside the hetero/homo binary. Even here, however, there are linguistic absences. As Frye noted, the lexicon of gay male sex refers primarily to *acts*. It is not a language of feeling, of sensation and emotion. [...]

It is within libertarian and queer writing that we find an emphasis on the potentially subversive effects of transgressive sexual acts. It is here, too, that some have found inspiration for 'queering' heterosexual sex. Yet rendering Queer so inclusive that it can encompass even heterosexuals must surely undercut its claims to radicalism. Moreover, equating the sexually transgressive with the progressive ignores the extent to which the heterosexual status quo can incorporate and defuse individualistic challenges.

[...]

In a context where heterosexual sex has come to be seen as something to be worked at in producing ever more skilled and varied performances, where the market in 'how to do it' manuals is huge (Jackson and Scott, 1997), heterosexual couples who expand their repertoire to include a few 'queer' practices are hardly radical subversives.

[...]

Carol Smart has reflected upon the implications of acknowledging that 'penetration is as heterosexual as kissing', that 'men penetrate men, women penetrate women and women can penetrate men' (1996a: 236), suggesting that it might help us to challenge both penetration's privileged place as the essential heterosexual act and its meaning as an 'invasion and colonization' of women's bodies. [...]

What Smart is suggesting is that, in disengaging penetration from hetero-sexuality and re-coding it as more sexually ambivalent, we may be able to move in the direction of a 'post-heterosexual' desire. [...] I would agree that transform-ing heterosex entails redefining penetration – but in the old feminist sense of dissociating it from the active (male)/passive (female) dichotomy, as well as in the newer queer sense of recasting it as no longer definitively heterosexual. I would also add that we should not lose sight of the long-standing feminist goal of deprioritizing penetrative sex, dislodging it from its privileged place as what sex *is*.

The potential for redefining penetrative sex within our existing, heterosexually ordered, society and culture is limited.[1]

After more than two decades of feminist attempts to redefine sex, more recent queer interventions and the challenge posed by HIV and AIDS, conventional heterosexual definitions of sex remain entrenched. We may have begun to erode them, but we still have a long way to go. For the here and now, we must be content with whatever pleasures are attainable, but remember to keep our critical faculties honed in the process and not assume that pleasure is anything more than a personal indulgence. We certainly should not kid ourselves that anything we do in bed (or in other erotic settings) will have any impact on the sexual lives of the majority of women – however radical it seems to us.

[...]

In my view, we should be aiming higher than simply destabilizing heterosexual erotic conventions – we should be working towards transforming them. This is unlikely to be achieved without a parallel transformation in heterosexuality as a social institution and the erosion of the gender hierarchy it entails. To think about this it is necessary to move beyond the narrow scope of the politics of pleasure and consider the ways in which heterosexuality is sustained. This brings me back to the two faces of heterosexuality which I outlined at the beginning of this chapter, heteronormativity and male domination, and to the centrality of gender.

## *Sustaining heterosexuality*

For heterosexuality to achieve the status of the 'compulsory', it must present itself as a practice governed by some internal necessity. The language and law that regulates the establishment of heterosexuality as both an identity and an institution, both a practice and a system, is the language and law of defence and protection: *heterosexuality secures its self-identity and shores up its ontological boundaries by protecting itself from what it sees as the continual predatory encroachments of its contaminated other, homosexuality.*

(Fuss, 1991: 2; my emphasis)

Aside from its personification of heterosexuality, this classically queer statement could be read as a simple reiteration of the old sociological truism that deviance functions to police the boundaries of normality. But more than this, Fuss is drawing our attention to ways in which homosexuality and heterosexuality serve to define each other, that the one can only exist in relation to the other, that neither makes sense without its other: they are co-constructed in a reciprocal, but hierarchical, relationship. Heterosexuality in these terms is sustained by silencing and marginalizing dissent, by naming the other as the outsider. Yet the presence of the other always threatens to undermine the heterosexual norm. It is the potentially destabilizing potential of this other which has preoccupied many queer theorists. [. . .]

But heterosexuality also, and very importantly, is sustained by maintaining a silence about itself. It dare not speak its name, for in so doing it makes evident what it keeps hidden, that it is only one form of sexuality. [. . .] Homosexuality, constituted as 'perversion', existed as a concept before heterosexuality and the latter still does not have the same currency as the former. 'Homosexuality' (or its more pejorative synonyms) is often mentioned in everyday straight talk, whereas the term heterosexuality is sometimes not even understood. Hence heterosexuals often do not know what they are; they do not need to know; they are simply 'normal'.

[. . .]

But heterosexuality does not sustain itself only by particular patterns of speaking and silence, nor just by keeping outsiders penned within their deviant enclosures. Fuss draws a parallel with gender, and I am sure she is well aware that both heterosexuality and homosexuality depend for their definition on gender. What she does not say – and this is indicative of Queer's preoccupation with heteronormativity alone – is that what is fundamental to heterosexuality, to what sustains it 'as an identity and an institution, both a practice and a system', is gender hierarchy. Its 'inside' workings are not simply about guarding against the homosexual other, but about maintaining male domination: and these two sides of heterosexuality are inextricably interwined.

I have argued that the intersection between gender and sexuality is a critical element in the analysis of heterosexuality, hence exploring the workings of this intersection is important. In much of my recent work, I have argued for the logical priority of gender (see Jackson, 1996a, 1996b; Rahman and Jackson, 1997). There are several reasons why I have consistently taken this position. Initially, I wanted to challenge the undue emphasis given to sexuality by feminists and non-feminists alike and to oppose those arguments which reduced women's oppression to any single cause, whether that be sexuality or any other. [. . .]

I would take the same view of more recent arguments which seek to challenge the concept of gender, replace it with 'sex', and then focus on its intersection with sexuality. Elizabeth Grosz, for example, deals with the blurring of the distinction between sex and gender in recent feminist theory by declaring the concept of gender redundant. She then defines 'sex' as referring to 'the domain of sexual difference, to questions of the *morphologies of bodies*' (1995: 213; her emphasis) and sexuality as 'sexual impulses, desires, wishes, hopes, bodies, pleasures, behaviours and practices.' [. . .] Almost the entire field of gender, as I would understand it, is erased. Who is doing the housework and raising children? Are wage differentials between women and men to be reduced to bodily morphologies? How are we to understand how bodies and sexualities figure in patterns of employment and workplace culture, for example, when the whole social world has been reduced to bodies?[2]

[. . .]

Part of the problem we have in thinking through the connections between gender, sexuality in general and heterosexuality in particular is that we do not all mean the same thing by these terms and are often talking about different objects at different levels of analysis. How the intersection works depends on precisely what we are talking about. The term 'heterosexuality' can be used in relation to the erotic or to denote an institution involving a much wider social relation between women and men. 'Sexuality' itself is sometimes understood primarily in terms of the hetero/homo binary, or the straight, gay or lesbian identities deriving from it, while others take it to encompass a fuller range of desires, practices and identities. 'Gender' can mean the division or distinction between women or men, whether this is seen as primarily a bodily difference or a social hierarchy, but also refers to the content of these categories, to what we understand as femininity or masculinity. I would always opt for the broader senses of these terms because to narrow them down risks losing sight of significant portions of social life. [. . .] As I use the term gender, then, it covers both the division itself and the social, subjective and embodied differences which give it everyday substance. Heterosexuality, as I have repeatedly argued, is not a simple monolithic thing, but a complex of institution, identity, experience, and practice, all of which intersect with gender, which is similarly sustained at a variety of levels. Moreover, heterosexuality is not only a means of ordering our sexual lives but also of structuring domestic and extra-domestic divisions of labour and resources. [. . .]

Some recent accounts have challenged the priority given to gender from perspectives which do incorporate broad definitions of both gender and heterosexuality, for example those of Tamsin Wilton (1996, 1997) and Chrys Ingraham (1996). Wilton's argument is that gender and heterosexuality are mutually defined and constituted to such an extent that neither can be accorded priority over the other. While she draws heavily on queer theory, and is therefore concerned with the issue of heteronormativity, she never loses sight of heterosexuality as an institution implicated in the subordination of women. Hence the 'disciplinary regimes of gender and the erotic are intrinsically co-dependent and foundational to the super-ordination of men to women' (Wilton, 1996: 126). [. . .] She develops her argument through the concept of 'heteropolarity', the socially constructed difference that positions men and women as complementary opposites, which is crucial for the maintenance of heterosexuality.

[. . .] I do not think the problem of the interrelationship between gender and heterosexuality can be resolved by collapsing both into one term – 'heteropolarity' – covering both gender difference and the ideologies and practices which tie that difference into heterosexuality. While gender and sexuality are so closely intertwined that it is not easy to unravel the connection, we need to retain the analytical capacity to tease out the tangled connections between them.

[. . .]

Ingraham's (1996) argument is that heterosexuality should displace gender as the central category of feminist analysis. Of all the analyses I have read which challenge my belief in the primacy of gender, it is Ingraham's which I find most convincing and hence difficult to contest. This is because, despite the almost opposite conclusions we come to, she is working within a sociological and materialist feminist framework very similar to my own. From this perspective she shares my scepticism about the sex – gender distinction and defines heterosexuality as an institution which regulates more than merely our erotic lives. Her concern is with the 'heterosexual imaginary' that masks the ways in which gender has consistently been defined from a heteronormative perspective. Like Wilton, she draws attention to the construction of 'women' and 'men' as mutually attracted 'opposite sexes', and argues that sociologists (including feminists) have failed to see the heterosexual ends to which this gender divide is directed.

As Ingraham points out, the definitions of gender employed by feminist sociologists indicate that it is a binary 'organizing relations *between* the sexes' (1996: 186; her emphasis). She goes on to suggest that heterosexuality 'serves as the organizing institution and ideology . . . for gender' (1996: 187). She sees heterosexuality implicated in the operation of all social institutions at all levels of society, from family to workplace to the state. [. . .]

I take Ingraham's point that heterosexuality is *an* organizing principle of many aspects of social structure and social life; this has, for example, emerged from some recent studies of workplace cultures (Adkins, 1995; Hearn et al., 1989), but I still have my doubts about according it primacy. Defining heterosexuality so broadly that it encompasses all aspects of gendered relations and then substituting it (or Ingraham's alternative, 'heterogender') for gender, raises some of the same difficulties as Wilton's conceptualization of heteropolarity – although

Ingraham's argument is far more internally consistent. It seems to me that it is
necessary to maintain an analytical distinction between gender, as the hierarchical relation between women and men, and heterosexuality, as a specific institutionalized form of that relation, and that not all gender relations are specifically
heterosexual.

[. . .]

## Doing and undoing gender and sexuality

Heterosexuality is sustained not only at the institutional level, but through our
everyday sexual and social practices, which indicates that, in some sense, it
requires our continual reaffirmation for its continuance. Most of the population
'do' heterosexuality every day without reflecting critically on that doing. Moreover, it is clear from the above discussion that whatever view we take on
heterosexuality and gender, they are interrelated. Hence 'doing heterosexuality'
is also about 'doing gender'. [. . .] If we 'do heterosexuality' and 'do gender' in our
everyday lives, to what extent can we 'undo' them?

[. . .]

Although there has been a great deal of emphasis in recent theory on destabilizing gender and heterosexuality, there is a reluctance to think about the possibility of thoroughly undoing them: doing away with them. The currently
fashionable ideas of performative subversions of gender and sexual binaries,
deriving from the work of Judith Butler, are not so much undoing gender as
doing it in new ways. [. . .] I find Butler's idea of gender as a performance, of
drag as a parody without an original to imitate, interesting and productive
(Butler, 1990). I also welcome her later emphasis on the constraining effects
of gender (Butler, 1993). But, quite apart from the absence of the social (beyond
the simply normative) in her work, the destabilizing effects she envisages for
such transgressive performances are limited. If Butler has a utopian vision, it
is a world of multiple genders and sexualities, not a world without gender
or heterosexuality. This she shares with many others writing from a queer
position.

[. . .]

I find it depressing that much of what passes as radical these days does not
envisage the end of gender hierarchy or the collapse of institutionalized heterosexuality, but simply a multiplying of genders and sexualities or movement
between them. [. . .] Seeking to undo binary divisions by rendering their boundaries more permeable and adding more categories to them ignores the hierarchical social relations on which the original binaries were founded. It fails to
address the ways in which heterosexuality and gender are sustained at the

macro level of structures and institutions as well as the micro level of our everyday social practices.

Our capacity to undo gender and heterosexuality is constrained by the structural inequalities which sustain them. Our ability to conceptualize their undoing is limited to the extent that our sense of ourselves has been constructed within a heterosexual, patriarchal social order. It may be this which accounts for the lack of vision which, in my view, underpins much queer writing, the failure to imagine a world without gender, without heterosexuality (and without other systematic inequalities deriving from a social order which remains capitalist and imperialist as well as patriarchal). Concern with material inequalities has given way to a preoccupation with difference as something to be valued and affirmed.

In my view there are dangers in endorsing too wholeheartedly 'the doxa of difference' (Felski, 1997) which has gained such a hold in feminist and queer circles. Certainly we should be cautious of affirming sources of difference which are themselves products of systematic inequalities. The theoretical impetus for this preoccupation with differences derives from postmodernism's scepticism about grand narratives purporting to reveal the 'truth' of historical, social conditions. The political impetus came from the realization that such truth claims were generally made from male, white, Western, heterosexual locations. Yet, as Rosemary Hennessy (1993) has argued, there are some totalities – capitalist, patriarchal, imperialist, racist – which continue to have pervasive, real and often brutal effects. Affirmation of 'difference' can simply lead to the acceptance of social divisions produced by these totalities. [...]

Utopian visions are no longer fashionable; most radical intellectuals have abandoned those metanarratives, such as Marxism, which once promised a better future, and have taken to heart Foucault's view that power is inescapable. We can resist, subvert and destabilize, but nothing much will change; or, if it does, there will be new deployments of power to be resisted, subverted and destabilized. This is a politics of resistance and transgression, but not a politics of radical transformation; its goal is permanent rebellion but never revolutionary change. It is ultimately a pessimistic politics. [...] I believe that it is crucially important, both politically and analytically, that we are at least able to *imagine* social relations being radically other than they are. If we cannot do this we lose the impetus even to *think* critically about the world in which we live.

## Notes

1   Rape is still endemic to most of the world's societies and still reaches epidemic proportions in times of war. We shouldn't need reminding of this in the context of the rape which has accompanied genocide in Rwanda and former Yugoslavia: this often entails men being forced to watch the raping of 'their' women before being killed, to emphasize their impotence in the face of the aggressor. Here rape is both a brutal physical act and a symbolic act whereby men demonstrate their power over women and over conquered men.

2   This critique of Grosz was developed in recent collaborative work with Sue Scott, in a paper entitled 'Putting the body's feet on the ground', presented at the British Sociological Association's Annual Conference in 1998.

## References

Adkins, L. (1995) *Gendered Work: Sexuality, Family and the Labour Market*. Buckingham: Open University Press.

Butler, J. (1990) *Gender Trouble: Feminism and the Subversion of Identity*. New York: Routledge.

Butler, J. (1991) 'Imitation and gender insubordination', in D. Fuss (ed.), *Inside/Out*. New York: Routledge, pp. 13–31.

Butler, J. (1993) *Bodies that Matter*. New York: Routledge.

de Lauretis, T. (1991) 'Queer theory: lesbian and gay sexualities, an introduction', *differences*, (5) 3: iii–xviii.

de Lauretis, T. (1994) 'Habit changes', *differences*, 6 (2 & 3): 296–313.

Dollimore, J. (1991) *Sexual Dissidence*. Oxford: Oxford University Press.

Felski, R. (1997) 'The doxa of difference', *Signs*, 23 (1): 1–22.

Frye, M. (1990) 'Lesbian "sex" ', in J. Allen (ed.) *Lesbian Philosophies and Cultures*. New York: New York University Press.

Fuss, D. (1991) *Inside/Out: Lesbian Theories, Gay Theories*. New York: Routledge.

Grosz, E. (1995) *Space, Time and Perversion*. New York: Routledge.

Halperin, D. M. (1995) *Saint Foucault: Towards a Gay Hagiography*. Oxford: Oxford University Press.

Hearn, J. et al. (eds) (1989) *The Sexuality of Organization*. London: Sage.

Hennessy, R. (1993) *Materialist Feminism and the Politics of Discourse*. New York: Routledge.

Holland, J., Ramazanoglu, C., Scott, S., Sharpe, S. and Thomson, R. (1990) '"Don't die of ignorance" – I nearly died of embarrassment': Condoms in Context*. London: Tufnell Press.

Holland, J., Ramazanoglu, C., Sharpe, S. and Thomson, R. (1991) *Pressure, Resistance, Empowerment: Young Women and the Negotiation of Safer Sex*. London: Tufnell Press.

Holland, J., Ramazanoglu, C., Sharpe, S. and Thomson, R. (1994) 'Power and desire: the embodiment of female sexuality', *Feminist Review*, 46: 21–38.

Holland, J., Ramazanoglu, C., Sharpe, S. and Thomson, R. (1998) *The Male in the Head: Young People, Heterosexuality and Power*. London: Tufnell Press.

Hollway, W. (1993) 'Theorizing heterosexuality: a response', *Feminism & Psychology*, 3 (3): 412–17.

Ingraham, C. (1996). 'The heterosexual imaginary', in S. Seidman (ed.), *Queer Theory/ Sociology*. Oxford: Blackwell, pp. 168–93.

Jackson, S. (1996a) 'Heterosexuality as a problem for feminist theory', in L. Adkins and V. Merchant (eds), *Sexualising the Social*. Basingstoke: Macmillan, pp. 15–34.

Jackson, S. (1996b) 'Heterosexuality and feminist theory', in D. Richardson (ed.), *Theorising Heterosexuality: Telling it Straight*. Buckingham: Open University Press, pp. 21–39.

Jackson, S. and Scott, S. (1997) 'Gut reactions to matters of the heart: reflections on rationality, irrationality and sexuality', *Sociological Review*, 45 (4): 551–75.

Jeffreys, S. (1994) 'The queer disappearance of lesbian sexuality in the academy', *Women's Studies International Forum*, 17 (5): 459–72.

Kitzinger, C. and Wilkinson, S. (1993) 'Theorizing heterosexuality', in S. Wilkinson and C. Kitzinger (eds), *Heterosexuality: A 'Feminism and Psychology' Reader*. London: Sage, pp. 1–32.

McRobbie, A. (1996) '*More!*: new sexualities in girls' and women's magazines', in J. Curran, D. Morley and V. Walkerdine (eds), *Cultural Studies and Communications*. London: Edward Arnold, pp. 172–94.

Rahman, M. and Jackson, S. (1997) 'Liberty, equality and sexuality: essentialism and the discourse of rights', *Journal of Gender Studies*, 6 (2): 117–29.

Rich, A. (1980) 'Compulsory heterosexuality and lesbian existence', *Signs*, 5 (4): 631–60.

Sedgwick, E. K. (1991) *The Epistemology of the Closet*. Hemel Hempstead: Harvester Wheatsheaf.

Segal, L. (1994) *Straight Sex: The Politics of Pleasure*. London: Virago.

Segal, L. (1997) 'Feminist sexual politics and the heterosexual predicament', in L. Segal (ed.), *New Sexual Agendas*. Basingstoke: Macmillan, pp. 77–89.

Seidman, S. (1997) *Difference Troubles: Queering Social Theory and Sexual Politics*. Cambridge: Cambridge University Press.

Smart, C. (1996a) 'Desperately seeking post-heterosexual woman', in Janet Holland and Lisa Adkins (eds), *Sex, Sensibility and the Gendered Body*. Basingstoke: Macmillan, pp. 222–41.

Smart, C. (1996b) 'Collusion, collaboration and confession: on moving beyond the heterosexuality debate', in D. Richardson (ed.), *Theorising Heterosexuality: Telling it Straight*. Buckingham: Open University Press, pp. 161–77.

Smyth, C. (1992) *Lesbians Talk Queer Notions*. London: Scarlet Press.

Thomson, R. and Scott, S. (1991) *Learning About Sex: Young Women and the Social Construction of Sexual Identity*. London: Tufnell Press.

Whisman, V. (1996) *Queer by Choice: Lesbians, Gays and the Politics of Identity*. New York: Routledge.

Wilkinson, S. and Kitzinger, C. (eds) (1993) *Heterosexuality: A 'Feminism and Psychology' Reader*. London: Sage.

Wilton, T. (1996) 'Which one's the man? The heterosexualisation of lesbian sex', in D. Richardson (ed.), *Theorising Heterosexuality: Telling it Straight*. Buckingham: Open University Press, pp. 125–42.

Wilton, T. (1997) *Engendering AIDS: Deconstructing Sex, Text and Epidemic*. London: Sage.

# 7

# When Bodies Come Together: Power, Control and Desire*

*Janet Holland, Caroline Ramazanoglu, Sue Sharpe and Rachel Thomson*

[...]

Feminist studies of heterosexuality have identified the physical body as a social site (Coveney *et al.* 1984: Thompson 1990; Hite 1987; Jackson 1982) and Foucault's (1979) conception of the 'micro physics' of power can be applied to these notions of women's bodies as sites of male domination. The identification of power as gendered links the disciplining of bodily activity to institutionalised heterosexuality, the 'beauty system', and women's consent and resistance to male hegemony (Bartky 1990; Bordo 1993; Martin 1989; Lesko 1988; MacCannell and MacCannell 1987).

Our analysis provides support for Foucault's theory that the body is the site where the large scale organisation of power is connected to the most minute and local practices, but feminists have noted that Foucault does not explain the link between male domination of sexual encounters and male power. He does not distinguish between men's and women's bodily experiences, nor does he investigate the reasons for the creation and persistence of male domination (Bartky 1990; Ramazanoglu 1993). In this chapter we trace critical connections between the embodiment and the male power of institutionalised heterosexuality.

[...]

The perceived opposition between essentialism and poststructuralism perpetuates a conceptual dualism between a natural, essential, stable, material body, and a shifting, plural, socially constructed body with multiple potentialities. If there is

*EDITORS' NOTE: Interviews quoted in the chapter are from the *Women, Risk and AIDS* and *Men, Risk and AIDS* projects during the early 1990s, in which 198 young people in the UK were asked about their sexual understandings and lives.

no simple conceptual dualism which allows us to distinguish the material, biological body from the social meanings, symbolism and social management of the
socially constructed body, then the material body and its social construction are
entwined in complex and contradictory ways which are extremely difficult to
unravel in practice.

> Biology provides a bedrock for social inscription but is not a fixed or static
> substratum: it interacts with and is overlaid by psychic, social and signifying
> relations. (Grosz 1990: 72)

Young people's bodies and their desires are given meaning through ideas about
the body and sexuality which are social, but these ideas are not entirely separable
from bodily constraints and possibilities. Foucault (1988: 120–1) suggests dissolving the appearance of two separate sides to sexuality – an essential versus
socially constructed sexuality – but this should not be taken as meaning that the
physical body can simply be dissolved *into* the social. Young people live with
their experiences of the physicality of bodily encounters, and often with physical
violence, in ways which are differently gendered.

[...]

## Disembodied femininity

[...]

A modest femininity requires a young woman to construct a disembodied sexuality that produces her as a passive body, rather than actively embodying feminine sexuality. While explicit accounts of young women's sexual activity are
largely missing from the interviews, they can be read as implying complex
interconnections of power and resistance, in which young women experience
and respond to social pressures to construct their bodies as passive and fragmented sexual objects. These fragments can become eroticised, but this is within a
'masculine appropriation of desire in a society that renders desire as power'
(Goldstein 1990). [...]

The young women did not easily discuss embodied sexuality, leaving it as
hidden, fragmented, alienated. For example, where they intimate that they enjoy
oral sex, they find it difficult to do more than hint at this in an interview. [...]

Oral sex was a particularly difficult area for women to negotiate openly with
men because making female sexual desire explicit could conflict with women's
expectations of men's desires. An unusual level of communication with their
partner is required for shared pleasure to be discussed. Lynne Segal (1992) has
pointed out that even when women know how to experience pleasure, they are
still constrained by the social construction of heterosexuality.

Although men's concern with their bodies appears to be growing in the 1990s,
women are still much more likely than men to be dissatisfied with their body and
to attempt to change it through dietary regimes and exercise (Martin 1989; Bordo

1988, 1993; McCarthy 1990). There are, at any one time, a limited range of potentially acceptable feminine images, including those specific to different cultural and sub-cultural groups, upon which young women can draw and which they can help to create. The images which they devise within these social constraints may be understood differently by the young women from the way in which they are read by the men who view them. A skilful representation of self as sexually knowing might be produced by a young woman, who is in fact unknowing. This disjunction between knowledge and self image can lead young women into sexually unsafe situations. Young women can spend a good deal of time on their outward appearance in order to construct a female body which will act as a magnet to attract men, but they may have little control over whom they attract, and the sexual expectations that they are then supposed to meet.

[...]

There is a related disengagement between the surface image of the body (the way femininity is socially inscribed on it) and the young women's sense of self. This is illustrated in responses to a direct question in the interview asking the young women for their own image of themselves. In no instance did they respond in terms of a physical image. In general they had difficulty in answering this question at all, but when they did manage to do so, tended to speak of their 'personality' or 'character' or what their friends thought of them. [...]

Young women can become conscious of their image as a construction when they make a distinction between the presentation of themselves that men respond to, and what they think of as their 'real self'.

> Oh, yeah. I mean at first like some of the people used to say, 'oh you're so nice and so gorgeous, you look so nice all the time', and at first I thought, 'oh, my God, it's so amazing', and then after a while it meant nothing. Like, 'yeah, you see this, but what am I really like, you know, who cares, you don't care'. ... I think with other boyfriends, I think Anne [her friend] found this as well, is that they like you when you're sweet and you're beautiful and, you know, whatever, you've got a new outfit on or whatever, whatever reason, but as soon as you feel depressed or down in the dumps or – I don't know, got a sudden rush of acne or something, they just don't want to know.
>
> (young woman, middle class, aged seventeen)

[...]

The power of masculine privilege in sexual encounters is often recognised by young women in terms of a 'double standard', but the extent to which they contribute to the reproduction of this power through their own femininity is much less clear to them. The surface image of the feminine body is literally made-up everyday, constructed to be socially acceptable, sexually desirable, or otherwise, in the here and now. This location in the immediate present combines with restricted knowledge of the possibilities of sexuality. The disembodiment which characterises the representation of femininity leaves many young women unprepared to become sexual, or to recognise themselves as sexual. One consequence can be the 'unreality gap' between expectations and experience recognised by so many in the behaviour of young women (e.g. Sharpe 1987). Their gendered understanding of sexuality can lead some to treat pregnancy and disease as events that cannot possibly happen to them.

[...]

### Embodied masculinity

While the demands of hegemonic masculinity (Connell 1993) may be as difficult to achieve for many young men as those of normative femininity are for many young women, social pressures inscribe a different set of requirements on the male than on the female body. Normative heterosexuality and the normative heterosexual act define young people in relation to each other: him as actor, her as acted upon; his agency, her subordination; her body for his pleasure. His body for his pleasure too. The young men's accounts communicate clear expectations that sex will be pleasurable. 'There's no point in sex if you don't have pleasure' (young man, working class, aged sixteen). There is an implicit assumption, gained from their sex education, that men are knowing sexual agents – that even when having intercourse for the first time, they will know what to do.

> Yeah, it was quite a good experience. I thought I'd done all right, like – never doing it before. I was quite pleased really.
>
> (young man, working class, aged eighteen)

The young men's accounts of first sex certainly express fears of failure, worries about what exactly to do, or apprehension about how they will cope when the time comes, but overwhelmingly, in contrast to the stories told by the young women, these are accounts of their agency and embodiment.

Also in contrast to the young women, the young men make much more explicit reference to the body and their own bodies. A few young men express dissatisfaction or concern, usually in relation to being too fat or too puny. But they are reluctant to relate these concerns to a need to be attractive to women. This young man spent some time discussing the different images he liked to portray, expressed in the type of clothing he wore:

> *Q:*  Do you think the way you look is important to you because of the way it will affect women or anything like that, the way you look to young women?
>
> *A:*  No, if the girls like you, they like your personality. I don't think looks matter that much.
>
> (young man, middle class, aged seventeen)

[...]

All the young people recognised the dominant definition of heterosexual sex as vaginal penetration, and this clearly places emphasis on the visible signs of male desire, arousal and performance, and women's accommodation to these. This emphasis on physical, embodied manifestation can also produce deep anxieties, and a recurrent theme in the young men's talk about their sexuality relates to penis size. Whatever the reaction – denial, derision, confidence, rebuttal, joking – penis size is an issue.

[...]

Despite considerable insecurity expressed about size, the emerging consensus from young men was that size is immaterial: what is important is how the body performs sexually. In this they feel they are supported by their girlfriends.

> When it comes to penis size, that doesn't bother me at all, because I have never measured it, but – I have measured it once and the size it was, I read in one of Rosa's magazines that it was standard size, so you know. That has never really worried me because if Rosa is satisfied....
>
>                                    (young man, middle class, aged eighteen)

[...]

While young men did express doubts and uncertainties about their physical attributes and performance, they presented themselves as unproblematically embodied, in marked contrast to the alienation from their bodies expressed by the young women.

It might seem that nothing could be more embodied than the female reproductive function: menstruation, fertilisation, growth of the foetus within the body, birth. And the discourse of difference through which these young people make sense of their bodies is rooted in the binary thinking of male–culture–mind opposed to female–nature–body. However, there is a paradox in this binary thinking, since the interdependence and interlocking of the two, to which deconstruction has alerted us, dissolves the dualism of male/female in favour of the male. In the social construction of heterosexuality it is the male who is embodied – in his body – and the female who is disembodied. Young people have to struggle with the construction of their sexuality as masculinity and the servicing of masculinity. These struggles raise critical issues of control.

## Power and control, pleasure and desire

Complex interrelations of power and control are played out upon the body in sexual relationships. As we have seen, women are under pressure to control the unruly body which may intrude upon the sexual encounter in unacceptable ways, and to subordinate their desire to men's. The following young woman gives an account of explicitly relinquishing lust and passion for the particular relationship that she was in and controlling her own passion to match that of her partner. She had been in a purely sexual relationship, and then moved into a more loving relationship with what she thought of as a 'normal sex life':

> I couldn't believe I'd gone from this really hot, sizzling relationship, to, you know like, I mean, if I ever played about in stockings or anything he just went, 'tut', you know like, – passion – you know I can't believe it, and I'm lying awake all night thinking any minute now, you know, it's just the difference but it's – I mean, I know it sounds daft saying well how you can have a purely sexual relationship, which is like lust with potential, and I prefer to go out with Dave and be able to talk to him and like, just have a normal sex life.
>
> (young woman, working class, aged twenty-one)

[...]

Men's power (however unwitting) to appropriate female desire, and women's part in accepting or resisting this power, raises issues of control in relation to the body. The embodiment of passion/desire in normative heterosexuality is paradoxical in that it requires both the exercise of control but also the loss of control. The relation between control/loss of control when two bodies meet cannot be disconnected from male dominance in gendered power relations and the silencing of female desire. [...]

About a quarter of the young women talked of sexual violence or various pressures to have intercourse when they did not want it, and clearly indicate a bottom line for the realisation of male power in sexual encounters.

[...]

But even where men use violence or pressure to subdue women, control of sexual encounters is a complex and contested process. While men may benefit from male domination in sexual encounters, they too are constrained by the social construction of heterosexuality. Women are both sexually subordinated by men, and drawn into the constitution of heterosexuality as male dominated, in part through the efforts they put into the construction of a passive femininity, which effectively silences their own desires. Women lose control of sexual encounters to men through self surveillance of their own bodies and desires. Male power constrains and controls, like a corset, but in accepting this constraint, in tightening the laces to enhance femininity, women lose the power of their muscles – the power of expressing their desires.

Tension is located at the point at which women are supposed to stay in control, for example by taking responsibility for contraception, while losing control through orgasm. This tension is one factor contributing to unsafe sex. The social construction of male sexual arousal means that men are supposedly in control at a rational level but also physically out of control, while women must respond to male arousal, but also control the rational man. For sex to be 'normal', the woman must lose control of the encounter so that the man can stay rational (Waldby *et al.* 1991: see also Nayak 1997 for a discussion of white masculinity in relation to black femininity).

Female desire is then both in the body and socially constructed. Young women are under social pressure (which they may or may not resist) to present male sexual partners with an idealised but material body for his pleasure. Any discourse or practice which legitimates *her* pleasure, acknowledges *her* sexual knowledge, values *her* performance or places it under *her* control, is potentially threatening to *his* masculinity. Young women can certainly enjoy sexual passion, but such enjoyment does not emerge from their interviews as the prime expression of their sexual experience.

### Her body subordinated to his pleasure

The following young woman, like several others, makes very explicit the subordination of female desire to male:

*Q*:  What did you expect from sex?

*A*:  Oh, gosh. On – when we do have any kind of sexual activity, for me the – the forefront of my mind is that I want – I want to make him happy, I want to – I – I think, you know, I want to do everything for him, you know.

(young woman, working class, aged nineteen)

[...]

Faking orgasm is a further way of meeting male needs, particularly when a man may be waiting for, or expecting the woman to reach, orgasm (see also Roberts *et al.* 1995). The following young woman underlines a common expectation amongst women that a man expects to have an orgasm as the culmination of intercourse, but that a woman does not necessarily do so. This young woman was accustomed to faking a climax and was taken by surprise by her first orgasm during intercourse:

if every time they had sex, you know like, for five years, and they never ever come, you know, they'd sort of like be out killing themselves, wouldn't they? But, you know, women do it for years and years, you know, it doesn't bother us, you know – well, as much as it might bother them, and – you know, like so when I did...I couldn't say to him 'oh, that's the first time I've had an orgasm [laugh], you know, so – but I was a bit surprised. I thought, 'oh, my God'.

(young woman, working class, aged nineteen)

[...]

Although these versions of female satisfaction are a dominant theme in both women's and men's interviews, there are also some points of resistance. These include explicit challenges to a male discourse of sex as his practice:

It was like as soon as he got an erection, that was all right, no matter how I was feeling, whether I was aroused or not, you had to do things because that was the point when things happened, when he was aroused, not when I was aroused.

(young woman, middle class, aged nineteen)

[...]

Foucault (1980: 57–8) argues that: 'nothing is more material, physical, corporal than the exercise of power', but that the ponderous forms of nineteenth century control are no longer necessary since industrial societies can manage with much looser forms of power: 'one needs to study what kind of body the current society needs...' (ibid.: 58). If we ask what kind of female body is required for the reproduction of male domination in intimate heterosexual social relations, then the disembodied, disciplined female body that is explicit in the young women's accounts of their sexuality is a socially appropriate response.

## Exercising and resisting male power

Many of the young men implicitly concur with the absence or subordination of female desire in the very commonly expressed view that, while men want sex, women want love and relationship. [...] Some saw themselves as able to change in this respect as they get closer to a girlfriend.

Blokes do not make love, they have sex. I suppose I try. I enjoy foreplay. I enjoy my girlfriend doing to me as doing it to my girlfriend. I suppose before this one, I wasn't...it was get it over as quickly as possible, it wasn't really hot on the foreplay.

(young man, working class, aged nineteen)

Like the young women quoted previously, this young man recognises both female compliance and the difficulty of making sense of his partners' responses:

I have spoken to girls about it, and you sort of say 'what do you want?' to the girl, and they say, 'I don't know, do what you want.'.... Most women have got a general idea how to please a man, because there ain't that much you can do to a bloke really, anything to do, but for a woman it's a bit more complex.

[...]

Lack of communication bothers many of the young men who have not developed communicative relationships. They are aware that differing expectations within a relationship can cause difficulties, but are not sure how this can be resolved:

Q: And did you find that girls generally enjoy it, like being done to them?

*A*:   Yes. Yes, no-one's told me to stop. I don't know, I'm not going to say yes, because women might be secretly thinking 'Oh, God, I wish he'd stop.' You never can tell. It's the most annoying thing, I don't know. If it's a relationship, you have to talk about it, what do you enjoy and what you don't enjoy. . . . My God, if they all fake, I'll die!

(young man, middle class, aged seventeen)

[. . .]

A masculine form of pretence is to fake the emotions that young men feel their partners expect as the price of intercourse. The following young man describes a girl as pursuing him and expecting sex; he does not want a relationship, but he likes the sex:

*Q*:   So you are quite happy to have the relationship?

*A*:   No, I'm not perfectly happy, but I do feel – it's just a completely silly thing, but it [the sex] is nice so there is no problem there in that respect. I enjoy it – there are too many other things you should enjoy about sex, but I just don't [in this relationship].

*Q*:   But there's not much emotion?

*A*:   There's fake emotion I suppose. . . . it's not really enough to be really intimate.

(young man, middle class, aged seventeen)

Where young people are able to discuss their desires openly with their partners, they give accounts of very positive experiences, but it is hard for most of them to develop this ability to communicate.

## Conclusion

The social construction of masculinity encourages young men's agency in exercising male power through management of the connections between material and gendered bodies. The social construction of femininity encourages young women not only to cede agency and submit to this male power, but also to contribute to it through their own disembodiment. Both men's power and women's resistance are contested and unstable, but the successful construction of femininity in relation to masculinity requires women to enable the exercise of men's power. We do not mean that all men control every sexual encounter, or that all women lose control of their bodies, or that women are the only losers. But the part played by femininity in producing hegemonic masculinity situates young people's bodies in an area of struggle over male power. Where young women's self esteem, self image, self knowledge and emotional needs are tied to a highly skilled but limited social construction of femininity, then women will continue to support men's power and their own subordination. The assertion of a need to take care of their bodies through safer sexual practices by young women challenges the disembodied femininity of conventional heterosexuality, and exposes the body as a still contested site.

Sex connects bodies, and this connection gives young people an intimate space within which men's power can be subverted and resisted. Where women do have a critical consciousness of the embodiment of their sexuality, and are comfortable with desires of their own, men's power can be directly threatened. Where young men fall in love or can talk to trusted female friends, they can begin to see beyond the boundaries of their masculinity. If young people can recognise and capture this intimate space, they can negotiate relationships which upset the gender hierarchy and so are potentially socially destabilising, but also potentially pleasurable for both men and women.

[...]

In Foucault's theory that power relations are unstable and resistance is perpetual and unpredictable (increasingly being adopted by poststructuralist feminists, see e.g. Hekman 1990; Sawicki 1991), male hegemony can exist but is precarious, and constantly diversifies in differing ways of doing masculinity (Morgan 1981). This view raises real political problems for feminism because it fails to account for the success and durability of supposedly precarious male dominance and the extent to which women strive to support rather than resist their feminine disembodiment and subordination.

Women's empowerment in confronting men's dominance begins with their ability to find their own voice, to reclaim their own experience and affirm their bodies as the site of their own desires. Female agency and the embodiment of female sexuality is necessary for the subversion of men's dominance at the level of everyday interactions, but it is not sufficient to dismantle the institutionalised male power of heterosexuality.

## References

Bartky, S. L. (1990) *Femininity and domination: Studies in the phenomenology of oppression*. London: Routledge.

Bordo, S. (1988) Anorexia Nervosa: Psychopathology as the crystallization of culture, in Diamond, I. and Quinby. L., *Feminism and Foucault: Reflections on resistance*. Boston: Northwestern University Press.

Bordo, S. (1993) *Unbearable weight: Feminism, Western culture and the body*. Berkeley: University of California Press.

Connell, R. W. (1993) The big picture: Masculinities in recent world history, *Theory and Society*, 22: 597–623.

Coveney, L., Jackson, M., Jeffreys, S., Kaye, L. and Mahoney, P. (1984) *The Sexuality Papers: Male sexuality and the social control of women*. London: Hutchinson.

Foucault, M. (1979) *Discipline and punish*. New York: Vintage Books.

Foucault, M. (1980) Body/power, in Gordon, C. (ed.), *Michel Foucault: Power/Knowledge*. Hemel Hempstead: Harvester Wheatsheaf.

Foucault, M. (1988) Power and sex, in *M. Foucault Politics, philosophy, culture: Interviews and other writings 1977–1984* (ed. Kritzman, L., trans., Sheridan, A. and others. London: Routledge.

Goldstein, L. (1990) Introduction, *Michigan Quarterly Review*, Fall: 485–9.

Grosz, E. (1990) Inscriptions and body-maps: Representation and the corporeal, in Threadgold, T. and Cranny-Francis, A. (eds), *Feminine, masculine and representation*. London: Allen and Unwin.

Hekman, S. J. (1990) *Gender and knowledge: Elements of a postmodern feminism*. Cambridge: Polity.

Hite, S. (1987) *Women and love*. London: Penguin.

Jackson, S. (1982) *Childhood and sexuality*. Oxford: Blackwell.

Lesko, N. (1988) The curriculum of the body: Lessons from a Catholic high school, in Roman, L. G. and Christian-Smith, L. K. with Ellsworth, E., *Becoming Feminine*. London: Falmer Press.

MacCannell, D. and MacCannell, J. F. (1987) The beauty system, in Armstrong, N. and Tennhouse, L. (eds), *The ideology of conduct*. London: Methuen.

Martin, E. (1989) *The Woman in the body*. Milton Keynes: Open University Press.

McCarthy, M. (1990) The thin ideal, depression and eating disorders in women, *Behavior Research Therapy*, 28 (3): 205–15.

Morgan, D. (1981) Men, masculinity and the process of sociological enquiry, in Roberts, H. (ed.), *Doing feminist research*. London: Routledge & Kegan Paul.

Nayak, A. (1997) Frozen bodies: Disclosing whiteness in Haagen-Dazs advertising, *Body & Society*, 3 (3): 51–71.

Ramazanoglu, C. (ed.) (1993) *Up against Foucault: Explorations of some tensions between Foucault and feminism*. London: Routledge.

Roberts, C., Kippax, S., Waldby, C. and Crawford, J. (1995) Faking it: The story of 'ohh!', *Women's Studies International Forum*, 18 (5/6): 523–32.

Sawicki, J. (1991) *Disciplining Foucault: Feminism, power and the body*. London: Routledge.

Segal, L. (1992) Sexual uncertainty, or why the clitoris is not enough, in Crowley, H. and Himmelweit, S. (eds), *Knowing women: Feminism and knowledge*. Cambridge: Polity in association with the Open University.

Sharpe, S. (1987) *Falling for love: Teenage mothers talk*. London: Virago.

Thompson, S. (1990) Putting a big thing into a little hole: Teenage girls' accounts of sexual initiation, *Journal of Sex Research*, 27 (3): 341–61.

Waldby, C., Kippax, S. and Crawford, J. (1991) Equality and eroticism: AIDS and the active/passive distinction, *Social Semiotics*, 1 (2): 39–50.

# 8

# Only the Literal: the Contradictions of Anti-Pornography Feminism

*Lynne Segal*

[...]

### Definitive ambiguities

Whatever the rhetorical interplay between pornography and anti-pornography, it seems hard to deny that the genre is notoriously difficult to define: its meanings shift, its productions diversify. Walter Kendrick's witty history of sex and censorship illustrates this well, as the many obscenity trials of the 20th century slowly uncoupled the 'pornographic' from anything 'experts' could affirm to be of 'scientific' or 'literary' value: 'pornography' officially became words or images designed primarily for sexual arousal, without redeeming social importance (Kendrick, 1987). In more detail, Linda Williams has mapped the continuous and continuing changes in pornographic productions, as new sexual questions and anxieties come into play (Williams, 1990). [...] Misogyny unquestionably pervades much of the genre, although the self-consciously pro-women pornographic productions that have recently emerged now attempt to represent female sexual agency always, only, as 'positive', hoping to subvert or resignify its traditional codings. The latter would include Candida Royalle's 'Femme Productions', Annie Sprinkle's 'Post-Porn Performances', Scarlot Harlot's 'postmodern prostitute art', and numerous other lesbian and straight creations designed primarily for arousing women. These all routinely encounter the censor's firm hand, both in the US and, when imported, here in the UK (Bell, 1994).

Williams herself, and many in her wake, argue that the greatest change in recent decades is that the 'pornographic marketplace is now almost as eager to address women as desiring consumers as it once was to package them merely as objects of consumption' (Williams, 1990: 230). [...]

Yet it still remains predominantly men who produce most of the sexual images of women: continually repositioned, passively, as object, icon and fetish of male desire – whether in pornography, cinema or elsewhere. In the stock top-shelf wank-mags, it is men's sexual needs and desires which are catered for, fuelling the prevailing pornographic narrative, with its own conventional code words and images. (Attempts to produce somewhat similar porn mags for women have so far met with little commercial success.) Here, as nowhere else in most men's lives, infantile grandiosity is fully catered for: men are inexhaustibly desiring, tumescent and irresistible; women insatiably available. Whether we respond with derision, sympathy, horror or indifference to what this suggests about men's ruling sexual trepidations will influence the stand we take on pornography.

[...]

## Feminist reappraisals

Sexuality was always accorded a central place in the analysis and politics of women's liberation. Feminists initially sought to celebrate female sexuality: liberating it from male-centred discourses and sexist practices to uncover women's own 'autonomous' sexuality. [...]

In *Straight Sex* (Segal, 1994) I traced the interconnecting strands leading towards the growth of a more pessimistic, sexual conservatism within feminist thinking from the close of the 1970s: the theoretical deficiencies of feminist borrowings from a behaviouristic sexology; the symbolic centrality of the hierarchical binaries roping gender to sexuality; the tenacity of men's power in relation to women, and their endemic abuse of it, especially in sexual matters; a more conservative political climate. Forceful feminist writing was soon reinscribing old patriarchal 'truths' centred on the polarizing of male and female sexuality – his: predatory, genital, exploitative and dominating; hers: gentle, diffuse, nurturing and egalitarian (Morgan, 1978: 181).

Coupled with shifts in feminist sexual politics and theory, pornography became *the* feminist issue of the 1980s, at least for its best-known (North American) white spokeswomen. This was the first of several theoretical reappraisals insisting that sexuality was the overriding source of men's oppression of women. Catharine MacKinnon later summarized this contentious rewriting: 'feminism is a theory of how the erotization of dominance and submission creates gender, creates woman and man in the social form in which we know them' (MacKinnon, 1987: 149). The second transformation cited 'pornography' as the cause of men's sexual practices, now identified within a continuum of male violence. Male 'sexuality' was irrevocably fused to 'domination', redefined as an urge to power.

Some feminists saw these moves, as I did, as part of a reaction to more conservative times, and the setbacks faced by feminist activism, especially in the US (where anti-pornography feminism arose at the close of the 1970s). 'Pornography', Ann Snitow suggests, became a metaphor for women's defeat, now that feminists in general were less confidently on the offensive. Isolating sexuality and men's violence from other issues of women's inequality was not only a defensive tactic for women, but one in perfect harmony with the rising tide of conservative backlash against radical politics generally (Snitow, 1986). The Right has always liked to demonize sexuality, and have us see it as the source of all our ills, ensuring that they would move swiftly into alliance with anti-pornography feminism. However vigorously we hear it denied, Dworkin and MacKinnon's alliance with the Moral Right is now well documented (Duggan and Hunter, 1995).

The strength of the new feminist discourses against pornography (once MacKinnon added her legal arguments to Andrea Dworkin's indictment of pornography as men's literal domination and torture of women) was to declare it a violation of women's civil rights (Dworkin, 1981; MacKinnon, 1987). It serves to convince men that women are inferior, and hence do not deserve equal rights. Pornography should not be seen as merely a form of representation – sexist and offensive images or words – but should be seen as *literally* harming women and creating gender inequality. [...]

Feminist anti-pornography arguments are seductive because most mainstream pornography obviously embodies the most outrageously sexist (often also racist) imagery. That is its function: to position women as – and only as – passive, commoditized, objects for men's sexual arousal. It does disturb many women (and many men as well). [...]

Pornography's standard servicing of men's narcissistic fantasies of female sexual availability was always an injurious affront to feminist attempts to eliminate sexual harassment, rape and violence against women. [...] It seems to offer, at the very least, a convenient scapegoat for rage against such abuses. Convenient, but also hazardous, when not directly menacing.

For if the force driving anti-pornography feminism is the belief that it is commercial pornography which lies behind the subordination and abuse of women in society, we are allowing ourselves to be seriously deluded. First of all, anti-pornography feminism has systematically misrepresented the content of mainstream pornography as 'violence' (Thompson, 1994). Secondly, it has consistently misrepresented studies of effects of pornography, falsely claiming that psychological and sociological surveys offer consistent and conclusive proof that pornographic images cause sex crimes ('not even courts equivocate over its carnage anymore' – MacKinnon, 1993: 37). Thirdly, it disavows all knowledge of the nature of fantasy and all recent theories of representation: where meaning is seen as never fixed in advance, but determined by its broader discursive context as well as its specific interpretive audience. Finally, and most fundamentally of all, however, anti-pornography feminism fails to address the elementary point that the role of commercial pornography in depicting a crude, imperious and promiscuous male sexuality, alongside female receptivity and vulnerability, is *completely* overshadowed by, and *entirely* dependent upon, the official discourses and imagery of science, medicine, religion and mainstream cultural productions (high or low), prevalent all around us.

## Pornographic imagery and gender discourses

The offensive codings of the sexually explicit significations of commercial pornography mimic, even as they sometimes function to unsettle, the ways in which women are subordinated in the heartlands of the most authoritative and revered (even sacred) discourses of our culture. Illustrations could be drawn from a whole range of genres, where the subordinating binaries of gender signification are always already in place. Popular biological texts, such as Donald Symons's *The Evolution of Human Sexuality*, for example, summarize human female sexuality as 'continuously copulable', human male sexuality as perpetually ready to copulate: 'women inspire male sexual desire simply by existing' (Symons, 1979: 284). This is not pornography, but 'science'; in fact, with the flowering of the oldest repetitions of social Darwinism in the current conceits of 'new evolutionary theory', it is once again becoming the most accessible scientific discourse around. [...]

Meanwhile, as sex therapists are all too well aware, outside the sexist metaphors and phallic hubris of scientific discourse (or their pornographic mirrorings), the hominoid penis is anything but permanently erect, anything but endlessly ready for unencumbered sex, anything but triggered by the nearest passing female: even when she happens to be his wife, mistress or lover – willing and eager for sex (Tiefer, 1995). This is the critical force behind Judith Butler's recent analysis of pornography, suggesting that it depicts just those 'unrealizable positions' that always already predetermine our social expectations of gender positions. But far from pornography itself constructing that social reality, it serves rather to mock the impossible distance between gender norms and practices 'that it seems compelled to repeat without resolution' (Butler, 1997: 69).

[...]

Pornography is thus only one of a multiplicity (the least esteemed, least convincing, often most contradictory) of phallocentric and misogynistic discourses fashioning our images of gender and sexuality. Those who are most eager to reiterate its unique offensiveness face the problem that surveys of what is packaged as pornography show that violent imagery is rare, rather than definitive, of the genre. Moreover, men are more likely than women to be depicted as 'submissive' in the S / M or bondage imagery available (McClintock, 1993: 6). This means, of course, that were there any truth in our direct mimicry of the pornographic, feminists should be out fly-posting this centuries-old dominatrix pornography, not trying to eliminate it. Again, at odds with its supposed 'addictive' nature, the violent imagery which does appear in pornography has been consistently found to be decreasing rather than increasing since 1977 (Howitt and Cumberbatch, 1990; Thompson, 1994). A host of empirical enquiries, from the Netherlands, Sweden, Denmark or the US, have all failed to find any consistent correlation between the availability of pornography and sex crimes against women; many indeed have found negative correlations (not that this tells us anything about causality) (Goldstein and Kant, 1973; Baron, 1990; Kutchinsky, 1990). Overall, the main finding from the avalanche of correlational studies carried out over the past 20 years is their inconsistency, both with each other, and with the claims of anti-pornography texts.

[...]

It is over a decade since MacKinnon and Dworkin first drafted their Model Ordinance, arguing that women can only assert their civil rights and become fully human once they win the battle against pornography. The Ordinance classifies pornography as sex discrimination ('the graphic sexually explicit subordination of women through pictures or words') and urges those who have suffered 'harm' from it to seek damages through the courts from its makers, sellers and distributors – public or private (MacKinnon 1987: 176). After initial success in Minneapolis, the Ordinance was eventually defeated in various states of the US following prolonged legal battles, but in Canada anti-pornography feminists (assisted by MacKinnon) have been victorious, with the adoption of a modified version of the Ordinance in the *Butler* Supreme Court decision in 1992. [...] Since the Butler decision, straight mainstream pornography is flourishing, but any representations of alternative sexualities are facing increasingly intense censorship, as Brenda Cossman and Shannon Bell document. Almost immediately, following the ruling, the gay and lesbian Glad Day Bookshop and Little Sister's Art and Book Emporium both faced harassment (the former brought to trial and convicted for selling the lesbian magazine *Bad Attitude*). [...] The misappropriation of this new Canadian law, not against most men's cosily familiar sexist pornography, but against the more unsettling productions of women and gay men which might work to subvert them, has been the precise and predictable outcome (Lacombe, 1994).

In the area of race, similar – not unpredictable – reversals occur in relation to whose speech remains protected (as before), and whose speech gets censored. Thus it is the performances of black rap groups 2 Live Crew and Salt n Pepa which have recently been targeted for censorship in US courts, fortifying hegemonic conservative racism: 'rap is the special contribution of blacks to American cultural degeneration', the conservative critic Stephen Macedo affirms (Macedo, 1997: 29). As Judith Butler explores in her latest book, *Excitable Speech*, once there is an overriding importance attached to individual speech utterances at the expense of collective action against underlying structures of sexism or racism, we get what she criticizes (perhaps to the surprise of some of her supporters and critics alike) as 'the "linguistification" of the political field': 'the dignity of women is understood to be under attack not by the weakening of rights to reproductive freedom and the widespread loss of public assistance, but primarily by African-American men who sing' (Butler, 1997: 74, 23). [...]

## Inscribing psychological reductionism

Part of the success of the anti-pornography movement over the past 15 years has been its ability to mobilize scientific research in support of its arguments, rather than the anecdotal narratives of harm it had previously relied upon. It is possible to connect the image of human beings in anti-pornography rhetoric with that which still dominates theorizing and research in psychology. In a recent essay, the Canadian researcher Thelma McCormack highlights the similarities, commenting upon the experimental studies of leading pornography researchers Donnerstein and Malamuth: 'The subjects in these experiments, almost always men, are excited by the sexual stimulus and respond on cue. There is no notion of vicarious experience, no concept of catharsis in what is a very rigorous positivist design' (McCormack, 1993: 14). As McCormack argues, the parallel between this type of reductive psychological research and the arguments of anti-pornography feminists is more than accidental.

[...]

The discourses and practices of many psychologists dovetail with MacKinnon's fanciful meditations. They are perfectly in harmony with the method and outcome of much psychological research on pornography which chooses, as its 'incontestably objective measures' of the effects of the genre on men's actions, responses of a wholly different order. Thus Eysenck and Nias, in the influential *Sex, Violence and the Media* (1978), draw their conclusions about the genre from measuring penile expansion (via a penis plethysmograph) as a response to depictions of sex acts – a response which, as others have noted, is as likely as not to be connected to the oddity of wearing the equipment in the first place. At the same time as warning their readers of the dangerous effects of pornography, however, Eysenck and Nias themselves take pains to reiterate the dominant message of straight pornography: drawing attention to men's sexual prowess. But whereas their discourse comes with the powerful cultural authority of 'scientific truth', the latter comes defined as officially 'worthless', the literally superficial. Thus Eysenck and Nias are quick to assure what they call 'women's lib' that 'high libido' is correlated with 'masculinity' (assuming feminists will dispute this). One might expect them to be a little disappointed that they actually found 'considerable overlap' in reported rates of male and female arousal to their images of sex acts, but instead they cheerfully dismiss this by questioning the 'typicality' of the women who volunteer for their research; although not, of course, the men (Eysenck and Nias, 1978: 236). Objective measurements hold no threat for those who know how to read them.

[...]

### The cunning of pornography

The most frustrating feature of both anti-pornography feminism and psychological research on pornography alike is that they lead us away from rather than towards any understanding of the issues we are supposedly addressing. The basis of the cosy alliance between mainstream psychological research and anti-pornography feminism is the literalist theory of language and representation they share. Rather than insight into the construction of meanings, what we get from positivistic psychology is the complete evacuation of any attempt to grapple with the dynamics of pornographic production and consumption – fantasy, projection, identification or representation – and the encouragement of modes of analysis that work to reduce, systematize and close off debate. What we get from MacKinnon and Dworkin, both experts at the art of arousal and manipulation, is the discursive mirroring of the most disturbing codes and conventions of pornography itself.

[...] As feminist philosopher Wendy Brown has recently argued, the theory of gender in anti-pornography feminism 'mirrors the straight male pornography it means to criticize': in MacKinnon and Dworkin's rhetoric women are always and only their sexuality; women exist in an 'always already sexually violated condition', the social construction of 'femininity' has no flexibility or complexity; there are no ways women can overturn this construction – lesbian sexuality, here, can no more escape the eroticization of dominance and submission than straight women who try to embrace sexual autonomy (Brown, 1995: 88). In this way, Brown concludes (inflecting Baudrillard on Marx), 'MacKinnon assists in the cunning of pornography', declaring women's emancipatory struggles deluded and impossible: 'MacKinnon formulates as the deep, universal, and transhistorical structure of gender what is really a hyperpornographic expression' (1995: 87).

[...]

## Rethinkings and resignifications

In the face of this orchestrated arousal of libidinal despair, what can those of us say who want to talk about the complex nuances of 'pornography'? In true behaviourist spirit, MacKinnon repudiates any psychological perspectives which try to shed light on the complexities of psychic life or the nature of fantasy. In particular, she has only the harshest criticism of Freud, who devised 'the theory of the unconscious', and 'invented fantasy', simply to hide the reality of men's continual sexual violation of women. [...] It is the light psychoanalytic reflection might shed on the 'pornographic' psychic life of women and men alike (most of whom are not 'forcing sex on women') which threatens MacKinnon's literality. [...]

Psychoanalytic readings suggest a way of understanding the bizarrely 'pornographic' nature of our fantasy life: where excitement and danger, pleasure and pain, adoration and disgust, power and powerlessness, male and female, even life and death, smoothly fuse and separate out again without damage or distress – except perhaps to our internal psychic censors troubled by incompatibilities, not with 'real life', but with internalized moral values. Moreover, in readings true to the complexity of Freud's own thinking on the topic, fantasy is not thought to be reducible to wishful thinking or daydreaming about some concretely desired experience. There is simply no straightforward connection between the dynamics of desire in fantasy and the satisfactions sought in material reality. [...]

Here too, men's fetishistic need for visual proof of phallic potency, alongside their craving for visual evidence of female desire, should be seen in relation to men's specific fears of impotence, feeding off infantile 'castration' anxiety and the threat women pose to their sense of manhood: through pornography real women can be avoided, male anxiety soothed, delusions of phallic prowess indulged. The more complex pleasures of bisexuality and the capacity for identification with the 'opposite' sex, as well as the enjoyment of passivity, the eroticization of penetration and pain, are all readily available psychoanalytic explanations of men's (and also women's) use of pornography.

Hence the serious danger of basing one's politics about pornography on assumptions of fixed identifications and aspirations. From this perspective, MacKinnon could hardly be more misleading in declaring 'fantasy' a simple expression of ideology (MacKinnon, 1987: 149). [...]

It is also relevant here that those who are socially powerful have not only always exploited the relatively powerless (in all ways, including sexual), but projected the troubling, 'dirty' aspects of sex onto them. This is why it is not only women's bodies, but black and working-class bodies, which are mythically invested with sexuality in dominant western discourse and iconography. It is the dynamic interplay between power and desire, attraction and repulsion, acceptance and disavowal, which eroticizes those *already* seen as inferior (and thereby gives them in fantasy a threatening power). It is not, as some feminists believe, the eroticizing of an object which creates it as inferior, but rather the other way around: assumed inferiority creates an erotic aura. [...]

Psychoanalytic reasoning suggests that infantile fears and desires, cross-sex identification (present in men's enjoyment of the ubiquitous lesbian number in pornography) and homosexual attachment (present in men's pleasure in watching other penises in action) all inform the content of pornography and men's and women's responses to it. But psychoanalysis has always had less of a purchase on the convoluted but nevertheless inevitable grounding of psychic experience in wider cultural meanings. Men's dread of 'femininity' and need for phallic reassurance is finally only comprehensible in the context of women's social subordination and the definitive ties of 'masculinity' to power and authority. Yet whatever men's social power (increasingly under threat for some men), their actual sexual potency has always been precarious. Rather than endorsing the myths carried by some of the most readily available pornography, and much else besides, we need to insist upon the precariousness of bodily masculinity and the possibilities for women's sexual empowerment. This returns us again to the incommensurabilities between gender norms and gender practices, especially marked in the sexual lives of men.

Instead of insisting upon the literal truths of pornography, other feminists (often combining psychoanalytic and deconstructive methods) have seen sexual representation as a site of political and discursive struggle – including struggle around just those sex acts which some find self-evidently 'degrading' and 'dehumanizing'. The theoretical inspiration behind Butler's recent foray into this area is precisely the suggestion that discourses do *not* fix meaning once and for all, which is why lesbians and gays have fought back as 'queer', just as certain racial signifiers have been reclaimed: to be hailed as 'black' was once the height of humiliating injury. [. . .] 'One is not simply fixed by the name that one is called', as Butler writes; 'the injurious address may appear to fix or paralyse the one it hails, but it may also produce an unexpected and enabling response' (Butler, 1997: 2).

From this perspective, if we want to keep any creative space open for ourselves as sexual agents (rather than encouraging fantasies of female victimization) the very last thing we want to do is remorselessly censor certain words and images: trying to fix their meanings, independently from seeking to understand their representational and social context, or complex psychic investments. This smacks of the very worst alliances between an unthinking psychology and a political culture of denial: premised on not wanting to understand or even acknowledge the underlying causes, or effects, of pervasive injustices, but seeking instead to locate familiar scapegoats. We saw its nadir in the media with the blaming of video-nasties for the shocking murder of the toddler James Bulger in Liverpool in 1993 (and the frightening clamour for vengeance), extinguishing any attempt at understanding the sad, impoverished, painful lives of the two 10-year-old children responsible for the murder.

## References

Baron, Larry (1990) 'Pornography and Gender Equality: An Empirical Analysis', *Journal of Sex Research* 27(3): 363–80.

Bell, Shannon (1994) *Reading, Writing and Rewriting the Prostitute Body*. Bloomington: Indiana University Press.

Brown, Wendy (1995) *States of Injury: Power and Freedom in Late Modernity*. Princeton, NJ: Princeton University Press.

Butler, Judith (1997) *Excitable Speech: A Politics of the Performative*. London: Routledge.

Duggan, Lisa and Hunter, Nan (1995) *Sex Wars: Sexual Dissent and Political Culture*. London: Routledge.

Dworkin, Andrea (1981) *Pornography: Men Possessing Women*. London: The Women's Press.

Eysenck, H. J. and Nias, H. (1978) *Sex, Violence and the Media*. London: Paladin.

Goldstein, Michael and Kant, Harold (1973) *Pornography and Sexual Deviance*. Berkeley: University of California Press.

Howitt, Donald and Cumberbatch, Graham (1990) *Pornography: Impact and Influences*. London: Home Office Research and Planning Unit.

Kendrick, Walter (1987) *The Secret Museum: Pornography in Modern Culture*. New York: Viking.

Kutchinsky, B. (1990) 'Pornography and Rape: Theory and Practice? Evidence from Crime Data in Four Countries where Pornography is Easily Available', *International Journal of Law and Psychiatry* 13(4): 409–27.

Lacombe, Dany (1994) *Pornography and the Law in the Age of Feminism*. Toronto: University of Toronto Press.

McClintock, Anne (1993) 'Sex Workers and Sex Work: Introduction', *Social Text* 37: 1–10.

McCormack, Thelma (1993) 'If Pornography Is the Theory, Is Inequality the Practice?', paper presented to the Senate Chamber of York University, Toronto, Canada, for discussion on '*The Limits of Freedom and Tolerance*', 20 October.

Macedo, Suzette, ed. (1997) *Reassessing the Sixties: Debating the Political and Cultural Legacy*. New York: W. W. Norton.

MacKinnon, Catharine (1987) *Feminism Unmodified: Discourses on Life and Law*. London: Harvard University Press.

MacKinnon, Catharine (1993) *Only Words*. London: Harvard University Press.

Morgan, Robyn (1978) *Going Too Far*. New York: Vintage Books.

Segal, Lynne (1994) *Straight Sex: The Politics of Pleasure*. London: Virago.

Snitow, Ann (1986) 'Retrenchment vs Transformation: The Politics of the Antipornography Movement', in Kate Ellis (ed.) *Caught Looking: Feminism, Pornography and Censorship*. New York: Caught Looking Inc.

Symons, Donald (1979) *The Evolution of Human Society*. Oxford: Oxford University Press.

Thompson, Bill (1994) *Soft Core*. London: Cassell.

Tiefer, Leonore (1995) *Sex Is Not A Natural Act*. New York: Westview Press.

Williams, Linda (1990) *Hard Core: Power, Pleasure and the 'Frenzy of the Visible'*. London: Pandora.

# 9

# Anomalous Bodies: Transgenderings and Cultural Transformations*

## Mark Johnson

[...]

### Viewing the denouement: ritual transformations in the tragi-comedy of gay beauty contests

There are two classes of *gay* beauty competitions in Jolo and Zamboanga. These are community-level contests held in the open air, usually at the community basketball court, and municipal competitions such as the Miss Gay International, Jolo, which are usually held in large auditoriums such as the Notre Dame de Jolo College gymnasium. [...] One of the differences between the community and town contests relates to the number and status of financial sponsors and the number and status of the judges, reflecting overall the greater 'prestige' value of the town contests for the *gay/bantut* contestants. Another difference is in the composition of the audience. In community contests, there is no admission fee, whereas 'in-town' competitions may charge anywhere from ten to fifty pesos depending on the venue. As a result, community-level competitions will usually attract a much more diverse audience, including those who might not otherwise pay to attend a downtown contest. With the exception of people on the extreme

---

*EDITORS' NOTE: Mark Johnson's research in the Philippines focuses on a group known as *bantut*, whom he describes as 'effeminate or transgenderally identified men' but who preferentially identify themselves as *gays* (Johnson 1997: 86–8). He emphasizes that local usage of the term *gay* is informed by a specific history of gender/sexuality and 'signals a range of semantic possibilities, including that of transvestism and transgendering' (Johnson 1997: 14). He notes: 'the term *bantut* is associated not only with cross-dressing and beauty but also with the vulgar and the sexually illicit', whereas 'the term *gay* [...] is used [...] by transgenderally identified men to distance themselves from the negative and socially circumscribing implications of the term *bantut*' (Johnson 1997: 89).

peripheries of towns and municipal centres, I would say that the majority of people have attended at least one community-level *gay* beauty contest or similar event, such as a talent or fashion show.

It is important to note here that there is no formal system or structure of competitive rank through which one moves, for instance, from being a local community winner to municipal, regional, national and thence on to an international arena. [...] What links the otherwise unrelated *gay* beauty pageants together is that it is, by and large, the same set of *gays* who organize and participate in the different beauty contests.

For *gays*, beauty contests are regarded as celebratory events or 'happenings' and are best expressive of what is for many, particularly younger *gays*, seen to be one of the defining characteristics of *gay* life, that is, being happy and having enjoyment (*nagenjoy*). Beauty contests encapsulate the sense of empowerment and pleasure articulated in the notion of 'exposing my beauty' which, as I have previously noted, is sometimes associated with and likened to sexual desire. As one younger *gay*, a frequent finalist and sometime winner of beauty contests, told me:

> First, I really wanted to go to school. Now my classes are gone to the wind and all I want to do is participate in contests, and I'm always thinking about when the next contest is. There is another contest in November. We are always looking and listening out for when the next contest will be. It has become like a sexual craving for me to participate. I want to 'expose my beauty'. It is enjoyment.

There is another aspect to this, however, inasmuch as beauty contests are, as the name suggests, competitive events in which *gays* invest considerable time, energy and money preparing costumes, rehearsing dance routines, and perfecting recitations. In fact, while in the run up to a beauty contest *gays* will often help each other out by exchanging clothing, accessories and make-up, at the beginning of a contest, camaraderie gives way to fierce competitiveness, so that, as they say, 'Good luck, may the best woman win', and *bahala' na sila*, 'to hell with the rest!'. [...]

It is useful here to compare *gay* performances in beauty contests with daily performances by *gay* beauticians working in the beauty parlours. I stress the performative nature of *gay* work in the parlour for several reasons. First, *gays*' body movements and speech are often extremely stylized, this being particularly the case in the beauty parlours, where even the simplest of actions, such as picking up a pair of scissors, potentially becomes a performative event of its own. *Gays* are continually posturing in front of the mirror, 'checking on my beauty,' as they often put it, combing and recombing their hair, applying and reapplying make-up, and in general examining their body from various perspectives while making alternately disparaging or adulatory comments to themselves and to one another. All this is done with great exuberance and dramatic flair. [...] Such performances are, of course, exaggerated characterizations, parodies of the stereotypically self-absorbed, sexually voracious and predatory *bantut* with which *gays* are commonly identified in mainstream culture. It is in beauty parlours, in fact, more than in beauty contests that the term 'camp' is probably most applicable, if by camp is meant 'the hollowing empty of an identity that has been given to one as subordinate' (Dollimore 1990: 226–30, cited in Garcia 1996: 169). This sometimes extends to the way *gays* treat their customers, where exaggerated flattery, for example, of a boy's manliness, is a pointed parody of the discourse of hyper-masculinity. In part, these re-presentations of and (dis)identifications with such stereotypes are clearly one way in which certain aspects of the dominant discourse may be destabilized. That *gay* banter in the parlours is characterized by underlying feelings of good-natured camaraderie, moreover, is, as I have already suggested, precisely because it is through these ironic redeployments, including the language of siblingship and gender, that *gay* kinship is established. [...]

Although not absent in *gay* beauty contests, the sense of parody and camp which characterizes *gay* discourse in beauty parlours is usually submerged by the much stronger sense of 'sentimentality and seriousness' at these events (Garcia 1996: 169). In fact, it is at beauty contests that intra-parlour rivalry emerges most clearly, since in many contests each parlour will sponsor one or more of their beauticians or another *gay* closely associated with it as their contestant, and the results of the beauty contests will often be discussed and debated among them for weeks and indeed months and years afterwards.

[...]

Contrary to what might be expected, *gays* are not battling over any monetary award. Only the finalists receive trophies, plaques, ribbons and special product-line packages, such as make-up and perfume from Avon dealers. Nor do *gays*, despite the widely articulated project of status transformation, see participation in beauty contests as a means out of 'poverty' or a peripheral 'backwater', as has been suggested of Thai transvestite (*kathoi*) beauty contestants (cf. Channel 4 production *Lady Boys*), since, unlike in Thailand, there are no national competitions from which to launch careers as entertainers in the metropolis. Rather, what *gays* are contesting is precisely their possession of, and hold over, the knowledge-power (potency) of America, which is demonstrated by their ability to embody and articulate, with apparently as little effort as possible, the total ensemble of elements in the beauty contests – beautiful faces, sculpted bodies, glamorous costumes, the English language and various performative talents. More specifically, their possession of beauty is demonstrated in their ability to evince and elicit the affirmation of these effects from the audience and the judges. [...]

On the other hand, what *gays* are contesting (both among themselves and with the audience) is not just the measure of potency they possess, but also the nature or quality of the transformation they see themselves enacting in exposing their beauty. [...] In *gay* imaginations America and beauty represent the possible / impossible site for the realization of their transgenderal projects (including true love relations). Nowhere is this more clearly articulated than in the context of beauty contests. As *gays* frequently put it, 'I want to expose my beauty, so the world will know that I am a woman.'

The particular image(s) of femininity which *gays* attempt to embody, although varied, draw on images which are commonly presented in the media, educational institutions and the political rhetoric of state institutions (cf. Blanc-Szanton 1990: 379–83). *Gays* clearly identify themselves as progressive, educated, and independent as well as glamorous, sophisticated and cosmopolitan women, as signalled by their *biodata*, their appropriation of *artistas'* (moviestars') names, educational qualifications and body measurements, as well as in the elaborate stage performances and wearing of 'cocktail' or 'evening' gowns and swimsuits. At the same time, however, *gays* also project a shy, quiet, self-effacing image of femininity, defined primarily in terms of motherhood and domesticity, creating what, following Blanc-Szanton, might be called an image of the 'modern woman of traditional virtue'. This image was seen to be exemplified, among others, by the then president, Cory Aquino, and was expressed not only by the frequent reference to familial obligations, civic responsibility and professional employment as teachers, nurses, doctors, etc., but also by the importance given to the displays of national and ethnic costumes and the rhetoric of national politics.

In aligning themselves with these images of femininity, and specifically in juxtaposing the glamorous with the maternal, what some *gays* are specifically attempting to do is to distance themselves from associations with the vulgar, indecent and 'overexposed', and to ally themselves with a socially acceptable but high status image of femininity. I asked Miss Gay International 1990 about beauty contests and the image of women purveyed in the contests:

> *MJ*:      So what is your vision of an ideal woman? When you are participating in the contest, what is it you're trying to portray? Woman as what? It's like this, I see these contests, and they say 'I am trying to be like a woman.' But obviously the woman they are portraying is not like the woman I meet everyday in the Philippines. [...]
>
> *Theresa*:  First thing, when I join a contest, I always make it a point that I will appear dignified, not being some sort of a leftover, not joining just to participate and then appearing with no personality at all. So I think my vision is that women should be proper. Especially when wearing the swimsuit and you are 'exposing' your body. So I tend to project myself as prim and proper as I can. And I am also trying to project myself not as a fashionable woman, but as a woman who can carry herself well. That's the first thing I do. I never try to 'over-expose' myself and then outdoing the other contestants. I just try to be as natural as a woman can be, and people notice me because of that. Not just run of the mill type *gay* or woman, I should say. Because even in female beauty contests you can see women walking like *gays*. Exaggerated. So I am trying to project a proper woman, which is the right thing for women to be even in public.

Yet it is precisely in respect of being a 'proper woman' that *gay* attempts such as Theresa's are thwarted, and h/er attempts to distance h/erself from the seriousness of the contest by calling attention to the irony of the contests are themselves doubly ironic, since s/he was at the centre of the dispute over who actually won the contest. On the one hand, the *gay/bantut* are regarded in the first instance as impotent men, signalled among other things in their bound penis, a frequent point of comment, among both men and women at the beauty contests, who sometimes suggested that the reason it was so easy for the *bantut* to conceal their genitals was because they were so small. Although never directly articulated as such, the bound and tucked-under penis of the *gay/bantut* beauty queens might also be seen as a striking symbolic inversion of the bound but erect penis of the ritual suicides (*parrang sabbil*), who, as I previously suggested, are sometimes eulogized as the aesthetic ideal of masculinity. On the other hand, the more the *gay* contestants strive to present themselves as respectable if cosmopolitan women, the more the MC, usually a straight man or woman, will, with the support of the audience, seek to draw out their sexuality, often with barely hidden references to anal intercourse, the latter read in terms not simply of sexual inversion, but also of the desecration of women's bodies, which are sacralized in Islamic ideology. This also articulates with the alternating desire for and appreciation of the elaborate costumes, beautifully made-up faces, perfected karaoke performances and well-recited answers, and the expectation, indeed anticipation, of the comic release which comes with the loose padded bra, lost heels, sagging hose, stuttered speech and rare but even more hilarious indiscreet genital, which is subject to the mimicry and laughter of the audience.

Here we confront the equivocation and ambiguity with which the *bantut* are locally regarded. I noted previously that there were two contrasting sets of discourses, beauty and vulgarity, which were seen to characterize the *bantut*. As in the remarks made about *bantut* beauticians, the one term that consistently arose in remarks made about *gay* beauty contests and which seemed to capture the contradictory sensibilities which the *bantut* were seen to embody was *maarte*. On the one hand, *maarte* is precisely about style, the trendy, beauty and glamour. On the other hand, *maarte* grades off into the affected and pretentious as well as the vulgar (*lumu', bastos*) and 'over-exposed', which is associated with X-rated film stars and prostitutes. In sum, *maarte* stands in opposition to the 'simple' and respectable, in signalling forms and formulations of sociality, including gender / sexuality, which are outside or along the boundaries of the ostensibly normative and conventional.

However, there are several ways in which this equivocation and ambiguity might be read. Viewed from the comparative perspective of 'traditional' Southeast Asian cosmologies, the seeming opposition in *gay* beauty contests between beauty and vulgarity – as between the refined transvestite singer and sucking whore transvestite in *ludruk* performances in Indonesia described by Peacock (1968) – might be interpreted less as a sign of, and for, deviant bodies or sexualities, but as signs of, and for, persons who possess extraordinary spiritual power and potency. This perspective certainly resonates with what I have described as the sense of empowerment and elation which, particularly younger *gays*, say they experience in beauty contests, as well as with the notoriety and seductive power *gays* achieve as persons who are *maarte*.

Nevertheless, as I also have suggested, there has been a further fixing of the meaning of the *gay/bantut* as ethnically and sexually deviant bodies. Viewed from this perspective, beauty and vulgarity are the primary means by which cultural crossing and ambiguities are kept at bay. Indeed, it is in the beauty contest, perhaps more so than anywhere else, that the *gay/bantut* are repeatedly constituted not only as creative producers of beauty, masters of the imaginary, but also as those who have been 'over-exposed' to, overwhelmed by and trans-formed into culturally unrecognized / unrecognizable women / men. It is against this backdrop – and drawing on the essentializing discourses of ethnic and gender / sexual identity, moreover – that the struggle and contest (among them-selves, as much as with the audience) for 'respectability' and legitimation as 'proper women' (as against *maarte*) is set. As I suggest below, however, it is precisely because they inhabit the boundaries of the conventional that the *gay / bantut* reveal, and may become sites for, contesting and refiguring exclusionary practices, which otherwise tend to be naturalized in the language and discourse of the 'real' and the 'simple'.

## Burning gender in the southern Philippines

In thinking about what is happening in these performances – in particular the dual movement by which the *gay / bantut* are at once celebrated and symbolically circumscribed within the domain of the vulgar and over-exposed – it is useful to compare local *gay*-transvestite beauty contests with the drag contests docu-mented in Livingstone's (1991) film *Paris is Burning*. The film is about drag balls in Harlem, New York City, which are attended and performed by African-American and Latino *gay* and / or transsexual / transgender men. Con-testants dress up and compete under a variety of categories such as 'executive', 'Ivy League' or 'glamour', and are judged on the basis of who can best approxi-mate or pass as 'real'. Although seemingly far removed from the discourses of gender transformation in the southern Philippines, the film raises issues which intersect in interesting ways with the ethnography presented here, not the least of which are the ways (White) 'America' figures as central symbol of these performances, and the way in which the term 'gay' is used to signal a variety of gender / sexual identities.

As Butler notes (1993: 122–40) in her critique of the film, 'Gender is Burning', the drag balls at once 'expose' (her term) the norms that regulate 'realness' as a naturalized, that is to say contingent and constructed, set of practices, and also serve to re-inscribe and re-idealize the norm. In effect, the performers affirm the 'real' and reproduce their own degradation – not just as *gays* but as ghettoized Black / Latinos – through their attempts to approximate and appropriate the 'real', a point reinforced by the film itself, which switches back and forth between ballroom drag scenes and shots of 'real' people moving in and out of expensive New York shops. In a similar way, one could argue that the transgenderal project expressed and articulated by many *gay / bantut* – in the beauty contest – and, in particular, the attempt to embody the refined and transcend the vulgar, merely reaffirms their socially circumscribed position in the field of liminal sexuality and gender. However, whereas the audience, judges and performers in drag balls in Harlem are all normatively excluded persons (although each represents or becomes for the others the normatively real in various ways), in *gay* beauty contests the contestants directly confront and are confronted with the 'normal' community. [...]

In fact, it is in and through their jointly produced quality of realness that *gay/ bantut* obtain a measure of success. Persons recognize, as they endow the *bantut* with, the power of self-transformation, of being able to appropriatively imitate and become that which they name. The sting, as it were, is that, in a kind of double mimesis (cf. Silverman 1992, cited in Weston 1993: 353; Taussig 1993) which turns back on itself, the *bantut* not only become more Woman than women themselves [...], but in the process become, as I have already suggested, a different category altogether, an alter-identity defined in terms of American style and beauty. The point is that the normal community (to appropriate Butler's [1993] language) in Sulu has a more immediate, if historically informed stake in *gay* productions of beauty than appears to be the case with the normal community in the drag balls of Harlem, the latter being largely unknown until Livingstone's film and the rise to stardom of Willie Ninja in Madonna's road show.

However, the audience at *gay* beauty contests in Sulu are not a singular entity, and it is important to explore further the different strategic positions and various interests at work in the 'normal community'. While men are as appreciative of *gay* talent at making beauty as women, their approach to the *bantut* is either, as is the case with older married men, critically to distance themselves (as is the case with their selection of the barber shop over the parlour) from what they regard to be the failed masculinity of the *bantut*, or, as is especially the case with younger men, to approach them (as in their accounts of their relationships with *gays*) as tricksters and jokesters. This can clearly be mapped out around the beauty contests, where older men will be found on the peripheries of the audience, viewing the proceedings from a disdainful distance, while younger men will either be found at the front or where possible hovering around the changing rooms making cat calls and other suggestive comments to the *bantut* while attempting to pinch, touch or fondle them as they go back and forth to the stage.

In fact, the relationship between young men and *gays* is complicated precisely because the *gay/bantut* represent such an immanent and familiar source of empowerment and desire. That is to say, while masculinity – the male body – is primarily identified with, and defined by, the defence of Islam, American *istyle*, and in particular those aspects of American style that are associated with an image of aggressive macho sexuality, are readily incorporated and have become a no less important source for defining the masculine body. Similarly, while young Muslim men deny that they would ever actively pursue a *gay* lover or develop any reciprocal emotional attachment or shared feelings with one, what is never denied by young men is the pleasure they receive at the hands of the *gays*. It is this mixture of affinity and desire, coupled with the potential danger of being contaminated (*nalamin*) by the *gay/bantut* – the danger not just of being effeminized, but more specifically of being 'over-exposed' to/completely trans- formed by cultural otherness – which informs the trickster scenario played out by young men. It is also a further expression, or 'testing' and development, of their masculinity.

Among women, there is also this dual movement of celebration and circum- scription, although it is structured and enforced in different ways. Women generally demonstrate a much greater affinity with *gays* than men. *Gays*, for instance, often cited the important influence of women in encouraging them either in childhood and / or during the 'coming out' of their *gay*ness. At beauty contests, not only is there usually a markedly higher proportion of older married women than older married men in attendance (with roughly equal numbers of young men / young women), but also women – especially wealthier, educated, professional women – are, apart from the *gays* themselves, usually among the major sponsors for such events and among the most vocal supporters of the 'third sex'.

One point of identification for women is the various and sometimes competing images of femininity which the *gays* purvey and which women (here as elsewhere) must continually negotiate, although in Sulu this is often formulated in terms of the competing demands and desires of *adat* (Muslim custom and traditions) and style (defined primarily in terms of an imagined American otherness). In fact, the images of femininity purveyed in *gay* beauty contests have much in common with local women's beauty contests, school talent and fashion shows and graduation events, not to mention 'native modern style' weddings. Moreover, there also is at times a clear point of identification with those aspects of *gay* performances which border on the vulgar and sexually illicit. According to many women and *gays*, a frequent topic of conversation among them pertains to sex, especially, but not exclusively, focusing on *gay*-men experiences. Several women told me, for instance, that their first experience of watching pornographic movies was with *gay* friends. Similarly, judging both by what women said and how they responded in the beauty contests, one of the things which women most anticipate in *gay* beauty contests is the ribald nature of the humour.

What I would suggest is that *gay* sexuality, engendered as an expression of unreproductive, ungifted, unendowed women – 'women as lovers but not as mothers' – as the *gays* sometimes put it, represents a kind of absolute freedom (Miller 1990) which women (no more or less than men) sometimes imagine but are only ever able to express and experience themselves in tension with other equally strong and normatively enforced interests in the reproduction and enhancement of familial prestige and local identity. In this respect, transvestite-*gay* beauty contests may be considered, in Garber's (1993: 17) terms, 'possibility spaces, structuring and confounding culture', an important forum not only for the formulation of feminine erotic desire, which is not defined exclusively in terms of reproduction, but also for reformulating dominant images of the feminine as guarantor and repository of cultural tradition and authenticity. In supporting the 'third-sex' and in drawing explicitly on sexual imagery, women are, in a double-edged manner, able to articulate this contradiction and vicariously to participate in the freedom represented by *maarte*, while at the same time clearly demarcating the boundaries of the reproductive and the unreproductive, that is to say, 'real' feminine sexuality, which distinguishes them from the *bantut*.

Gender and sexuality are, of course, just one vector in the play of strategic relations, and it is useful to indicate here the way in which other interests, simplistically mapped along the lines from the poor, under-educated, non-professional, non-elite, to the more affluent, educated, professional and / or political-economic elite, inform and / or provide alternate interpretative possibilities with respect to the *gays* and *gay* / *bantut* beauty contests. The elite, who figure prominently in beauty contests as sponsors and/or judges, and whose names and positions are often read out several times throughout the contests, are a mirror image of the conceptual order of beauty which is signalled and indexed by the *gays* in the parlours and on the stage. In fact, it is the strategic interests of these elite individuals as the representatives, the embodiments, of the state and state institutions, that is the Christian Philippine state – who are, quite literally in some instances, the gate-keepers of state funds and favours, through which the wealth, goods and images purveyed in these beauty contests (and women's beauty contests, school talent shows and weddings) flow – which, more than any other relationship, creates and subverts the transformative mimesis at work in the beauty contests.

On the one hand, elite persons frequently upheld such performances by the 'third-sex' as an example of a progressive and tolerant society, even while they basked in the reflected glory of their glamorous performances. [...] On the other hand, however, the 'third-sex' is often derided as ignorant, a view expressed, for instance, by the chairperson of the board of judges and headmistress of the school, who laughed at the inability of the 'uneducated' *bantut* to answer the questions she had set them in the beauty contest. Other things suggested about the *bantut*, particularly by the educated elite, was that they were 'psychologically maladjusted', 'imbalanced', 'the product of failed upbringings'. At the same time, they were, as more generally, considered to be vulgar, indecent, irreligious and 'over-exposed'. It is in fact primarily among the wealthy educated elite, who have and maintain connections with metropolitan culture, that the discourse of sexual inversion circulates and has become tied to the discourse of ethnically deviant bodies.

Similarly to what Butler (1993) argues is the case in *Paris is Burning*, in a move in which the *gays* collude, the elite, as judges – both in the literal sense that they are actually the judges in the contest and in the figurative sense reflected in elite commentaries about *gay* ignorance, etc. – are instantiated and naturalized as the source and arbiters of the real, the refined and the original, which in the process denies the *gays* the full potential of their performances. At the same time, they also suggest, along with others, that the *gay/bantut* have not just been exposed but over-exposed to, overwhelmed and completely transformed by, cultural otherness. This move allows the elite to draw on and endow the *gay/bantut* as creative producers of 'native modern style', transcending and negotiating their position as functionaries of the Christian Philippine state and staking out their claims to be arbiters of local identity.

On each count, the *gay/bantut* are circumscribed in the domain of *maarte* and 'over-exposed', while the elite claim to be, to possess, the 'real', the 'simple'. More than that, they are claiming ownership and possession over the *gays*, over the transformative potential of the imaginary they represent. This does not mean, however, that either their possession of the *gays* or the space of the imaginary is complete or that their claims to the simple, to the real, remain uncontested, although it is not the *gays* themselves who actively challenge their position. Rather, it is individuals who identify themselves as 'the poor' (*kamiskinan*) who continually call into question and challenge the cultural order of difference which the *gays* purvey on stage and which the wealthy claim to possess in practice.

Viewed from the perspective of the poor and powerless (*miskin way kusug*), the black humour of the *gay/bantut* beauty contest – that is, the dual movement in which the *gays* are alternately celebrated and laughed at, mocked and sometimes even forced to leave the stage – might be seen as embodying the tragic aspect of personal and community life, the frustration of unobtainable aspirations and desires (e.g., wealth and glamour), and, one might add, the failure of state institutions to deliver education and true democracy, themes which are also enshrined in the ideology of beauty which is purveyed by the *bantut* and represented by the elite. However, there are other aspects to this. More than anything else, what the poor celebrate and call attention to in these contests is, as with everyone else, precisely *maarte*, which on the one hand signals the potency and potential of appropriative transformation and on the other the 'over-exposed' potency which in and of itself is considered to be outside the transactional relations through which social memory – remembrances – are produced.

Unlike the elite, whose discourse of 'support' for the 'third sex' is belied by the fact that they sit in judgement upon and distinguish themselves from the vulgarity and over-exposure of the *bantut*, those who identify themselves as poor adopt one or more different positions. On the one hand, they sometimes identify with what is perceived to be the abjected status of the *gay/bantut*, upholding their rights, whatever else might be said about them, to be treated as persons like themselves, a discourse which I also heard in relations to distinctions of ethnicity. On the other hand, this appeal to a common humanity underlying various and varied manifestations was often placed alongside other, more critical comments which drew a homology between the glamour and falsity of both the elite and the *bantut*.

This circumscription of the politically dominant within the domain of *maarte* and the homology often drawn between them was most clearly demonstrated in the run-up to the national and local elections of May 1992. In particular, an explicit link was often drawn between political campaigning and the *kursinada* scenario, in which for a period of time people were said to become the 'target' or *kursinada* of the politicians who attempted to win their votes through money or gifts. Just as young men represented their relations with *bantut* as being one in which they allowed the *bantut* to masturbate them in exchange for money or other goods, in a similar way political campaigns were seen as being a prime time for making money (*hikasin*), a time to be masturbated or fellated by as many of the political-economic elite as possible, who were, during election time at least, reduced to being *manupsup*, 'cock-suckers'.

The point is not whether this constituted a genuine threat to the instrumental or economic power of the elite. Clearly it did not, nor was it meant to. Rather, I would suggest that in drawing the homology between the politico-economic elite and the *bantut* and circumscribing both within the domain of *maarte* and the 'over-exposed', the poor are, on the one hand, contesting and drawing attention to the moves of the wealthy elite to naturalize difference and distinction within the terms of those state institutions, such as democracy, education and bureaucracy, which they see as largely ineffective and corrupt. On the other hand, they are also challenging and making claims on the higher status of the wealthy in terms of their failure to acknowledge them as a constitutive part of that status.

In other words, what is being said to the wealthy is that while they may be powerful and have acquired the power of self-transformation, and may even be able to attract an audience, this does not in and of itself constitute a socially legitimate status. Nor is it simply seen as a matter of earning or obtaining social legitimacy through charity: rather, it is a matter of 'remembrancing', of sharing substance, of reciprocal recognition and the creation of social memory through ongoing gifting transactions. [...] In sum, the *beauty and glamour* which the *bantut* create in the beauty contest and within which the powerful are circumscribed belies the pathos of a situation in which power is at times seen by the poor as increasingly employed, and wealth increasingly accumulated, outside the boundaries, and without respect to the order of either *adat* (custom or tradition) or *istyle* (that is, American style). In each case the poor are making claims upon those more powerful, more wealthy and of higher status than themselves in terms of human sociality, and the transactions through which human sociality is seen to be achieved – affirming their own, while leaving open the question and possibility of the humanity of the other. This takes us back, however, to the *gay/bantut* embodiments of *maarte tuud* – *maarte* in the extreme, power without relation – for while the challenges, claims and appeals to human sociality are part of the ongoing contest for social recognition between persons who are variously and differentially located with respect to each other along the continuum from poor to wealthy within local communities, the *gay/bantut* are more generally and systematically excluded from and denied the possibility of realizing a socially accepted status or identity. The paradoxical position of the *gay/bantut*, which structures the contradictory nature of *gay* experiences and *gay's* expressed transgenderal project – alternately celebratory and tragic – is that they have been constituted as the embodiment of a potent cultural otherness, within and for, but never completely accepted by, their own cultural community.

## Summary and conclusion(s): there is nothing ambiguous about ambiguity

Traditionally, anthropological contributions to debates surrounding gender and sexuality have often, although not always, consisted of pointing out that in such and such a society the practice of same-sex sexuality was valued and valorized in altogether different ways from the way it was in another culture or society, including the anthropologists' own. What anthropologists have been much slower to recognize are the shifting historical contexts and spatial fields in which such categories and practices have emerged not as *sui generis* but as the specific product of political and cultural entanglements (cf. Thomas 1991). As others have argued, it is no longer either theoretically sound or empirically valid to treat various forms and formulations of gender and sexuality as isolated and self-perpetuating islands of desire and desirability.

This is not to say that the interpenetration of gendered signs and sexual spaces have necessarily produced the post-modernist panacea of cultural hybridity and reflexive subjectivities (cf. Lash and Urry 1993). On the contrary, there appears to be no diminution in the production and circulation of essentializing discourses of identity, part of social and symbolic worlds which, while ever shifting, are still characterized by the politics of centres and peripheries, majorities and minorities, belonging and exclusion. This is no less true of gender and sexuality than it is of ethnic and national identities and identifications. Indeed, as the symbolic circum-scription of the *bantut* in the discourse of ethnonationalism attests, these are rarely separate or separable processes (Parker, Russo, Sommer and Yaeger [eds] 1992). Nevertheless, in highlighting the entanglement of cultural economies, I am suggesting that one can only begin fully to understand the dynamic of gender and sexual diversity in a particular locale by exploring the ways in which visions of the local, including local '*gay*' identities, are produced through opposition to, juxtaposition with, and / or exclusion from own or other worlds, and the ways in which dominant versions of locality are reformulated and rearticulated at various levels in the experience and retelling (retailing) of, to rephrase Anna Tsing (1996), alien encounters (real and imagined), including those with anthropologists. In sum, sexuality and gender, like ethnicity, are most usefully thought about not in terms of static boundaries and isolated 'it' entities (cf. Herdt 1991). Rather, they emerge, among other places, in the telling and retelling, mapping and remapping of forms of love and desire, as multi-dimensional cartographies of identity and identification.

[...]

In summary, I have argued that transvestism and transvestite effects (by which I refer to various forms and formulations of gender transformations) are not, as Garber (1993) would have it, the universal fount of cultural transformation. Rather, what this study has suggested is that transvestites and transvestite performances may usefully reveal certain aspects of the way in which the liminal, that is to say the transitional and transformational, are themselves culturally engendered. In this respect, the marginalization and enforced liminality of the *gay / bantut* might be said to be both culturally and historically overdetermined (Althusser 1969: 106–13). That is to say, not only have they been repeatedly constituted as occupying the boundary or border between 'own' and 'other' in the contemporary cultural economy, but also, and more fundamentally, they have come to occupy the boundary between discourses of identity and identifications premised on hierarchy and the possibility of encompassment – in which they figure as signs of cosmic unity and incorporation, something for which people strive to achieve – and discourses of identity premised on separateness and distinction, in which they figure as markers of identity crisis, the focal point of cultural alarm and panic. Moreover, inasmuch as the meaning of transvestites and transvestite performances are a site for contesting and refor-mulating social classifications – a 'possibility space' – what is being contested and negotiated is the meaning and process of cultural transformation itself. The point is that there is nothing ambiguous about ambiguity, sexual or otherwise. Rather, it is the specific product or effect of different historical relations of power and resistance through which cultural subjects are created and re-create them-selves.

# References

Althusser, L. 1969. *For Marx*. London, Allen Lane.

Blanc-Szanton, C. 1990. 'Collision of Cultures: Rhetorical Reformulations of Gender in the Lowland Visayas, Philippines', in S. Errington and J. Atkinson (eds), *Power and Difference: Gender in Southeast Asia*. Stanford, Stanford University Press.

Butler, J. 1993. *Bodies That Matter*. London, Routledge.

Dollimore, J. 1990. *Sexual Dissidence: Augustine to Wilde, Freud to Foucault*. Oxford, Oxford University Press.

Garber, M. 1993. *Vested Interests: Cross-Dressing and Cultural Anxiety*. London, Penguin.

Garcia, J. N. C. 1996. *Philippine Gay Culture: The Last Thirty Years*. Quezon City, University of the Philippines Press.

Herdt, G. 1991. 'Representations of Homosexuality in Traditional Societies: An Essay on Cultural Ontology and Historical Comparison, Part 1'. *Journal of History of Sexuality* 1: 481–504.

Johnson, M. 1997. *Beauty and Power: Transgendering and Cultural Transformation in the Southern Philippines*. Oxford, Berg Publishers.

Lash, S. and J. Urry 1993. *Economies of Signs and Space*. London, Sage.

Miller, D. 1990. 'Fashion and Ontology in Trinidad'. *Culture and History* 7, 49–68.

Parker, A., M. Russo, D. Sommer and P. Yaeger (eds) 1992. *Nationalisms and Sexualities*. London, Routledge.

Peacock, J. L. 1968. *Rites of Modernization: Symbolic Aspects of Indonesian Proletarian Drama*. Chicago, University of Chicago Press.

Silverman, K. 1992. *Male Subjectivity at the Margins*. London, Routledge.

Taussig, M. 1993. *Mimesis and Alterity: A Particular History of the Senses*. London, Routledge.

Thomas, N. 1991. *Entangled Objects*. Cambridge, Mass., Harvard University Press.

Tsing, A. L. 1996. 'Alien Romance', in L. J. Sears (ed.), *Fantasizing the Feminine in Indonesia*. Durham, N C, Duke University Press.

Weston, K. 1993. 'Lesbian / Gay Studies in the House of Anthropology'. *Annual Review of Anthropology* 22, 33–67.

# Part III

# Sexual Identities

Identities are usually seen as basic to who or what we are, and, in relation to sexual identities, it has been traditional to see an automatic relationship between desire and self-description, self and social identity. But the evidence for this has always been problematic, as the work of Kinsey and his colleagues in the 1940s made dramatically clear. They recognized both the spectrum of sexualities and the disjunction between sexual behaviour and sexual identity. This issue has become the focus of considerable debate since the 1970s, and has given rise to political mobilization. For many socially marginalized groups the assertion of distinctive sexual identities has been a critical aspect of the struggle for freedom of choice. For lesbians and gays in particular, but also for bisexuals, transgendered people and a proliferation of even more marginalized groups, it has been critical to assert the significance of organizing a sense of self around a sense of one's needs and desires. Identities have been struggled for, often against extremely forceful and imposed norms. In the modernist project, of which in some ways the sexual movements of the 1970s were heirs, it was taken for granted that the historical distinction between heterosexuality and homosexuality would be reflected in homogeneous identities of, for example, heterosexuals, lesbians and gays. In recent years this has met a dual challenge. The emergence from the late 1980s of 'queer' political movements radically challenged the homogeneous nature of the identities that existed, and constituted a self-conscious refusal of identity on the part of many younger people. An even more significant challenge has come from a growing recognition that the meanings developed around sexual identity in the West were of little relevance to many marginalized people from minority ethnic communities within the Western world, or to many people in other cultures. The complexity of the relationship between the development of Western norms and the experience of colonialism has given rise to a more sophisticated and complex post-colonial theorization of sexual identities. The export of sexual identities from the developed to the developing world must now be assessed in the context of an understanding of neo-colonial power relations, though without seeking to idealize those identities associated with pre-colonial traditions and indigenous cultures.

The first two articles in this section take up the theme of identity most explicitly. Jeffrey Weeks's article explores the paradoxes of sexual identity. Sexual identity assumes fixity and uniformity but confirms unfixity, diversity and difference. Sexual identities are deeply personal, but tell us about multiple social belongings. Sexual identities are simultaneously historical, shaped in specific histories, but also contingent; there is no necessary relationship between behaviour and identity. Weeks concludes that sexual identities are fictions, stories we tell each other about who and what we are, but they are necessary fictions. We might continually question identity, but it is apparently very difficult to escape the concept and the importance it has to our everyday positioning in society.

Arlene Stein continues this theme by exploring the 'identity work' involved in becoming 'lesbian'. Her article examines one of the most fascinating social experiments of recent times, the development of political lesbianism within the second-wave feminist movement, which represented a remarkable example of self-conscious reinvention of the self by a mass movement of women. Like Plummer in part 1, Stein emphasizes the significance of the stories that women tell one another, and explores shifts in the form of these stories over the past generation. She suggests that identities are shaped through a process of negotiation, especially within the wider sense of the community that makes possible contemporary stories. The recognition of how identities are made in specific circumstances has underlined the necessity of seeing identity as multi-dimensional.

The sexuality of people with disabilities has historically often been denied or problematized, yet until recently this has been a neglected area in sexuality research. Tom Shakespeare's chapter rejects the medical model of disability, in which disabled people are cast as victims, in favour of a social model in which the problems faced by the disabled are seen as socially produced. He explores the sexual stories of disabled people, through which their agency in negotiating their sexual identities finds a voice.

Merl Storr examines the emergence of contemporary bisexual identities in an essay which reflects upon the relationships between bisexuality, queer theory, postmodernism and postmodernity. She suggests that bisexualities are shaped within the postmodern flux of sexualities, yet are theoretically obscured by writings about the postmodern. Bisexuality, then, is a phenomenon of post-modernity which, she argues, opens up new possibilities for challenging the rigid dichotomies of modernist theories of sexuality.

Finally, two contributions drawing upon post-colonial theory focus on historical and contemporary developments in formerly colonized states. Oliver Phillips offers a case study of contemporary Zimbabwean attitudes to homosexuality, in a chapter that illustrates the increasing richness and interdisciplinarity of contemporary research on sexuality in the fields of law and socio-legal studies. He reveals the intricately intertwined combination of nationalist, racial, gender and sexual discourses that shape the state's response to sexual diversity. Ironically, in attempting to extirpate homosexuality as a remnant of British imperialism, the

Zimbabwean state effaces the patterns of same-sex behaviour that existed in Africa prior to the colonial encounter.

M. Jacqui Alexander explores the sexual politics of Caribbean states, focusing on Trinidad and Tobago and the Bahamas. She suggests that they have developed *national* identities, but have failed to develop notions of full citizenship for those whose sexual behaviour does not fit into the nationalist image, in particular lesbians and gay men. She asks why the state has marked sexual inscriptions of normality particularly upon the female body, and she suggests that state nationalism and its sexualization of particular bodies is part of an international struggle for legitimation which reconfigures the nation as heterosexual. This is simultaneously a legacy of and a reaction to colonialism. The nation has come to be shaped by what it opposed. But there is a deep paradox in this. The nationalist state has legislated against certain sexualities which are regarded as deviant. At the same time, because of integration into the globalized economy and a reliance upon women's sexualized bodies in the pursuit of the tourist market, it has produced a political economy of desire which is intimately linked with private capital accumulation and denies full citizenship to its own nationals. Alexander suggests that the work of decolonizing the body after 500 years of colonial influence has been disrupted by new forms of state building.

# 10

# Necessary Fictions: Sexual Identities and the Politics of Diversity

*Jeffrey Weeks*

### *Identity trouble*

Sexuality has become a constitutive element in postmodern politics. The politics of the right is preoccupied with sex education, abortion, the threat of the 'gay agenda', the dangers of single parenting and the underclass and the need to shore up the family and its 'traditional' assignment of gender and childrearing responsibilities. The politics of the left is challenged by the claims of women and erotic minorities for rights, and faced by the need to translate its discourse of fairness and equality into an understanding and endorsement of sexual change. In both directions we see a conventional politics having to confront and come to terms with an increasing erotic and cultural diversity. Nor is this challenge limited to the boundaries of the traditional polity. [...]

In this new and unprecedented situation it is not surprising that it is the radical agenda of those who extol the virtues of choice, personal autonomy and the value of diversity who have become the target of hostile moral attack. The radical sexual movements that have sprung up since the 1970s have been the site for some of the most sustained interrogation of values and ethics during the past generation (Seidman 1992). Questions about sexual practices, relationships and lifestyles raised by feminism, lesbian and gay politics, and to a lesser extent by other 'erotic minorities', have in turn fed into mainstream culture, in the form of fashion, representation, sexual techniques, political strategies and moral debate. The responses to these influences have been mixed: from stylistic absorption or dialogue to explicit opposition and outrage. But there has been a sustained common element in the subsequent flurries. In one way or another, they have all raised issues about identity: who we are, why we are, in what ways should we live, how we should love, have sex...

The problematic nature of sexual identity has become the fulcrum of wider debates about the meaning and direction of sexual values, and of the politics of the erotic. This is not because of the power of radical ideas alone, or possibly at all; rather the radical questions raised by recent sexual politics have fed into a much wider uncertainty about the stability and fixity of our sexual belongings and identifications, and hence of who we are and should or could be.

[. . .]

Contemporary identities are hybrid, made of many fragments of history and of social and personal experience; they are heterogeneous, establishing many possible identifications across the boundaries of many potential differences; they are often political in the broadest sense, making links which defy the neat categorizations of social policy and social science, and challenging settled power relations (Rutherford 1990). Yet they are personally knitted together into narratives which give coherence to individual lives, support and promote social agency, and express certain values: values which we share with those with whom we identify, and which differentiate us from countless others with whom we do not, often cannot, identify.

Because of these complexities, identities are troubling. We search for them, claim them, assert and affirm them, usually with all the passion and personal conviction we can command. They provide a bedrock for our most fundamental being and most prized social belongings. Yet we are often forced to question them, or have them questioned for us, remake and reinvent them, search for new and more satisfying personal 'homes', all the time. Questions of identity, personal and collective, are flashpoints for some of the most poisoned and violent disputes across the world: 'intercommunal strife', 'ethnic cleansing', the reassertion of 'lost' or more likely invented national or tribal traditions, have become tokens of our apparent inability to live with diversity, to tolerate the existence of different identities. Simultaneously, new political and cultural identities have proliferated, around race and ethnicity, gender and sexuality, HIV and AIDS, among other collective identities, which have emerged to confirm and promote common human interests, to challenge frozen hierarchies of power and, implicitly or explicitly, to argue for autonomy, diversity and choice. But they in turn generate new types of controversy, around 'identity politics', 'political correctness', the threat to the 'natural order' of sexuality and the like. Not all identities are harmless and enabling. Identities can be battlegrounds. So is the trouble worthwhile?

## The paradoxes of identity

Identities are troubling because they embody so many paradoxes: about what we have in common and what separates us; about our sense of self and our recognition of others; about conflicting belongings in a changing history and a complex modern world; and about the possibility of social action in and through our collective identities. And few identities are so paradoxical as sexual identities.

Sexual identities have a special place in the discourse of identity. They are like relay points for a number of interconnected differences, conflicts and opportunities. For the past few centuries, at least, sex may have been central to the ~~fixing of the individual's place in the culture, but it has not been simply a categorization and placing for a *sexualized* identity (as male or female, normal or pervert, heterosexual or homosexual), rather for a whole set of social positionings. Concepts of national identity have been intricately bound up with notions of appropriate gendered or sexualized behaviour~~ (Parker et al. 1992). The injunctions of nineteenth-century imperial propagandists to the young innocent – to 'be a man' and eschew masturbation, homosexuality or nameless other secret sins, or to embody motherhood and purity for the sake of the race – brought together class, race, gender and sexuality into a potent brew which locked normality and sexuality into a fixed hierarchy that few could escape from even if not so many lived up to it.

[…]

Sexuality is woven into the web of all the social belongings we embrace, and that is why the emergence over the past two hundred years, and in a rush since the 1960s, of alternative or oppositional sexualized identities – lesbian and gay, 'queer', bisexual, transvestite and transsexual, sadomasochistic, an exotic parade dancing into history with a potentially infinite series of scripts and choreographies – is seen as subversive by sexual conservatives. They breach boundaries, disrupt order and call into question the fixity of inherited identities of all kinds, not just sexual, which is also the reason, no doubt, for identities being so problematic to those committed to sexual change. If they are asserted too firmly there are dangers of fixing identifications and values that are really necessarily always in flux; yet if their validity is denied, there is an even greater danger of disempowering individuals and groups from the best means of mobilizing for radical change (Weeks 1991).

Identities are paradoxical, and they raise paradoxes. I want to illustrate this by exploring four key paradoxes.

***Paradox 1:***   *Sexual identity assumes fixity and uniformity while confirming the reality of unfixity, diversity and difference*   Many of us in the West like to say who we are by telling of our sex: 'I am gay/straight'; 'I am male/female'. It places us securely in recognized discourses, embodying assumptions, beliefs, practices and codes of behaviour. Yet the truth is rather more complex. 'Possibility and many-sidedness', Rosenblum (1987, p. 149) has argued, 'are built into the very idea of identity formation'. This is especially true of sexual identities. Academically and theoretically, we increasingly recognize both the diverse desires, needs and passions of individuals and the diversity of (often conflicting) social obligations and belonging, pulling us in a variety of directions. Is being a member of an ethnic or racial minority community more important than a sexual identification? Do class or community loyalties take precedence over identification with the aims of a political movement such as feminism? Such anguishings have characterized the sexual politics of the past thirty years. We fear the uncertainty, the abyss, the unknown, the threat of dissolution that not having a fixed identity entails. So we often try to fix identities, by asserting that what we are now is what we have really, truly always been, if only we had known.

But consider the realities. [...] Since the nineteenth century the placing of individuals into clearly demarcated sexual categories, and hence identities, has gone hand in hand with the presentation of plentiful evidence detailing the fluidity and uncertainty of desire and cultural loyalties (Weeks 1985). It is difficult to fit neatly into the social categories which define and limit possible identifications. The binary divisions that many of us in Western countries take for granted, between men and women, heterosexual and homosexual, normal and perverse, provide barriers against, in the words of Epstein and Straub (1991, p. 14), 'the uncontrollable elasticity and terrifying lack of boundaries within or between bodies'. [...] But those barriers are often fragile, inadequate blocks to the flux of contemporary life, and the range of possible ways of being. The repressed usually returns, sometimes in distorted and damaging ways (such as the homophobia of the 'repressed homosexual'), sometimes in liberating and creative ways, in the elective communities where dissident or oppositional sexual identities, at least, are forged and confirmed. Then identities can become enabling. Yet, I would argue, they are still only ever provisional. We can put on a good performance with them. But we should never believe they are final, or embody some unique truth about ourselves.

***Paradox 2:*** *Identities are deeply personal but tell us about multiple social belongings* All cultures seem to depend on their members having a secure sense of self, and a placing in the order of things. But there is no reason to think that the modern individual is a reflex product of his or her 'instincts'. Self-identity, at the heart of which is sexual identity, is not something that is given as a result of the continuities of an individual's life or the fixity and force of his or her desires. It is something that has to be worked on, invented and reinvented in accord with the changing rhythms, demands, opportunities and closures of a complex world; it depends on the effectiveness of the biographical narratives we construct for ourselves in a turbulent world, on our ability to keep a particular narrative going.

We apparently need a sense of the essential self to provide a grounding for our actions, to ward off existential fear and anxiety and to provide a springboard for action (Giddens 1991; Cohen 1994). So we write into our personal narratives the elements which confirm what we say we are. And here our bodily feelings and presence become central. In a world of apparently constant flux, where the fixed points keep moving or dissolving, we hold on to what seems most tangible, the truth of our bodily needs and desires, or, in the age of AIDS, our vulnerabilities. It is not surprising that the making and remaking of the body then becomes so basic to our assertion of identities. We worry about its health and the forces that can undermine it (smoking in relative private becomes more tabooed than having sex in public, our cholesterol levels more important than our protein intake); we run and do exercises to ward off its infirmity and temporality (even as we collapse from exhaustion, sore feet or painful muscles); we adorn it in clothes that affirm our sense of individuality (but which also provide a badge of our belonging to one subgroup or another, or our enslavement to the whims of the market-place); we assert the imperatives of its desires and potentiality for pleasure (though they as often wrack us with their contradictory messages as confirm a single bodily truth). For the body is seen as the final court of judgement on what we are or can become. Why else are we so worried if sexual desires, whether homosexual or heterosexual, are inborn or acquired? For what other reason are we so concerned whether gendered behaviour corresponds with physical attributes? Only because everything else is so uncertain do we need the judgement that our bodies apparently dictate.

[...] But the body is a fickle master or mistress: its needs change; it falls prey to want or plenty; to sickness and physical decay; its sources of pleasures can be transformed, whether through chance, training, physical alteration, mental control – or, increasingly, the demands of a new regime of 'safer sex'. Even the apparently most decisive of differences between biological men and women, reproductive capacity, is now subject to major medical intervention and potential manipulation. [...]

The body is no more immune to the power of culture, and its transforming possibilities, than our mental attitudes or social identifications. The body, as Giddens suggests, 'in late modernity becomes increasingly socialised and drawn into the reflexive organisation of social life' (1991, p. 198). Yet we necessarily use the body as the focus of our sense of biographical continuity, while implicitly acknowledging our social belongings and cultural baggage. The body, marked by gender, race, age, subject to pleasure, pain and ultimate extinction, is the site for the inscription of difference, the battleground for conflicting cultural meanings.

[...] The socio-sexual identities we adopt, inhabit and adapt, work in so far as they order and give meaning to individual needs and desires, but they are not emanations of those needs and desires. Indeed they have no necessary connection at all to the contingencies of the body. The sources of the narratives that keep us going, that make sense of our individual peculiarities, are deeply historical, dependent on social bonds that provide the map for personal meaning and cultural identification. And those bonds are multiple: we come from different nations, classes, statuses, religions, racial and ethnic groupings, different genders and generations and geographical areas, each of which provides a sliver of experience, a residue of a personal history, which we try to integrate into our personal biographies, to shape our individual identity. Sexual identity involves a perpetual invention and reinvention, but on ground fought over by many histories.

**Paradox 3:** *Sexual identities are simultaneously historical and contingent* The idea that sexual identities are not simple expressions of bodily truth but are historical phenomena – and therefore constantly changing – is a relatively recent one, pioneered largely by feminist and lesbian and gay scholars (see for example, Duberman, Vicinus and Chauncey 1989). Its origins were largely political, demonstrating the historicity and potential ephemerality of the categories we take for granted as natural and inevitable, even as their power was acknowledged. [...] Sexual identities embody power relations, products of imposition *and* agency, and are rooted in many histories.

We still know more about the constitution of Western homosexual identities over the past few hundred years than about any other, particularly the overarching categorization of heterosexuality and heterosexual identities (but see essays in Peiss and Simmons 1989; Katz 1995). Nor is this surprising, for the dominant or hegemonic form of any social position becomes the given, the taken for granted, part of the air we breathe, from which everything else becomes a deviation at best or a perversion at worst. [...] We are increasingly accustomed to seeing sexuality as a spectrum along which lie many potential sexual desires and many different identities. But that easy pluralism obscures the fact that historically sexual identities have been organized into violent hierarchies, where some positions are marked as superior (more natural, healthier, more true to the body than others). The shaping of a distinctive categorization of 'the homosexual' over the past century or so in the leading Western countries (but not, until recently, others) has been an act of power, whose effect, intended or not, has been to reinforce the normality of heterosexuality. [...] In other words, the apparently neutral description of men as either homosexual or heterosexual conceals the intricate play of power, of domination and subordination, which minoritizes the homosexual experience, and consolidates male power in a new, effective pattern. In the same fashion, the categorization, in psychology, sexology and a variety of other social practices, of some women as homosexual and others as very definitely not, breaks the continuum of all women, and hence serves further to consolidate the sexual power of men (Smith-Rosenberg 1985).

The fact that such arguments are still not only controversial in themselves but contested even as a starting-point for debate is a testimony to the power of the categories that have become sedimented in our consciousness during the twentieth century, and to our cultural preference for neat divisions of people and identities: you are either this or that. [...] There are two related points that must be made here.

The first is that the discursive construction of categories of sexual subjects is a constant process, and involves a struggle over definitions on a sexual-political terrain that is ever shifting. The agents of sexual regulation, whether state, churches or other institutions such as those of medicine or psychology, are involved in an effort of definition that is never ending, and the reason for this is quite simply that sexual identities, including (perhaps especially) heterosexual ones, are profoundly unstable.

[...]

The second point is that these categorizations and imposed definitions cannot and do not exhaust the actual lived experience of sexuality or the proliferation of oppositional identities. In the case of homosexuality, there is plentiful evidence that cultures of opposition, pleasure and self-identification were emerging before and then against the opprobrious categorizations that emerged in the law, medicine, sexology and so on in the course of the nineteenth century (see, for example, Bray 1982). It is characteristic of what Dollimore has called the 'perverse dynamic' (1991, p. 160) that a political and sexual ordering is always internally disordered by the very perversities it produces, and sets up against itself. The power to define may have set the limits on what could be said, done or spoken, but those apparently fixed by the definitions nevertheless produced their own resistances and identities. More recently, the emergence of a distinctive identity politics around sexuality has articulated a growing recognition that the power to define itself combines a multiplicity of powers and hierarchies, not only around gender and sexuality, but also around race and ethnicity, class and status, which in turn has produced new frontiers in sexual politics, and new forms of resistance. Sexual identities are enmeshed in relations of domination and subordination, where many histories intertwine. [. . .]

Yet if histories (rather than History) and various forms of power relations (rather than a single Power) provide the context for sexual identities, our assumption of them is determined not by the past but by the contingencies, chances and opportunities of the historic present. As I have already suggested, there is no necessary relationship between a particular organization of desire and a social identity. Many people who practise various forms of homosexual activity fail to recognize themselves in labels such as 'homosexual', lesbian and gay, queer, or whatever the available identity is at any particular time, even in the West, where such descriptions and self-descriptions are hegemonic. In other parts of the world, homosexual practices, where they are not banned totally, are integrated into various patterns of relations, without giving rise to Western-style identities, though other forms of identity do of course exist (Herdt 1994).

This has become particularly crucial in the age of AIDS. It has sometimes been said that HIV and AIDS, in its spread across the world, tells the truth about identity, revealing in infection what is concealed in social life. But it is more accurate to say that HIV reveals the truth about often concealed sexual activities. The assumption that evidence of certain practices reveals the prevalence of identities is not only a fallacy but a dangerous one when it comes to health and safer-sex education, because it assumes that people will recognize themselves in social identities that are peculiar to very specific parts of the world. [. . .]

Available identities are taken up for a variety of reasons: because they make sense of individual experiences, because they give access to communities of meaning and support, because they are politically chosen (Weeks 1985). These identities can, however, equally be refused, precisely because they do not make sense to an individual, or because they have no cultural purchase. Identities necessarily differentiate. They also have differential weight for individuals and collectivities at different times. The positive assertion of sexualized identities is more likely to be a result of a sense of exclusion, denial or threat than an easy acceptance of one's lot. By and large the heterosexual majority have not felt it necessary, until the challenges of recent years, aggressively to assert their heterosexual identities, simply because they set the norm. It was not until the twentieth century that women asserted their sense of themselves as sexual beings, because while before that women may have been regarded as 'the sex', their sexuality was generally during the nineteenth century not seen as autonomous but responsive to that of men (Bland 1996). Similarly, the differential emergence of distinctive male homosexual and lesbian identities can be related to the separate experiences and histories of men and women (Weeks 1977/1990).

[. . .]

The challenge is always one of shaping usable narratives that can make sense of the present through appropriating a particular history. Not surprisingly, one of the first signs of the public emergence of new identities is the appearance of works that detail the 'roots' of those hitherto obscured from recorded or respectable history: history as a way of legitimizing contingency.

***Paradox 4:*** *Sexual identities are fictions – but necessary fictions* Sexual identities are historical inventions, which change in complex histories. They are imagined in contingent circumstances. They can be taken up and abandoned. To put it polemically, they are fictions. This is not of course how they are seen or experienced, or what we wish to believe. Worse, in the age of uncertainty through which we are currently struggling, to say this often seems a betrayal of what we need most desperately to hold on to, an arid intellectualism which leaves minorities without hope, and the vulnerable defenceless. As HIV disease visibly and remorselessly spread in the male gay communities of the West from the early 1980s, it was the existence of strong lesbian and gay communities and identities which provided the essential context for combating the virus: in providing social networks for support and campaigning, in developing a grammar for safer sex, in promoting a language of resistance and survival. The homophobia that was encouraged by AIDS demanded, and in fact greatly strengthened, lesbian and gay identities; without them, it often seemed in the embattled 1980s, there was nothing. To say that all this was a fiction seemed perverse.

But to say that something is a historical fiction is not to denigrate it. On the contrary, it is simple to recognize that we cannot escape our histories, and that we need means to challenge their apparently iron laws and inexorabilities by constructing narratives of the past in order to imagine the present and future. Oppositional sexual identities, in particular, provide such means and alternatives, fictions that provide sources of comfort and support, a sense of belonging, a focus for opposition, a strategy for survival and cultural and political challenge. Such a view of identity does two things. First of all it offers a critical view of all identities, demonstrating their historicity and arbitrariness. It denaturalizes them, revealing the coils of power that entangle them. It returns identities to the world of human beings, revealing their openness and contingency.

Second, because of this, it makes human agency not only possible, but also essential. For if sexual identities are made in history, and in relations of power, they can also be remade. Identities then can be seen as sites of contestation. They multiply points of resistance and challenge, and expand the potentialities for change. Identities, particularly those identities which challenge the imposing edifice of Nature, History, Truth, are a resource for realizing human diversity. They provide means of realizing a progressive individualism, our 'potential for individualization' (Melucci 1989, p. 48) and a respect for difference.

Frank Kermode (1967) has made a useful distinction between myths and fictions. Myth, he argues:

> operates within the diagrams of ritual, which presupposes total and adequate explanations of things as they are and were: it is a sequence of radically unchangeable gestures. Fictions are for finding things out, and they change as the needs of sense-making change. Myths are the agents of stability, fictions are the agents of change. (1967, p. 210)

From this viewpoint, the dominant (hetero)sexual identities in our culture have some of the qualities of myths: they speak for an assumed naturalness, eternity and truth which belie their historical and contingent nature. The radical, oppositional identities which have arisen in and against the hegemonic ones can be seen as fictions: they offer narratives of individual life, collective memory and imagined alternatives which provide the motivation and inspiration for change. In that sense, they are not only fictions – they are necessary fictions. Without them we would have no basis to explain our individual needs and desires, nor a sense of collective belonging that provides the agency and means for change.

The danger is that these historical inventions, these fictional unities, become closed, the exclusive home of those who identify with them. [...] But if their historicity, openness, flexibility and conditional nature – fictional qualities – are acknowledged fully, they provide the opportunity for thinking about not only who you are, but also about who you want to become. They reveal the power relations that inhibit change, by making power visible. And once we accept that sexuality takes its form from historically specific power relations, then it becomes possible to imagine new forms of desire which are not blocked by a sense of powerlessness and inevitability. Oppositional sexual identities in their collective form provide vistas for different futures. By interrogating and challenging normalizing and imposed forms of identity, it becomes possible to invent oneself anew.

Identities in this sense are less about expressing an essential truth about our sexual being; they are more about mapping out different values: the values of autonomy, relationships, of belonging, of difference and diversity. They provide continuous possibilities for invention and reinvention, open processes through which change can happen. [...] That, of course, means that sexual identities are more than troubling on a personal level; they also cause trouble on a social level. I agree with Judith Butler's summing up of the paradox of identity:

> I'm permanently troubled by identity categories, consider them to be invariable stumbling-blocks, and understand them, even promote them, as sites of necessary trouble. (1991, p. 14)

It is the necessary trouble caused by the paradoxes of identity that makes the politics of sexuality so fraught with tensions, but so important for rethinking the nature of our social and cultural values.

[...]

# References

Bland, L. 1996, 'The shock of the *Freewoman* journal: feminists speaking on heterosexuality in early twentieth-century England', in J. Weeks and J. Holland (eds), *Sexual Cultures: Communities Values and Intimacy*, London, Macmillan.

Bray, A. 1982, *Homosexuality in Renaissance England*, London, GMP.

Butler, J. 1991, 'Imitation and gender insubordination', in D. Fuss (ed.), *Inside/Out: Lesbian Theories, Gay Theories*, New York and London, Routledge.

Cohen, A. P. 1994, *Self Consciousness: An Alternative Anthropology of Identity*, London and New York, Routledge.

Dollimore, J. 1991, *Sexual Dissidence: Augustine to Wilde, Freud to Foucault*, Oxford, Clarendon Press.

Duberman, M. B., Vicinus, M. and Chauncey, G. (eds) 1989, *Hidden from History: Reclaiming the Lesbian and Gay Past*, New York, New American Library.

Epstein, J. and Straub, K. (eds) 1991, *BodyGuards: The Cultural Politics of Gender Ambiguity*, London and New York, Routledge.

Giddens, A. 1991, *Modernity and Self-Identity: Self and Society in the Late Modern Age*, Cambridge, Polity.

Herdt, G. (ed.) 1994, *Third Sex, Third Gender: Beyond Sexual Dimorphism in Culture and History*, New York and Paris, Zone Books.

Katz, J. N. 1995, *The Invention of Heterosexuality*, New York, NAL/Dutton.

Kermode, F. 1967, *The Sense of an Ending: Studies in the Theory of Fiction*, London, Oxford and New York, Oxford University Press.

Melucci, A. 1989, *Nomads of the Present: Social Movements and Individual Needs in Contemporary Society*, London, Radius.

Parker, A., Russo, M., Sommer, D. and Yaeger, P. (eds) 1992, *Nationalisms and Sexualities*, London and New York, Routledge.

Peiss, K. and Simmons, C., with Padgug, R. 1989, *Passion and Power: Sexuality in History*, Philadelphia, Temple University Press.

Rosenblum, N. 1987, *Another Liberalism: Romanticism and the Reconstruction of Liberal Thought*, Cambridge, MA, Harvard University Press.

Rutherford, J. (ed.) 1990, *Identity: Community, Culture, Difference*, London, Lawrence and Wishart.

Seidman, S. 1992, *Embattled Eros: Sexual Politics and Ethics in Contemporary America*, London and New York, Routledge.

Smith-Rosenberg, C. 1985, 'The female world of love and ritual', in *Disorderly Conduct: Visions of Gender in Victorian America*, New York and Oxford, Oxford University Press.

Weeks, J. 1977/1990, *Coming Out: Homosexual Politics in Britain from the Nineteenth Century to the Present*, London, Quartet.

Weeks, J. 1985, *Sexuality and its Discontents: Meanings, Myths and Modern Sexualities*, London and Boston, Routledge and Kegan Paul.

Weeks, J. 1991, *Against Nature: Essays on History, Sexuality and Identity*, London, Rivers Oram Press.

# 11

# Becoming Lesbian: Identity Work and the Performance of Sexuality

*Arlene Stein*

[...]

### Identity work

Lesbian feminists [in the USA in the 1970s] imagined 'coming out' as a journey that began with a discovery of the lesbian within one's sense of self and proceeded through time, as the individual moved from an oppressive environment to one that permitted freer and bolder self-expression.[1] Coming out signified the claiming, or reclaiming, of that which is essential, true, unchanging. But coming out is as much a practical creation of the self, a 'be-coming out,' as a matter of revealing or discovering one's sexuality.

'Coming out is partially a process of revealing something kept hidden, but it is also more than that,' writes political philosopher Shane Phelan. 'It is a process of fashioning a self—a lesbian or gay self—that did not exist before coming out began.'[2] Identities do not spring forth effortlessly from individuals: individuals reflexively effect change in the meanings of particular identities. Becoming a lesbian always entails participating in particular communities and discourses, conforming to historical and localized norms for 'being' a lesbian. A lesbian identity is learned and performed in many different ways. Particularly for women who 'originally' experienced themselves as heterosexual or bisexual, and who became lesbians very selfconsciously, through the influence of feminism, coming out as a lesbian often entailed a great deal of work.

Sociologist Barbara Ponse describes 'identity work' as the 'processes and procedures engaged in by groups designed to effect change in the meanings of particular identities.'[3] I use the term similarly, to signify the process by which many individuals sought to make their subjective sense of self congruent with their emergent social identity as lesbian and to narrow the experiential gap separating them from other, more experienced lesbians. [...]

Erving Goffman has shown that on the surface level, individuals use gestures and symbols, 'signs that convey social information,' as means of self-presentation. This type of identity work signals membership in the group to others.[4] A second dimension, emotion work, concerns 'deep acting,' the attempt to alter one's inner thoughts so as to feel differently and also look as though one feels differently.[5] Arlie Hochschild proposes that people are more likely to seek interactional rules for both of these levels in 'times of great social transition,' when they often find themselves in new situations with no social rules at hand. An emergent culture would need to codify rules for management of both symbols and emotions in order to organize members' interactions successfully.[6]

Indeed, my interviewees described a period, the 1970s, when new gender norms were devised through feminist practice. Acts of identity work conveyed membership and position within the lesbian subculture to other members, while at the same time communicating information about this stigma to members of the larger society. They also effected change in personal identities, altering the ways in which individuals thought about themselves. In terms of surface identity work, individuals changed their dress and mannerisms to conform more closely to what a 'real' lesbian 'looked like.' They also engaged in the public telling of coming out stories. But the work also went deeper, as individuals consciously altered not only such relatively superficial characteristics as symbols or gestures but also inner characteristics, such as emotions and desires. By looking at these performances, we can more fully grasp the complexity of sexual identity formation.

## Telling stories

Modern life offers individuals numerous opportunities to 'confess' the 'truth' of our lives. The Catholic confessional, in which individuals speak of dark secrets in order to expunge their sins, is joined by the psychoanalytic couch, where the analysand is encouraged to probe the depths of her unconscious. Among lesbians and gay men, the coming out narrative has become a kind of collective confessional that seeks both to free the individual from her or his sexual repression and, at the same time, to build a culture and community around a 'reverse affirmation' of shared stigma.[7]

Many women who came of age during the 1970s were introduced to the idea of coming out through their participation in feminist 'consciousness-raising.' Women talked together about their personal problems as women—their unsatisfying relationships with men, their feelings of inferiority and powerlessness. Within the context of a 'consciousness-raising group,' 'small group,' or 'rap group,' as they were sometimes called, many women came to recognize that the 'personal is political' and began to think of themselves as members of a collectivity of women. They also came to recognize their deep feelings for other women. [...] As gender and sexual boundaries were breaking down and the meanings of sexuality were being redefined, consciousness-raising groups often became coming out groups in which individuals were socialized into the lesbian world. In the language of the day, discovering one's lesbianism was a matter of unearthing that which was repressed and hidden, that which was negated by the compulsory heterosexuality of the dominant culture.

[...] As a 1972 lesbian feminist tract explained, this passage entailed the fashioning of a self that, though new, was actually 'truer' to the individual than had been the formerly 'feigned' heterosexual self: 'Readiness to become an acknowledged Lesbian seems to involve a personal and emotional restructuring of values, often with the help of friends or a consciousness-raising group.... The transition from a feigned heterosexual identity to a Lesbian identity may constitute a period of considerable confusion. There is a time when a Lesbian feels she is nobody, nowhere—on a bridge between an old self and a new self.'[8] [...]

The coming out story, the account of the passage into the lesbian/gay world, was the gay community's 'development myth.' It was an account of heroism in the face of tremendous odds and societal pressure: based on the ideal of being 'true to oneself' and expressing one's 'authentic' self, it invoked a central theme in American culture.[9] [...] The telling of coming out stories was a public act, serving as a type of 'identity announcement' that directed an individual's conduct and influenced that of others. Telling one's coming out story in effect announced one's membership in the group to others. But it also defined and sharpened the teller's interest in a situation, thus focussing attention more acutely on those situated events that are relevant to that identity.[10] In telling these stories, individuals ordered their subjective reality; isolating and recalling the defining events, contexts, or ideas gave symbolic order to their lesbian trajectory. This telling served to reinforce the teller's commitment to a lesbian identity. As Judith Butler suggests, 'it is through the repeated play of this sexuality that the "I" is insistently reconstituted as a lesbian "I."' In other words, the repetition of a culturally constructed characteristic produces a lesbian identity.[11]

[...]

Symbolic interactionist literature on identity construction describes how people experiencing 'conversions' of identity are prone to 'recasting the past' to bring it into line with the present.[12] Coming out stories, like all narratives of the self, are incomplete, selective renderings of personal history, shaped by the needs of the present as much as by the past.

[...]

## Defining desires

Lesbian feminism normalized relationships among women by deprecating heterosexual relationships and by generating a culture and vocabulary that valued and even *idealized* lesbianism. Feminists privileged lesbianism as the most effective challenge to compulsory heterosexuality. They attributed a woman's heterosexual past to some 'preenlightened phase' and created a new cultural repertoire of desire, a new set of 'sexual scripts' that would guide sexual desire and behavior and provide an alternative to the dominant, heterosexual schemas.[13]

For many women, exclusive commitment to homosexuality was never in question. But for others, including some of those who came out through feminism, heterosexual desires persisted beneath the surface, despite their best efforts. Even as they identified as lesbians, some women reported experiencing a sense of 'role distance.' They felt that the term *lesbian* did not fully express 'who they were.'

[...]

Unconscious fantasies tend to pose intractable problems for 'politically correct' voluntarism.[14] Among feminist lesbians, heterosexual desires were seen as evidence of 'internalized oppression.' Once they were recognized and brought to consciousness, it was imagined that internalized heterosexuality, much like internalized homophobia, could be overcome.

[...]

Having heterosexual desires was one thing, and acting on them was quite another. While conducting fieldwork in a lesbian community in the mid-1970s, Barbara Ponse found strong norms among lesbians prohibiting heterosexual contacts and mandating a high degree of consistency among identity, behavior, and practices. 'The importance placed on lesbian identity,' she concluded, 'would tend to limit experimentation with heterosexual relationships once a woman had made the identification[:]... a lesbian who engages in relationships with men could expect censure from other lesbians.'[15]

[...]

The gay liberation movement had initially supported bisexuality as the ideal form of sexuality, a mode that transcended binary identity categories, questioned the homosexual/heterosexual dichotomy, and affirmed polymorphously perverse pleasures. But by the early 1970s, in many lesbian circles bisexuality was anathema: bisexuals were at best inferior lesbians and at worst collaborators with the enemy. [...] In the terms set forth by the 'gay trajectory,' women who harbored continued heterosexual desires were imagined as 'having trouble dealing with their gayness.'[16] Faced with these negative sanctions, some believed that even if they were originally attracted to men, and their initial lesbian experiences were not entirely positive, they could resocialize themselves to be sexually interested in women. They believed that they were originally bisexual, but had been socialized to be straight. Coming out therefore entailed identity work designed to 'get in touch with one's lesbianism' and resocialize oneself to be gay.[17]

[...]

Laura Stone recalled that she 'started out somewhat repulsed when I saw lesbians with each other' and through the movement became 'sensitized to the possibility of sexuality being changeable. . . . It wasn't a "wow" experience at first. But I was under the sway of the idea that it's the most natural thing in the world to do with someone you're close with. So even though the sexual experience wasn't "wow," I began to think about how great it was to be having sex in such a "natural" way.' Even though she 'found a lot of feminists very attractive, not just physically,' Laura said she was 'more comfortable sexually with men.' In her circle, she was known 'as a straight woman who was sleeping with lesbians,' or as a 'political lesbian.' But over time, she began to think of her heterosexuality as a product of socialization. [. . .] 'I began to think of my heterosexuality as a temporary aberration, a product of internalized homophobia. I didn't believe that there was some kind of primary sexual identification. I thought it was changeable.' What began as 'deep acting' actually resulted in a changed perception of sexuality.

'After three or four sexual experiences with women,' Laura said, she 'started to get turned on by it. . . . and there were many times that it was great sexually.' [. . .] In retrospect, Laura thought of herself as someone for whom lesbian desires were 'produced' by a sense of lesbian identity: 'I would not say that my sexuality preceded my identity. My identity as a lesbian preceded my sexuality. And my sexuality was just trying to catch up. I was more mutable than other people. It seemed to me that I was a case of someone who was proof of the socialization theory.'

## Doing gender

[. . .]

Codifying and eroticizing gendered differences have long been central to lesbian subcultures. The most visible manifestation of lesbian 'gender' is tied to appearance. [. . .] Members of prefeminist working-class bar subcultures eroticized gender differences. Butch-femme roles, which adapted conventional gender roles to the lesbian context, were in Nestle's words 'a conspicuous flag of rebellion' in a highly stigmatized, secretive world, a means of survival in an age when gender rules bore down heavily.[18] Being a butch, or 'mannish woman,' was an assertion of strength against very narrow conceptions of what it meant to be a woman. To wear a leather jacket and slick back one's short hair weren't simply experiments with style – it was an embrace of one's 'true nature' in the face of the dominant culture's notions of 'woman': feminine and coy.

Nearly twenty years later, in the context of the women's liberation movement, a very different politics of gender and the body emerged. Seventies feminists attempted to free women's bodies from their possession by men, which they viewed as being synonymous with their sexualization.

Women looked at their vulvas and cervix, examined their breasts and took up sports and recreational activities. . . . How we lived in our bodies, not only how we thought about our bodies, was transformed. A growing awareness of alienation from and oppression to our bodies was met not only by a new consciousness in our minds, that is, new ideology and new information, but by a new set of practices that enabled women to both learn about their bodies and live differently in them.[19]

As part of a movement devoted to empowering women by reconstituting gendered bodies, lesbian feminists attempted to erase gender differences, to recodify gender and sexuality, and to position themselves outside the dominant culture. Early lesbian feminists saw themselves as the embodiment of the androgynous ideal of a world without gender. Minimizing the differences between women and men, they embraced an antinatalist, antihousewifery politics that placed lesbians in a cross-gender position. [...]

For feminists, who were committed to minimizing gender differences, the exaggerated gender roles of butch-femme were little more than a self-hating reflection of the dominant heterosexual culture. Butches, some charged, were 'male-identified' in the truest sense: they looked and acted like men. Femmes were little better. [...] In contrast, feminists wished to free themselves from norms that associated women with their bodies and made a fetish of personal appearance. They tried to remove all traces of what R. W. Connell has called 'emphasized femininity,' or hegemonic rules for female gender.[20] The practice of femininity, they believed, constrained women and encouraged them to display sociability rather than technical competence, to accept marriage and caring for children rather than combat labor market discrimination against women, and to organize their lives around themes of 'sexual receptivity' and 'motherhood.'

Jackie Henry, a therapist, remembered the scorn meted on feminine-appearing women in feminist circles in the Midwest in the early 1970s. 'Where I was, you wouldn't dare wear nail polish. You really wouldn't. If you were brave enough and tough enough, you would do it anyway, and nobody would tell you you couldn't. But you would not be approved.' [...]

Feminist lesbians wished to free themselves not only from gender roles but from high fashion altogether, which they saw as synonymous with women's oppression. Toward this end, they embraced androgynous self-presentation. They wore jeans and t-shirts, flannel shirts and work boots. They wore their hair relatively short. They forged a style that embodied ideals of authenticity and naturalness against what was seen as the artificial, feigned styles of both butch-femme and 'normal femininity.' [...] Styled after simple, functional working-class clothing, the lesbian look represented the wish of many middle-class lesbians to be downwardly mobile, or at least to identify with less fortunate members of society. [...] Clothing was an emblem of refusal – a blow against the twin evils of capitalism and patriarchy, against the fashion industry and the female objectification that fueled it.[21]

Several women who had thought of themselves as tomboys from an early age spoke about the 'lesbian look' in much the same terms as they described their own coming out: as a 'coming home.' [...] But this sense of self-recognition was not universal. Though the 'dyke uniform' was intended to minimize the differences among lesbians, disparities of style persisted and sometimes posed problems. Thirty-four-year-old Dale Hoshiko arrived in San Francisco in the mid-1970s from Hawaii, eager to become a part of the lesbian/gay scene. A friend from Hawaii, a lesbian, showed her around when she arrived, but, Dale recalled, 'she didn't like hanging out with me because it pointed to the fact that we were both Asian. People would ask if I was her sister. She liked to view herself as white.' Because Dale was Asian American, she said she was viewed as an oddity on Castro Street, in the heart of the gay ghetto. 'The men looked at me strangely. They couldn't figure out what I was doing there. I didn't have the lesbian look. I carried a handbag. I wasn't seen as a lesbian. I was seen as an Asian woman.' The women's community of San Francisco, which was at that point fairly distinct from the gay male ghetto, was much more receptive and welcoming toward Dale. But [. . .] Dale's comments suggest that dominant visual codes in lesbian/gay communities, which determined 'what a lesbian looked like,' often assumed whiteness and marked women of color as heterosexual. The identity work required of women of color was therefore doubly demanding.

[. . .]

Although they sought to neutralize gender (and race), many women experienced a continuing disjunction between the person they were and the person they wished to be. Some changed their gendered self-presentation, or 'surface identity,' but still felt that 'deep down' they could never entirely free themselves from gender roles. One needed to be butch to subvert femininity, but butch-femme roles were generally anathema to baby boom women. As Gayle Rubin has noted, 'In spite of their prevalence, issues of gender variance are strangely out of focus in lesbian thought, analysis, and terminology. The intricacies of gender are infrequently addressed.'[22] Despite their ostensible attempts to erase gender differences, recodify gender and sexuality, and position themselves outside the dominant culture, lesbian feminists were ultimately utterly dependent on the gender codes they tried to subvert.

### Finding an 'other' lover

For women of the baby boom cohort, recasting the past, resocializing one's sexual attractions, and changing one's appearance were important steps toward developing a lesbian identity. But perhaps the most important step was the establishment of a same-sex relationship, which was often virtually synonymous with involvement with an identifiable lesbian community. Many women described the erotic flavor of community interactions, the fusion of the personal and the political that made lesbianism a plausible and even exciting alternative.[23] [. . .] The community provided an alternative sense of self and a sensibility that valued lesbianism and deprecated mainstream values.

If the community was in some sense a 'significant other,' which fused personal and political relationships and provided a source of potential lovers and friends, the building block of the community was the couple. For sexually inexperienced women, entry into a romantic relationship with another woman was one way of gaining membership into the lesbian subculture. Many women spoke of the importance of their first relationship, as distinct from a first sexual experience that may or may not have been considered to be significant. So Laura Stone:

> I wouldn't say that once I had good sex with women I became gay identified. [...] it really took my relationship with Nora for me to feel 'permanently' gay. I feel like I got married to this woman. I thought I was going to be with her for the rest of my life. We had a kid together. Now, I was a lesbian, I thought. So that's when I really came out.

Women who experienced their sexuality as relatively fluid and their lesbianism as largely 'elective' often formed an emotional attachment with a more experienced lesbian. The more experienced lesbian helped construct the new lesbian's coming out experience and participated in the formation of her new sexual identity. No one said that she consciously became involved with a woman for this reason alone; nonetheless, many of my interviewees were highly conscious of the role that this dynamic played in their attractions and relationships.

[...]

More than half of the women who described their lesbianism as 'elective' identified similar patterns in their relationships. They found themselves consistently attracted to and involved with 'more experienced' lesbians. Many 'new' lesbians described their involvement with 'old gay' women who had then come into the women's movement. Others chose as lovers women of their own age, but 'new gay' women for whom lesbianism was a 'coming home' experience. Several women reported that more experienced, more internally driven lesbians courted them, attracted to what was seen as their femininity. They, in turn, were attracted to what they perceived as the more 'androgynous' or masculine sense of self of lifelong lesbians.

[...] The eroticizing of difference flew in the face of the ideology of lesbian feminism, which imagined lesbian attachments, in contrast to those of heterosexuals or even butch-femme lesbians, as a partnering of equals, united in their similarity.

[...]

### The actors behind the acts

The dominant sociopsychological conception of lesbian development, reflected in stage models of sexual identity formation, claims that lesbian identity forms in an objective, unilinear process that ends at the moment at which one 'comes out,' or consciously identifies as lesbian. As the preceding suggests, such models offer little insight into the production of gendered and sexed subjectivity, with all of its inconsistencies. Identity is not a 'truth' that is discovered: it is a performance enacted. [...] One is not born a lesbian; one becomes a lesbian through acts of reflexive self-fashioning. The formation of a lesbian identity is at least partly a matter of developing proficiency in manipulating codes and symbols. It involves conforming to historically specific and localized norms of identity and culture.

Women of the baby boom performed their lesbianism by rewriting their autobiographies, or by consciously trying to resocialize themselves to be sexually attracted to women and to repress their feelings for men. Sometimes they changed their self-presentation to bring it more into line with what they considered to be 'authentically' lesbian. At other times they pursued relationships with women whom they identified as 'real' lesbians. In the 1970s, when feminism and gay liberation were very influential, such performances took place within a system that highly valued authenticity – the idea of being 'true to oneself.' Lesbian feminism was founded on the belief that women could retrieve a self that had been denied to them by the dominant culture. Authenticity was an important criterion for building trust among individuals within lesbian communities, particularly as the stigma of lesbianism persisted. By the standards of the dominant culture, lesbians often felt like inauthentic, deviant, 'failed' women, but within the lesbian subculture, they imagined that it was possible to 'be themselves.' The effect of this identity work was often, paradoxically, to impose a rather rigid normative conception of what it means to be a 'lesbian.' To become a lesbian in the context of the gender / sexual politics of the 1970s was to be implicated in that which one opposed: binary sexual and gender categories.[24]

While identity may consist of a string of performances made coherent only through their repetition, individuals varied in terms of their 'skills' as performers and the success of their performances. For many women, performing lesbianism came relatively easily and effortlessly; becoming a lesbian meant reengaging with what they already believed to be their authentic self and claiming their long-standing, if secret, desires. It permitted them to adopt a *surface* identity as a lesbian that matched the *deep* sense of difference they already possessed.

To others, who had experienced themselves as originally heterosexual or bisexual, coming out meant 'discovering' their lesbianism. For these women, desire was often not the primary determinant of a deep identification as lesbian; first, they identified with lesbianism as a sociosexual category. Even after having come out, some in this group felt that their sense of lesbian self was inauthentic; it seemed that they were just 'going through the motions.' They felt compelled to undertake much more rigorous 'identity work.'

By engaging in such identity work, some individuals in this latter group were able to narrow the experiential gap separating them from other, more experienced lesbians. They 'became lesbians.' But others continued to suffer a dissonance between who they felt that they 'were' and who they wished to 'become.' Identity work did not make their subjective sense of self match the sociosexual typology 'lesbian.' For some of these women, lesbian identity often felt 'put on' or 'not part of them.'[25] They changed their self-presentation, which operated as a surface identity, but still felt that 'deep down' they could never entirely free themselves from their essential selves. For them, gender and sexuality inhered in traits 'possessed' rather than in presentations enacted.[26]

## Notes

1  Zimmerman 1990, 34–75.
2  Phelan 1993, 774.
3  Ponse 1978, 91.
4  Goffman 1959 distinguishes between use of symbols to denote prestige and stigma. A prestige symbol serves to 'establish a special claim to prestige, honor, or desirable class position,' while a stigma symbol 'draw[s] attention to a debasing identity discrepancy' (43–44).
5  Here 'the actor does not try to seem happy or sad but rather expresses spontaneously' (Hochschild 1983, 35).
6  Hochschild 1992.
7  Plummer 1995 situates the confessional mode of sexual storytelling in late modernity.
8  Abbott and Love 1972, 223.
9  For examples of this 'development myth,' see Stanley and Wolfe 1980.
10  Hewitt 1989, 167.
11  Butler 1991, 18.
12  Berger and Luckmann 1966; Ponse 1978.
13  Gagnon and Simon 1973 conceptualized the 'sexual script' as a counterpoint to 'drive theory,' suggesting that sexual behavior is, for the most part, a simple, everyday occurrence that is constructed from variable social motives and settings. Also see Plummer 1982.
14  See Segal 1983.
15  Ponse 1978, 184.
16  Ponse 1978, 189–92.
17  Risman and Schwartz 1988 suggest that lesbians' 'transformation of sexual orientation to suit political beliefs deserves more analytical attention' (138).
18  Nestle 1981, 21.
19  Gerson 1995, 3.
20  Connell 1987.
21  Stein 1992.
22  Rubin 1992, 468.
23  See Lorde 1984 for a holistic definition of lesbian eroticism.
24  On the 'paradox of performativity,' see Butler 1993, 241.
25  Hochschild 1983, 36.
26  Weston 1993, 13.

## References

Abbott, Sidney, and Barbara Love. 1972. *Sappho Was a Right-On Woman*. New York: Stein & Day.
Berger, Peter, and Thomas Luckmann. 1966. *The Social Construction of Reality: A Treatise in the Sociology of Knowledge*. New York: Anchor Books.
Butler, Judith. 1991. 'Imitation and Gender Insubordination.' In *Inside / Out: Lesbian Theories, Gay Theories*, ed. Diana Fuss. New York: Routledge.
Butler, Judith. 1993. *Bodies That Matter*. New York: Routledge.
Connell, R. W. 1987. *Gender and Power*. Stanford: Stanford University Press.

Gagnon, J. H. and William Simon. 1973. *Sexual Conduct: The Social Sources of Human Sexuality*. Chicago: Aldine.

Gerson, Deborah. 1995. 'Speculums and Small Groups: New Visions of Women's Bodies.' Department of Sociology, University of California, Berkeley. Photocopy.

Goffman, Erving. 1959. *The Presentation of Self in Everyday Life*. Garden City, N. Y.: Doubleday.

Hewitt, John P. 1989. *Dilemmas of the American Self*. Philadelphia: Temple University Press.

Hochschild, Arlie. 1983. *The Managed Heart: Commercialization of Human Feeling*. Berkeley: University of California Press.

Hochschild, Arlie. 1992. 'Gender Strategies in Women's Advice Books.' Paper presented at the annual meeting of the American Sociological Association, Atlanta, Georgia.

Lorde, Audre. 1984. *Sister Outsider*. Trumansburg, N. Y.: Crossing.

Nestle, Joan. 1981. 'Butch – Fem Relationships: Sexual Courage in the 1950s.' *Heresies* 3(4): 21–4.

Phelan, Shane. 1993. '(Be)Coming Out: Lesbian Identity and Politics.' *Signs* 18: 765–90.

Plummer, Ken. 1982. 'Symbolic Interactionism and Sexual Conduct: An Emergent Perspective.' In *Human Sexual Relations*, ed. Mike Brake. New York: Pantheon.

Plummer, Ken. 1995. *Telling Sexual Stories: Power, Change, and Social Worlds*. New York: Routledge.

Ponse, Barbara. 1978. *Identities in the Lesbian World: The Social Construction of Self*. Westport, Conn.: Greenwood.

Risman, Barbara, and Pepper Schwartz. 1988. 'Sociological Research on Male and Female Homosexuality.' *Annual Review of Sociology* 14: 125–47.

Rubin, Gayle. 1992. 'Of Catamites and Kings: Reflections on Butch, Gender, and Boundaries.' In *The Persistent Desire: A Femme-Butch Reader*, ed. Joan Nestle. Boston: Alyson.

Segal, Lynne. 1983. 'Sensual Uncertainty or Why the Clitoris Is Not Enough.' In *Sex and Love*, ed. Sue Cartledge and Joanna Ryan. London: Women's Press.

Stanley, Julia Penelope, and Susan J. Wolfe. 1980. *The Coming Out Stories*. Watertown, Mass.: Persephone.

Stein, Arlene. 1992. 'All Dressed Up, But No Place to Go? Style Wars and the New Lesbianism.' In *The Persistent Desire: A Femme-Butch Reader*, ed. Joan Nestle. Boston: Alyson.

Weston, Kath. 1993. 'Do Clothes Make the Woman?: Gender, Performance Theory, and Lesbian Eroticism.' *Genders*, no. 17: 1–21.

Zimmerman, Bonnie. 1990. *The Safe Sea of Women: Lesbian Fiction, 1969–1989*. Boston: Beacon.

# 12

# 'I Haven't Seen That in the Kama Sutra': the Sexual Stories of Disabled People

*Tom Shakespeare*

## Introduction

Over the last fifteen years, disabled people around the globe have issued a major challenge to their oppression (Driedger, 1989; Coleridge, 1993). Particularly in Britain and America, this popular movement has produced an academic discourse, disability studies, which seeks to retheorize disability and more adequately represent disabled people's experiences (Davies, 1997; Shakespeare, 1998). The basis of these shifts has been the recognition that people are disabled by society, not by their bodies. A distinction is made between impairment (medical state) and disability (social experience) which echoes the feminist distinction between sex and gender. This 'barriers' approach, or social model, has replaced the prevailing 'deficit' approach, or medical model, in many fields (Swain et al., 1993).

However, feminist disabled writers have suggested that the social model gives too much space to structural factors and neglects the personal experience of disabled people, particularly issues such as the body, impairment, sexuality, relationships and family (Crow, 1996; Morris, 1991). The American disabled feminist Ann Finger argues that the disability rights movement has not put sexual rights at the forefront of its agenda:

> Sexuality is often the source of our deepest oppression; it is also often the source of our deepest pain. It's easier for us to talk about – and formulate strategies for changing – discrimination in employment, education, and housing than to talk about our exclusion from sexuality and reproduction. (Finger, 1992: 9)

As a result of this gap in theory and practice, understandings of disabled sexuality remain limited, and often medicalized (Shakespeare 1996). This chapter will draw on research with British disabled people in an attempt to begin to construct a social model of disabled sexuality. Although a small sample are quoted here, the project involved forty-four people with a variety of impairments and social characteristics (gender, ethnicity, sexuality, age). The research involved gathering personal stories via interview, questionnaire and self-generated accounts, following the example of Plummer (1995). This article summarizes an argument and quotes testimonies presented at greater length elsewhere (Shakespeare et al., 1996).

A key finding of the research was that disabled people reported that their gender and sexuality were disregarded by non-disabled people. Beth, a professional woman with MS, told us:

> I am sure that other people see a wheelchair first, me second, and a woman third, if at all. A close friend assumed that, for me, sex was a thing of the past. I think that this is a view shared by the majority. It may have little reality, but influences my self-image.

In exploring the importance of sexuality in the lives of disabled people, this article attempts to challenge this traditional neglect and exclusion.

## Focus on function

> This head waiter that I knew well, I could speak Italian and we got on reasonably well, and he came up to me and said, 'You can't, can you . . .?' I said, 'Can't what?' . . . I knew what he meant. I thought, I'll drag this out a bit, and he said, 'Well, you can't have sex, can you?' And I said, 'Why ever not?' And he said, 'Well, you can't walk . . .' And I said, 'You walk while you're having sex? I haven't seen that in the Kama Sutra!' (Paula)

Dominant ideas about disabled sexuality are medicalized: disabled people are regarded as having sexual problems as a consequence of physical deficits or inabilities. Partly because women generally are less likely to be regarded as sexual subjects, these prejudices work differently for men and women. Popular notions of disabled masculinity focus obsessively on perceived impotence and lack of manhood. The novel *Lady Chatterley's Lover*, and films such as *Waterdance* and *Forrest Gump*, reinforce the idea of disabled men being excluded from sexual activity because of erectile failure, and consequently of being less than men. Such an approach often also ignores the experiences and desires of women, with or without impairment, and reinforces a patriarchal and heterosexist construction of normal sexual activity.

The psychologist Leonore Tiefer has criticized the medicalization of male sexual dysfunction, arguing that human sexuality has been reified and that much sexology is more to do with patriarchal and heterosexual ideology than any actual appropriate or effective sexual functioning. This narrow notion of normal sexuality – which is focused primarily on the male erection – is detrimental to the sexual and psychological health of both men and women (Tiefer, 1995). Disabled sexuality is all too often reduced to a question of male erectile function. The mechanistic approach to sexuality underlying this conception is epitomized by some of the work of the British organization SPOD (Sexual Problems of the

Disabled), which gives advice on sex aids such as artificial penises and vaginas (*Disability Now*, Feb 1993: 16). For most disabled people, it's not how to do it which causes the main problems, it's finding someone to do it with. Problems of erectile function are more easily resolved – by medications such as Viagra and Papaverine, or by vacuum pumps or implants – than problems of isolation and exclusion.

Caroline, a respondent with arthritis, criticized the medicalization of disabled sexuality:

> My view was that I go to my doctor about medical matters, and as far as I'm concerned sex is not medical.... The medical profession is not, in my opinion, the appropriate source of wisdom regarding sex.

Her feeling was partly shaped by a bruising encounter with a doctor after she mentioned that pain sometimes prevented enjoyment of sex:

> When I saw the doctor, he noticed this response and said that it must be because I don't love my husband. I was horrified! I was so upset that I have never even told my husband what the doctor said – I haven't told anyone until now. Sadly, every time I find I am unable to have sex because of pain in my back and hips, the idea crosses my mind that perhaps I don't love my husband.

This anecdote shows some of the prejudice faced by disabled people, and the dangers of professionals assuming they know what is best. The limitations created by Caroline's impairment were relevant to her sexual expression, but the major problem was caused by an inappropriate medical response.

The critique of the medical model of disabled sexuality has focused on the ways in which the 'functional' approach can be applied inappropriately. However, it can also be demonstrated that an obsession with impairment neglects the other social and contextual factors which impinge on a disabled person's experience of sex. In the research, it was found that people with the same impairments had very different attitudes and experiences. For example, Beth told us:

> I have always been my own person and without the MS I would start again. I would seek to meet my emotional and sexual needs elsewhere. Now I feel unable to do this. At the same time I cannot describe how awful it feels sometimes to have to allow a man who insists that he loves, and must see, another woman, to put me to bed, turn me over at night, get me up in the morning, or carry out any of the other tasks that are essential.

However, Paula, who has had MS for a similar period of time, had been able to develop a positive approach:

> ...I refused to be sick, it was like, I am not going to let this beat me. But I also didn't have a boyfriend for two years, nobody asked me at all. It was because I closed down on myself, I had ceased to perceive myself as an attractive human being. I couldn't project myself, and I just wanted people not to notice me. I wanted to disappear, and I think it took me many years to actually get to the stage of

saying, well it's here, it's part of who I am, it has formed a lot of what I have done.
So I am disabled, it is not a character trait that I can work on so, like it or lump it,
it's here and as far as partners are concerned I have said that too.

Significantly, we found that people with very profound impairments could
nevertheless have active sexual lives, given the right situation. Juniper is a
respondent who uses a wheelchair, who communicates via an alphabet board,
and who relies on personal assistants: in his own words, he is 'helpless as a small
child'. Yet he told us about the sexual relationships which he had experienced
with several of the women who had worked as his carers. Our research included
people with visual impairments, hearing impairments, epilepsy, muscular dys-
trophy, spinal injury and other significant restrictions to their physical capacities,
who nevertheless had achieved similar levels of sexual expression and satisfaction
to non-disabled people.

As Caroline's account reminds us, it would be unhelpful to suggest that
impairment did not have any impact on the experience of sexuality, although it
is vital to show that it does not rule out sexual expression and sexual pleasure.
Sara's account demonstrates the ways in which disabled people can negotiate and
resolve physical problems:

> Sex can be difficult due to severe pain. Being aware of positions I can and can't do
> helps. Being stuck in a position or having to stop half way through due to pain or
> because my joints have locked or because I'm exhausted are complications I experi-
> ence. . . . What is important for me is having a relationship with your sexual partner
> which enables you to stop. To consider your needs, to share anxieties without
> becoming uptight about sex or deciding never to have sex again. . . . My partner
> sometimes needs to assist me to undress and make myself ready for sex. This for me,
> means I am supporting my partner to understand that I do wish to have sex and can
> have sex, but just need a bit more time and assistance.

Our research demonstrates that the circumstances and social relations of a
particular individual will determine their outlook and opportunities to a greater
extent than the physical attributes of their body, which underlines the need for a
social model approach.

## Social model of disabled sexuality

An approach which focuses on the context, not the person, enables the real
obstacles to be identified and appropriate interventions made. The main barriers
to disabled sexuality include dominant discourses about disabled people being
asexual, or needing to be protected from sexual knowledge. Sometimes, these ideas
connect to eugenic fears that disabled people might exercise their sexuality and
become parents. As a result of prejudicial views, disabled people in residential
institutions are often prevented from having emotional and sexual relationships.
This might also mean that disabled-relevant sex education, and information about
safer sex, is denied to disabled people. For example, Caroline told us:

I'd like to be able to declare that, as a disabled woman, I have a happy and fulfilled sex life. Sadly, however, that is not true. Although everyone can now say 'condom' without any difficulty or embarrassment, the idea that disabled people have sex is still taboo. My dream is to open a magazine and think 'I could try that', instead of saying 'You must be joking – I can't even look up at the chandelier, let alone swing from it!' Information is power, and disabled people still don't have enough of it.

A second set of problems concern the widespread social discrimination which means that disability is the experience of poverty and marginalization. This impacts on disabled people's sexuality in various ways. Because disabled people are denied access both to work and to leisure settings, they sometimes do not have opportunities to meet others or make the friendships which can lead to sexual and emotional relationships. They may lack the income to spend on leisure and social activities. We also found that many disabled people had problems accessing transport, particularly in the evenings, and in getting into bars, restaurants and clubs. Sometimes this was to do with lack of physical access, sometimes it was due to the negative views of the people running these leisure facilities. So, for example, Sara said:

> I've dragged myself along floors to loos, pulled myself up stairs on my bum, lifting my legs, step by step. I've pulled my arm muscles doing this and injured my sacrum as well as worsening pressure sores.

Dafydd highlights the way that barriers can also be social:

> Going into a crowded night club, people trip over you, they are pissed, they are cruising, you get this look that basically lets you know you're not welcome. It's like 'you are reminding us of something unsexy, get out of the way.'

Inaccessible facilities, lack of transport in the evenings, and lack of money to spend on social activities all undermine the possibility of pursuing sexual relationships.

A third problem is that initiating relationships requires a considerable degree of confidence and assertiveness. Because disabled people are often socialized into dependency and have low self-esteem, it may be more difficult to make contact or develop friendships. The disabling ideology of inferiority and incapacity dominates in contemporary society, and disabled people have often internalized these messages. Moreover, disabled people often experience prejudice from others, and the combination of these internal and external factors interfere with normal interaction (Keith, 1996).

A further obstacle in the lives of some disabled people may be the experience of physical and sexual abuse. It is now becoming clear that many women and men have been the victims of abuse, both in childhood and in adulthood. For reasons which are again predominantly social, not physical, disabled people are more vulnerable. Thus Mark told us:

> I was sexually abused when aged six. It often happened. If I tried to resist I was hit very hard. Even these days I still have nightmares.

This may be one of the reasons that he has faced difficulties in forming relationships:

> ...being disabled means no sex...my body does not belong to me.... People look at you in a 'different way'. ... A lot of times I have had to try and hide my disability. I haven't found it easy to find lovers.

Disabled people who have experienced abuse may be wary about making themselves vulnerable. They may have psychological difficulties associated with their body, or with intimacy, which can undermine their ability to relate effectively to significant others.

Not all disabled people experience social oppression around sexuality, or experience it in the same ways. Discourses around the sexuality of people with learning difficulties, for example, are different from those around people with spinal-cord injury. The former tend to be infantilized and protected, whereas the latter may experience sympathy from those who feel that their sexual lives must now be finished. Yet, in general, the problems of disabled sexuality are not caused by the impairment itself, but by the way people with that particular impairment are viewed and treated in society.

### Experiencing disabled sexuality

So far, the argument has centred on the need to shift from a medical to a social understanding of disabled sexuality. Another dimension of the debate is the continuum between what we could call 'victims' and 'agents'. It is important not to replace a traditional account of disabled people as tragic victims of bodily restrictions with a radical account of disabled people as inevitable victims of social oppression. Any account of being disabled in contemporary society needs to include a notion of disabled people resisting and exercising agency. We found that many people were having positive sexual experiences and developing good relationships, and even having families. The disability movement itself, by bringing people together and by empowering people, had significantly contributed to this improvement in disabled people's lives.

People had developed coping strategies and found new techniques to enjoy sex. Penny told us:

> For me, sex is about pleasure, humour and respect. It is with these factors in mind that I approach any seeming 'difficulty' my impairments present me. Of course, there are techniques and positions I will never manage to do. But I know this is true of most people, along that huge scale of physical variety that in reality exists in human beings. Some activities I choose not to do, because I have no taste for them. This is as it should be. But I also know my open attitude to my sexuality, arising because I am a disabled person, often defines sex for me as a much more celebratory and explorative experience than for many non-disabled people.

Her account suggests something which other people highlighted: that there may be positive benefits in disabled sexuality.

This may relate to a third analytical dimension, namely the continuum between 'normality' and 'abnormality', or, perhaps more accurately, 'normality' and 'difference'. When we asked Kirsten about images of disabled people, she felt they were:

> Very unsexy, but also slightly monstrous and very perverted. Which always makes it a bit of challenge being a lesbian actually, because they think you are being utterly perverse and perverted. The image of a disabled person is not a sexual being, it's not someone attractive and beautiful.

Whereas disabled people have been seen as abnormal, particularly in terms of sexual activity, perhaps it would be more helpful to deconstruct notions of normality and move towards an understanding of disabled sexuality as just another one of the many sexualities which are possible.

For example, some disabled people have found different ways of being male and female, partly in response to a society which cannot accept them as real men or women. So Juniper said:

> We so often find ourselves in situations where we are exposed and naked and vulnerable. This leaves us open to domination, and even abuse. Our general existential situation is quite different from that of the non-disabled male, and has some similarities with the vulnerability of women.

Jazz told us: 'I think disability is a breed on its own, neither masculine nor feminine.' Gay men commented on their different masculinity, as in this comment from Jeremy:

> It has taken ages just to think of myself as a man. I don't actually think of myself, because when you say a man, you think of someone who's strong, the usual stereotypes, but I'm not any one of those, although I am male.

But so also did some heterosexual men, such as Eddie:

> One of the interesting things, I feel, is that, with the exception of gays, males don't get hassle, whereas you suffer a form of sexual oppression as a disabled man. I very much see myself as a disabled man, not a heterosexual man.

For some lesbian women, there was a feeling that their disability was used to explain their sexuality: 'you are not a real woman, so the only person that you can find to fall in love with you is another woman.' Disability, gender and sexuality are interacting in the lives of these respondents in complex ways: disabled sexuality can expand our understanding of how gender and sexuality operate, as well as our approach to disabled identity.

Related to this is the way in which being disabled can release people from expectations and pressures around physical appearance. Some male respondents felt that they were not expected to conform physically to macho stereotypes: alternatively, some women who used wheelchairs commented on their muscular arms and shoulders as challenging conventional femininity:

I think the fact that I have arms like Arnold Schwarzenegger is probably not one of my plus points.... I have to be careful about some things that I wear. I rarely wear clothes now that are off the shoulder because I look like Mr Motivator [television exercise guru].

Many men and women were redefining ideas of attractiveness, or taking an individualist approach, as this man suggested:

I am me, and do not want to fit into someone else's idea of me. ... I feel good about myself..... The idea of the Body Beautiful is very dangerous. .... I don't try to project an image, I project myself.

Finally, some disabled people, being forced to improvise around sexual activity, may have to move away from standard (hetero) sexual patterns of intercourse. Having an impairment means many people actually become less inhibited and self-conscious. For example, Paula talked about her lack of inhibitions consequent on her physical experience of MS. 'Before I got MS I was OK. My sex life was pretty good, I suppose, but I was thirty and I had MS for eight years before I became multi-orgasmic.' She felt that her sexual life was more varied and interesting, that she was more likely to initiate sex, and that she had been liberated by having been able to accept her physical difference: her sexual partners also felt freer, and under less pressure to 'perform'.

Sometimes, physical restrictions lead to people being more experimental and imaginative, trying alternative ways of giving pleasure, and communicating more: this parallels the idea that the restrictions imposed by HIV and the need for 'safer sex' might actually lead to better sex. A recognition of the continuum of sexual practices – of which penetrative sex is only a part – and a greater willingness to embrace diversity and experimentation might be of value to all sexually active people, not just to those who happen to have impairments.

Possibly because of these benefits to disabled sexuality, many respondents preferred to have sexual partners who were also disabled. This was because they felt freer and more equal, did not have to explain everything, and could expect acceptance and imagination. Paula reported:

I just think that, actually the two probably most successful sexual relationships I have had have been with wheelchair users. Often disabled men are more erotic and caring. The two men that I have had sexual relationships with who were wheelchair users gave me the most mind-blowing sexual experience that I have ever had in my life.

The suggestion that there are distinct advantages to disabled people's sexuality is very challenging to the medical deficit model with which the paper commenced. It should not be concluded that all disabled people are having brilliant sex: for many people, the obstacles outlined mean that they do not have access to sexual expression at all. Yet there is not a qualitative difference between disabled people and non-disabled people in terms of the potential for sexual expression, even though there be a quantative difference in the likelihood of achieving it. The considerable number of respondents who reported good experiences show that the potential is there for all disabled people, and that the change required is the removal of social barriers, not the development of medical miracles.

## Conclusion

I've always assumed that the most urgent Disability civil rights campaigns are the ones we're currently fighting for – employment, education, housing, transport etc., etc., and that next to them a subject such as sexuality is almost dispensable. For the first time now I'm beginning to believe that sexuality, the one area above all others to have been ignored, is at the absolute core of what we're working for. [...] It's not that one area can ever be achieved alone – they're all interwoven, but you can't get closer to the essence of self or more 'people-living-alongside-people' than sexuality, can you? (Crow, 1991: 13)

Disabled sexuality is an important issue which should be prioritized by the disability movement and service providers. Like non-disabled people, disabled people need sexual expression: when they do not achieve it or have sexual difficulties, this is often due to social and psychological issues, not medical problems.

Change should be based on barrier removal, education and information about sexuality, and empowerment of disabled people. Work on sexuality and disability should be led by disabled people wherever possible. Rather than fearing disabled people's sexual expression, families and agencies should empower and enable people to engage in age-appropriate sexual activity in a safe and non-abusive context.

Disabled people need access to sexual expression, because sex is a normal human activity. Wolfensburger's (1972) notion of normalization suggests that the key to integrating disabled people is to facilitate them to follow normal patterns of behaviour. But normalization has often failed to encompass sexual rights for people with learning difficulties and other disabled people. The notion of 'normality' is a dangerous one, particularly where it leads to the imposition of narrow notions of morality or conduct (Brown, 1994). Not all disabled people will want to be heterosexual or monogamously pair-bonded. Rather than disabled people being integrated into the dominant modes of sexuality, it may be more appropriate for notions of sexuality to be expanded to include the variations implicit in disabled sexuality.

The onus for change rests with society. So many of the problems – from the acute issue of abuse, to the general negative attitudes of doctors and other professionals – are nothing to do with the disabled person themselves, but are a product of the social context. Therefore education of those who work with disabled people is a major priority. At last, the civil rights of disabled people are on the political agenda: it is time that the sexual rights of disabled people were also considered.

# References

Brown, H. (1994) 'An ordinary sexual life?': a review of the normalisation principle as it applies to the sexual options of people with learning disabilities. *Disability and Society*, 9, 123–44.

Coleridge, Peter (1993) *Disability, Liberation and Development*. Oxford: Oxfam.

Crow, Liz (1991) 'Rippling Raspberries: Disabled Women and Sexuality', unpublished MSc dissertation, South Bank Polytechnic.

Crow, Liz (1996) Including all of our lives: renewing the social model of disability. In Colin Barnes and Geof Mercer (eds), *Exploring the Divide: Illness and Disability*, Leeds: Disability Press.

Davies, Lennard (1997) *The Disability Studies Reader*. London: Routledge.

Dreidger, Diane (1989) *The Last Civil Rights Movement: Disabled Peoples' International*. London: Hurst & Co.

Finger, Ann (1992) Forbidden fruit, *New Internationalist*, 233, 8–10.

Keith, Lois (1996) Encounters with strangers: the public's responses to disabled women and how this affects our sense of self. In Jenny Morris (ed.), *Encounters with Strangers*, London: Women's Press.

Morris, Jenny (1991) *Pride against Prejudice*. London: Women's Press.

Plummer, Ken (1995) *Telling Sexual Stories*. London: Routledge.

Shakespeare, Tom, Gillespie-Sells, Kath, and Davies, Dominic (1996) *The Sexual Politics of Disability*. London: Cassell.

Shakespeare, Tom (1996) Power and prejudice: issues of gender, sexuality and disability. In Len Barton (ed.), *Disability and Society: Emerging Issues and Insights*. Harlow: Longman.

Shakespeare, Tom (ed.), (1998) *The Disability Reader*. London: Cassell.

Swain, John, et al. (1993) *Disabling Barriers, Enabling Environments*. London: Sage.

Tiefer, Leonore (1995) In pursuit of the perfect penis. In *Sex is Not a Natural Act*, Boulder, CO: Westview Press.

Wolfensburger, W. (1972) *The Principle of Normalisation in Human Services*. Toronto: NIMR.

# 13

# Postmodern Bisexuality

## *Merl Storr*

Bisexuality has come a long way in recent years. A few years ago in an article on this topic the only thing I would have felt able to say about bisexuality would have been to defend the viability of saying anything about it at all. Even, or perhaps especially, in Britain and North America, which have been the (almost exclusive) contexts for the formation of bisexual identities and politics as such, bisexuality has been a fraught topic. It is easy to forget, in the present climate, just how hostile academia in general, and lesbian and gay studies in particular, were to the very idea that bisexuality might be considered a serious topic of discussion. [. . .]

That climate of outright and unabashed hostility is changing, at least in the academic field in the US and UK. Nowadays it seems to be *de rigueur* for lesbian and gay and/or queer textbooks to include one (but usually only one) essay about bisexuality (e.g. Hemmings, 1995), usually (though not always) sympathetic. At a simple, day-to-day level the new surge of interest in bisexuality feels to me like progress, both academically and personally. But I remain suspicious of 'progress' in general and of bisexual progress in particular. Why bisexuality, and why now? [. . .]

One rather obvious answer to this question which bisexual theorists have clearly found tempting is to align bisexuality with the postmodern – to explain the new interest in bisexuality as part of a wider academic interest in postmodern identities and ideas. [. . .] Dollimore suggests that the recurrent temptation to posit bisexuality as 'sexually postmodern' (1996: 526) stems from a more general weakness in contemporary theory for a kind of intellectual radical chic, where the term 'postmodern' is invoked for the purposes of alibi rather than analysis. Dollimore's discussion of this trend in bisexual theory ends with a mixture of elegy and warning: 'It is difficult to be against fashion; as someone once said, you have to forgive it because it dies so young. But what, in the context of wishful theory, has died with it is the theoretical commitment to engaging with the cultural real in all its surprising diversity and mysterious complexity' (p. 533).

With this elegiac warning in mind, I want to probe here the relationship between bisexuality and the postmodern. What I wish to suggest is that the key term in this relationship is not, in fact, postmodern*ism* but postmodern*ity*, and that it properly lies not in the realm of cultural and/or queer theory but in, precisely, the cultural – and indeed the social – real.

In making this claim I find myself face-to-face with a number of conceptual and methodological problems, all of them weighty and well-rehearsed. Of course it is impossible to draw a stable distinction between the theoretical on the one hand, and the social and cultural real on the other hand. The positions we occupy in the real inform our theoretical perspective, and vice versa: we all know by now that scholarship is not about attaining some impossible 'God's eye view' of the world (Nicholson, 1990: 2). [...]

The fact that the distinction between the theoretical and the real is unstable and sometimes difficult to discern does not mean that it is not there at all. It is in this spirit that commentators such as Kumar (1995) have drawn a distinction between postmodern*ism* as a cultural and/or aesthetic movement and postmodern*ity* as a specific set of material conditions. According to this schema, the characteristic concerns of postmodernism include notions such as fragmentation, instability, anti-foundationalism, loss of and/or evanescence of identity; postmodernity is characterized by such features as the emergence of post-Fordist regimes of production and exchange including the so-called flexible labour market, the rise of niche marketing and of minutely segmented and sophisticated patterns of consumption (including the self-reflexive creation of identity through consumption). Like the parallel terms *modernism* and *modernity*, postmodernism and postmodernity are not always easy to distinguish, and they interact with and mutually affect each other in unpredictable ways. [...]
The distinctions between postmodernism and modernism, and between postmodernity and modernity, are themselves fuzzy rather than sharply defined. The transition from modernity to postmodernity, or from modernism to postmodernism, is not a sudden break or rupture: in each case there are strong continuities and commonalities, with the postmodern re-examining and re-working modern themes in new ways (Huyssen, 1984/1990). In this respect the prefix 'post' is to be regarded as a marker of continuity as much as it is one of change.

With all these caveats and provisos, then, my hypothesis is two-fold:

1   The emergence of bisexuality – in the sense of self-conscious bisexual identity, rather than simply of bisexual behaviour – in (primarily) Britain and North America during the late 20th century is a phenomenon of postmodernity.
2   The dominance of postmodernism in British and North American queer theory in general, and bisexual theory in particular, has paradoxically acted to obscure (1) from view.

Let me outline each of these hypotheses in turn.

## First hypothesis: bisexuality is a phenomenon of postmodernity

A compelling piece of evidence for the postmodern nature of bisexuality can be taken from Ken Plummer's insightful work on sexual identity narratives. In *Telling Sexual Stories* (1995), Plummer analyses three everyday forms of contemporary sexual story-telling: lesbian and gay coming out stories, women's rape stories, and stories of recovery through counselling / self-help programmes (such as the famous 'women who love too much' movement). Drawing on the work of Propp, Plummer argues that these stories, while all very different, can be said to fall into the broad category of 'modernist tales'. Such tales have three underlying structural elements: 'there is always a *suffering* which gives the tension to the plot; this is followed through a crisis or turning point or *epiphany* where something has to be done – a silence broken; and this leads to a *transformation* – a surviving or maybe a surpassing' (Plummer, 1995: 54). [...]

Most of Plummer's book is taken up with a detailed and illuminating examination of these modernist tales. Towards the end of the book, however, he turns his attention to what he sees as new forms of sexual story-telling now appearing on the cultural horizon. These new stories 'shun unities and uniformities; reject naturalism and determinacies; seek out immanences and ironies; and ultimately find pastiche, complexities and shifting perspectives' (p. 133). Plummer explicitly identifies these as 'postmodernist stories' (pp. 131–3).[1]

What is very striking about *Telling Sexual Stories* is the almost complete absence of bisexuality. [...] How does this absence of bisexuality affect the book's argument? I suggest that the absence serves to preserve intact the book's characterization of its other forms of story-telling (coming out stories, rape stories, recovery stories) as modernist. Two factors are of importance here: firstly, Plummer's explicit periodization of gay and lesbian coming out stories as such as a post-Stonewall phenomenon whose heyday was the 1970s and 1980s (p. 82); secondly, Plummer's subsequent statement that 'I do not think there are as yet many everyday folk – outside of the art and intellectual worlds – telling stories like [the postmodern narratives]' (p. 142). These two factors situate the post-Stonewall era as modern rather than postmodern, while insisting that the postmodern is still barely on the horizon in 1995.

In fact, scholars of postmodernity have argued that the 1960s and early 1970s are far from unambiguously modern, but are instead a crucial period of transition from modernity to postmodernity and as such are far more contradictory and polyvalent than Plummer's 'modern' framing of them suggests. [...] [This] time frame of the transition to modernity must surely throw into question Plummer's claim both that coming out (and other) stories are 'a relatively new historical story-form' (p. 60) emerging from the late 1960s and early 1970s, *and* that that story form is 'modernist'. (Indeed alternative analyses of such stories, which place them in a postmodern rather than a modern frame, can and have been offered by other authors, e.g. Marcus, 1992.)

[...]

Plummer lists some major characteristics of the new postmodern stories as he sees them (pp. 138–42). At no point does he mention bisexuality as an example of any of these characteristics, although he gives many examples of other kinds of sexual story. They are, however, characteristics which commonly appear in accounts of bisexuality given by self-identified bisexuals. For example, Plummer states that postmodern stories are articulated around fragmentation, rather than around modernist notions of a sexual 'truth' or 'core' in or for each individual. This is common in bisexual descriptions of bisexuality, either in everyday self-descriptions as 'half heterosexual and half homosexual', 'having masculine and feminine sides' and the like (see Ault, 1997: 453–4), or in more theoretical discussions of bisexuality as fragmented, impermanent or incomplete (Hemmings, 1995: 49). Plummer also states that, unlike the more linear and unitary modernist stories, postmodern sexual stories are full of indeterminacies, multiple possibilities and multiple choices, and recount the blurring or changing of identities. Indeterminacy has of course often been hailed as a peculiarly bisexual trait, by both detractors of bisexuality (who accuse bisexuals of indecision, fence-sitting, unreliability) and its defenders (who celebrate its fluidity, its freedom from constraint). Many personal narratives of bisexuals also include stories of identity change, particularly among so-called hasbians (women who formerly identified as lesbian), for whom the change from lesbian to bisexual identity is a significant and often painful event (Chater and Finkler, 1995; Clarion, 1996). Another characteristic of postmodern sexual stories suggested by Plummer is the collapse of grand narratives, a feature most obviously present in bisexual narratives in the collapse of grand narratives of homosexuality. [. . .]

Thus these and other characteristics of postmodern sexual stories as described by Plummer – the indeterminacies, the multiplicities, the flux and disunity – can all readily be found in many published accounts of bisexuality, although I have only had space to outline a few of them here. In other words, narratives of bisexuality produced by bisexuals themselves are often markedly postmodern according to Plummer's criteria, and the exclusion of such bisexual narratives from *Telling Sexual Stories* serves to sustain the book's claim that other kinds of narrative, such as coming out stories, are 'modernist' rather than postmodern. [. . .]

I am arguing, then, that narratives of bisexuality in the US and UK have been newly audible in recent years because – in part, at least – they are part of a more generalized (and, of course, still very incomplete) shift from the modern to the postmodern which began to pick up speed around the time of Stonewall. In this sense one might argue that [. . .] it is lesbian and gay coming out stories, rather than the more postmodern bisexual narratives, which might perhaps be seen as anomalous and even anachronistic: they may be the products of a relatively short-lived period of social and cultural transition between the post-war years and the early 1970s (Huyssen, 1984/1990), the crises and confusions of which provided a window of opportunity for all those 'new' movements and 'new' identities which have subsequently and rather unsatisfactorily become identified with the symbolic date '1968' (Mercer, 1994: 287–308). Now that crucial transition period may be over. With the early stages of postmodernity proper underway, coming out stories – or, at any rate, their linear 'modern' form – may be heading for obsolescence. Indeed the UK has seen a recent spate of both journal-istic and academic work making precisely this suggestion: that the model of gay identity that was born after Stonewall is heading for its demise (Northmore, 1998). [. . .] The debate itself marks a potentially huge turning-point in the history of sexual identity and politics, and one which is making the articulation of bisexual identity increasingly possible.

## Second hypothesis: postmodern theory obscures postmodernity

So far I have been identifying the new audibility of bisexual voices with a more general and long-term shift to postmodernity, which many commentators have dated from around the mid-1970s. But I began this article by claiming that the marked upsurge of bisexual audibility in academia is a more recent phenomenon which really began only during the early 1990s. This seeming anomaly highlights the distinction between postmodernity and postmodernism discussed earlier, and so brings forward my second hypothesis: that postmodern *theory*, which as such is postmodern*ist*, far from illuminating the conditions of postmodernity, has tended rather – at least in the field of theories of sexuality – to obscure them. Thus I am arguing that the postmodern sexual theory of the 1990s (much of which can be more or less designated under the rubric of 'queer theory') has provided a forum within academia where bisexuality can appear, but has done so in such a way that the import of postmodern*ity* – the material conditions of society and culture – has been lost. This is why bisexual theory has tended to lapse into 'wishful theory', as Dollimore diagnoses it, and to fail to engage with the material on any significant level.

This failure to engage with the material is not peculiar to bisexual theory, and in fact many commentators on sexual or 'queer' theory – not just Dollimore (1996: 531–3) but also, for example, Tim Edwards (1998), Rosemary Hennessy (1995) and Steven Seidman (1995) – have already noted this trend with alarm. Indeed, a similar trend in postcolonial theory is diagnosed by Anne McClin-tock [. . .] (McClintock, 1995: 63). As Dollimore, Hennessy, Seidman and McClintock all suggest (albeit from different theoretical and political stand-points), this is a general problem of contemporary theory, or at any rate of those current versions of it committed to an emphasis on the discursive over – sometimes even to the exclusion of – the material. Such theory renounces the difficulties of coming to grips with the distinction and the interdependence between the material and the discursive, in favour of the much easier solution of collapsing the former into the latter.

Thus the malaise of bisexual theory can be understood as a particularly virulent strain of a malaise afflicting contemporary theory more generally, especially insofar as it addresses sexuality as a central concern in the guise of 'queer theory'. That this malaise has afflicted us specifically in the 1990s is not a historical accident. As Michael du Plessis writes, 'The rise of queer theory in the United States may be linked to an increased loss of political force and direction inside the United States academy . . . In such a context, joining "theory" to some almost all-purpose "queerness" seems to promise a kind of magical resolution to conflicts over the social role of the university by granting whoever purveys "queer theory" the illusion of direct action *via* theory' (Du Plessis, 1996: 25). The applicability of this US scenario to the UK is obvious to anyone who has experienced the UK academy in the past 20 years. The UK situation has recently received extensive commentary from Joanna de Groot (1997) who – significantly for my argument – gives it a precise historical location, stating that 'It was the period *from the mid-1970s to the early 1990s* which saw the dramatic shifts which opened up the university system and its denizens to much more forceful intervention by governments and "markets"' (p. 133; my emphasis). Queer theory, then, has established itself at a time when academics are trying to find ways (both consciously and unconsciously) to cope with the underfunding and concomitant marketization of the academy – at a time, that is, of reaction among academics to material changes wrought by the shift to postmodernity. [. . .]

Thus it is arguable that the effects of postmodernity on the academy itself have played a part in the rise of a body of queer theory which, to put it crudely, needs to convince itself that it has a greater (actual or potential) impact upon the material than it has, and which does so by positing the realm of abstract theory – or, more generously, of cultural signification – as the primary or even the only site of political action. Seen in this light, the abandonment of the material in favour of the discursive in postmodernist academic theory seems, to say the least, somewhat overdetermined by the conditions of postmodernity itself. Indeed it calls to mind Frederic Jameson's (1984) famous claim that one of the defining characteristics of postmodernity is that 'capitalism has no outside'. The culture and aesthetics of modernism, Jameson argues, were able to offer a critique of modernity – specifically of its 'low-brow' mass-market consumption patterns, fed by Fordist mass production. Postmodernism, on the other hand, is unable to achieve any critical distance from the commodified consumer-oriented, society which produces it, since it is itself commodified and consumer-oriented, explicitly rejecting the distinction between 'high' and 'low' culture on which modernism rested. Postmodernism, according to Jameson, is so completely 'inside' postmodernity that it cannot really 'see' it. This argument is suggestive in the context of postmodernist queer theory, which seems to have found it strangely difficult to get to grips with the material in general, and with postmodern capitalism in particular.

Here, again, bisexual theory offers some notable examples of the more general difficulties of queer theory. On the rare occasions when bisexual theory acknowledges capitalism at all, it does so by positioning itself as either perpetually on the verge of disrupting it (especially where capitalism is conceived of as structured by 'western dualism', to which bisexuality is alleged to pose an inherent challenge (Sturgis, 1996)), or indeed as precisely *outside* it. One bisexual commentator who explicitly allies himself with 'queer' even writes, 'I have rejected marriage and consumerism, and I revel in pleasure. I do drugs and publish pornography' (Pritchard, 1995: 178), without noticing that drugs and pornography situate him as both producer and consumer in postmodern, consumer-oriented capitalism. [. . .] It is symptomatic that among the many interrelated forms of identity and/or oppression invoked by bisexual theory, the issue of class is rarely mentioned and even more rarely given substantive discussion. [. . .]

Postmodernity is the location not just of the emergence of (or at any rate the audibility of) narratives of bisexuality; it is also the location of what Rosemary Hennessy analyses as an 'aestheticization of daily life' through commodification and consumption, the drive to (re-)configure our selves, including our queer selves, through consumption and lifestyle choices' (Hennessy, 1995: 162–7). Given this location, bisexual theory urgently needs to enquire into the ways in which postmodern capitalism shapes sexual identity in general and bisexual identity in particular – that is, to the specific ways in which, as I have been arguing, bisexuality is a phenomenon of postmodernity. For example, I would suggest that the hyperbolic excess of much bisexual theory, and in particular the 'sexual revolution'-style visions of a sexuality without limits championed by bisexual heroines such as Annie Sprinkle (1991) and Susie Bright (1992: 150–7), present what Jo Eadie (personal communication, 1996) has called a 'spend spend spend' model of bisexuality ideally suited to, and thoroughly complicit with, the postmodern ethos of consumer capitalism. In this case postmodernist bisexual theory can easily be seen as instantiating rather than analysing the nature of bisexuality in postmodernity – as being a symptom rather than a diagnosis. [...] Regarded in this light, the insistence of some bisexual and/or queer commentators that their sexual identity and/or preferences situate them outside of capitalism appears not merely as naivete, but as mystification, or even as fetishism in Marx's sense (Hennessy, 1995: 161–2), an inability or refusal to see the material conditions which lie behind one's enjoyment of consumer goods such as pornography and drugs (the production and, perhaps more especially, the exchange of both of which are often exploitative)$^2$ – or for that matter of sex toys, leather gear, or latex products involved in safer sex practices.

If this sounds like a glorified version of the old accusation that bisexuals are 'just being greedy', I can only point out that bisexuals are by no means the only queers – and that queers may not be the only sexual subjects – who are currently framing the demand for more or better forms of pleasure as a political demand in and of itself (Rubin, 1993). [...] Despite all the references to Foucault, a great deal of postmodernist queer theory and politics still tends to reify sexuality and sexual pleasure into things which need to be pursued or even liberated for their own sake. As Connell points out, 'the goal [of radical sexual politics] cannot be the "liberation of sexuality" from social constraint. The only thing that can be liberated is people' (Connell, 1995: 390). [...]

## Postmodern bisexuality

Bisexuality *is* postmodern. Of course, the idea of bisexuality has a history no less long and complex than that of homosexuality or heterosexuality (Hall, 1996), and the meaning of the term 'bisexuality' has undergone a series of shifts and transformations since the late 19th century (Storr, 1999). But the existence of a self-conscious bisexual identity, and of recognizable forms of bisexual community, organization and politics, are very clearly rooted in early postmodernity, from the mid-1970s onwards. [...]

The recognition that bisexuality, or any other contemporary form of sexuality, is postmodern in this sense is not, however, in itself a cause for celebration. The characteristics of indeterminacy, instability, fragmentation and flux are not ipso facto politically radical or challenging to the conditions of postmodernity that have produced them. It is not, by the same token, a cause for despair either. Postmodernity, like modernity before it, is full of both good and bad, liberating and oppressive elements: our task is to begin to find out which is which, and what we can do with them. [...]

## Notes

1   In fact Plummer prefers to use the term 'late modernist', partly because he deplores the kind of excesses of postmodern theory also identified by Dollimore and partly because he wishes to avoid the implication of a radical *break* with modernity that the prefix 'post' might imply. [...] While I share many of Plummer's well-founded reservations about it, for clarity of exposition I continue to use the term 'postmodern' throughout.
2   By this I do not mean to align myself with the argument (e.g. Dworkin, 1981) that pornographic images are exploitative (specifically, exploitative of women) merely in and of themselves; rather, I am referring to the material conditions of pornography's production and exchange.

## References

Ault, Amber (1997) 'Ambiguous Identity in an Unambiguous Sex / Gender Structure: The Case of Bisexual Women', *Sociological Quarterly* 37(3): 449–63.
Bright, Susie (1992) *Susie Bright's Sexual Reality: A Virtual Sex World Reader*. San Francisco: Cleis Press.
Chater, Nancy and Finkler, Lilith (1995) ' "Traversing Wide Territories": A Journey from Lesbianism to Bisexuality', in Bisexual Anthology Collective (eds) *Plural Desires: Writing Bisexual Women's Realities*. Toronto: Sister Vision.
Clarion, Meg (1996) 'The Hasbians', in Sharon Rose, Cris Stevens et al. / Off Pink Collective (eds) *Bisexual Horizons: Politics, Histories, Lives*. London: Lawrence & Wishart.
Connell, R. W. (1995) 'Democracies of Pleasure: Thoughts on the Goals of Radical Sexual Politics', in Linda Nicholson and Steven Seidman (eds) *Social Postmodernism: Beyond Identity Politics*. Cambridge: Cambridge University Press.
De Groot, Joanna (1997) 'After the Ivory Tower: Gender, Commodification and the "Academic" ', *Feminist Review* 55: 130–42.
Dollimore, Jonathan (1996) 'Bisexuality, Heterosexuality and Wishful Theory', *Textual Practice* 10(3): 523–39.
Du Plessis, Michael (1996) 'Blatantly Bisexual: Or, Unthinking Queer Theory', in Donald E. Hall and Maria Pramaggiore (eds) *RePresenting Bisexualities: Subjects and Cultures of Fluid Desire*. New York: New York University Press.
Dworkin, Andrea (1981) *Pornography: Men Possessing Women*. London: Women's Press.
Edwards, Tim (1998) 'Queer Fears: Against the Cultural Turn', *Sexualities* 1(4): 471–84.
Hall, Donald E. (1996) 'Graphic Sexuality and the Erasure of a Polymorphous Perversity', in Donald E. Hall and Maria Pramaggiore (eds) *RePresenting Bisexualities: Subjects and Cultures of Fluid Desire*. London: New York University Press.

Hemmings, Clare (1995) 'Locating Bisexual Identities: Discourses of Bisexuality and Contemporary Feminist Theory', in David Bell and Gill Valentine (eds) *Mapping Desire: Geographies of Sexualities*. London: Routledge.

Hennessy, Rosemary (1995) 'Queer Visibility in Commodity Culture', in Linda Nicholson and Steven Seidman (eds) *Social Postmodernism: Beyond Identity Politics*. Cambridge: Cambridge University Press.

Huyssen, Andreas (1984/1990) 'Mapping the Postmodern', in Linda J. Nicholson (ed.) *Feminism/Postmodernism*. New York: Routledge.

Jameson, Frederic (1984) 'Postmodernism, or, the Cultural Logic of Late Capitalism', *New Left Review* 146: 53–92.

Kumar, Krishan (1995) *From Post-Industrial to Post-Modern Society: New Theories of the Contemporary World*. Oxford: Blackwell.

McClintock, Anne (1995) *Imperial Leather: Race, Gender and Sexuality in the Colonial Conquest*. London: Routledge.

Marcus, Sharon (1992) 'Fighting Bodies, Fighting Words: A Theory and Politics of Rape Prevention', in Judith Butler and Joan W. Scott (eds) *Feminists Theorize the Political*. New York: Routledge.

Mercer, Kobena (1994) *Welcome to the Jungle: New Positions in Black Cultural Studies*. London: Routledge.

Nicholson, Linda J. (1990) 'Introduction', in Linda J. Nicholson (ed.) *Feminism/Postmodernism*. New York: Routledge.

Northmore, David (1998) 'Will We Ever Be "Post-Gay"?', *Pink Paper* (24 April): 9–10.

Plummer, Ken (1995) *Telling Sexual Stories: Power, Change and Social Worlds*. London: Routledge.

Pritchard, Mark (1995) 'Liberating Pornography', in Naomi Tucker (ed.) *Bisexual Politics: Theories, Queries, and Visions*. New York: Harrington Park Press.

Rubin, Gayle (1993) 'Thinking Sex: Notes for a Radical Theory of the Politics of Sexuality', in Henry Abelove, Michele Aina Barale and David M. Halperin (eds) *The Lesbian and Gay Studies Reader*. London: Routledge.

Seidman, Steven (1995) 'Deconstructing Queer Theory or the Under-Theorisation of the Social and the Ethical', in Linda Nicholson and Steven Seidman (eds) *Social Postmodernism: Beyond Identity Politics*. Cambridge: Cambridge University Press.

Sprinkle, Annie (1991) 'Beyond Bisexual', in Loraine Hutchins and Lani Ka'ahumanu (eds) *Bi Any Other Name: Bisexual People Speak Out*. Boston: Alyson Publications.

Storr, Merl (1999) *Bisexuality: A Critical Reader*. London: Routledge.

Sturgis, Susan M. (1996) 'Bisexual Feminism: Challenging the Splits', in Sharon Rose, Cris Stevens et al./Off Pink Collective (eds) *Bisexual Horizons: Politics, Histories, Lives*. London: Lawrence & Wishart.

# 14

# Zimbabwean Law and the Production of a White Man's Disease

*Oliver Phillips*

> ... to support the presence of these people (gays and lesbians) in this country is to be an accomplice in promoting lechery. ... It means, if we support them, we want our nation to be vile. We want our nation to be unchaste. We want our people to be animal-like and immoral in behaviour. In cultural terms, what it amounts to is that the homosexuals are like a witch weed in Zimbabwe, which in Shona we call 'bise'. It is therefore supposed to be eradicated. The moment you see it you eradicate it. ...
>
> The whole body is far more important than any single dispensable part. When your finger starts festering and becomes a danger to the body you cut it off. ... The homosexuals are the festering finger endangering the body and we chop them off. (Anias Chigwedere, MP, *Zimbabwe Parliamentary Debate* on motion of 'The Evil and Iniquitous Practice of Homosexualism and Lesbianism', *Hansard*, 28 September 1995: 2779–81)

In August 1995, the usually uncontentious Zimbabwe International Book Fair (ZIBF) erupted into controversy as the organizers obediently carried out a government order to expel the Gays and Lesbians of Zimbabwe (GALZ) from the fair, despite the dedication of that year's fair to the theme of 'Human Rights and Justice' (Dunton and Palmberg, 1996). In defending the expulsion of GALZ from this event, President Mugabe asserted that it was 'outrageous' and 'repugnant' that homosexual rights should have any advocates whatsoever, adding 'I don't believe they should have any rights at all' (ZIBF Opening Speech and Press Conference, 1 August 1995). This saw the start of a deluge of homophobic outbursts by the President and other senior Zimbabwean politicians, the content of which invariably 'whitewashed' homosexuality as a 'sickness' imported by white settlers. President Mugabe denounced 'sodomists and sexual perverts' (*The Herald*, 2/8/95: 1) as 'behaving worse than dogs and pigs' (*The Herald*, 12/8/95: 1); he referred to homosexuality as a threat to the moral fibre of society and proclaimed a return to 'traditional' culture, saying: 'We have our own culture, and we must rededicate ourselves to our traditional values that make us human beings' (*The Citizen*, 12/8/95).

This vituperation is evidence of attempts to reject homosexual behaviour as extrinsic to Zimbabwean culture, relying on the notion that it 'is mainly done by whites and is alien to the Zimbabwean society in general' (President Mugabe, GALZ *Newsletter*, Issue 11, 1/94: 13). This was amplified through repeated use of the metaphor of homosexuality as a white man's disease infecting the African nation's virtuous heterosexual inclination. In this way, homosexuality has not only been treated as something *un*Zimbabwean and *un*African, but as something specifically *anti*Zimbabwean and *anti*African. This portrayal of such a confluence of racial and sexual degeneration was intended to carry the twin implications that, first, white western European 'culture' is depraved as it corrupts other cultures with the 'evil' practice of homosexuality; and that, second, homosexuals must be white, as they are, by definition, 'depraved'. Thus, the signifier of homosexuality is used to denounce 'white culture', and the colouring of homosexuals as 'white' is used to denounce them as non-Zimbabwean.

This article sets out to explore the manner in which the law and the social context of its enforcement contributes to a 'racially contoured... monochromatic image of homosexuality' (Eaton, 1995: 47) of the kind articulated by President Mugabe. Through an analysis of court records and socio-economic context, it can be seen that the law is heavily implicated in the production of such a discourse through rendering visible the 'unnatural offences' of men who are predominantly white.

[...]

### 'Alien to Zimbabwean culture'

> I just want to warn our heroic people that if we allow or condone such bastardly acts under the so-called human rights banners, if we are not careful, we shall also have rapists, murderers, criminals and those sodomists who are militating to have sex with four year olds claiming to have human rights. ... In our African cultural inheritance, there is no room for such devients [sic] in culture, this abominable practice of homosexualism and lesbianism is totally foreign to the African culture, it encourages devilish acts and in my view, it should be thoroughly punished. (Mr Mudariki, MP, *Zimbabwe Parliamentary Debate* on 'Homosexualism and Lesbianism', *Hansard*, 6 September 1995: 2513)

Claims that homosexuality is 'alien to Zimbabwean culture' suggest a confusion between an identity which might not have existed traditionally, with a practice which certainly did. [...] Just as the notion of a singular 'African' culture dangerously misrepresents the wide variety of a multiplicity of African cultures, so it is misguided to assume that the same behaviour will be construed as 'sexual' within different locales. Before the arrival of white settlers in the area now known as Zimbabwe, the social reaction to (what are now more commonly understood to be) homosexual acts is difficult to state with any degree of clarity, but it would be wrong to suggest that they did not take place at all. Across the continent of Africa, homosexual acts took place in various social contexts with differing reactions. While some groups paid it no attention, others, like the Azande, whose warriors had boy-wives, institutionalized it (Evans-Pritchard, 1970: 1428; Seligman and Seligman, 1932: 506–7). Similarly the Ekkpahians, the Abuan and the Western Ikwerri devoted considerable resources to the construction of lavish buildings specifically for the purposes of male homosexual sex, as it was believed to increase crop and human fertility by magical means (Talbot, 1967: 35–6). [...] Others, like the Mandari (Buxton, 1973: 22), were said to severely punish homosexuality as non-procreative and destructive (De Rachewiltz, 1964; Pittin, 1983; Greenberg, 1988).

What is clear is that to suggest that homosexual acts are against 'African culture' is to misrepresent Africa as statically monocultural, to ignore the richness of differing cultural constructions of desire, and in suggesting such a totalized notion of African culture, one simply replicates much of the colonial discourse on African sexuality. More specifically, while attitudes towards homosexual sex among Shona or Ndebele people could have been prohibitory or permissive, to claim that they never experienced any homosexual sex prior to the arrival of white settlers is to deprive them of a corporeal imagination enjoyed by the rest of the continent.

## Colonialism and the 'civilizing mission'

Rather than new activities or behaviours, what is more likely to have been imported by Victorian colonials, taught to feel guilty after the most solitary masturbation, is the eroticization of repression. Through the notion that 'innocence' was a 'natural' state ignorant of the 'dangers' of lust and the pleasures of the flesh, and the concomitant creation of a cognitive concept of a sexuality in need of policing as an object in itself, ideas and practices around sexual morality were considerably changed. Prior to colonialism, the emphasis had been on the reproduction of the patrilineal order through the regulation of reproductive relationships; procreation and social alliances directed men's selection of heterosexual partners for themselves or their daughters / wards, and sexual behaviour was regulated at the level of the body with the primary purpose of protecting a man's exclusive access to his wife / wives. What was important was consequential physical activity rather than projected cognitive desire.

But with the arrival of European settlers came a whole new concept of 'sex' which, in the nineteenth century, was being formulated into a 'sexuality' – and this was a sexuality regulated not just through the structure of reproductive relationships but through fantasy and denial, giving it the capacity alternatively to create or censure identities. It is this western conjuring of sexuality and power, conducted through a discourse of repression, which reached its apotheosis in the nineteenth century, and was central to the whole notion of a 'civilizing mission' – repression and discipline being two definitive ingredients constituting Victorian ideals of 'civilization'. Add to this the proselytizing of the Christian notion of sin and the introduction of a capitalist economy, and it suggests the development of a consciousness based on the commodification of sex and the erotic regulation of individual desire rather than the prioritizing of procreation and the making of social alliances.

The arrival of Christian 'civilization' and colonial authority also brought with it the imposition of an 'anatamo-politics' (health and hygiene [Burke, 1996], work, efficiency, morality, production) of the individual body as well as a demographic regulation (land apportionment, pass laws, curfews, compounds, etc.) of the social body, in an attempt to produce self-disciplined 'obedient subjects' (Foucault, 1978: 139–41). Rather than being perceived as just symbolic of life and causative of procreation, sex slowly began to be reconceptualized as the location of truth; a treasure trove of dangerous but vital secrets in need of investigation, monitoring and correction through techniques which would render truth rational, engender discipline of the self and carry through the sexual erethism of the nineteenth century. Thus, while the possibilities of different sexual activities remained the same, they were excitedly 'discovered' to be imbued with new associated labels of perversion:

> The growth of perversions is not a moralizing theme that obsessed the scrupulous minds of the Victorians. It is the real product of the encroachment of a type of power on bodies and their pleasures. It is possible that the West has not been capable of inventing any new pleasures, and it has doubtless not discovered any original vices. But it has defined new rules for the game of powers and pleasures. The frozen countenance of the perversions is a fixture of this game.
>
> (Foucault, 1978: 48)

For instance, in Zimbabwe oral historians have suggested that sexual activity between children of the same sex was expected as 'normal' behaviour, particularly around the age of puberty, but that thereafter 'it was frowned upon' (Chavanduka *Interview*, 1993; see also Colson, 1958: 272, 274; Wilson, 1951: 87, 196–7). [. . .] It is clear that rituals of circumcision and ceremonies of initiation were substantially changed and in some cases became extinct, on account of missionaries' objections to what they saw as 'lascivious songs' and 'immoral acts' which accompanied the celebrations (Bullock, 1950: 45, 50).

Thus, the first censure of local sexual practices by European morality took place not through the law but through the salvatory mission of Christianity. But the arrival of pioneer settlements, with the bureaucratic apparatus of civil and criminal regulation, meant that Christian morality soon had the backing of a nascent infrastructure. Attempts by missionaries to 'civilize' through the construction of sin and the regulation of individual bodily practices were supplemented by the developmental requirements of colonial capital – the bureaucratic regulation of the social body. One instrument inextricably engaged in this process is the law. The charter of the white settlers provided that, in civil cases between 'natives', the courts were to be guided by 'native law', only insofar as that law was 'not repugnant to natural justice or morality' (1889 Charter of the British South Africa Company). The process of deciding what constituted valid 'native law' took place in an arena in which many contesting interests attempted to assert their particular claim to truth (Chanock, 1982; 1985). More significantly, the repugnancy clause meant that homosexual acts would be criminalized in the same manner as they were criminalized under the common law of the Cape of Good Hope (which the charter proclaimed to be the common law of Southern Rhodesia), whatever the situation might have been under African custom. Thus, the notion of sin became reinforced with a legal definition of a 'natural' morality, as any act between men which could be construed as sexual was classified as an 'unnatural offence' under the Roman-Dutch law of *venus monstrosa*.[1]

## Legal regulation

This prohibition was not something which affected only white men indulging in a 'decadence' from which black men were miraculously excluded. Indeed in the very first year of operation of the colonial courts in Southern Rhodesia, the courts heard five cases (1.5% of all criminal court cases that year) of sodomy and indecent assault between males, and none of the people involved was white (Epprecht, 1998). Between 1892 and 1923, there were approximately 250 cases of 'homosexual crimes' tried in the magistrates' courts, and of these, only 22 involved white men (Epprecht, 1998). [...] Epprecht's research into prosecutions for 'unnatural offences' between black men in the first 30 years of colonial rule shows that the relationships between these men varied from casual to long-term, from loving to coercive, from discreet to openly acknowledged, and were certainly not restricted to conditions where men were grouped together in compounds. The constant reference point in all this is not the race, not the activity and not the type of relationship; the only place in which 'total' exclusions constantly apply is in the prohibition – the law.

The proscription of homosexuality as *venus monstrosa*, under the common law of 'unnatural offences', has remained constant in Zimbabwe since the start of colonial rule. 'Unnatural offences' include three categories of acts: sodomy (anal penetration) between two men; bestiality; and a 'residual group of proscribed "unnatural" sexual acts referred to generally as "an unnatural offence"' (Hunt, 1982: 270). This last category refers to any sexual act between men which does not amount to sodomy, and is deliberately vague in definition in order to serve as a catch-all provision (Phillips, 1997). There is no mention of sex involving two women, no case has been prosecuted, and it would seem that the law does not proscribe sex between women (Feltoe, 1980: 246, 251). However, 'unnatural offences' between men are still prosecuted whenever possible (Derks and Anor., 1984; *S* v. *Roffey*, 1991; and also Omerjee *Interview*, 1993), and consent provides no defence. [...] The same law is used to punish both consensual and non-consensual acts, and the use of force or violence or a great disparity in ages are all seen as simply aggravating factors to the main charge of the commission of a sexual act between two males (Phillips, 1997).

'Unnatural offences' are generally tried in the magistrates' courts. [...] Cases of this nature only reach the High Court through the processes of review or appeal. When a sentence of longer than six months is handed down by a magistrate, it is automatically reviewed by a judge of the High Court; but unless the accused is represented or the judge feels that legal argument is necessary, a review is not heard in the High Court itself, but is dealt with by a judge in chambers and so is not published. The court of ultimate appeal is the Supreme Court.

As the common law is established through precedent, legally significant rulings of the High and Supreme Courts are published in the Zimbabwe Law Reports, while all other cases heard in the High Court are only available as cyclostyled judgments on specific request. [...] A magistrate is expected to apply, rather than set, precedent and so the magistrates' courts records are not published at all but are kept at the courts of origin. [...] Public impressions of conviction trends are therefore based mainly on the cases in the higher courts, as reported through the press and legal publications. [...]

Epprecht's (1998) research found a predominance of black men convicted in the magistrates' courts for 'unnatural offences' in the first 30 years of colonial rule. This is in direct contrast to the conviction rates of recent years as reflected in law reports. During the 28-year-period 1966–1994, all but three of the 21 convictions for 'unnatural offences' published in the Law Reports and cyclostyled judgements involve a white man as an offender. [...] In a country where white people make up less than 1 per cent of the total population, this is remarkable. Without doubt, there are convictions of men who are not white, which took place in regional or local magistrates' courts, but as these did not progress into the higher courts, they remain unpublished. [...]

## 'White man's disease'

[...] For example, without exception all the reported and cyclostyled convictions in the 14 years prior to Independence in 1980 involve a white man.[2] The judgements in some of these cases make clear that where sex took place between two men of different races the court took a more serious approach to the matter (*S* v. *K*, 1972; *S* v. *C*, 1976). This was ostensibly on the grounds that the socio-economic differences between the participants vitiated against the defence that consent was freely given.

> It must be remembered that the appellant was a European of some 52 years of age, while the complainant was a humble African domestic servant of 21 years of age, the sort of man who would be likely to yield easily to persuasion of this sort.... I point out, however,... that this is not a case where force, or threats of force were used in order to induce the complainant to submit.
>
> (Beadle, C.J. in *S* v. *K*, 1972, 80E)

While the courts certainly did find themselves obliged to provide protection to workers vulnerable to the unsolicited advances of both heterosexual and homosexual men, it is impossible, in the context of a society as racist as white Rhodesia, to ignore the increased 'offensiveness' of inter-racial sex. For a white man to have sex with a black man was not only construed as taking advantage of a position of power, and a neglect of the responsibility of patronage, it also offended directly the racial hierarchy. [...] The efforts of the courts to protect both vulnerable people and a vulnerable ideology meant that cases involving two people of different races were more likely to be dealt with at a higher jurisdication and so would be published in law reports or cyclostyled judgments.

Since 1980, I know of several men, who are not white, who have been convicted of sodomy and unnatural offences, but as these prosecutions took place in the lower courts, they are unreported and go unnoticed. There have been three published convictions of men who are not white in courts of a higher jurisdiction (*S v. Beli Enock Dube*, 1987; *S v. Stanford*, 1992; *S v. Magwenzi*, 1994). *S v. Magwenzi* involved a boy of 8 years old, and *S v. Stanford* involved a boy of 14 years old, while Beli Enock Dube committed what would amount to male rape. These disparities in age in *Magwenzi* and *Stanford*, and the threat of violence in *Dube's* case were aggravating factors which led them to be referred to the High Courts for sentencing and review. [...]

In comparison, since 1980, there have been four convictions of white men dealt with in higher courts and so recorded in law reports (Le Roux, 1981; Derks & Anor., 1984; Mackie, 1990; *S v. Roffey*, 1991). All of these cases involved consensual acts and have gone as far as the High Courts (where they would be published) on review, or on appeal as a result of legal representation. Representation is a luxury few can afford in Zimbabwe. [...] This is one of the main reasons for the disproportionate number of white men whose convictions for 'unnatural offences' [...] proceed as far as the higher courts and are published in law reports and cyclostyled judgments. [...]

The end result of this disparity in convictions is that it contributes to a discourse of discrimination which produces homosexuality as 'a white man's disease'. [...] The cases passing before the senior judiciary, receiving publicity in the media, being recorded in public law reports, coming to the attention of government, and featuring in the market-place discussions of an insatiably curious populace are those which involve the participation of a white man. Public discussion of homosexuality becomes fueled with racial epithets, and the primary definition of the issue includes the presence of a white man, and the relative obscurity of black men.

### Social order of black invisibility

[...] Traditional Shona and Ndebele culture were and in many cases still are patriarchal, gerontocratic and polygynous, with women transferred by men into marriage to create links between different kinship networks (Folbre, 1988: 62–7; Jacobs, 1984: 33–4). A system of dowry (*lobola/roora*) lends marriage great significance in local economies and in the fortunes of whole communities. [...] Furthermore, marriage and the production of children is the primary medium through which the independent status and power which constitute adulthood are achieved, and at the heart of marriage is the objective of raising children, rather than the western construction of romantic love. Marriage is therefore more than expected, it is virtually an obligation. [...] The strength of heterosexual marriage as an institution has a number of significant repercussions regarding the visibility of same-sex lovers.

First, it means that most of the black men having sex with men are married. While extramarital heterosexual sex for men is common (but usually discreet), homosexual sex is considerably more furtive as it is both extramarital and same-sex oriented. Second, there is no easy space for a late twentieth-century gay identity to develop. For Shona or Ndebele men to remain unmarried is extremely difficult and often achieved only at the expense of one's kinship ties, support network and the gender-normative power wrought by men in a highly patriarchal society. [...] Third, it means that the possibilities of gay identities and same-sex domestic partnerships are seen by traditionalists as threatening to what is presently established as 'traditional' culture.

[...]

## Inventing Zimbabwe: 'tradition' in late modernity

The clarion call around which issues of gender and sexuality are discussed in Zimbabwe is clearly that of 'tradition', and notions of equity, justice or liberation battle to be heard among the resounding proclamations of what this 'tradition' might be. The strength which notions of 'traditional' culture wield over the discourse around modern Zimbabwean identities owes something both to the entrenched position of those dependent on 'traditional' structures of power (particularly elder men such as chiefs and headmen), and also to the void left by the disappearance of apartheid in South Africa. [...] For not only did the apartheid government provide Zimbabwe with an external military, economic and political threat on which to focus, but it presented the Zimbabwean government with a moral high ground easily occupied. Both of these factors provided a moral-political impetus and a certain cohesion to government and society in the newly liberated Zimbabwe, as well as sometimes excusing or distracting from internal problems. However, the new South Africa has a constitution which explicitly premises itself on 'diversity' [...] [This] is specifically enshrined in Chapter 2 of the Constitution, a 'Bill of Rights' which contains the 'Equality Clause' prohibiting discrimination on many grounds, including sexual orientation, ethnic origin and language (the constitution recognizes 11 official languages).

This approach to traditions in the new South Africa is in striking contrast to the current climate in Zimbabwe, where difference or marginality is viewed with suspicion. 'Traditional African culture' is regularly invoked as a monolithic symbol of historical purity. [...]

In Zimbabwe there was never any similarly far-reaching and deep-seated attempt to reconcile through the telling of truths and the open discussion of responsibilities. At the end of the liberation war in 1980, the new government under President Mugabe pursued a policy of reconciliation with white settlers, but did nothing so dangerous as to institute a 'Truth Commission'. Initially, with the release from military obligations, the flight of the most racist white Rhodesians, and the lifting of the international isolation of the 1960s and 1970s, the atmosphere was one of euphoria. Social boundaries were thrown into question, briefly delivering an 'alternative' social scene, more mixed both in terms of sexuality and race, but with the notable absence of black (apart from 'coloured' or Asian) gay men or lesbians (Gay Men *Interviews*, 1991). But by the mid-to-late 1980s, once the honeymoon period was over, it became increasingly clear that this reconciliation had been carried out in such a way that the effect was to paper over the social cracks. Zimbabwe continues to be a country riven with enormous social segregation and vast disparities in wealth. [...] The labouring classes are still exclusively black, and to be white, Asian or of mixed race is to be middle class. This has significant consequences in terms of the general visibility of different gay men and lesbians, and consequently within the law as well.

## Class, race and sexual identity

[...] The corruption that has been 'imported' is not the homosexual act, but rather the growth of the bourgeois notion of sexuality as constitutive of social truths, and the concomitant need to declare and control these truths through such categorical mechanisms as a hetero / homosexual dichotomy. This is a need manifested both by government, in their emphatic censure of homosexuality, and also by those young urbanized Zimbabweans who proclaim their sexuality. [...]

The negotiation of identity in Zimbabwe's nascent 'lesbian / gay community' is one differently experienced by different individuals within the collective of people having same-sex relationships and, therefore, incorporates varying levels of Afro-centricity and Eurocentricity. What is clear is that there is no mysterious Shona exemption from homosexual desire, for this desire certainly exists and is acted upon. This is illustrated by the increasing number of working-class black men who specifically identify themselves as gay. Communities of young gay men who have either left or been expelled from their families on account of their sexuality are to be found in the larger cities. While some have managed to find employment, or form manufacturing cooperatives in order to generate enough income to survive, others become sex workers on the streets. Prostitution is illegal in Zimbabwe and these young men are prosecuted for 'unnatural offences'. While their clients range across the spectrum of Zimbabwean men, the most valued tend to be the more 'out' white middle-class men and foreigners. This is on account of their affluence, their ability to supply accommodation (however temporary), and their reliability in terms of payment (Gay Men *Interviews*, 1991). It also means that white men become the most visible employers of gay sex workers, fueling media and public perceptions of homosexuality as a white man's proclivity into which black men are drawn by economic need (*Daily Gazette*, 19 / 1 / 93: 1).

[...]

## Conclusion

The vilification directed at gay men and lesbians in Zimbabwe recently is not the result of an increase in the commission of or convictions for unnatural offences, so much as a growth in the visibility of lesbians and gay men. There does not appear to be a marked increase in attempts to arrest or prosecute men for sexual acts. What is being more actively censured, through less formal mechanisms, is the identity of being lesbian or gay, for it is this identification of sexuality as signifying a social truth, and defining a particular lifestyle, which seems to carry the most significance. In both 1995 and 1996, the Zimbabwe International Book Fair was an occasion where the government's actions were specifically aimed at silencing people who identified themselves as gay or lesbian. Initially, it was suggested by political commentators that the government was using this identity as a whipping-boy to give vent to its own prejudices and to divert attention away from pressing economic and political problems. A closer consideration suggests the more sinister project of marginalizing a vulnerable minority group to re-inforce the frontiers of a consensual hegemonic national identity.

[...]

In Zimbabwe the prevalence of the notion that homosexuality is a white man's disease corrupting local innocents has been used to shore up a national identity appropriate to the maintenance of a hegemonic masculinity. This notion is clearly an unsustainable fiction, premised as it is on an absurdity, and ironically pa-trolled by laws imported with colonialism. As an increasing number of black men and women move from discreet homosexual activity to a more open espousal of same-sex relationships, it will become clear that the real battle concerns an identity which must jostle for space in a dynamic and fast-changing culture. Conservative forces have made themselves the primary definers of a reinvented traditional culture. Such neo-traditionalism will best be countered through the effective combination of revealing the existence of same-sex relationships within a traditional local context and simultaneously emphasizing the indigenous produc-tion of those contemporary Zimbabwean identities continually being constructed through participation in a global culture.

## Notes

1   A category of acts deemed to be 'unnatural' at various stages of the development of Roman Dutch law were all grouped together as '*Sodomie*', '*Onkuisheid tegen die natuur*', or '*venus monstrosa*'. Over the centuries different jurists included various activities within this category, including self-masturbation, heterosexual sodomy, sexual acts between women and heterosexual acts between Jews and Christians (see Hunt, 1982: 266–90).
2   See Flanagan, 1966, 96; *R* v. *Stephen*, 1966, 271; *R* v. *B*, 1969, 212; Da Silva, 1970, 94; Addison, 1971, 65; Henriques, 1971, 94; Bartlett, 1972, 30; Kladides, 1972, 141; Maritz, 1972, 98; Valades, 1972, 574; Amos, 1974, 98; Jordan, 1975, 7; *S* v. *C*, 1976, 55; *S* v. *Meager*, 1977, 327.

## Cases cited

Addison AD-65-71.
Amos GS-98-74.
Bartlett AD-30-72.

Da Silva AD-94-70.
Derks & Anor. HC-B-124-84.
Flanagan AD-96-66.
Henriques AD-94-71.
Jordan AD-7-75.
Kladides AD-141-72.
Le Roux S-172-81.
Mackie HC-B-54-90.
Magwenzi HH-59-94.
Maritz AD-98-72.
*R* v. *B* [1969] (2) Rhodesia Law Reports 212.
*R* v. *Stephen* 1966 Rhodesia Law Reports 271.
*S* v. *Beli Enock Dube* HC-B-94-87.
*S* v. *C* [1976] (1) Rhodesia Law Reports 55.
*S* v. *K* [1972] (2) Rhodesia Law Reports 78.
*S* v. *Meager* [1977] (2) Rhodesia Law Reports 327.
*S* v. *Roffey* [1991] (2) Zimbabwe Law Reports 47.
*S* v. *Stanford* [1992] (1) Zimbabwe Law Reports 190.
Valades GD-574-72.

## Newspapers

*The Citizen*, Johannesburg, South Africa.
*The Daily Gazette*, Harare, Zimbabwe.
*Newsletter of the Gays and Lesbians of Zimbabwe*, Issue 11, January 1994.
*The Herald*, Harare, Zimbabwe.

## Interviews

Director of Public Prosecutions (Mr Yunnus Omerjee), 26/1/93.
Gay Men in Zimbabwe, January 1991.
Past Chairman of Zimbabwe Natural and Traditional Healers Association (Professor
    Chavanduka), 28/1/93.

## References

Bullock, C. (1950) *The Mashona and the Matabele*. Cape Town: Juta & Co.
Burke, T. (1996) *Lifebuoy Men, Lux Women: Commodification, Consumption, and Clean-
    liness in Modern Zimbabwe*. London: Leicester University Press.
Buxton, Jean (1973) *Religion and Healing in the Mandari*. Oxford: Clarendon.
Chanock, M. (1982) 'Making Customary Law: Men, Women, and Courts in Colonial
    Northern Rhodesia', in M. J. Hay and M. Wright (eds) *African Women and the Law:
    Historical Perspectives*. Boston, MA: Boston University Papers on Africa VII.
Chanock, M. (1985) *Law, Custom and Social Order: The Colonial Experience in Malawi
    and Zambia*. Cambridge: Polity.
Colson, E. (1958) *Marriage and the Family among the Plateau Tonga of Northern Rho-
    desia*. Manchester: Manchester University Press.

De Rachewiltz, B. (1964) *Black Eros: Sexual Customs of Africa from Prehistory to the Present Day* (tr. P. Whigham). London: Allen & Unwin.

Dunton, C. and M. Palmberg (1996) 'Human Rights and Homosexuality in Southern Africa', *Current African Issues* 19. Uppsala: Nordiska Afrikainstitute.

Eaton, M. (1995) 'Homosexual Unmodified: Speculations on Law's Discourse, Race, and the Construction of Sexual Identity', pp. 46–73 in D. Herman and C. Stychin (eds) *Legal Inversions: Lesbians, Gay Men and the Politics of Law*. Philadelphia, PA: Temple University Press.

Epprecht, M. (1998) '"Good God Almighty, What's This": Homosexual "Crime" in Early Colonial Zimbabwe', in S. Murray and W. Roscoe (eds) *African Homosexualities*. New York: New York University Press.

Evans-Pritchard, E. E. (1970) 'Sexual Inversion among the Azande', *American Anthropologist* 72: 1428–34.

Feltoe, G. (1988) 'A Guide to the Criminal Law', *Zimbabwe Law Journal* 20: 246, 251.

Folbre, N. (1988) 'Patriarchal Social Formations in Zimbabwe', in S. B. Stichter and J. L. Parpart (eds) *Patriarchy and Class: African Women in the Home and the Workforce*. Boulder, CO: Westview.

Foucault, M. (1978) *The History of Sexuality: An Introduction*. London: Penguin.

Greenberg, D. F. (1988) *The Construction of Homosexuality*. Chicago, IL: University of Chicago Press.

Hunt, P. M. A. (1982) *South African Criminal Law and Procedure* (2nd ed.). Cape Town: Juta & Co.

Jacobs, S. M. (1984) 'Women and Land Resettlement in Zimbabwe', *Review of African Political Economy* 27/28: 33–50.

Phillips, O. C. (1997) '"Venus Monstrosa" and "Unnatural Offences": Homosexuality and the Law in Zimbabwe', in R. Green and D. J. West (eds) *Socio Legal Implications of Homosexual Behaviour*. London: Plenum.

Pittin, R. (1983) 'Houses of Women: A Focus on Alternative Life-Styles in Katsina City', in C. Oppong (ed.) *Female and Male in West Africa*. London: Allen & Unwin.

Seligman, C. G. and B. Z. Seligman (1932) *Pagan Tribes of the Nilotic Sudan*. London: Routledge.

Talbot, P. A. (1967) *Some Nigerian Fertility Cults*. London: Frank Cass.

Wilson, M. (1951) *Good Company: A Study of Nyakyusa Age-Villages*. London: Oxford University Press.

# 15

# Not Just (Any) *Body* Can be a Citizen: the Politics of Law, Sexuality and Postcoloniality in Trinidad and Tobago and the Bahamas

*M. Jacqui Alexander*

I am an outlaw in my country of birth: a national; but not a citizen. Born in Trinidad and Tobago on the cusp of anti-colonial nationalist movements there, I was taught that once we pledged our lives to the new nation, 'every creed and race [had] an equal place.' I was taught to believe 'Massa Day Done', that there would be an imminent end to foreign domination. Subsequent governments have not only eclipsed these promises, however, they have revised the very terms of citizenship to exclude me. No longer equal, I can be brought up on charges of 'serious indecency' under the Sexual Offences Act of 1986 and, if convicted, serve a prison term of five years. In the Bahamas, I can be found guilty of the *crime* of lesbianism and imprisoned for twenty years.[...] Why has the state marked these sexual inscriptions on my body? Why has the state focused such a repressive and regressive gaze on me and people like me? [...]

In what follows, I want to suggest a way of thinking about state nationalism and its sexualization of particular bodies in Trinidad and Tobago and the Bahamas in order to determine whether such bodies are offered up, as it were, in an internal struggle for legitimation in which these neo-colonial states are currently engulfed. What kinds of reassurances do these bodies provide, and for whom? The state's authority to rule is currently under siege; the ideological moorings of nationalism have been dislodged, partly because of major inter-national political economic incursions that have in turn provoked an internal crisis of authority. I argue that in this context criminalization functions as a technology of control, and much like other technologies of control becomes an important site for the production and reproduction of state power.

Although policing the sexual (stigmatizing and outlawing several kinds of non-procreative sex, particularly lesbian and gay sex and prostitution) has something to do with sex, it is also more than sex. Embedded here are powerful signifiers about appropriate sexuality, about the kind of sexuality that presumably imperils the nation and about the kind of sexuality that promotes citizenship. Not just (any) *body* can be a citizen any more, for *some* bodies have been marked by the state as non-procreative, in pursuit of sex only for pleasure, a sex that is non-productive of babies and of no economic gain. Having refused the heterosexual imperative of citizenship, *these* bodies, according to the state, pose a profound threat to the very survival of the nation. Thus, I argue that as the state moves to reconfigure the nation it simultaneously resuscitates the nation as hetero*sexual*.

[...]

In the section that follows, I analyse the ways in which naturalized heterosexuality shapes the definitions of respectability, Black masculinity and nationalism. We come full circle, then, as I argue that the effects of political economic international processes provoke a legitimation crisis for the state which moves to restore its legitimacy by recouping heterosexuality through legislation. I end by suggesting that the process of decolonization, which the nationalist state had claimed as its own, has been seriously disrupted and I draw out the implications for oppositional movements and analyses.

## Naturalizing heterosexuality as law

In 1986, the parliament of the Republic of Trinidad and Tobago scripted and passed the Sexual Offences Act: 'An Act to Repeal and Replace the Laws of the Country relating to Sexual Crimes, to the Procuration, Abduction and Prostitution of Persons and to Kindred Offences.' This gesture of consolidation was, in the words of law commissioners, an attempt 'to bring all laws dealing with sexual offences under one heading.' It was the first time the neo-colonial state confronted earlier colonial practices which policed and scripted 'native' sexuality to help consolidate the myth of imperial authority.

Many of the thirty-five provisions of the legislation, then, had prior lives, and were being reconsolidated under a different schedule of punishments. Prohibitions regarding sexual violence within the family (incest), and against women who exchanged sex for money (prostitutes) and those who aided them (brothel-keepers), or those who exploited them (pimps) had long been established in the emendations to the Offences Against the Person Acts, that one-sided pivot of British jurisprudence. In keeping with its allegiance to hegemonic masculinity, the script upheld a prior provision that defined anal intercourse between men as buggery, outlawed it, and affixed a penalty of ten years imprisonment, if convicted. It moved, in addition, to criminalize new areas of sexual activity. [...]

Three years later, the parliament of the Bahamas scripted and passed its own version of the Sexual Offences Act, cited as the 'Sexual Offences and Domestic Violence Act of 1989', *its* gesture of consolidation, formulated by law commissioners 'as an attempt to provide one comprehensive piece of legislation setting out sexual offences which are indictable', seeking, in its words, 'to make better provision in respect of the rights in the occupation of the matrimonial home.' As in the case of Trinidad and Tobago, it was the first attempt to impose a veiled sexual order on the chaotic legacy of colonialism. [...]

Its thirty-one provisions bore close resemblance to those of Trinidad and Tobago in terms of the injunctions, prohibitions and schedule of punishments against prostitution, incest, and sexual harassment and assault in the workplace. It too, conflated buggery, bestiality and criminality: 'If any two persons are guilty of the crime of buggery – an unnatural crime, or if any person is guilty of unnatural connection with any animal, every such person is guilty of an offence and liable to imprisonment for twenty years.' [...] The law also moved to imprison (for five years) anyone with HIV infection who had consensual sex without disclosing their HIV status.

Its new provision, relating to domestic violence, made it possible for *any* party in the marriage to apply to the Supreme Court for an injunction that would restrain the other party from molestation and from using violence in the matrimonial home. What is remarkable about this act that calls itself a domestic violence act is that nowhere is there a definition of domestic violence. Rather the majority of the provisions focus upon the disposition of private property and on the minute distinctions among 'dwelling, estate, apartment', etc. These were not the terms on which the women's movement in the Bahamas had pushed for the criminalization of domestic violence. [...] It would seem then, that even in the face of violent disruptions in marriage, conjugal heterosexuality is most concerned with the patrilineal transfer of private property.

Legislative gestures fix conjugal heterosexuality in several ways. Generally, they collapse identities into sexual bodies which, in the particular case of lesbian and gay people, serves to reinforce a fiction about promiscuity: that sex is all of what we do and consequently the slippage, it is all of who we are. Yet lesbian and gay sex, the 'pervert', the 'unnatural' are all indispensable to the formulation of the 'natural', the conjugal, the heterosexual. This dialectic must be made visible, for there is no absolute set of commonly understood or accepted principles called the 'natural' which can be invoked definitionally except as they relate to what is labelled 'unnatural'. [...]

Conjugal heterosexuality is frozen within a very specific and narrow set of class relations between 'husband' and 'wife' in 'marriage', narrow because the majority of heterosexual relationships are in fact organized outside of this domain. Even while the Bahamian legislation might appear to address violence in all 'domestic' domains, its skewed emphasis on private property immediately renders it class specific. For working-class women who do not own property and are beaten by the men with whom they live, this legislation offers no protection. And even for middle-class and upper-middle-class women who are beaten by their husbands and might own property, the problem they face is how to disentangle the web of well-connected social relationships that protect *their* middle-class and upper-middle-class husbands from being prosecuted as criminals. For most women who stand outside of the legal definitions of 'parties to a marriage', they can make no claims for relief from the state. Thus, domestic violence works as a proxy for class and facilitates the reallocation of private property in disruptive conjugal marriage.

Both pieces of legislation systematically conflate violent hetero*sexual* domination, such as rape and incest, with same-sex relations, thereby establishing a continuum of criminality among same-*sex* rape, domestic violence, adultery, fornication and dishonesty. On this continuum the psyche of homosexuality becomes the psyche of criminality. By criminalizing perverted heterosexual sex, the legislation aims to expunge criminal elements from the heterosexual so that it could return to its originary and superior moral position. [...]

Outside the boundaries of the legislation, yet informing it, state managers generated a simultaneous discourse invoking nostalgia for a Bahamas and Trinidad and Tobago when there were ostensibly no lesbians, gay men and people with AIDS. In this move, heterosexuality becomes coterminus with and gives birth to the nation. Its antithesis can unravel the nation. [...] Yet, the state simultaneously enacts the dissolution of the nation through a series of political-economic gestures (adherence to the narratives and practices of modernization through allegiance to multinational capital, tourism, etc.) that it ideologically recodes as natural, even supernatural, as the salvation of the people. In this equation, tourism, foreign multi-national capital production and imperialism are as integral and as necessary to the natural order as heterosexuality. But before examining these twin processes of sexualization and internationalization more closely, one would have to understand why conjugal heterosexuality is so important for nationalist state managers and the role it plays in constituting respectable masculinity. [...]

## State nationalism and respectability, Black masculinity come to power 1962, 1972

[...] We can frame hegemonic definitions of masculinity and femininity by examining what Kobena Mercer and Isaac Julien have called the 'hegemonic repertoire of images' which have been forged through the histories of slavery and colonization in order to identify the sexual inheritances of Black nationalism as well as its own inventions. (Mercer and Julien, 1988: 132–5). [...] What is crucial for my argument is the intransigence of dominance and, in this instance, the continuities and discontinuities between the practices of the colonial and the 'postcolonial' around those very images.

In the repertoire of images that developed during the organization of slave-plantation economy and in the consolidation of imperial rule, the English gentleman was given primacy. [...] Colonial rule simultaneously involved racializing and sexualizing the population, which also meant naturalizing whiteness. There could really be no psycho-social codices of sexuality that were not simultaneously raced. In general terms, these codices functioned as mythic meta-systems fixing polarities, contradictions and fictions while masking as truth about character. [...]

Here, too, identities were collapsed into bodies. Black bodies, the economic pivot of slave-plantation economy, were sexualized. Black women's bodies evidenced an unruly sexuality, untamed and wild. Black male sexuality was to be feared as the hypersexualized stalker. These dominant constructions worked to erase indigenous (Lucayan, Carib and Arawak) sexualities. Indentured Indian femininity (in Trinidad and Tobago) was formulated as dread and desire, mysteriously wanton, inviting death and destruction, although it could also be domesticated. Indian manliness was unrestrained, violent and androgynous, the last construction drawn from Britain's colonial experience in India. Free coloured women, who outnumbered Black women in the Bahamas, and their counterparts in Trinidad and Tobago [. . .] were also sexualized, but positioned as potential mates (Saunders, 1985; McDaniel, 1986). [. . .]

It would indeed require a complicated set of cognitive and ideological reversals for the British to turn the savage into the civilized, to turn those believed incapable of rule into reliable rulers. Herein lies the significance of socialization into British norms, British manners, British parliamentary modes of governance; into conjugal marriage and the 'science' of domesticity. [. . .] Whereas in Europe these processes were indigenous to the formation of the middle class, in the Caribbean it was imported through imperialism. The Black middle class would be schooled in the definitions of morality, civility and respectable citizenship in the metropolis, in the company of the British, while 'women of reduced means' and the working class would be trained at 'home'. [. . .]

It was the élites of the middle class who established the nationalist parties which later became part of the state apparatus. They mobilized consensus for nation building, moulded psychic expectations about citizenship and therefore consolidated their own internal power on the ideals of sovereignty, self-determination and autonomy from foreign mandates. Ostensibly, this was a neutered invocation to citizenship; yet it was in the creation of the women's wing of these parties and in their organization of 'culture' that one begins to detect a gendered call to patriotic duty. Women were to fiercely defend the nation by protecting their honour, by guarding the nuclear, conjugal family, 'the fundamental institution of the society', by guarding 'culture' defined as the transmission of a fixed set of proper values to the children of the nation, and by mobilizing on the party's behalf into the far reaches of the country. [. . .] Patriotic duty for men, on the other hand, consisted in rendering public service to the country, and in adopting the mores of respectability.

[. . .]

If, as Toni Morrison has suggested, rescue and indebtedness sometimes sediment as part of the psychic residue of the process of colonization, then respectability might well function as debt payment for rescue from incivility and from savagery (Morrison, 1992: vii–xxx). But a rescued masculinity is simultaneously an injured masculinity; a masculinity that does not emerge from the inherited conditions of class and race privilege. And it is injured in a space most vulnerable to colonial constructions of incivility. At one time subordinated, that masculinity now has to be earned, and then appropriately conferred. Acting through this psychic residue, Black masculinity continues the policing of sexualized bodies, drawing out the colonial fiction of locating subjectivity in the body (as a way of denying it), as if the colonial masters were still looking on, as if to convey legitimate claims to being civilized. Not having dismantled the underlying presuppositions of British law, Black nationalist men, now with some modicum of control over the state apparatus, continue to preside over and administer the same fictions.

To the extent that the sexual offences legislation polices non-procreative, 'non-productive' sex especially in relationship to women, the neutered invocation to citizenship becomes transparent. In fact, we can read state practices as attempts to propagate fictions of feminine identity, to reconfigure women's desire and subjectivity and to link the terms of the nation's survival to women's sexual organs. [...]

State claims of a non-productive femininity are deceptive in a number of different ways. Both the People's National Movement (PNM of Trinidad and Tobago) and the Progressive Liberal Party (PLP of the Bahamas) could not have consolidated their power or secured support for popular nationalism without women's labour, women who ironically would later have to struggle for citizenship. Yet once installed, state nationalism came to stand in an authorial relationship to women's interests and women's agency. The claim also works to mask women's labour in other areas of the economy, particularly in the tourist sector where women are the majority of a proletarianized and superexploited workforce. [...]

### (Inter) national boundaries and strategies of legitimation

I wish to foreground the effects of international political economic processes in provoking the legitimacy crisis nationalist states are currently confronting, and argue that the sexual is pivotal in state orchestration of a new internal struggle whose contours are different now than they were at the moment of flag independence. In an almost ideal-typical sense, the nation had come to be shaped by what it had opposed (Anderson, 1983). Public opposition to the British had provided powerful ideological fodder for independence. We had all suffered colonial injustice together, and it was out of that experience of collective suffering that a collective vision of sovereignty could be built. Since 'independence', the state has colluded in adopting strategies that have locked these nations into a world economic and political system, the effect of which is re-colonization. [...]

But this is not how state managers see the crisis. Both in Trinidad and Tobago and the Bahamas they sound the danger of cultural contamination from the 'West' which they depict simultaneously as sexual intemperance, the importation of AIDS and the importation of feminism (read lesbianism). [...]

State nationalism in Trinidad and Tobago and the Bahamas has neither reformulated nor transformed the fundamental premises upon which economic and material exchange is based. Its secular adherence to a linear definition of 'development' and progress has continued to imagine an (il)logic of a movement from 'tradition' to 'modernity' in which industrialization presumably serves as the motor for economic success. The contemporary version of development now called structural adjustment finds expression in a powerful, yet unequal alliance among foreign multinational lending agencies such as the International Monetary Fund (IMF), the World Bank, the United States Agency for International Development (USAID), the American state and neo-colonial regimes. Their aim is to impose a set of lending arrangements that would ostensibly reduce the foreign debt [...] (McAfee, 1991:67–79). In particular, the programmes have been organized to reduce local consumption by devaluing currency, increasing personal taxes and reducing wages. [. . .]

Although the Bahamas has not formalized 'structural adjustment' programmes (SAP), the continued subordination of its economy to the political and economic imperatives of the United States has resulted in an economic infrastructure that bears all the marks of a country that has actually adopted structural adjustment. The most dramatic shift is evident in the displacement of capital and labour forces from agrarian production to service, which now employs more than 50 per cent of the workforce, massive increases in the size of the food import bill (people are no longer able to feed themselves), the consolidation of foreign transnational capital in the tourist industry (hotels, airlines, services and tour operators, international finance capital, real estate), and the expansion of off-shore companies.

But perhaps the most significant and dramatic effect of SAP is that it has exacerbated the triple processes of proletarianization, superexploitation and feminization of the workforce which began in the mid-1960s.

[. . .]

It is difficult to imagine that massive economic disjunctures with corresponding deterioration in the quality of people's daily lives, precipitated by SAP, would not provoke a major political crisis for the state. Emerging within this crisis are serious contestations to the state's right to rule. The question is how do these movements frame their opposition to the state? Even with the importance of the material deterioration of people's lives, one of the more crucial elements uniting these varied constituencies is the urgency to move beyond questions of survival to, as Joan French has argued, 'creating, building community, deepening the under-standing of oneself and of others, developing local, regional, and international structures for communication and participation' (McAfee, 1991: 188). The focus of the challenges, therefore, is to transform the nature and definition of develop-ment from profit and exploitation to holistic, participatory models, the maps of which are still being worked out (Antrobus in McAfee, 1991: 187). [. . .]

## State nationalism, globalization and privatization

State-supported globalization of capital is crucial not only because of the internal political effects I outlined earlier, but also because these international processes help to refigure definitions of masculinity and femininity, and simultaneously undermine the ideological bases upon which the state organizes, separates and draws from the 'public' and 'private' domains. International practices dovetail with state ideologies about masculinity and femininity, and in particular with ideological constructions of women's work. The most significant retrenchment with the adoption of SAP has taken place in those sectors which have been historically coded as women's work: health, clinic and hospital service, caring for the sick and elderly, social services and education. As women continue their work in the home and their work in the private or public service sector, they work, in addition, to care for the sick and elderly, and to continue the education of their children without state subsidies. The state relies upon and operates within these dominant constructions of a servile femininity, perennially willing and able to serve, a femininity that can automatically fill the gaps left by the state. Quite the opposite of a 'non-productive' femininity drawn in the legislation, these are women doing work, and ironically, state work.

[. . .]

We can now return to one of the central paradoxes this paper raises, that of the nationalist state legislating against certain sexualities while relying upon women's sexualized body and a political economy of desire in private capital accumulation. Tourism is the arena in which the moves to privatize the economy through foreign investment, imperial constructions of masculinity and femininity and state constructions of sexualized woman all intersect.

[. . .]

How does one prepare citizens for self-determination by depending on its antithesis – tourism – the practice of servility and serviceability, the production of maids, washers, cooks? In this economy, Black women braid white women's hair as they flirt with Blackness, for African styles can only be adopted far away from home. Difference is exotically and fleetingly adopted. These are a complicated set of psycho-sexual gestures converging in this (hetero) sexual playground, this arena which Caribbean state managers see as the economy of the future; where Black masculinity manages phantasmic constructions of Black femininity, satisfying white European desire for restless adventure, satisfying white European longing for what is 'rare and intangible' (hooks, 1992: 21–39).

## Mobilizing heterosexuality: post-colonial states and practices of decolonization

My analysis suggests that the archetypal source of state legitimation is anchored in the heterosexual family, the form of family crucial in the state's view to the founding of the nation. This consolidation of domesticity in the very process of nation-building is the sphere in which a certain kind of instrumental legitimation is housed. There is an evident relationship among monogamous heterosexuality (organic representation of sexuality) nationhood and citizenship. [. . .] Nothing should threaten this sphere of family, not the single woman, the lesbian, the gay man, the prostitute, the person who is HIV infected. The state must simultaneously infiltrate this domain in order to recoup its original claim to it. It must continue to legislate its existence.

[. . .]

Part of the difficulty we face as feminists doing this kind of analysis, and ironically one of the reasons the state can at least be partially successful in mobilizing heterosexuality, is the persistence of the belief in naturalized heterosexuality, the belief that it lies outside of the sphere of political and economic influence and therefore state influence. In the absence of any visible lesbian and gay movements in the Caribbean, state managers believe they can rely upon heterosexuality even more heavily. [. . .] Radical lesbian and gay movements in metropolitan countries which have demystified heterosexuality must now take on board analyses of colonization and imperialism, for the effects of these processes loop back to the centre from which they originated. These movements in metropolitan countries need to work assiduously, however, not to reproduce practices of imperialism. [. . .] If sexualization and internationalization have been linked in the strategies of domination, *we* must link them in our strategies for liberation, although admittedly along different registers (Moraga, 1983). It might help to reduce the impulse to conflate capitalism with democracy and the more pervasive feminist theorizing of liberal *democratic* advanced capitalist states.

[. . .]

It is both analytically and therefore politically necessary to disentangle the processes of decolonization and nation-building. In a real sense, the work of decolonization (the dismantling of the economic, political, psychic and sexual knowledges and practices that accompanied the first five hundred years of conquest) has been disrupted, especially in light of the map I have drawn of these new sexualized strategies of recolonization and the commodification of alienated sexual desire in tourism within nation-states that are infiltrated by corporate globalization politics. Since women's bodies have been ideologically dismembered within different discourses – the juridical, political-economic, religious and popular – the work of decolonization consists, as well, in the decolonization of the body.

## References

Anderson, Benedict (1983) *Imagined Communities: Reflections on the Origin and Spread of Nationalism*. London: Verso.

hooks, bell (1992) *Black Looks Race and Representation*. Boston: South End Press.

McAffe, Kathy (1991) *Storm Signals: Structural Adjustment and Development Alternatives in the Caribbean*. Boston: South End.

McDaniel, Lorna (1986) 'Madame Phillip-O: Reading the Returns of an 18th century 'Free Mulatto Woman' of Grenada' (unpublished manuscript).

Mercer, Kobena and Julien, Isaac (1988) 'Race, sexual politics and Black masculinity: a dossier,' in Chapman, Rowena and Rutherford, Jonathan (1988) *Male Order: Unwrapping Masculinity*. London: Lawrence & Wishart.

Moraga, Cherríe (1983) *Loving in the War Years*. Boston: South End Press.

Morrison, Toni (1992) *Race-ing Justice, En-gendering Power: Essays on Anita Hill, Clarence Thomas, and the Construction of Social Reality*. New York: Pantheon.

Saunders, Gail (1985) *Slavery in The Bahamas*. Bahamas: The Nassau Guardian.

# Part IV

# Globalization, Power and Resistance

A post-colonial perspective is closely related to a recognition of the growing importance of globalization in relation to the organization of sexualities. A globalized world is one in which Western categorizations of sexuality increasingly interact and interpenetrate with those operating in other sexual cultures, and in which new categorizations emerging worldwide – whether being universalized or asserted in opposition to one another – are increasingly interconnected across cultures. Globalization is not of course new in the field of sexuality. It is often forgotten that in the earlier part of the twentieth century an international discourse had emerged around common sexual issues. Magnus Hirschfeld's World League for Sexual Reform brought together people not only from the industrialized countries in Western Europe and America but also from Asia, Africa and Latin America. The agenda that then developed – for example, over the sexual exploitation of young children, the recognition and rights that should be accorded self-defined homosexuals, sexual disease, birth control and abortion, marriage and divorce   strikingly resembles the issues that are central to contemporary debates about globalization and sexuality.

A globalized world is a world in which the nature and experience of risk has changed. The spread of the HIV / AIDS epidemic since the 1980s to become a global pandemic is a vivid and tragic illustration of this. Sexual behaviour has of course always been associated with risk: the risk of unwanted pregnancy, of disease, of exploitation, of prejudice and oppression. These risks did not disappear with the emergence of a new discourse of sexual rights over the last thirty years. But the risks have changed their forms, giving rise to new forms of conflict – over, for example, the rights and roles of women in non-industrialized societies, and the responsibility of the developed world to the South in relation to matters such as the population explosion. These often become central to political differences on a global scale, such as the postulated conflict between Western and Islamic values. Conflicts over sexuality have become integral to the emergence of fundamentalist politics both within Western societies and elsewhere around the world. Fundamentalism, it has been suggested, is about the refusal of dialogue, the declaration of absolute values in relation to a perceived relativism. The relativization of sexual values has accompanied the recognition of a plurality of sexualities in Western societies, and this has led to issues of the family, traditional gender relations, sex education and homosexuality becoming central preoccupations of fundamentalist movements. Many of these movements are transnational, with identities organized around the great religious faiths such as Hinduism and Islam that have bridged divisions between the North and the South in global terms (see Bhatt's article in this book, chapter 17). And yet processes of engagement between cultures and movements on an international scale have in turn given rise to new discourses of human rights on a global scale, which are already having a significant impact on sexual politics within specific countries. We think, for example, of the impact that Britain's involvement in the European Union is having on debates on sexuality in the United Kingdom (Waites 2001). We can also cite the global fight against AIDS, or the globalization of concern with child sex abuse, so that one country may take action against its citizens for offences committed against children in other parts of the world. And yet struggles over human rights are themselves not unproblematic. A recognition of the human rights of women, for example, does not mean that as yet it is possible to develop a common assumption about what those rights mean in practice.

The first article in this section explicitly introduces the concept of globalization, and hence provides a context for subsequent articles which address a variety of dynamics implicitly related to the same theme. Globalization, Dennis Altman suggests, redistributes difference on a global scale. The HIV / AIDS epidemic provides a stark case study of the processes at work. Linking globalization and AIDS throws new light on the epidemiology of a sex-related set of diseases; the processes of mobilization which have combated the epidemic on a transnational scale; and the dominance of certain ways of understanding the epidemic which are gendered, ethnicized and embody certain assumptions about sexuality. AIDS provides a reminder of the uneven development of societies, and the necessity for both international and specific local responses that this engenders. Through these, sexual behaviours and identities are being contested and reconstructed.

Chetan Bhatt, in his contribution, uses a detailed study of Hindu nationalist fundamentalism, one of the world's most significant cultural movements over recent decades, to illustrate the symbiotic relationship between transnational movements and religious and ethnic foundationalisms. Central to extreme Hindu nationalism, Bhatt suggests, is a political language of the body, in which nationalism is symbolized. The sexual body is to be disciplined, contained, silenced, obscured or eradicated. Women's bodies in particular become the site of revivalist agitation. Sexuality is produced even as it is denied, especially through processes which define and categorize feared or despised 'others'. An ironic effect is that, in the course of reaffirming Hindu identity, many of the forms of the British colonialist discourses on sexuality are reproduced.

Julia O'Connell Davidson's contribution explores the international patterns of prostitution which have developed in an increasingly globalized world. She rejects what she sees as two extreme ways of understanding prostitution: one which views the prostitute as always entirely the victim in sexual and economic interactions; and another which perceives sex work as a way for women to take control of their destinies as free labourers. Against these O'Connell Davidson explores the complex and relational nature of power, through a series of comparative studies of the patterns of brothel prostitution in different states. Her diverse examples are suggestive of the different ways in which sex markets are transformed by globalization processes in different contexts.

Harriet Evans continues this theme by exploring women's sexuality in China in the wake of its market reforms from the 1980s. Her chapter can be seen as addressing a central question in contemporary debates over sexuality which is not only applicable to China, but also relevant worldwide: what are the effects of capitalism, commodification and sexual markets as they operate on an increasingly global scale? In China, argues Evans, the resulting patterns of prostitution and representations of women simultaneously recall pre-revolutionary traditions and respond to the international representations of female sexuality which have been allowed to circulate by liberalizing shifts in Chinese government policy. The effect, she claims, is to perpetuate the construction of women either as naturally dependent and passive subjects, or as dangerous perpetrators of social chaos.

In her article, Rosalind Petchesky charts the new forms of resistance that have developed in an ever more globalized world, which are increasingly international in organization and global in extent. The specific focus is the international campaign for 'reproductive rights', which brings together women from both the North and the South. Petchesky suggests that there is a double push in this global movement: for bodily integrity and the right of women to control their own body; but also the negotiation of wider social, economic and cultural challenges. As a result, while a common discourse on reproductive rights is emerging, particularly in the language of international human rights, the meanings vary across different societies, dependent on different traditions, circumstances, and relations of power. The success of the ongoing dialogue among women of many cultures that Petchesky describes is that not only are there successful moves to reinterpret and amend international human rights law, but that women's sense of entitlement to reproductive rights is also increasing.

## Reference

Waites, M. 2001: Regulation of sexuality: age of consent, Section 28 and sex education. *Parliamentary Affairs*, 54, 495–508.

# 16

# Globalization, Political Economy and HIV / AIDS

*Dennis Altman*

## Conceptualizing AIDS

The rapid spread of HIV means that AIDS[1] is looming as a huge threat to most developing countries, particularly in Africa and south Asia, where it threatens to assume epidemic proportions far beyond the resources of governments to control. Responsible United Nations officials have compared AIDS to the great plagues of history, with some countries close to an adult infection rate of 25 percent;[2] and the UN Population Division estimates that life expectancy is falling in 29 African countries due to AIDS.[3] The particular nature of the transmission of HIV through intimate personal connections raises immediate questions about appropriate public health responses, and the balance between human rights and respect for existing religious and cultural norms. In developing countries particularly AIDS poses central challenges to existing social, economic, and gender relations. For all these reasons the unprecedented degree of involvement of community-based activity in United Nations AIDS programs has implications for both the creation of new forms of global cooperation and the idea of global citizenship.

The dominant paradigms in 'social' research around HIV / AIDS have been psychological, focusing heavily on questions relating to 'risk,' individual behavior and how to change it. Although writings on HIV / AIDS in poor countries have tended to have a larger appreciation of the social and economic contexts, they tend to focus on the development of programs for behavior change, less commonly on care and support for those already infected.

However there is another strand of analysis that seeks to place HIV / AIDS within far broader categories, to link its spread, impact, and governance to the sociopolitical changes of the post-Cold War world and to the rapidly developing literature of 'globalization.' It is the argument of this article, first, that the rapid spread of AIDS to become a global pandemic can only be understood within this larger picture, and, second, that AIDS is a remarkably useful case study through which to understand the diverse meanings of 'globalization.'

[...]

There exists, therefore, a considerable need to bring together two strands of academic discourse, and, indeed, to integrate them with a third, the language used by community-based and people with HIV / AIDS organizations as they seek to develop and strengthen their activities. [...]

## Globalization and the AIDS epidemic

There is, of course, a vast literature on 'globalization,' and it has become a term used loosely to encompass every aspect of social, political, economic, and cultural life. At its simplest, globalization means, to quote Paul Kennedy: 'the inter-connectedness of capital, production, ideas and cultures at an increasing pace.'[4] In a globalizing world, it is argued, time and space themselves take on different meanings,[5] and no aspect of life is untouched by global forces. The impact of multinational firms, able to move capital and factories across the world in search of both markets and cheap workers, of electronic media, of the vast apparatus of consumerism, means that increasingly national boundaries are unable to contain either ideas or money. In general, they remain more successful at containing populations, despite the vast movement of people, both legal and illegal, which is itself a marker of globalization, whether in the form of mass tourism or of large numbers of people moving from south to north in search of economic survival. Most writers agree that globalization involves the simultaneous strengthening and weakening of national and state boundaries. [...]

Ironically, globalization is often taken to mean a certain homogenization of cultures just when the influence of post-modern thought is to focus on difference, hybridity, pastiche.[6] Yet the point is not that globalization abolishes difference as much as it redistributes it, so that certain styles and consumer fashions are internationalized, while class divides are strengthened, often across national boundaries. [...]

I use the term 'political economy' to signal that globalization is multi-faceted, and impacts on all areas of human life. The impact of globalization includes the *economic*, as the complex mix of growing affluence and greater inequality allows – and forces – new ways of organizing 'private' life; the *cultural*, as images of different ways of life are rapidly diffused across the world; and the *political*, in that state regulation plays a crucial role in determining the limits within which new social structures and identities will be developed. To take an example closely related to HIV / AIDS, it is clear that globalization impacts upon sexuality in all three ways. Economic changes mean that sexuality is increasingly commodi-fied, whether through advertising or prostitution, which, as in the nineteenth century, is closely linked to economic dislocation and change. Cultural changes mean that certain ideas about behavior and identity are widely dispersed, so that new ways of understanding oneself become available that often conflict bitterly with traditional mores. [. . .] And the political realm will determine what forms are available for sexual expression, so that there is a far more overt 'gay' world in Manila than in Singapore, despite the considerable gap in wealth, in part because of different political regimes.

[. . .]

How does AIDS fit these various understandings of 'globalization'? I would suggest in a number of ways, including its epidemiology, the mobilization against its spread, and the dominance of certain discourses in the understandings of the epidemic.

Reports of a new infectious and potentially fatal disease date from 1981, when young men were diagnosed as suffering from severe immune deficiency on both coasts of the United States. It is almost certain that HIV/AIDS had long existed in Africa.[7] Its rapid spread in the past two decades is closely related to the forces of 'development,' and to global population movements. It is probable that the virus was spread beyond its original home through urbanization and population shifts, and that its rapid dispersion across the world is closely related to the nature of a global economy. HIV followed the huge population movements of the contemporary world, whether these be truckers moving across Zaire and India,[8] women taking up sex work as a means of survival as old communities and social order crumbled, men seeking work on the minefields of South Africa and Zimbabwe, or tourists (for example Americans in Haiti), refugees (Haitians fleeing to the United States), and soldiers (Cubans serving in Angola) moving across national boundaries. [. . .] Thus, AIDS ironically linked the least developed and the most developed regions of the world, and despite attempts to close borders to its spread (as in the restrictions on entry of HIV-positive people applied by many countries) the spread of the virus made a mockery of national sovereignty. [. . .]

The growing internationalization of trade in both sex and drugs has played a major role in the diffusion of HIV, and its rapid spread into almost every corner of the world. It has been argued that 'patterns of use of illicit drugs are becoming globalized and "standardized."' [9][. . .]

Moreover, the very policies urged by international bodies and economic theorists to promote faster development have added to the conditions that make people vulnerable to HIV infection. Under conditions of social dislocation, poverty, and the absence of health services, HIV will spread much faster (it is known that other untreated sexually transmissible diseases increase susceptibility to HIV infection). [. . .]

[. . .] Global mobilization around the demands of a biomedical emergency has inevitably meant the further entrenchment of Western concepts of disease, treatments, and the body. [. . .]

The first significant international response to the new epidemic came in 1986 when the World Health Organization established the Global Program on AIDS (GPA), based in its Geneva headquarters. GPA had three clear achievements: the establishment of an international discourse around HIV/AIDS that stressed the language of empowerment and participation; technical support for a number of developing countries in a range of policy and program areas; and mobilization of donor countries to support a multilateral response to the epidemic.[10]

It was in large part due to the Global Program that the non-government sector was recognized as legitimate internationally. There are some tensions between the various groups that could be fitted under the umbrella of 'NGOs,' whether between those who are seropositive and negative, between those who stress activism as against service delivery, or between small community-based organizations and large international development NGOs. [...]

Building on the strength of local and national community organizing around AIDS, GPA encouraged the formation of networks such as the Global Network of People Living With AIDS (GNP Plus), the International Council of AIDS Service Organizations (ICASO) and the International Community of Women Living with HIV / AIDS (ICW). [...]

Equally a particular set of discourses were universalized by the actions of state and international agencies. These included the basic biomedical analyses that explained AIDS through infection by blood-borne transmission of a retrovirus – a form of explanation quite alien to the 'commonsense' understandings of many societies and epistemologies – as well as an emphasis on education and various forms of community mobilization to counter the spread of infection.

[...] Programs around HIV / AIDS have done a great deal to further the spread of identities such as 'sex worker' or 'gay men' / 'bisexuals' / 'men who have sex with men,' and the further globalization of movements based on such identities.[11]

[...]

As programs are developed to encourage 'safe' (or safer) sex, they also tend to spread the reach of the state apparatus – even though the agents of such programs are often NGOs with their own complex relations to state authority – and hence of a globalizing set of discourses and behaviors. [...]

In similar ways the dominance of Western discourses around HIV / AIDS meant the introduction of human rights as a major issue, often linked to the so-called 'new public health' based on ideas of empowerment and community control.

[...]

During the 1990s there was increased involvement of UN agencies – especially the United Nations Development Program and more recently the World Bank – and growing dissatisfaction among some donor governments with the workings of the GPA, seen as hamstrung by its place within WHO and unable to work cooperatively with other UN agencies. Thus, a number of donor countries proposed the creation of a 'joint and co-sponsored program' of the United Nations, UNAIDS, which began operations in 1996. UNAIDS is meant to coordinate the activities of seven of the international agencies involved in AIDS work – the World Health Organization; the United Nations Development Program; the United Nations Children's Fund; the United Nations Population Fund; UNESCO; the World Bank, and the UN International Drug Control

Program. As its Mission states, UNAIDS is meant to act as 'the main advocate for global action on HIV/AIDS.'

[...] The incorporation to an unprecedented degree of NGO involvement and the attempt to act as a coordinating body across the United Nations system makes the creation of UNAIDS an experiment with implications for the entire international system. [...]

## The relevance of political economy

A Canadian expert in health promotion, Ronald Labonte, has written that: 'Most of what creates 'health'...lies beyond organized health care sectors. Poverty, income inequalities, social inequalities, environmental pollutants/degradations, violence and other complex social phenomena are far more important health determinants than access to health care services.'[12] I want to tease out this argument as it might apply to HIV/AIDS.

I have already suggested that 'development' is often a major determinant of the spread of HIV. In the same way HIV impinges on economic growth, both slowing it and distorting the allocation of resources because of the demands it places on health and care systems. There exists a limited amount of analysis of the economic impact of HIV, most of it concentrating on the decline in life expectancy and production in some key sectors of the economy. For example, UNAIDS has calculated that: 'In Botswana life expectancy, which rose from under 43 years in 1955 to 61 years in 1990, has now fallen to levels previously found in the late 1960s'.[13] [...] More generally attempts to combine political and economic analysis are largely underdeveloped in respect of AIDS.

[...]

A political economy approach would stress the significance of political as much as economic factors: the extraordinary importance of political space for the discussion and articulation of ways to respond to the threats of HIV, as well as the need for sufficient resources to support these responses. In many parts of the world, the greatest problems are a compound of a lack of political will, the existence of barriers (usually religious or cultural in origin) against admitting the causes of infection and addressing them in practical ways, the severe stigma directed against both those with HIV and those from groups associated with AIDS (sex workers, needle-users, homosexuals, etc.) and – often underlying all of these – the pressure for survival on large numbers of people who are poor, homeless, and ill educated.

[...]

In short, effective AIDS interventions depend upon a number of variables most of which are outside the control of those immediately concerned with HIV/AIDS programs and their delivery. These center around the resources available to mount both prevention and care programs, resources in this case encompassing cultural and political factors as much as economic. Indeed Jonathan Mann argued that there is a basic link between a strong civil society that protects human rights and vulnerability to HIV infection.[14] Yet in many countries it is not the absence of civil society that is involved, but rather the reality that the organizations that civil society comprises will not necessarily be in agreement.

[…]

There is little doubt that some of the worst affected countries, particularly those in tropical Africa, could not provide effective medical care for the majority of those infected with HIV even if the entire government budget were devoted to that end. Much richer countries – Thailand, say, or South Africa – do not possess the necessary resources to meet the standards of care now available in most of the first world. Even rich countries have constantly to make decisions about the allocation of resources for – and within – their health sectors, and these decisions will directly determine who will live, and under what conditions others will die.

[…]

The common rhetoric around inequality in access to healthcare tends to reflect a rather simplistic analysis of imperialism, in which 'developing' countries are seen as powerless in face of the dominant capitalist order. There is some support for this view in the ways in which 'structural adjustments' imposed by the World Bank and the IMF have both increased the vulnerability of many to infection and limited the resources available for public health.[15] In recent years the Bank has itself admitted the validity of some of these criticisms, and indeed a major loan from the World Bank to Brazil has made it possible to provide considerable therapeutic support for those with HIV. Moreover, current international trade and patent laws prevent the production of appropriate drugs more cheaply in a number of affected countries (e.g., Thailand, India, South Africa).

But too often governments use global inequality as an alibi to excuse their own failings. Poor countries differ dramatically in their response to the epidemic, particularly in their willingness to admit the seriousness of the epidemic and to encourage effective measures to address it. Compare, for example, the support for effective intervention in Uganda against the general denial at government level in Kenya,[16] or the much stronger support for HIV programs in the Philippines as against Indonesia. […] We badly need research that might suggest what factors make for an effective government response, taking into account available resources. Such factors would undoubtedly include some respect for human rights of the sort Mann stressed (see note 14). […]

Around the provision of treatments, the example of Costa Rica and perhaps other Latin American countries, as well as the UNAIDS and French initiatives, suggest that the political arena may be as significant as financial restraints in determining what sort of treatments are made available and to what extent. A fuller analysis would need to incorporate the role of the large pharmaceutical companies in drug development and marketing. […]

The irony of seeing AIDS as a global epidemic is that in practice the global response is largely at a rhetorical level. At the 1996 International AIDS Conference in Vancouver (whose slogan was 'One World, One Hope') one plenary speaker pointed out that the cost of bringing her to speak for twenty minutes could have supplied food and medicines to her and her family for a year. Indeed, the constant advances in biomedicine's ability to manage infections, leading to a lengthening life span for those who are positive *and who have full access to the latest medical technologies* is increasing the gaps between two epidemics, one for the rich and one for the poor. These gaps raise practical and moral questions both for official and non-official responses to the epidemic, and, indeed, for theories of globalization themselves.

## AIDS and theorizing globalization

[...]

I argue that three key propositions stem from this study of HIV/AIDS: that the political/cultural arena remains as important as the economic in understanding processes of globalization; that globalization impinges on everyday life through the ways we create and understand identities and emotions; and that globalization urgently requires the creation of effective mechanisms for international governance in areas other than those traditionally viewed as global security or economic concerns.

Firstly, there is a tendency to see globalization as not only leading to an integrated world market but in the process obliterating cultural and political differences. [...] Processes of globalization simultaneously reinforce cultural differences while they disseminate certain images and consumer goods that create the appearance of homogenization.

Although the *vulnerability* of people to HIV varies greatly and is closely linked to their socioeconomic status, the *response* to AIDS is closely related to cultural and political factors. Thus Thailand, which was the first country in Asia to experience a major epidemic, was also able to mobilize a reasonably effective response. This mobilization was due to a number of factors, including strong commitment by several senior government figures, a culture that allowed comparative freedom in discussing sexuality, and sufficient resources to finance an effective intervention program.[17] Even allowing for the relative scale of the epidemic, not all rich countries can match Thailand's achievements.

Implicit in most discussion of HIV/AIDS is the view that there is a huge gap between the epidemic in 'developed' and 'developing' countries. In terms of access to the increasingly sophisticated and apparently effective drugs now available against HIV, this is true. Yet in other areas of AIDS policy, such as education interventions and prevention of discrimination, the correlation between 'development' and policy options is less clear. [...]

Secondly, as Richard Parker has written: 'In little more than a decade the rapid spread of the international AIDS pandemic has profoundly changed the ways in which we live and understand the world. Never has a common, global problem so clearly drawn attention to the important differences that shape the experience of diverse cultures and societies. And nowhere is this more true than in relation to our understanding of human sexuality.'[18] AIDS has entered the global imaginary, using this term in Appadurai's sense of 'a constructed landscape of collective aspirations ... the imagination as a social practice.'[19]

This is clearest in the growth of community-based politics around HIV and the corresponding push to construct universal identities around HIV status, sexuality, drug use, and sex work. [...] The creation of the 'Person Living With HIV / AIDS' as a specific identity clearly drew on earlier gay models of 'coming out' and has been a significant factor in breaking down the medical dominance of the epidemic. [...]

The internationalization of sexual identities, above all 'gay' identities, have been hastened by the requirements of HIV surveillance and prevention. [...] Equally, particular images of the epidemic have been universalized through global media, ironically often leading to false perceptions given the very different epidemiological patterns in different parts of the world. [...] Yet it remains true that in most parts of the world the dominant media images of the epidemic are unlikely to reflect the local situation accurately, thus allowing claims that 'AIDS couldn't happen here ...' or that it is spread by foreigners. At the same time the proliferation of particular Western constructs of the self, implicit in organizing around sexuality, sex work, or sero-status, means changes in the emotional lives of those involved, even though they are never as simple as merely duplicating what happens elsewhere. One of the traps in the signs of globalization is that we too easily assume that the Nike sneakers or baseball caps carry the same meanings in the slums of Jakarta that they do in Bedford-Stuyvesant.

Finally, AIDS might seem to bear out Bryan Turner's comment that 'there are no national solutions to world problems, precisely because it is difficult to imagine what a "national problem" would look like.'[20] Yet states do deal with AIDS as if it were a national problem, seeking to insulate themselves from outside forces even where they receive considerable foreign assistance.

Thus the political dilemma posed by globalization: it weakens the powers of the state without offering any effective substitute. In a globalized world, the state is increasingly squeezed between international capital and local holders of power, so that in some parts of the world NGOs and international agencies provide the only effective governmental structure.

[...]

The rapid spread of HIV, particularly in southern Africa, south and southeast Asia, and the Caribbean represents for many of the countries involved a major threat to their social and economic fabrics, and hence to their very survival. Increasingly the world will face issues like AIDS / HIV, which by their very nature go beyond the ability of national governments to control, and require coordinated and well-funded international responses. Similar arguments could be made around environmental issues, narcotics, and crime, or the ability of capital to move rapidly across the globe without meaningful restraints or supervision. Whether the attempts to create new international structures to meet the challenges of the AIDS epidemic succeed will have implications for areas far beyond those of the epidemic.

## Notes

1 While HIV is the basic cause of AIDS, there are some problems in the way in which the two terms are conflated. See Anthony Smith, 'AIDS is...,' *International Journal of Health Services* 28/4 (1998): 794.

2 Laurence Altman, 'AIDS Is on Course to Ravage Africa,' *International Herald Tribune* (24 June 1998).

3 On the epidemiology of HIV/AIDS, see J. Mann and D. Tarantola, editors, *AIDS in the World II* (New York: Oxford 1996) and regular updates from UNAIDS.

4 Paul Kennedy, 'Forecast: Global Gales Ahead,' *New Statesman & Society* (31 May 1996): 28.

5 See, e.g., David Harvey, *The Condition of Postmodernity* (Oxford: Blackwell, 1989).

6 See the discussion of this in Joel Kahn, *Culture, Multiculture, Postculture* (London: Sage, 1995), 128–35.

7 See M. Grmek, *History of AIDS* (Princeton: Princeton University Press, 1990).

8 See Ted Conover, 'Trucking through the AIDS Belt,' *New Yorker* (16 August 1993).

9 See 'The Hidden Epidemic,' *Asian Harm Reduction Network Newsletter* no. 10 (Jan./Feb. 1998).

10 On GPA, see J. Mann and K. Kay, 'Confronting the Pandemic: The WHO's GPA 1986–9,' *AIDS* 5/Suppl. 2 (1991): S221–9; D. Tarantola, 'Grande et petite histoire des programmes sida,' *Le journal du sida* no. 86/7 (June/July 1996): 109–16.

11 See Dennis Altman, 'Political Sexualities: Meanings and Identities in the Time of AIDS,' in R. Parker and J. Gagnon, editors, *Conceiving Sexuality* (New York: Routledge, 1994), 97–106.

12 R. Labonte, 'Health Public Policy and the World Trade Organization,' speech delivered in Melbourne, 1997 (http://www.vichealth.vic.gov.au/docs/wto.htm).

13 UNAIDS Press Release, 26 November, 1997.

14 J. Mann, 'Solidarity and the Future of the Global AIDS Movement,' Lecture at XI International AIDS Conference (Vancouver: July 1996).

15 Antonio Ugalde and Jeffrey Jackson, 'The World Bank and International Health Policy: A Critical Review,' *Journal of International Development* 7/3 (1995): 525–40.

16 See, e.g., 'Serial Killer at Large,' *The Economist* (7 February 1998).

17 There is an extensive literature on HIV in Thailand. See, e.g., Y. Porapakkham et al., *The Evolution of HIV/AIDS Policy in Thailand: 1984–1994* (Arlington AIDSCAP/Family Health International, 1996); A. Pramualratana, 'HIV/AIDS in Thailand,' UNAIDS Position Paper (January 1998).

18 R. Parker, 'Sexual Cultures, HIV Transmission and AIDS Prevention,' *AIDS* 8, Suppl. 1 (1994): S312.

19 Arjun Appadurai, *Modernity at Large* (Minneapolis: University of Minnesota Press, 1996), 31.

20 Bryan Turner, *Orientalism, Postmodernism and Globalism* (London: Routledge, 1994), 113.

17

# The Land, the Blood and the Passion: the Hindu Far-Right

*Chetan Bhatt*

[. . .]

## The sangh parivar: *visceral mutilation, radical difference and ethnic death*

[. . .]

During the 1960s [in India] the RSS (Rashtriya Swayamsevak Sangh – the National Volunteer Servers' Organization) expanded its activities by forming several affiliated organizations, of which the Vishwa Hindu Parishad (VHP – World Hindu Council) and the political party the Jan Sangh were the most important. This was the formative period of the Hindu nationalist social movement. The VHP was a federation of Hindu religious leaders whose activities were to dominate Hindu revivalism in the 1980s and 1990s. The Jan Sangh [. . .] was to become part of the ruling Janata coalition following the defeat of Indira Gandhi's Congress Party in 1977. The RSS membership of Jan Sangh MPS was at the root of the attacks upon it by other Janata partners and led to the dissolving of the coalition and its consequent defeat at the polls. Subsequently, the Jan Sangh reformed itself as the Bharatiya Janata Party (BJP – Indian People's Party) in 1980 under the leadership of Lal Krishnan Advani. From 1985, the BJP committed itself to the late Deendayal Upadhyaya's philosophy of 'integral humanism'. Integral humanism is a self-consciously modern, holistic and developmental vision of the social totality in which individuals and collectives are seen as interdependent and should be mutually non-conflictual under the greater principle of nation. The basis of conflict is indeed seen as a weakening of nationalism and *dharma* among individuals, and consequently some form of *Dharma Rajya*, which Upadhyaya insists is not a theocratic state, needs to be established. [. . .] Interestingly, the

Darwinian metaphor, together with various organicist and biological tropes, is heavily employed in integral humanism (Upadhyaya et al. 1979)

[...] The BJP has risen spectacularly in Indian national politics since 1980. Its two seats in parliament in 1984 increased to 89 seats in 1989 (and almost 120 seats following political realignments in 1991). It has seen similar successes in state assembly elections, including control of the prize state Uttar Pradesh.[1] [...] In 1995, it won a two-thirds majority in Gujarat state and took control of Maharashtra state in a coalition with the fascist Shiv Sena.

The broader 'family', or *sangh parivar*, of contemporary Hindu nationalist organizations in India are mainly aligned to the RSS–VHP–BJP axis. The RSS has about two million members in India and its role has been to advise, guide and organize the other revivalist formations. These have grown rapidly since the 1970s.

[...]

The Vishwa Hindu Parishad, the Bharatiya Janata Party, the Rashtra Sevika Samiti (the RSS' women's affiliate), the violent Bajrang Dal ('Hanuman's army', the youth wing of the VHP), the Durga Vahini (the young women's wing of the VHP), the Mahila Mandal (the VHP's women's section formed in 1980), as well as the organizations formed to destroy the Babri masjid were the most active during the late 1980s. Other older organizations such as the Arya Samaj are also relevant. In addition, there are thousands of local organizations, including welfare, cultural, student, peasant, farmer, tribal, youth, trade union, women's and religious organizations, some of which are explicitly linked to the formations mentioned, or sympathetic to them and others that use alternative local epithets but are essentially branches or local projects of the RSS and the VHP. Importantly, various older missionary movements, including the Swaminarayan Mission and the Chinmaya Mission, undertake joint projects with the VHP, and in many cases the exact organizational boundaries and personnel affiliation between the RSS and (especially) the VHP and other groups has dissolved. [...]

This is a practical demonstration of a strictly hegemonic political strategy in which diverse, eclectic and unrelated strands are knitted together into an overarching political discourse within which their discursive unity 'makes sense'.

[...]

While communalist language and violence has been a part of Indian post-Independence politics, the more recent activities of the *sangh parivar* have framed this within a larger metanarrative of Hindu nationalism, Hindu superiority and mass social movement. Since the 1960s, communal violence against Muslim communities and beatings and murders of Muslims have been framed within the discourse of 'necessary punishment' for a minority that is 'too vociferous' and 'unruly' and too demanding of 'special privileges' and 'rights' that are 'denied' to the Hindu majority. A formative point for this new Hindu communalist language was the war between India and Pakistan in 1965. [...] Further wars with Pakistan, Indian support for Bangladesh's separation, the intensification of the conflict in Kashmir, the growth of Islamic revival in the Subcontinent following the Iranian revolution and the war in Afghanistan resulted in further Hindu nationalist resentments.

Three events in the 1980s, all of which centred on the purity of the body, were extremely important for both Hindu and Muslim revivalists (Chhachhi 1991: 162) – the mass conversion of 'untouchables' to Islam in Meenakshipuram, Tamil Nadu, in 1981, the Supreme Court ruling on the Shahbano case in 1985 and an incident of self-immolation by a widow in Rajasthan in 1987. The Tamil Nadu incident directly changed the work of the VHP towards massive conversion, fundraising, Ekatmata ('Integration') and 'Hindu Enlightenment' campaigns all over India. In Rajasthan, a young Hindu woman (Roop Kanwar) immolated herself on the funeral pyre of her husband and was hailed as a *sati*, leading to huge feminist and secular protests. These protests were interpreted by Hindu nationalists as 'Hinduism under threat' and the suicide-murder was militantly defended as Hindu Rajput 'tradition'. Shahbano, an elderly Muslim woman, was divorced and abandoned by her husband and she subsequently filed a petition for alimony. The case went to the Indian Supreme Court which, in April 1985, ruled in her favour, overturning the legitimacy of Muslim Personal Law in India. This was seen as both a victory against Muslims by Hindu revivalists and a victory for women by feminist and progressive organizations. However, after considerable lobbying by Islamic organizations, especially the Indian Jamaat-i-Islami and the (Deobandi) Jamaat-i-Ulema-i-Hind, Rajiv Gandhi's government intervened and overturned the court ruling by introducing new legislation.

We should note that it was virtually this same Islamic coalition which formed around the Shabano case that was also directly involved in starting the Rushdie affair in India and in Britain. Almost the same coalition was involved in political agitation in defence of the Babri masjid against Hindu fundamentalists. An extremely important political thread links Shahbano with Salman Rushdie and with the Babri masjid and emphasizes the fundamental importance of Hindu-Muslim communal relations in South Asia in shaping the global form of religious-political activism by Muslims and Hindus. In this register, incidents in the Middle East become less important in comparison with those in South Asia, as the Rushdie affair and the destruction of the Babri masjid demonstrated.

Many Indians viewed the government's intervention in the Shahbano case as an unjust concession to Islamic fundamentalists, an attack on women's rights and an opportunist strategy by the ruling Congress (I) Party to keep the Muslim 'vote bank' (Muslims have traditionally voted Congress). Hindu nationalists saw this as a further appeasement towards a backward, intransigent Muslim minority: why should Hindus have to follow a 'secular' common civil code but Muslims have their own separate legislation in matters of family law, divorce, polygamy and alimony? [...] In Hindu nationalist political language, this is the 'pseudo-secularism' that 'keeps Hindus enslaved in their own country'. The similarity between this discourse and new-right and far-right racial discourse in the West should be apparent. Just as central are the personal politics of Roop Kanwar's death, the Shahbano case and the religious conversion cases in framing the national agendas of both Islamic and Hindu fundamentalists. In Hindu nationalism, as in Islamism, the personal is intensely political. Importantly, both the Shahbano ruling and Roop Kanwar's suicide-murder critically expose the recent fabrications of Hindu nationalism around women's rights. The same Hindu nationalist claims justified both these incidents. If Hindu nationalism could claim ownership of women's rights in the Shahbano ruling, it also vigorously defended the grotesque mass public spectacle of the murder of a woman in Rajasthan.

It is the way in which these recent developments have been articulated through a new Hindu tradition based on mythic history, new conceptions of blood superiority and new ideas of Hindu nationalism that has led to the political language of the body in Hindu nationalism becoming especially violent. In the chants at Ayodhya, Muslims were called 'the sons of Babar', who must 'pay with their blood'. [...]

At the core is the theme of essential belonging by virtue of blood and soil to 'Bharat'. Indian Muslims do not belong to 'Bharat' since 'they are Pakistanis': 'If they wanted a separate state why don't they go and live there now? Why do they remain in India' – 'our' nation?

Alongside this *Hindutva* political language resides a vast repertoire of prejudice that would be instantly familiar to students of racism and ethnic hatred. Muslims are 'intolerant' or 'dirty', responsible for crime, prostitution, drug trafficking, they take away 'our' jobs and homes, they have four wives or child brides, their population will overtake us (the fertility trope), they get favourable treatment and special rights, the state favours Muslims, Muslims have an absolute political veto, multiculturalism favours Muslims' culture, equal opportunities policies and job reservations favour Muslims, secularism discriminates in favour of Muslims and against Hindus, Muslims are fundamentalists, Muslims are proselytizing and converting *'our* Hindus, *our* untouchables'. Racist languages are themselves highly structured and extraordinarily capable of dismissing realist history or sociology. Hence, factors such as the higher levels of unemployment among Muslims compared with Hindus, or the roughly equal incidence of polygamy among Hindus and Muslims, are elided. One route of escape from the brutality and prejudice of the Hindu caste system for many *dalits*, lower-caste Hindus, and *adivasi* (tribal) peoples was to convert to Buddhism and Islam within which they have, technically, formal gender-differentiated equality. In Hindu nationalism this simply becomes Islamic fundamentalist proselytizing.

The political rhetoric of murder and death to the body of 'the other' has always accompanied communal violence. But its articulation in this new Hindu nationalist metanarrative is often explicitly genocidal. Communal violence is manifestly about the recognition of difference in civil society, and the legitimation of physical attacks on, and murder and rape of those who are different. Aside from a few extremely important interventions (Das 1992), it has been common on the Indian left to view communalism as 'false consciousness' (Vaniak 1990: 153), a strategy of the state or ruling class to divide the masses along communal lines. Communalism is also invariably viewed as a phenomenon that commenced with, and was a strategic practice of, British rule in India. It is also common to view communalism as an ideological epiphenomenon rather than a material practice carried out by cognitive agents who are not simply uncritical bearers of discursive formations that reside outside their communities. However, a common thread in most assessments of communalism is that, despite its 'external' or institutional causes, a reservoir of violence lies just below a deceptively thin surface of peace and it requires a relatively minor incident ('a Muslim-owned dog bites a cow') or intervention ('a speech by Advani or Shahabuddin') to trigger it. Most assessments of communalism combine this reservoir–tinderbox view with an explanatory paradigm of external institutional cause.

However, communalism highlights important factors about the structuration of many modern, civil societies and the identities that are reproduced within them. Communalism is manifestly a problem of modern urban civil society. It is a highly dynamic cultural-political formation that may (or may not) be related to state ideology or social policy but is strictly autonomous from it. Significantly, communal violence is not generally directed against the state. Identities are thus formed not through eternal ethnic traditions but through new forms of difference constituted as martial territorialization of the urban city and routine acts of semi-organized and disorganized violence against affiliates of another identity. Murder might be terrifying but it becomes essentially mundane. In important ways, some civil societies are organized through the enactment of communal violence against others so that disorganized or semi-organized collective violence can become a permanent constitutive mechanism of identity formation in complex modern civil societies.

[...]

Another important aspect of communal violence is the celebration of visceral mutilation and the annihilation of the body of the other, an obsessive fixation on the body within a modern urban ritual of carnage and bloodshed. Importantly, there is an embedded aspect to disorganized collective violence that is about ecstatic 'joy' and 'rapture' in the riotous situation (cf. Gilroy's discussion of riots in Britain (1987: 238)). Communal violence is also a highly gendered phenomenon that focuses on the meaning of masculinity in a complex social formation where gendered difference is continually overdetermined by other differences. However, recent acts of communal violence in India have involved women as core mobilizing agents of men, as well as agents themselves of communal violence. The hate-filled political rhetoric of the VHP 'sanyasinis', Sadhvi Rithambara and the (conveniently named) BJP MP Uma Bharati has been absolutely fundamental to this process. The reproduction of Rithambara's inflammatory and genocidal rhetoric by audio-cassette has been seen as fundamentally sufficient to create a permanent wall of communal hatred. [...]

In much Hindu nationalist activity, Hindu women are frequently placed in important leadership, organizing or activist positions and very much *not* in the home. At Hindu rallies women speakers, often the main mobilizing speakers, taunt, abuse and insult the predominantly male audience: 'Are you cowards?', 'Are you real men?', 'Are you effeminate weaklings?', urging them to commit acts of violence against Muslims – 'can't you do any better than that, you pathetic idiots?' Similarly, during communal riots, women on the sidelines taunt and encourage men and women participants to go further. This includes the raping and murder of Muslim women and children, rapes of other women being justified because they are major violations of Muslim womanhood and consequently major indignities for their husbands or family. Women are mobilized in huge numbers under a powerful and violent conception of Hindu womanhood and are encouraged to engage in acts of violence against Muslims. In the communalist idiom, it becomes productive to efface Sita and Lakshmi – instead it is the *duty* of women to become Durgas:

> Just now you tried weapons but they were only wooden. Now you need to learn to use real weapons. The time to use them is coming, the nation is in crisis.[2]

The activities of the Rashtrasevika Samitis (RSS-affiliate women's organizations) and the Durga Vahini have created a major problem for secular Indian feminism which has never witnessed anything like this mass mobilization of Hindu women before.[3] [...] This novel Hindu nationalist discourse around womanhood extends to the BJP, which can talk openly about 'women's liberation' and 'womanpower', and about the necessity of bringing women into the political, educational, economic and social processes. Both these aspects can be articulated as part of the same discourse. The extremely visible and militant presence of Hindu women in Hindu nationalism has led some commentators to view this as an unforeseen but progressive and emancipatory development because Hindu women are being mobilized in huge numbers under a militant and active conception of womanhood, political participation and women's rights. However, at the same time, and through the same process, the most brutal and violent masculinities are being constructed. Similarly, a 'naturalized' understanding of women as 'homemakers' is still dominant, especially in strictly religious Hindu nationalist ideology. Moreover, Hindu nationalist womanpower is a deeply particularist understanding of women's liberation that is completed and hermetically sealed before the moment that Muslim women can be articulated within it. This creation of Hindu sex/gender systems is a novel rehearsal of Hindu 'tradition' in modern civil society.

One extremely important gendered trope for Hindu communalist agitation has been that of 'Bharatmata' – 'Holy Mother India'. The Motherland definition that is essential to Savarkar's *Hindutva* is hugely influential in contemporary discourse. 'India' is represented as a frequently chained, bound or gagged woman and the Muslim presence within it is thus signifies 'a pollution', 'a rape'. The intended conclusion is elementary – 'Hindu womanhood is being raped', or, more powerfully, 'your mother is being raped' by Muslims and she is powerless to resist because she has been bound and chained like a slave by secularists and Hindu traitors. Similarly, Partition is often represented as the beheading of a sobbing, grieving Hindu woman. One popular VHP hoarding portrays a beautiful woman having her head slowly sliced off by secularists with a massive tooth-saw. [...] She is looking down at her bloodied body ('India') but her arms and legs are shackled and she can do nothing but cry. Her tears intermingle with her pure, wasted, Hindu blood.

It does not require a major leap to relate the visceral and intensely sexualized nature of these national symbols of Hindu nationalism, especially the continual representation of appalling and horrifying acts of mutilation of the body, to the actual practice of communal violence. Communal violence celebrates the frenzied mutilation of the flesh and destruction of the human body of 'others', a tragic form of 'personal politics'. Of particular relevance to its reproduction is the importance of sexual narrative in constructing both the visceral symbols of communalist agitation and in providing various explanatory methods for local communalist violence. In the communalist idiom, sex, gender, femininity, masculinity, fertility, death and blood are used in both metonymic and metaphoric senses. These intensely libidinal tropes that are used in Hindu communalist agitation are the paradoxical end-products of a founding discourse that actually claims to suppress and 'order' sex and sexuality. Golwalkar, for example, was quite explicit about the destructive nature of sexuality and the need to repress it:

> The 'modern fashion' of young men is to appear more and more feminine. In dress, in habits, in literature and in every aspect of our day-to-day life 'modernism' has come to mean effeminacy. 'Sex' has become the one dominating theme of all our 'modern' literature. History of countries the world over has time and time again shown that sex-dominated literature has been an unfailing precursor to the ruin of nations and civilisations. (Golwalkar 1966: 230)

The iterative, semiotic nature of communal violence also significantly evades a moral and ethical dimension about the killing of humans and the worth of human lives. Religious discourse, in its capacity to decentre the subject, also naturally and powerfully displaces philosophical humanism. While, indeed, the defeat of communalism requires a political strategy within the *personal* institutions of civil society, it is difficult to view such a strategy as simply one that stresses secularism – the ideal of a non-religious ethic – when communalism is so firmly fixed on the highly gendered and sexualized destruction of the body through an autonomous dynamic of local myth, rumour, memory and fabricated histories of purity.

### Conclusion: modernity and the violence of purity

In both Hindu and Islamic fundamentalism the obsession with the body is strikingly repressive and violent. There is little celebration in revivalist discourse of the real erotic traditions of Islam or Hinduism, of the sexual pleasures of the human body. The sexual body is instead to be disciplined, contained, silenced, obscured or erased. However, just as important for communalist symbolism and mobilization is the continual manufacture of visceral symbols through which subjects are mobilized against 'others'. These symbols are explicitly libidinous and constituted through barely disguised sexual narratives. In this symbolism, the woman's body often becomes the privileged site of revivalist agitation. In both the Shahbano case and the Rajput Hindu glorification of the *sati*, the woman's body became the territory on which Islamic and Hindu neotraditions condensed. The identification in revivalist discourse of women as the bearers and reproducers of culture, and of women as equivalent to tradition, has a contrary side because women are also explicitly identified with unrestrained sexuality, and relentless temptation. In neofoundational discourse, women represent both the tradition that is to be preserved and are at the same time constitutive of the transgressive sexuality that is to be repressed. This is a ruptured and unsettled identification. Consequently, neotraditional discourse has to keep reproducing sexual narratives of the gendered body even as it ostensibly claims to repress sexuality. This pivotal place of sexuality in otherwise righteous revivalist discourse forms a core aspect of its obsessions with purity.

Noting the importance of sexuality and purity to neofoundationalist discourse is far easier than explaining it. There are several themes that appear to be important, though they barely constitute an explanation and require further discussion. The regulation of sexuality is a characteristic feature of modernity (Foucault 1981) that, in the West, has had complicated historical links with the establishment of racial and class purity (Weeks 1981: 126–38). The creation of Hindu and Muslim Personal Codes and legislation dealing with sexuality, the family, polygamy, *sati*, and so forth in nineteenth-century India was informed by essentially British colonial mappings of sexual discourse that instituted British regulations of sexuality as an ideal. These British colonial codes are still considerably influential today and, arguably, dominate Indian regulations of sexuality. In this sense, the 'traditional' purity strand within Hindu revivalist constructions of sexuality is essentially a Puritan strand. In important ways, British colonial codification of sexual morality and sexual practice also dovetailed into some forms of traditional *brahminic* asceticism and sexual renunciation. The colonial frontier also becomes important in another sense. The importance of slavery and colonization in constituting a sexual narrative for the West's sense of its own racial identity has been noted by numerous writers. However, what is at least as important is how these narratives impacted on the populations they colonized and instituted indigenous constructions of sexuality as a marker of communal difference within the social formation. Nineteenth-century colonial discourse imposed – possibly for the first time ever – legislated differences between different Indian communities through the narratives of sexuality, sexual practice, reproduction, fertility and the family. There is a deep link between British constructions of communalism and the sexual narratives of modernity. Indeed, it is instructive that contemporary Hindu nationalist constructions of Muslim 'difference' reinstall aspects of British colonial discourse about Muslim sexual practice.

'Hindu communalism' has rarely acquired its potency in a *foundational* way, except perhaps during the period of Partition. It has, even during national waves of communal violence, tended to reactively follow localized or singular national or international events. However, today communal rhetoric is deployed within a metanarrative of Hindu revivalism that structures quite neatly the legitimacy of killing within an overall explanatory and generalized modality. The complex social formation acquires elementary intelligibility as a somatic 'polluted' totality. This Hindu neotradition is not reducible to previous examples of communalism. Instead, Hindu communalism is legitimized within a systematic, ruthless formation of superiority, prejudice, state power and 'Hindu revolution' (*kranti*). This modernist will to totalitarian power has deliberately created a dangerous gaze on an underprivileged minority 'Other'. The great challenge is in promoting a new counter-hegemonic 'culture of social change' that embraces new political visions. This oppositional task is not restricted to secularists and progressive activists within India. The ideologies, organizations, political language and activities of Hindu nationalism have been hugely influential in diasporic communities outside India, just as Islamic revival has impacted on Muslim communities across the globe. [. . .]

## Notes

1   Uttar Pradesh contains not only Ayodhya but also Mathura, Krishna's alleged 'birthplace', and numerous other sites that revivalist Hindus are contesting.
2   An RSS affiliate gymnasium instructor speaking to a group of young women being trained in Indian martial arts, quoted in *Assignment*, BBC2, 15 June 1993.
3   Madhu Kishwar, 'Hindu nationalism and women', paper presented at the University of California at Berkeley, 5 May 1993.

## References

Chhachhi, A. 1991. Forced identities: the state, communalism, fundamentalism and women in India. In *Women, Islam and the state*, D. Kandiyoti (ed.), 144–75. Basingstoke: Macmillan.

Das, V. 1992. Introduction: communities, riots, survivors – the South Asian experience. In *Mirrors of violence: communities, riots and survivors*, V. Das (ed.), 1–36. Delhi: Oxford University Press.

Foucault, M. 1981. *The history of sexuality*, vol. I. Harmondsworth: Pelican.

Gilroy, P. 1987. *There ain't no black in the Union Jack: the cultural politics of race and nation*. London: Hutchinson.

Golwalkar, M. S. 1966. *Bunch of thoughts*. Bangalore: Vikrama Prakashan.

Upadhyaya, D., M. Golwalkar, D. B. Thengdi 1979. *The integral approach*. New Delhi: Deendayal Research Institute.

Vaniak, A. 1990. *The painful transition: bourgeois democracy in India*. London: Verso.

Weeks, J. 1981. *Sex, politics and society: the regulation of sexuality since 1800*. Harlow: Longman.

# 18

# Prostitution, Power and Freedom

*Julia O'Connell Davidson*

What kind of power do clients and third parties exercise over prostitutes? Can human beings freely consent to their own prostitution? For some feminists these questions are relatively clear cut. Carole Pateman (1988), for example, holds that the prostitution contract establishes a relationship within which the prostitute is unambiguously subject to the client's command. The client exercises powers of mastery over her. There is equally little room for ambiguity in Kathleen Barry's treatment of prostitution. Sexual exploitation violates human rights to dignity, she argues, and there can therefore be no 'right to prostitute' and no distinction between 'free' and 'forced' prostitution [...] (Barry, 1995, pp. 304–6).

This kind of analysis rests on certain assumptions about the essential properties of prostitution (that it *necessarily* subordinates the prostitute to the client's will, that it *necessarily* involves inhuman and degrading treatment) and on an undifferentiated view of power. There is nothing in the account provided by Barry, for example, which would allow us to distinguish between the kind of powers that are exercised over a debt-bonded child prostitute and those exercised over an adult who prostitutes independently or voluntarily enters into an employment contract with a third party, and it is this which so infuriates those feminists who campaign for legal rights and better working conditions for 'sex workers'. Barry, and the US-based Coalition Against Trafficking of Women with which she has been heavily involved, stands accused of pursuing an underlying moral agenda of 'abolishing prostitution ... by linking all forms of the sex trade with an emphasis on emotive words like "trafficking, slaves, and child prostitution"' (Perkins, 1995). For most prostitutes' rights activists, it is the laws that criminalize prostitution, rather than anything inherent in the prostitution exchange, which make prostitutes so vulnerable to coercion, abuse and exploitation. Prostitution should therefore be recognized as a form of work that can be actively chosen and prostitutes accorded the rights and protection that is given to other groups of wage workers.

Although 'abolitionist' and 'pro-sex worker' feminists clearly hold divergent moral and political understandings of prostitution, it seems to me that the view of power implicit in both lines of analysis is equally unidimensional. The former offers a zero-sum view of power as a 'commodity' possessed by the client (and / or third-party controller of prostitution) and exercised over prostitutes, the latter treats the legal apparatuses of the state as the central source of a repressive power that subjugates prostitutes. [However,] the power relations involved in prostitution are far more complicated than either of these positions suggest. [...]

## The faces of power

The social relations of prostitution vary. To begin with, we can note a distinction between independent, self-employed prostitutes and those who are controlled by a third party. So far as the latter group are concerned, we can further distinguish between those who are subject to what Truong (1990, p. 184) terms 'relations of confinement' (wherein third parties use physical force and / or debt to prevent individuals from exiting from prostitution, even in the event of an alternative means of subsisting becoming available to them) and those who are subject to 'enterprise labour relations' (which involve individuals who are, in a formal sense, free to exit from prostitution and which take a form similar to direct or indirect 'employment relations' in other capitalist enterprises). This means that there is a continuum within third-party controlled prostitution in terms of the formal freedoms that prostitutes exercise over their own persons and also that there is variability within prostitution in terms of the extent and degree to which prostitutes are subject to the *personalistic* power of third parties. Some prostitutes are directly forced into particular kinds of transactions and a given work rate by one or more individuals. Others are not.

While the formal social relationship between prostitutes and third party has an important bearing upon the type and degree of compulsion to which prostitutes are subject, it is not the *only* external constraint operating on them. Prostitutes are also subject to *materialistic* forms of domination; that is to say, economic pressures operate as another form of compulsion upon them. This is not simply true of those who prostitute independently. Prostitutes who are employed and even those who are enslaved are typically subject to both materialistic and personalistic forms of power. [...]

Next we should note that the relationship between prostitute and third party, as well as that between prostitute and client, takes place in a specific legal, institutional, social, political and ideological context, and that this represents another set of external constraints upon those relationships. In many cases, for example, prostitution is legally regulated in ways which so heavily penalize independent prostitution that law / law enforcement effectively operates as a pressure on prostitutes to enter and remain in third-party controlled prostitution no matter how exploitative the third party may be. Equally significant in shaping the relative powers enjoyed by prostitutes and third parties are broader ideological and political factors. [...]

In short, there is no single, unitary source of power within prostitution that can be seized and wielded by third party, client or prostitute. Rather, prostitution as a social practice is embedded in a particular set of social relations which produce a series of variable and interlocking constraints upon action. Finally, we should note that, as Layder (1997, p. 147) puts it, 'power spans both the objective and subjective aspects of social life', and this too has implications for the degree of unfreedom experienced by prostitutes. People come to prostitution as *individuals* with particular personal histories and subjective beliefs, and some people's psychobiographies and attitudes leave them far more open to abuse and exploitation than others. I want to flesh these points out by looking at some examples of different types of brothel prostitution in the contemporary world.

## Brothels as business enterprises

Prostitution involves the transfer of certain powers of command over the persons of prostitutes in exchange for money and / or other material benefits, but the actual prostitute–client exchange is necessarily surrounded by various other activities, such as soliciting custom, negotiating contracts, providing a setting for executing those contracts, managing the throughput of customers, and so on. In brothel prostitution all or some of these functions are undertaken by a third party – the brothel owner or her / his agents. The dictionary definition of 'brothel' is 'a house of prostitutes', and we might add to this that a brothel constitutes premises at which clients can view, select, arrange and execute a transaction with prostitutes.

[...]

Whether it does so overtly or covertly, the brothel is an organization which facilitates numerous prostitute–client exchanges and through which some or all of the activities that surround those exchanges are brought under the central co-ordination of a third party. Brothel owners [...] take it upon themselves to orchestrate prostitute–client exchanges out of economic self-interest, and it is therefore important to consider how, exactly, the brothel owner can make a profit from these exchanges.

[...]

The basic concepts of 'necessary' and 'surplus' economic activity can be applied to prostitution (Dixon, 1988). Assume that, in a given country, the minimum 'rate' for a trick is $x$ and the cost of an individual's daily subsistence is $4x$. In order to live, and so reproduce herself and her capacity to continue working each day, a prostitute must therefore enter into four client transactions daily. If she enters into more than four transactions, and / or manages to get clients to pay more than the minimum rate, she will generate an economic surplus. We can also argue that, just as the capitalist labour process is designed to facilitate the production and appropriation of surplus value, so the social relations and organization of third-party controlled prostitution are fundamentally geared towards this same end, for it is only if third parties can get prostitutes to generate a surplus and surrender that surplus to them that they can hope to profit from the prostitution of others. [...]

As the examples provided below will show, brothel owners typically manage to siphon off a profit from prostitution by inserting themselves as intermediaries in the prostitute–client exchange and demanding payment from either the client or the prostitute, or both, for 'facilitating' each exchange. [...] Depending upon the broader structural context in which brothel prostitution is set, the brothel owner's essential goals can be pursued in different ways and can imply different configurations of power between brothel owners, prostitutes and clients.

## Massage parlours in England

Under the law of England and Wales, 'prostitution itself is not a criminal offence, but public manifestations of prostitution: soliciting, advertising, making agreements with clients, brothel-keeping, and living on the earnings of prostitution are illegal' (Bindman, 1997, p. 14). The law further stipulates that it is an offence 'for men and women to exercise control over prostitutes . . . and for men and women to procure' (Edwards, 1993, p. 115), and thus it formally proscribes all forms of brothel prostitution. In England, then, brothels are typically operated behind the front of another business that offers legitimate services / facilities – most commonly massage or saunas. This makes it possible for the owner to contract women legitimately as masseuses, and to argue that 'these legitimate and licit activities comprise the "core" of parlour work. Any prostitution exchange that may take place is extra to this contract; it is negotiated privately between the worker and the client' (Phoenix, 1995, pp. 72–3).

'Stephanie's', a massage parlour in a midlands town in England, is fairly typical of this form of brothel. [...] Prostitutes working at Stephanie's have to pay a 'shift fee' of £20 for the privilege of working there at all, and they are then charged a 'punter fee' of £5 for each client that they see. As well as this, they are expected to pay £25 per shift, supposedly for the receptionist's services. In short, they cover the expenses of running the parlour, and by the time they see their first client they will have incurred 'expenses' of £50 (£10 more than the rate for penetrative sex set by the owner).

On a good day, a prostitute at Stephanie's sees seven clients during a shift. If every client pays the full price for the most expensive 'service' – penetrative sex – then the prostitute will end up with £200 at the end of her shift, while the owner will pocket £125. If the prostitute sees fewer clients, say five, and if they negotiate for cheaper services or to pay lower rates, say £25, then she will walk away from the shift with a mere £55. However, since the owner does not vary the punter fee or the shift fee, she will still pocket £95. On days when there is very little custom it is possible for prostitutes to end up owing money to the parlour owner.

[...]

What is it that assures parlour owners a steady supply of 'employees'? To begin with, employment opportunities for unskilled women in England are limited, and those which do exist are usually extremely low paid. Moreover, the English welfare system barely assures a subsistence to single adults, and is even more inadequate in respect of lone parents. The financial situation of many women is therefore so desperate that prostitution often appears to be the best of a poor bunch of economic alternatives (McLeod, 1982; Edwards, 1987). It clearly makes more financial sense for women to prostitute independently rather than allow a third party to siphon off a portion of their earnings, and many do exactly this. But economically vulnerable women are, by definition, unlikely to be in a position to set up their own private brothel and, since law-enforcement practice in England consistently targets street prostitutes rather than brothel owners or pimps (see Edwards, 1993; Smart, 1995), independent street prostitution carries with it legal as well as other risks. [...]

The [brothel] prostitute is directly constrained by the employment relations and practices adopted by the parlour owner. To begin with, the prostitute must relinquish control over her own work rate, which is determined in large part by the parlour owner's decisions about how many prostitutes to employ per shift. When parlour owners operate with a low prostitute:client ratio, each prostitute will have to enter into a large number of transactions per shift, and refusal to do so will place her continued employment at risk. When the owner operates with a high prostitute:client ratio, each prostitute will be restricted in terms of the number of transactions she can enter into. In neither case can she work or earn at a rate of her own choosing.

Massage-parlour prostitutes also find it more difficult to exercise control over the terms and limits of each individual prostitute–client exchange than do independent, self-employed prostitutes. [...] Though, in theory, prices for specific 'services' are set by the owner, she does not actually make any attempt to enforce the rates set for anything other than the 'massage fee'. It is up to the prostitute to negotiate the terms and limits of the exchange once alone with the client, and, in practice, both prostitute and client often haggle over the set rates. [...] Since it is quite possible for prostitutes to end up owing money to the owner at the end of a shift, there is often a very powerful pressure on the prostitute to enter into transactions that are either dangerous or underpriced (or both) in order to cover the shift fee and receptionist's pay. [...]

## The Genelev system in Turkey

In Turkey, prostitution is regulated by commissions for the prevention of venereal diseases and prostitution, which are established in each municipality, and prostitutes are controlled as a distinct class of persons. They are denied free movement and required to register with the commissions, undergo medical checks and so on. Once registered, 'they exchange the identity card carried by every ordinary citizen for special ones identifying them as prostitutes' (Bindman, 1997, p. 25). Brothel keeping is not illegal providing it conforms with the 126 articles laid down in the decree entitled *Statutes Concerning the Prostitutes,*

*Regulations which Brothels will Comply with, and the Prevention of the Infectious Venereal Diseases Resulting from Prostitution* (Willey, 1993, p. 15). These articles are designed, among other things, to ensure that brothel keepers are licensed, to regulate the physical location and environment of brothels, to oblige brothel keepers to exercise certain control functions on behalf of the state (such as notifying the police within twenty-four hours if a prostitute has moved brothel, failed to go for required medical checks, or failed to register with the commission), to prevent the prostitution of minors in brothels, and to compel brothel keepers to pay fees and taxes (Willey, 1993, p. 16). A common form of brothel prostitution in Turkey is referred to as a *genelev*, which is:

> a walled off complex in or near a town which consists of a number of houses where prostitutes work ... These licensed brothel complexes are all privately owned, very often by a group of proprietors; or a single proprietor may own one or two houses within a particular complex.
>
> (Willey, 1993, p. 9).

In the past, *genelev* prostitutes are believed to have been effectively confined in brothels by debt, but it is thought that most now enter them 'voluntarily' and are technically free to leave at will (Bindman, 1997). *Genelev* proprietors typically exercise close control over the work rate of the prostitutes they exploit. Women interviewed by Anti-Slavery International researchers stated that they worked a twelve-hour day and entered into transactions with a minimum of ten customers daily and a maximum of fifty or sixty. They 'are not allowed to refuse a customer unless he requests services which are considered sexually deviant, or is drunk or violent' (Willey, 1993, p. 13). Rates are generally set by the brothel owner, and prostitutes receive:

> only 40 to 50 per cent of the set price paid at reception. Upstairs, the women bargain for tips, which are also shared with management ... In addition, a significant charge must be paid daily to the management for tea, electricity, water, paperwork and other overheads.
>
> (Bindman, 1997, pp. 25–6)

Again, the massive asymmetry of power between brothel proprietors and 'employed' prostitutes is a function of a range of social, economic, legal, political and ideological factors. The 'long-standing inequitable social and economic position of women in Turkish society ... severely restricts the average woman's opportunities to earn, especially in times of recession' (Willey, 1993, p. 26), and once a woman has started to prostitute in Turkey, it is not only extremely difficult for her to exit prostitution altogether, but also difficult for her to leave a particular brothel. This is first of all because prostitutes are treated as a distinct 'class' of persons, and as such are excluded from the social security system, and second because 'once a woman is a registered prostitute she will always be regarded as an outcast and if she leaves the *genelev* and tries to get another job she is bound to be found out as a former prostitute; her record will be checked against police files and she will be sacked immediately' (Willey, 1993, p. 29). The legal regulation of prostitution reflects and reproduces profoundly gender discriminatory social attitudes and practices, within which women who are deemed sexually 'impure' are completely marginalized. In such a context brothel owners can force prostitutes to accept a phenomenally high throughput of clients when demand escalates and can extract a large proportion of the surplus this policy generates. [. . .]

## The bar system in the Philippines

Prostitution is illegal in the Philippines, but since 1972 legal recognition has been given to those prostitutes deemed 'hospitality workers' (Chant and McIlwaine, 1995, p. 212). To attain this status the prostitute has to work from a designated bar or other establishment, and must also register at the social hygiene clinic (SHC), where she will be required to undergo a chest X-ray, smear and blood test. After this:

> she . . . receives a card indicating that she is clean and is required to report for a VD smear twice a month and a chest X-ray and AIDS test twice a year . . . The workers pay for the tests at the SHC themselves. If a smear is positive, the bar is contacted and the woman must report for treatment and stop working until she is cured.
> (Sturdevant and Stoltzfus, 1992, p. 45)

Bar brothels typically offer prostitutes direct employment, ostensibly as cashiers, waiters, go-go dancers or hostesses. However, the wages paid are either nominal or well below subsistence level, and employees are usually – but not invariably – expected to make up their income by entering into prostitution contracts with the bar's customers. These transactions are not normally executed on the premises of the brothel, but in a hotel room or other location of the client's choosing. The client is expected to pay what is known as a 'bar fine' before taking a prostitute from the bar for the night or a short time, and:

> Women earn primarily by commission on ladies' drinks and bar fines. A ladies' drink is a mixed drink that the customer buys for a woman when he wants to talk with her . . . In both cases, the woman receives a commission of less than half the cost . . . If a customer is not satisfied . . . he may ask for his money back from the bar fine. If the bar owner agrees, the bar fine is charged to the woman.
> (Sturdevant and Stoltzfus, 1992, p. 46)

Bar owners also impose fines on women for other 'misdemeanours', such as lateness, improper dress, and so on. This kind of close control is not exercised over the details of prostitute–client exchanges. Other than specifying a time limit to the transaction, the bar owner places no boundaries upon what the client can and cannot demand from the prostitute in exchange for the set bar fine. It is up to the prostitute to attempt to negotiate limits to the powers of command that are transferred to the client once alone with him. The loose and open contractual arrangement struck between bar owner and client places the prostitute at a massive disadvantage within her actual transactions with clients. Many clients assume that they have paid for powers of command that are limited *only* by time; in other words they assume that, within the set time period, they can do whatever they choose, as many times as they choose. If the prostitute contests this assumption, she may well find that the client complains to the bar owner and demands a refund. Very similar arrangements and power relations are to be found in bar brothels in Thailand and the Dominican Republic (O'Connell Davidson, 1995; O'Connell Davidson and Sánchez Taylor, 1996), and many of the hostess clubs which are to be found in most of the world's major cities are effectively brothels run along much the same lines as those described here.

[...] A high level of demand for prostitution was created first by the establishment of US military bases in the Philippines and then by a form of tourist development which capitalized on the existence of a well-established sex industry. Chant and McIlwaine (1995, p. 45) observe that, 'as of 1990, the Philippines had one of the lowest per capita GNPs (US$760) in the East Asia and Pacific region and was one of the most heavily indebted countries in the world', and such economic conditions, along with various other structural factors, ensure that a supply of women, children and men exists to meet this demand. [...] Non-registered prostitutes 'are illegal and therefore subject to arrest and imprisonment' (Sturdevant and Stoltzfus, 1992, p. 45), and the criminal law thus helps designated third parties virtually to monopolize the stream of demand, thereby constructing a huge asymmetry of power between prostitutes and 'employers'.

But, as ever, it is not merely economic and legal factors which empower third-party controllers of prostitution. Gender ideologies which devalue women in general and denigrate prostitute women in particular and which encourage men to abuse and neglect wives, partners and children help to construct the kind of personal biographies which underpin the entry of women and children into prostitution and their vulnerability within it. [...]


### 'Confined' brothel prostitution

It is probably true to say that in every country of the world there are instances of third parties who make money by prostituting individuals who are kept in conditions of confinement (by which I mean conditions that prevent exit from prostitution through the use of physical restraint, physical violence or the threat thereof, or through the threat of other non-economic sanctions, such as imprisonment or deportation). But there are also regions of the world where confinement is known to be more systematically used within prostitution. [...]

Individuals who are confined in brothels may be victims of abduction, entrapment or debt bondage. In many parts of Latin America, as well as South-East Asia and the Indian subcontinent, there are 'recruiting agents' who use the promise of employment to draw young people from impoverished rural areas into their power. Recruits may be promised work as domestics, bar staff or dancers in a city of their own country or abroad; others know that they will be working as prostitutes but do not realize they will be confined and otherwise abused by their 'employers'. Once they arrive at their destination they are either incarcerated and physically coerced into prostitution, or told that they owe the agent a large sum of money for the cost of their travel as well as other expenses which may have been advanced to them, and that this sum will have to be worked off through prostitution. Where individuals have been trafficked into confinement across national borders, their vulnerability in relation to the third party is usually further reinforced by the removal of their identity papers, by their status as undocumented migrants in the 'host' country, and by their complete isolation from all that is familiar.

Loans are also used as a means of securing 'labour', preventing voluntary exit from the brothel and ensuring the continuous production and appropriation of surplus, and this method can be more systematically employed by brothel keepers and procurers in regions of the world where artificially induced indebtedness is more widely used as a means of enslaving the rural poor. [...] While some debt bondees are condemned to what is effectively lifelong slavery (a condition frequently passed on to their children, who 'inherit' the parent's debt), others are bonded for a specified and limited time period, or (at least in theory) are paid wages which go towards the liquidation of the debt. [...]

Thailand and India are perhaps the best-known examples of countries where prostitution is one of several economic sectors in which workers may be subject to forms of debt bondage. [...] In India brothels are prohibited by the 1956 Suppression of Immoral Traffic Act, and debt bondage is officially outlawed by the 1933 Children (Pledging of Labour) Acts and the 1976 Bonded Labour System (Abolition) Act, yet both the general phenomenon of debt bondage and the more particular one of debt-bonded prostitution persist (Sawyer, 1986; Fyfe, 1989; Singh, 1989). [...]

In Thailand both prostitution and debt bondage are also officially outlawed, and yet there are many prostitutes who are bonded to brothel owners through debt. [...] Agents recruit in the desperately poor regions of Thailand and/or travel across borders into Laos, Burma, China and Cambodia (Phongpaichit, 1982; Asia Watch, 1993; Ren, 1993; Hengkietisak, 1994; GAATW, 1997).

[...]

## Power, oppression, the subject and the law

My purpose has been to provide a series of examples which highlight the fact that brothel prostitutes can be subject to a range of different types of compulsion to conform to brothel owners' wishes, that within this they can be subject to those pressures to different degrees, and that the types and degree of compulsion to which prostitutes are exposed are powerfully affected by broader, structural features of the society in which they are prostituted. Here, I want briefly to make some more general points about power and oppression in prostitution.

### Idioms of power

It has been seen that brothel owners who control confined prostitutes can and do exercise direct forms of personalistic power over those they exploit, and very often physical force, or the threat of it, is used to subjugate prostitutes to their will. However, those who exploit confined prostitutes also often include economic sanctions and incentives in their repertoire of 'labour discipline', and this, I would argue, tells us something about the relational nature of power. A number of theorists have pointed out that, even where huge asymmetries of power between two people or groups of people exist, other than by murdering them it is impossible for the powerful party *actually* to transform their subordinates from subjects to objects or to eradicate their free will (see Sartre, 1966; Giddens, 1984; Layder, 1997). The human subject of power can, in the final instance, (almost) always choose death in place of submission. This fact is, of course, of small comfort to those who are the victims of the most extreme forms of oppression, but it *is* significant for the oppressor in terms of the control strategies he or she chooses to adopt.

Given that psychological responses to the trauma of being either sold or kidnapped or held hostage, then serially raped, include extreme forms of anxiety and withdrawal, thoughts of suicide, and so on, it is reasonable to assume that brothel owners use economic sanctions and 'incentives' partly because of the normalizing and legitimizing effect they can have upon abuse. If a person is told that they are working off $x$ sum from their debt or that they will receive $x$ sum every time they submit to sexual violation, then their desire to be free of debt or to have money on which to live or perhaps escape starts to take on the appearance of consent to their sexual violation. Equally, the relationship between captor and captive takes on a new aspect when the captor apparently pays, charges and fines the victim according to set rates, rather than abusing in an arbitrary and wholly unpredictable fashion. It begins to seem that the victim has some control, no matter how minuscule, over her fate. [. . .]

Clearly, it is in the brothel owner's interests to manipulate the subjective experience of captive prostitutes in this way. If such prostitutes accept their condition as a legitimate form of servitude or work, they are less likely to resist through escape or suicide and so require less surveillance, and they are more likely to co-operate with the brothel owner's attempts to maximize the throughput of clients. This reduces the costs associated with the process of generating and extracting surplus. [. . .] Better to induce both hope and despair in proportions that encourage compliance, to offer hope of redemption in the form of remuneration for co-operation, then claw back some or all of the payment in the form of charges for subsistence, fines for 'misbehaviour' and the like.

Just as it is important to recognize that confined prostitutes are subject to power in both its materialistic and personalistic idiom, so we should note that those who are not technically confined by brothel keepers can sometimes be physically coerced, as well as being under an economic compulsion, to conform to a given regime. It is known, for example, that Mafia-like criminal organizations are involved in trafficking women from Eastern to Western European countries, and, though brothels in the latter are not usually operated by these organizations, women exploited therein can be under Mafiosi control. They may therefore be compelled to work by the threat of violence, even death (Eurofile, BBC Radio 4, 22 November 1997; Butler, 1997). [. . .] There are contexts in which the employed prostitute's dependence upon one particular employer is so great that the employer's freedom to employ various violent and / or intimidatory tactics of control is almost as great as it would be if the prostitutes were formally bonded to them in some way.

Although some brothel keepers provide prostitutes in their employ with a degree of protection from abusive clients, they do not always take precautions or action to protect the physical safety of the prostitutes they exploit. *Genelev* prostitutes report frequent incidents of being beaten up by clients (Willey, 1993), something which could easily be avoided if the brothel owners took even elementary steps to protect them; escort-agency workers report agency owners who fail even to keep records of violent or abusive clients; and the organization of many English massage parlours leaves prostitutes vulnerable to attack. Nor can brothel keepers be relied upon to insist that the client fulfils his obligations to the prostitute or to intervene to ensure that the client respects certain limits to the contract or that clients observe safer sex precautions. Prostitutes who are most exploited and most unfree in relation to third parties and clients are the least able to insist upon condom use as a condition of contract, enforce that condition and freely retract if the client refuses to comply, and are therefore the most at risk of contracting AIDS and other STDs. This helps to explain the findings of research which concludes that 'Thirty per cent of Bombay's 100,000 prostitutes, who serve a combined average of 400,000 clients per day, are HIV positive. Thirty per cent of Thailand's 800,000 prostitutes are infected with HIV' (Le and Williams, 1996, p. 244).

[...]

### Power and the law

While the types and degrees of compulsion which operate on brothel prostitutes vary, formally organized, third-party controlled prostitution always and necessarily implies constraints upon prostitutes' freedoms. [...] I want to conclude by noting that, vital as it is to campaign for an end to legal discrimination against prostitutes, such campaigns cannot and will not put a stop to the oppression involved in prostitution. [...]

### References

Asia Watch, 1993: *A Modern Form of Slavery: trafficking of Burmese girls and women in Thailand*. New York: Women's Rights Project of Asia Watch.
Barry, K., 1995: *The Prostitution of Sexuality*. New York: New York University Press.
Bindman, J., 1997: *Redefining Prostitution as Sex Work on the International Agenda*. London: Anti-Slavery International.
Butler, K., 1997: Tricked, beaten and sold as a sex slave – the diary of Mia, aged 14. *Independent on Sunday*, 12 October.
Chant, S. and McIlwaine, C., 1995: *Women of a Lesser Cost: female labour, foreign exchange and Philippine development*. London: Pluto Press.
Dixon, R., 1988: *Production, Distribution and Value: a Marxian approach*. Brighton: Wheatsheaf.
Edwards, S., 1987: Prostitutes: victims of law, social policy and organized crime. In P. Carlen and A. Worrall (eds), *Gender, Crime and Justice*. Milton Keynes: Open University Press.

Edwards, S., 1993: England and Wales. In N. Davis (ed.), *Prostitution*. Westport, CT: Greenwood Press.

Fyfe, A., 1989: *Child Labour*. Cambridge: Polity.

GAATW, 1997: *Newsletter*, 7, April–June. Bangkok: Global Alliance Against Traffic in Women.

Giddens, A., 1984: *The Constitution of Society*. Cambridge: Polity.

Hengkietisak, K., 1994: A green harvest of a different kind. *Bangkok Post*, 20 March, p. 17.

Layder, D., 1997: *Modern Social Theory: key debates and new directions*. London: University College.

Le, N. and Williams, D., 1996: Social factors and knowledge of HIV / AIDS in Vietnam. In J. Subedi and E. Gallagher (eds), *Society, Health and Disease*. Upper Saddle River, NJ: Prentice Hall.

McLeod, E., 1982: *Working Women: prostitution now*. London: Croom Helm.

O'Connell Davidson, J., 1995: British sex tourists in Thailand. In M. Maynard and J. Purvis (eds), *(Hetero)Sexual Politics*. London: Taylor & Francis.

O'Connell Davidson, J. and Sánchez Taylor, J., 1996: *Child Sexual Exploitation in the Dominican Republic*. Bangkok: ECPAT.

Pateman, C., 1988: *The Sexual Contract*. Cambridge: Polity.

Perkins, R., 1995: Alleged trafficking of Asian sex workers in Australia. *Prostitutes Education Network*. <http: / / www.bayswan.org / Austraf.html>.

Phoenix, J., 1995: Prostitution: problematizing the definition. In M. Maynard and J. Purvis (eds), *(Hetero)Sexual Politics*. London: Taylor & Francis.

Phongpaichit, P., 1982: *From Peasant Girls to Bangkok Masseuses*. Geneva: International Labour Office.

Ren, X., 1993: China. In N. Davis (ed.), *Prostitution*. Westport, CT: Greenwood Press.

Sartre, J. P., 1966: *Being and Nothingness*. London: Methuen.

Sawyer, R., 1986: *Slavery in the Twentieth Century*. London: Routledge & Kegan Paul.

Singh, S., 1989: *Exploited Children in India*. Calcutta: Shila Singh.

Smart, C., 1995: *Law, Crime and Sexuality*. London: Sage.

Sturdevant, S. and Stoltzfus, B., 1992: *Let the Good Times Roll: prostitution and the US military in Asia*. New York: New Press.

Truong, T., 1990: *Sex, Money and Morality: prostitution and tourism in Southeast Asia*. London: Zed Books.

Willey, P., 1993: *Forced Prostitution in Turkey*. London: Anti-Slavery International.

# 19

# Sex and the Open Market

## Harriet Evans

The 1980s market reforms in China put into acute relief a fundamental paradox in the relationship between the state and women. As the state intensified its intervention in women's lives – their choices, their bodies, their identities – through its fertility limitation programme, its disengagement from total control over labour, land and markets created new spaces for the construction of women as commodities for sale – and often violent abuse – on the open market. The commercialization of women for their sexual value has many different facets, from the banal use of pretty women to advertise fashions and domestic appliances to the violation of women's basic rights to bodily integrity. In particular, the violent abduction and sale of young women and girls into marriage, concubinage and prostitution have caught the headlines of the national and international press in recent years. Such 'feudal practices', as they are often described, have been reported in every province of China. [...] If these abuses of women's rights seem to mirror pre-revolutionary practices in a changed socio-economic context, other forms of commercial appropriation of women's bodies are more immediately associated with China's new market environment. The production and trafficking of pornographic materials is a thriving business in many parts of China, aided, according to many accounts, by the international trading opportunities offered by the open-door policy. Prostitution also flourishes throughout China, in as wide a variety of forms as is suggested by the market disparities between wealth and poverty. The increasing incidence of rape and other sexual crimes against women is also widely associated with the impact on social and sexual behaviour of the commercialization of sex. As in other instances of the violation of women's rights, extensive media coverage is given both to the sufferings of the victims and to the punishment of the offenders.

The different constitutions of female sexuality implicit in the uses and abuses of women's bodies encouraged by commercial opportunity converge in a number of important aspects. They all represent women's sexuality in some way or other as being available for male consumption, whether as an item to be purchased on the market or as a body to be brutalized. The women in such representations appear either as vulnerable victims or as wilful examples of moral turpitude – on the one hand, whose condition has arisen out of ignorance, and, on the other, whose victimization is the consequence of deliberate non-conformity to the dominant sexual order. [...] The lack of an adequate gender analysis to explain these representations effectively perpetuates the naturalized construction of women as dependent subjects or as dangerous perpetrators of social chaos.

## Women for sale

'Marriage by sale' (*maimai hunyin*) – the term used by the communist authorities to denote a marriage that was 'arranged or coerced by a third party for the purpose of obtaining property' (Ocko 1991, 321) – and other venal practices involved in the negotiations of marriage were outlawed by the 1950 Marriage Law.[1] In particular, the law targeted those who demanded a bride-price or gifts as a condition for agreeing to the marriage of their daughter (Meijer 1971, 172). However, despite claims to have eradicated such 'feudal' anachronisms, and assertions that the collective structures of production and distribution in the countryside had destroyed the economic rationale sustaining the exaction of goods in relation to marriage, the 'buying and selling of wives continued' (Ocko 1991, 320–1); the multiple interests sustaining marriage as an economic transaction between households and families were temporarily obscured, rather than eliminated, by the collective structures of the previous two decades. [...] In conditions of extreme poverty and geographical isolation, where marriage is near universal and where surname exogamy and virilocal marriage are standard practices, the procedures of marriage can be demanding and economically crippling. Some physical or mental disability might further impair a person's marriageability. The 'sale' of daughters may represent a means for poor parents to finance a son's marriage as well as a last-resort response to economic deprivation.[2] However, a survey of venal marriage practices commonly found in rural areas suggested that [...] contrary to the widely held assumption that 'feudal' customs victimize mainly the uneducated and the underprivileged from the countryside, increasing numbers of the women and children affected come from the urban sector, and include students and foreigners as well as unemployed workers. [...]

Extensive media publicity has been given to the abduction and sale of women in recent years. Articles in the national press publish details of the numbers of women released from captivity, and of gangsters executed for their crimes, often specifying the age and education of those involved. Though there are major loopholes in legislation against the kidnapping of women, figures are often produced to testify to the government's commitment to eradicating this brutal abuse of women's rights. In 1991 and 1992 alone, according to police statistics, 50,000 cases of abduction of women and children were reportedly solved, and 75,000 people connected with the traffic were arrested (*Survey of China Mainland Press*, 5 November 1993). [...] Descriptions of the conditions in which women are kept, and the violent abuse to which they are subjected by their husbands and husbands' relatives, are also common. Horrifying accounts of individual women's experiences are published as warnings to unsuspecting young women whose innocence may lead them to make fatal decisions. Alternatively, disguised as legal case histories for the education of the readers, they are specifically designed for their sensationalist value.[3]

[...]

The rural–urban opposition invoked in contemporary Chinese discourses about social and cultural matters is a frequent metaphor for backwardness and feudal tradition on the one hand, and modernity, progress and development on the other. The inscription of this opposition in the figure of the abducted women functions as a clear marker distinguishing the wiser, better-educated and urban women from their innocent and ignorant rural cousins. In these contexts, woman becomes a signifier for all that is categorized as 'backward' by the exponents of market reform.

[...]

Media reports about the re-emergence of the abduction and sale of women give a privileged place to the socio-economic factors involved. Rural poverty, lack of education, urban employment opportunities, and marketization of the economy are the conditions generally emphasized in explaining this particular form of gender exploitation. Little space is given to the argument that the continued abuse of women's basic rights in this particular form is grounded in hierarchical gender structures and ideologies. [...] The attribution of the practice to the pernicious influence of history effectively invalidates the view that, as an aspect of gendered power relations, it is also produced and sustained by structures and discourses situated in the current, radically different socio-economic context. The significance of gender in analysing this particular form of gender subjugation is obscured by a discursive emphasis on the primacy of socio-economic factors.

[...]

## Prostitution

'China is a country that once proclaimed that it had eradicated prostitution and venereal disease . . . Thirty years passed and to their astonishment people discover that prostitution has revived and that sexual diseases are once again spreading, at an alarming speed' (Wang Xingjuan 1992, 420). The assumptions embedded in this comment, made by one of China's pioneer researchers in prostitution and female crime, are common to many contemporary views about the history and recent resurgence of prostitution in China. According to these, the early years of the People's Republic, the period when prostitution was largely eliminated, was a time when purity of spirit was reflected in unimpeachable morals, and when ordinary women and men shared at least some of the collective ideals extolled in official rhetoric. By contrast, the reappearance of prostitution in the past fifteen years is identified with policies and practices legitimizing individual desire over collective commitment within a context of flourishing commercial opportunity. [. . .]

Within little more than two months of the founding of the PRC, a series of measures outlawing prostitution adopted by the central communist authorities resulted in the closure of some 220 brothels in the capital, the 'salvation' (jiejiu) of 1,200 prostitutes and the sentencing of more than three hundred brothel owners and pimps (Wang Xingjuan 1992, 420). By 1951, similar actions had been taken in Shanghai, the thriving centre of China's sex industry, resulting in the 'salvation' of more than 7,000 prostitutes. [. . .] By 1958, when the eradication of prostitution in Shanghai was announced, prostitution was already presented to the public as a practice of the feudal past. The culminating act indicating the success of the official onslaught on the 'system of prostitution' was the declaration in 1964 that, with the closure of the country's last hospital for venereal diseases in Shanghai, venereal diseases no longer existed in China (Quanguo renda changweihui fazhi gongzuo weiyuanhui xingfa shi 1991, 1).

Since the early years of the post-Mao reform programme, prostitution has once again caught the authorities' attention. According to official figures, between 1986 and 1990 the numbers engaged in prostitution increased fourfold over the previous five years, despite repeated crackdowns and police raids (Quanguo renda changweihui fazhi gongzuo weiyuanhui xingfa shi 1991, 12). [. . .] Not only has prostitution continued to flourish, particularly in the commercial zones of the south and southeast, but its social composition has expanded. A publication explaining the clauses of the 1991 Decision on the Prohibition of Prostitution contained the following view: 'In the past, [prostitutes] came principally from the unemployed and the poorly educated; a few were foreign. But now, in addition to these, employees from state, collective and private enterprises, party and state, cadres, intellectuals, science and technology personnel, and even university students and researchers, are becoming prostitutes' (Quanguo renda changweihui fazhi gongzuo weiyuanhui xingfa shi 1991, 12). [. . .] Recent evidence suggests that increasing numbers of educated and upwardly mobile young women are joining the sex trade, since prostitution offers more lucrative prospects than the relatively meagre incomes afforded by other professions. [. . .]

The changing social composition of sex work in recent years has introduced new elements into public discussion. Dominant representations now clearly situate prostitution as an aspect of the aspirations and practices encouraged by the commercial possibilities of the market economy. Prostitution is a symbol of both the possibilities and the dangers of modernity. Though the rural background of the majority of sex workers may suggest a different story, young women who become prostitutes are commonly described as well educated, with aspirations for a university education and travel abroad.[4] They are also invariably described as urban-based, with easy access to the economic opportunities offered by the private sector. Indeed, their introduction into sex work is frequently associated with their access to private entrepreneurs (geti hu). However, the prostitute also emerges as a sign for the moral dangers associated with commercialization. [...] Some commentators have argued that, since the women who become prostitutes are 'not without employment, nor are they poor, and even less are they the target of social disdain and oppression', the main reasons explaining their position is 'first and foremost [the fact that they are] morally degenerate (*daode zhuiluozhe*), and secondly that they are individualistic pleasure seekers' (Kang Shuhua, Liu Lanpu and Zhao Ke 1988, 55). The appropriation of the prostitute for the purposes of moral control is also apparent in the view that the recent increase in prostitution is an aspect of the corrupting influence of 'sexual liberation' from abroad (Kang Shuhua, Liu Lanpu and Zhao Ke 1988, 155–7; *Gongren ribao* sixiang jiaoyu bu 1983, 38–9). Indeed, the entire programme of moral and ideological education which prostitutes are obliged to undergo as part of their rehabilitation is premised on the supposition that, as prostitutes, their outlook has been tainted by undesirable tendencies. The idea that 'sex work' might be a legitimate form of employment that should enjoy the same legal and social status as any other is, by definition, excluded from this construction.

[...]

The visibility of prostitution in Chinese society has brought with it fears about physical as well as moral contamination. References to prostitution rarely fail to include some warning note about sexually transmitted diseases, often by pointing out the percentage of prostitutes affected. The link made between disease and prostitution underlies the control of prostitution as one of the key features of government policies to monitor and reduce the spread of STDs and AIDS. Legal regulations introduced in 1991 permit specific penalties for women for working as prostitutes if they have a sexually transmitted disease. [...] The dangers of prostitution are, by extension, also linked to eugenic considerations. Much in the terms used by the social reformers of the 1930s, who linked venereal disease with gruesome consequences for the individual, family and 'race' (Dikötter 1995, 126–37), the evil of prostitution is thought to derive from its capacity to attack the health of the nation – 'the health of our sons' and grandsons' generations' – as much as from its threat to the social and moral order (Wang Xingjuan 1992, 421).

[...]

### Yellow materials

Immediately after its violent suppression of the 1989 democracy movement, the government launched a nationwide campaign against the 'six evils', one objective of which was to 'sweep away the yellow' (*sao huang*) and rid society of pornographic materials.[5] The timing of the campaign was not coincidental; as the state tried to convince the public of the legitimacy of its actions, it sought to vilify the political arguments of its opponents by linking them with the erosion of moral standards. The proliferation of 'social ills' in China was in large part the result of the 'open-door policy' and the invitation it gave to unmonitored influences from beyond China's borders. The circulation of pornographic materials was thus explicitly linked with the bourgeois potential within Chinese society – represented particularly by the young supporters of the democracy movement – and the commercial infiltration of salacious influences from abroad. [...] Considerable publicity has also been given to the legal penalties faced by producers and distributors of pornographic materials. In an article about the effects of 'sexual publications' on their audience, Pan Suiming noted that at least twenty persons were put to death in 1989 for selling pornographic materials (Pan Suiming 1993, 59). [...]

Discussion about pornography in China is complicated by problems of definition. Official texts commonly apply the term 'yellow' to all visual, written and audio materials that explicitly describe sexual behaviour. Hence 'yellow' materials can include the erotic images of women found in the fashion advertisements of women's magazines as well as the pornographic videos sold on the black market. [...] Works of art that contain sexually explicit images may also be condemned as pornographic; as far as the censors are concerned, aesthetic distinctions do not apply to representations of the human body. [...]

State control of representations of the sexualized body has been a consistent aspect of official discourses on sexuality since 1949. Between the 1950s and the late 1970s, any reference, whether narrative or visual, to explicitly erotic interests was subject to stringent censorship. [...]

Since the early 1980s, however, the marketization of the economy has given a new public prominence to sex, and pornographic publications flourish on the black market. Thus, although during the Cultural Revolution pornographic materials circulated clandestinely, particularly among young people in the towns and cities, it has only been since the introduction of the post-Mao reforms that pornography has become an issue of explicit official concern. The government's response to the prevalence of erotically suggestive images has veered between bans on the importation of 'yellow' materials and crackdowns on those involved in the domestic pornographic industry. [...]

The official objection to representations of the sexualized body depends on a simple categorization of the images of the naked, invariably female, body as a source of moral corruption and shame, regardless of the place or narrative context within which it appears, and regardless of the different meanings that the viewer might read into it. Without clothes, the female body must be banned, despite the sexualized meanings that might be inscribed in fashion photographs of the clothed female body; it is the perpetrator of depravity and danger. Such a position makes no distinction between hard pornography, in which women's bodies are subjects of physical brutality as well as sexual titillation, and images of the female body which are constructed for aesthetic purposes. Nor is it accompanied by any critical discussion about the gender and social issues involved in the production and consumption of pornographic materials. Indeed, the official ban on pornographic materials seems only incidentally to have anything to do with women and hierarchical gender relations. [...] The 'yellow female' thus emerges as a generic signifier of degeneration, vulgarity and criminality. The failure to approach pornography as a gender issue, rather than as an issue of social morality and control, reinforces the negative attributes, already widely represented in public images, associated with female gender and sexuality.

## Rape and sexual violence

After years of very scant media coverage, sexual violence against women has recently become a prominent issue of public debate, in large part inspired by the debates that took place in the run-up to the Fourth UN Conference on Women held in Beijing in September 1995. Unofficial women's groups have pointed out that the international focus on women in 1995 gave them their first opportunity to bring the issue into the public arena. Discussions have begun to focus on women's experiences and difficulties in reporting rape that signify a qualitative difference from the more distanced, 'factual' reporting of the mid-1980s. However, government publications indicate that the issue of sexual violence against women has been a significant – though maybe not prime – concern for the past decade or so. In August 1983, as alarm about the rate of sexual crimes began to penetrate official bodies, the government took the decision to identify rape as one of the most serious. Accordingly, the criminal law identified different categories of rape which carried sentences of varying severity. Rape 'by violence, coercion, or other means' carried three to ten years' imprisonment. Sexual relations with children under the age of fourteen was categorized as rape, 'and is to be given a heavier punishment'. 'Especially serious circumstances', when rape involves a 'person's injury or death', and cases of multiple and gang rapes carried life imprisonment or even the death sentence (Article 139). Liu Dalin estimated that the incidence of rape showed an increase of 345 per cent between 1979 and 1983, a significant proportion of which was committed by juveniles (Liu Dalin 1987). Official statistics of the late 1980s showed that, in terms of numbers of cases reported according to categories of crime, rape was second only to robbery, with reported instances rising in the spring and summer months (Wang Ranji et al. 1990, 3). Figures for domestic violence, including wife battering and sexual abuse, also indicate an increase, leading to public discussion of questions like 'Is the family a special zone of violence?' (Chen Huilin 1984, 26).

Media coverage of rape cases in recent years suggests varying analyses of its causes and effects. Condemnation of rape and other forms of sexual violence frequently accompanies reports about the 'feudal' maltreatment of women, alongside their abduction and sale into marriage and prostitution. Alternatively, it is explained as a result of the social dislocation engendered by reform policies, and as a significant factor in a large proportion of murder and assault cases (Amnesty International 1995, 2). [...]

[...] While the popular press doubtless derives considerable financial gain from publishing detailed accounts, often semi-fictionalized, of rape cases, other publications have a more didactic and moralistic purpose. A main objective of many such reports, for example, often noted in an introductory paragraph, is to warn young women of the perils of mixing with certain types of people, of indulging in certain fashions and leisure activities, or of entertaining upwardly mobile social aspirations. Many accounts seek to expose the inefficiency and unwillingness of local authorities to investigate rape cases, and to criticize the pressures and interests which effectively prevent young women from reporting rape to the authorities. [...]

Many reports, however, leave the reader with a somewhat ambivalent understanding of the principles on which accusations are made. Indeed, even when a commentator's ostensible purpose is to expose discriminatory attitudes, the narrative techniques used in describing the details of a particular case may suggest otherwise. A typical mode of this is the narrative use of personal characteristics – appearance, marital status, sexual history – of the victimized woman to contextualize the description of a case. Descriptions of 'a dark slippery road' along which an unsuspecting young woman walks 'in high heels' give a particular framework to accounts of resistance against an assailant, which implicates the woman in responsibility for her own misfortune (Jia Zheng 1987). [...] The appearance of words like 'error' or 'mistake' (*cuo*) to describe women's role in being raped further suggests the lingering influence of notions of female guilt. [...]

There is a prominent contrast in these articles between the attention given to describing the personal attributes and responsibilities of the victim and the lack of interest in formulating a gender analysis of rape. [...] Few articles approach sexual violence against women in terms which challenge the gender hierarchy represented in the dominant discourse of sexuality. Simple comments to the effect that a rapist enjoyed reading pornographic materials, or that he had no knowledge of sex education, or that his parents had not brought him up properly, hardly compensate for this lack. Nor do general comments that seek explanations for rape in, for example, the social disruption caused by the Cultural Revolution, or the pressures of living in a rapidly changing social environment in the late 1980s.

One explanation for this lack lies in the reluctance of party-state institutions to undertake any serious gender analysis except in contexts that are deemed to have a significant bearing on economic and political developments. Considerable official attention has been devoted to women's education, employment and migration, health and childcare, and so on. However, analyses of women's disadvantaged position in all these areas have tended to focus on factors such as the lack of resources, inequalities in development and population pressure rather than on gender – even though, in both its construction and effects, gender necessarily intersects with other discourses. Discussion about gender issues considered to have only a tenuous relationship to the broader, more pressing matters of economic and social development – sexual violence, abduction of women, the increase in venal marriage practices, and female infanticide, to name but a few – is often subsumed under general categories such as 'social ills'. Even in cases such as female infanticide, where the issue of sexual discrimination is at its most basic, substantive analysis of the gender issues involved continues to be secondary to the imperatives of population control. In line with these general approaches, discussion about rape is oriented either to the elucidation of general problems of social order or to the inadequacies of the legal system and the public's legal understanding. Suggestions that rape might be avoided if women were less ingenuous and ignorant do not really contribute much to a gender analysis.

Recent debate about non-consensual sex within marriage represents a contestation of this position. In the early 1980s, the definition of rape set out in the legal press included coercive sex between betrothed and divorced couples, but it did not include rape within marriage. [...] Liu Dalin, however, pointed out that rape and sexual abuse in marriage is quite widespread, and commonly coincides with the husband's assumption that his wife is his sexual property. Liu Dalin further cited evidence from divorce cases brought before the courts to argue that, while women commonly assume that sexual intercourse is a wifely duty, whether they want it or not, increasing numbers of women are expressing their dissatisfaction with an abusive relationship (Liu Dalin 1992, 425, 599–600). In defence of the category of marital rape, one commentator wrote that 'sexual autonomy [means] the right to voluntarily participate in and refuse sexual relations. Today's imbalance in sexual relations is principally manifested in a depreciation and lack of respect for a woman's sexual rights' (Song Meiya 1991). [...]

The brutal lives that countless numbers of women and men live in every part of the world defy representation. That girls and women are killed, abandoned, abducted, sold, raped, violently abused, commodified and objectified for their sex alone reinforces the difficulties of representation. Many of the issues examined in this essay constitute a terrible violation of women's basic rights to physical and sexual integrity. However, little of the publicity given to the crimes against women affords any indication of the extent and the depth of the brutality suffered. The figures the government produces for numbers of criminals executed or sentenced for rape or abduction provide little indication of an attempt to analyse the gender issues at stake in the abuse of women's rights. Although the government repeatedly declares its commitment to eradicating crimes enacted against women on the grounds of their sex, this cannot compensate for the horrific wounds women suffer for the simple fact that they are female.

The above analysis – brief though it is – shows that there is a very limited field of meanings associated with being female in recent discussions about gender and sexual violence against women. Women are represented as guileless victims, taken in by good looks and power, or motivated by social and material aspirations. Representing women as either the victims of patriarchal structures of power or as malicious perpetrators of disease and degeneration caricatures the realities of women's lives. The subject positions constructed for women here neither coincide with those identified by real live women nor grant any space for women's own voices. [...]

The most disturbing aspect of such representations is the disjuncture between the repeated brutality against women and the government's failure to extend any real gender analysis of the realities involved. The government has consistently ignored the gender issues present in the commercial and violent abuse of women, defining them instead as social, economic or moral issues. The condemnation of prostitution, pornography and sexual crime is part of an official discourse that is moulded more by moralistic assumptions about sexual propriety, women's in particular, than by an understanding of gender hierarchy. Official statements situate the policy of suppressing prostitution within an ideological framework which views the feudal past and the bourgeois present as a dual repository of depravity and corruption. While a rhetoric of gender equality continues to establish the parameters within which discussion about women takes place, standard analyses of commercial practices which exploit women neglect the crucial function of gender hierarchies of power in favour of generally articulated ideological injustices.

## Notes

1    For a brief review of the literature on the different kinds of monetary transaction that marked the entry of wives, concubines and maids into a household in the Hong Kong region in the early part of this century, see Watson 1991, 239–41.
2    The sale of daughters as concubines and as maids (Watson 1991, 231–55) into the despised 'minor marriages' and as domestic slaves (*mutsai*) (Jaschok and Miers 1994) represented some of the alternatives available to families who could not sustain the appropriate bridal costs.
3    This genre of writing, known as *fazhi wenxue* (legal literature), provides a common outlet for sensationalist and pornographic materials, often exploited by ordinary publishing companies for profit.
4    These descriptions abound in a series of interviews Liu Xiaocong held with prostitutes sent to reform through education camps (Liu Xiaocong 1991).
5    Launched in August 1989, the campaign against the 'six evils' targeted pornography, prostitution, gambling, drugs, abduction and selling of women and children, and profiteering from superstition.

## References

Amnesty International (1995), *Women in China*. London: Amnesty International.

Chen Huilin (1984), 'Jiating shi baoli tequ ma?' (Is the family a special zone of violence?), *Zhongguo funu* (Women in China) 12, 26–9.

Dikötter, Frank (1995), *Sex, Culture and Modernity in China*. London: Hurst.

*Gongren ribao* sixiang jiaoyu bu (1983) (Thought and Education Department of the *Workers' Daily*), *Aiqing, hunyin, daode* (Love, marriage, morality). Beijing: Gongren chubanshe.

Jaschok, Maria and Miers, Suzanne, eds (1994), *Women and Chinese Patriarchy: Submission, Servitude and Escape*. London: Zed Books.

Jia Zheng (1987), 'Dang tamen miandui qiangbao de shihou' (When they [women] come face to face with violence), *Zhongguo funu* (Women in China) 3, 26–7.

Kang Shuhua, Liu Lanpu and Zhao Ke (1988), *Nüxing fanzui lun* (On female crime). Lanzhou: Lanzhou daxue chubanshe.

Liu Dalin (1987), 'Xingkexue yu funü jiefang' (Sexology and women's liberation), *Shehui kexue zhanxian* 1, 120–5.

Liu Dalin, ed. (1992), *Zhongguo dangdai xing wenhua – Zhongguo liangwan li 'xing wenming' diaocha baogao* (Sexual behaviour in modern China – a report of the 'sex civilization' survey on 20,000 subjects in China). Shanghai: Sanlian shudian.

Liu Xiaocong (1991), 'Maiyin funü xintai lu' (Records of prostitutes' state of mind), *Nuxing yanjiu* (Women's studies research) 3, 12–15; 4, 15–17.

Meijer, M. J. (1971), *Marriage Law and Policy in the People's Republic of China*. Hong Kong: Hong Kong University Press.

Ocko, Jonathan K. (1991), 'Women, property and law in the People's Republic of China', in Rubie S. Watson and Patricia Buckley Ebrey, eds, *Marriage and Inequality in Chinese Society*. Berkeley: University of California Press, 313–46.

Pan Suiming (1993), 'China: acceptability and effect of three kinds of sexual publication', *Archives of Sexual Behaviour* 22, 1, 59–71.

Quanguo renda changweihui fazhi gongzuo weiyuanhui xingfa shi (The Criminal Law Office of the Legal Work Committee of the Standing Committee of the National People's Congress) (1991), *Guanyu yan jin maiyin piaochang de jueding, Guanyu yan cheng guaimai bangjia funü ertong de fanzui fenzi de jueding* (Decisions on strictly prohibiting prostitution and decisions on strictly punishing criminals who abduct and kidnap women and children). Beijing: Zhongguo jiancha chubanshe.

Song Meiya (1991), 'Yi zhuang zhangfu qiangjian qizi an' (A case of marital rape), *Zhongguo funu* (Women in China) 1, 14–15.

Wang Ranji, Zhang Zhiyou, Cui Jin and Wan Chun (1990), *Qiangjian zui de rending yu fangzhi* (Defining and preventing the crime of rape). Beijing: Zhongguo huaqiao chubanshe.

Wang Xingjuan (1992), 'Guanyu maiyin piaochang wenti de yanjiu' (Research on the problem of prostitution), in Xiong Yumei, Liu Xiaocong and Qu Wen, eds, *Zhongguo funü lilun yanjiu shi nian* (Ten years of theoretical studies of Chinese women). Beijing: Zhongguo funü chubanshe, 420–41.

Watson, Rubie S. (1991), 'Wives, concubines and maids: servitude and kinship in the Hong Kong region, 1900–1940', in Rubie S. Watson and Patricia Buckley Ebrey, eds, *Marriage and Inequality in Chinese Society*. Berkeley and Los Angeles: University of California Press, 231–55.

Zhang Ping (1992), *Kuang fu yuan nü: daling weihun wenti toushi* (Carefree bachelors and worried spinsters: a perspective on the problem of the older unmarrieds). Xi'an: Shaanxi renmin jiaoyu chubanshe.

# 20

# Negotiating Reproductive Rights*

*Rosalind Petchesky*

Although the origin of the term 'reproductive rights' may be traced to movements
that initially surfaced in North America and Europe, similar yet distinct movements on behalf of women's reproductive health and rights rapidly formed
during the early-to-mid 1980s in Latin America and the Caribbean, Asia and
Africa.[1] As Garcia-Moreno and Claro (1994:48) have observed, while the principles embedded in reproductive and sexual rights are often labelled a byproduct
of Western culture, this view distorts both history and the varieties and local
roots of feminist movements: 'While Western ideas have played a role, women in
Southern countries have generated their own analyses, organizations, and movements, with and without exposure to the West, and there has been considerable
cross-fertilization of ideas – across many countries and continents.' Women's and
gay and lesbian rights movements in countries where the Catholic Church is
powerful – such as the Philippines, Brazil, and Mexico – have struggled to legalize
abortion, reduce maternal mortality and educate about safer sex and condom
use. In Bangladesh, women's organizations have publicly countered brutal
attacks on women accused by Islamic religious tribunals of transgressing sexual
norms (Amin and Hossain 1995). In Africa and the Middle East, campaigns by
women's groups against female genital mutilation (FGM) have focused both on
the procedure's suppression of women's sexual pleasure and on its severe risks
to their health (Toubia 1995; Tambiah 1995). Women-of-color organizations
in the United States, like women's groups in India, have vigorously opposed

*EDITORS' NOTE: Rosalind Petchesky is the founder and former international co-ordinator of the
International Reproductive Rights Research Action Group (IRRRAG), which conducts research
into a variety of reproductive and sexual health issues in many countries. In this article she describes
the collective approach to reproductive rights developed by IRRRAG and draws on research
undertaken within this framework. IRRRAG's model for international collaborative research and
the results of its research are described further in the book from which this introduction is drawn.

sterilization abuse and the coercive or nonconsensual promotion of long-acting contraceptives by family planning programmes (Hathi 1996; Srinivas and Kanakamala 1992; United States Women of Color Delegation 1994).

These practical campaigns and theoretical reconceptions nourished the forcefulness of the women's coalitions at the World Conference on Human Rights in Vienna in 1993, the International Conference on Population and Development (ICPD) in Cairo in 1994, and the Fourth World Conference on Women (FWCW) in Beijing in 1995. Representing women from both the global South and the North, those coalitions worked to replace the old population-and-family-planning discourse with a broad concept of reproductive and sexual health and rights that links sexual and reproductive freedom to women's human rights.[2] At the core of that concept lies a principle that as recently as the mid-1980s, in nearly all countries and political systems, was widely deemed unacceptable if not unthinkable: that even the most intimate areas of family, procreative and sexual life are ones where women's human rights to self-determination and equality must prevail. This principle, and the success of women's movements in gaining international recognition for it, is embodied in a historic paragraph adopted by government delegates in Beijing:

> The human rights of women include their right to have control over and decide freely and responsibly on matters related to their sexuality, including sexual and reproductive health, free of coercion, discrimination and violence. Equal relationships between women and men in matters of sexual relations and reproduction, including full respect for the integrity of the person, require mutual respect, consent and shared responsibility for sexual behaviour and its consequences.[3]

Yet, while Southern women and women of colour in the North in the 1980s and 1990s affirmed the critical importance of women's control over their fertility and sexuality, they were pushing for a much broader approach. That approach would integrate issues about abortion, contraception, childbearing and sexuality – the politics of the body – into a larger framework that emphasizes 'the transformation of state social, demographic and economic development policies to incorporate women's social and economic rights'. As DAWN's (1995) platform puts it, 'women's reproductive health must be placed within a comprehensive human development framework that promotes all people's well-being and women's full citizenship' (Corrêa 1994:64). This suggests that the concept of reproductive and sexual rights must be seen through a double lens, and that its personal and social dimensions, rather than being in conflict, are mutually dependent.

On the one hand, a double perspective on reproductive and sexual rights embraces the feminist ethics of bodily integrity and personhood that permeates the Cairo and Beijing documents and directly challenges the moral arsenal of Christian, Islamic and other fundamentalists. Such a feminist ethics requires not only that women must be free from abuse and violation of their bodies but also that they must be treated as principal actors and decision makers over their fertility and sexuality – as the ends and not the means of health, population and development programmes. And it applies this imperative not only to states and their agents but to every level where power operates, including the home, the clinic, the workplace, the religious centre, and the community. On the other hand, this feminist perspective links the rights of the body and the person directly with the social, economic and political rights – the enabling conditions – necessary to achieve gender, class and racial-ethnic justice (Corrêa and Petchesky 1994).

Having achieved considerable success at the level of theoretical visions and United Nations rhetoric, feminist activists in all the world's regions now face the problems of turning reproductive and sexual rights into concrete realities in women's everyday lives. In so doing, they confront several major obstacles. First, in most countries, due to hegemonic capitalist markets and the declining role of the state, the availability and quality of public health services continue to deteriorate, especially burdening low-income women. For women's reproductive and sexual rights to be implemented in practice will require not only supportive laws and policies (still to be enacted within most countries) but also a thorough transformation of existing global, regional and national economic structures (Bandarage 1997; Corrêa 1994; Sparr 1994). Individual women cannot exercise their reproductive and sexual rights without the necessary enabling conditions for their empowerment. These include both material and infrastructural supports (such as reliable transport, child care, and jobs as well as accessible and adequate health services); and cultural and political supports (such as access to education, self-esteem, and political power). In turn, such conditions for the vast majority would require a reordering of international and national economic policies to abandon debt servicing and militarism in favour of social welfare and primary health care (Corrêa and Petchesky 1994). Yet economic and social policies continue to move in the opposite direction: towards structural adjustments that dictate privatization and reduction of social services, deference to corporate interests and transnational capital, and high levels of military spending.

Second, resurgent fundamentalisms in many countries, claiming ultimate authority over religious doctrine and moral values, actively challenge the recognition of reproductive and sexual freedom as a basic human right. Whether Christian, Hindu, Islamic, Buddhist or Jewish, these fundamentalist currents reinforce traditional patriarchal views of women's 'natural' subordination and the primacy of a male-dominated, procreative, heterosexual family form. Despite their religious facade, the impact and aims of today's fundamentalist movements are overwhelmingly political: to influence or take over state power, to buttress the authority of religious laws and courts over all family and sexual relations, and to reshape national policies and international norms in a conservative mould. During the mid-1990s, the Vatican and its Catholic state allies formed an outspoken alliance with Islamist regimes in order to influence the Cairo and Beijing conferences – and especially to oppose the notions of reproductive and sexual rights, individual rights, and diversity of family forms. Although they lost the contest over words in the United Nations documents, these forces continue to wield considerable power and to influence governments, legislation and popular opinion (Amin and Hossain 1995; CFFC 1995; Freedman 1996).

Finally, these economic and political obstacles to realizing reproductive and sexual rights are reinforced by the deep cultural and social roots of gender inequality. The misbelief (going back to Aristotle) that women are mainly private actors incapable of, or uninterested in, public debate acts as a brake on the power of many women in all societies to articulate and embrace their rights and make claims on public agencies to enforce them; that is, to act as citizens in defence of their own bodily integrity and personhood (Peters and Wolper 1995; Nelson and Chowdhury 1994). For reproductive and sexual rights to become practical realities for all women, such rights must be fully integrated into the agendas of social justice and democratization movements. In the first instance, this means mobilization of women's groups into strong alliances and actions that can secure government and international enforcement mechanisms – in other words, that can stimulate political will where such will is lacking.

Ultimately, however, political action can be effective only if masses of women believe in and own their rights. They must have a conviction that they are entitled to be treated as primary decision-makers over their own bodies and reproductive capacities. [...]

## Conceptual framework

[...] Despite its widespread use since the Cairo conference, the concept of reproductive rights is by no means universally accepted among feminist groups around the globe. For some, it evokes a highly Westernized and narrow frame of reference that reduces reproduction at best to fertility control and at worst to the single issue of abortion; or it evokes an even more devious scenario that masks racist and eugenic population control behind 'a feminist face' (Akhter 1994; Hartmann 1994). For others, any rights discourse is suspect if not objectionable, either on philosophical and political grounds (because of its association with individualistic, privatized, adversarial meanings derived from Western law and ethics); or on pragmatic grounds (because of its lack of any meaning to grassroots women). Still other feminists are troubled by the focus not on rights but on reproduction, insofar as it may reinforce the ideological bias that reduces women to one aspect of their being and occludes other aspects, particularly (nonprocreative) sexuality (Patcman 1988; WGNRR 1993).

[...]

In recent years, numerous well-documented studies and journals have explored diverse feminist perspectives on reproduction in an international context laying a solid analytical basis for further empirical and cross-cultural research.[4] [...]

### Rights

Since the 1970s, women's movements have played a leading role in securing recognition in international instruments for matters of personal and bodily integrity, health and reproduction. They have also helped to promote the principle of the indivisibility of such 'personal' rights from the more established civil and political as well as economic, social and cultural rights.[5] Early documents such as the founding Charter of the World Health Organization (1946), the Universal Declaration of Human Rights (1948), and the International Covenant on Economic, Social and Cultural Rights (1967) contain language inscribing 'the enjoyment of the highest attainable standard of health' and the right to 'life, liberty and security of the person' as fundamental human rights. The American Convention on Human Rights (1970) and the African Charter on Human and People's Rights (1982) also refer to the inviolability of the person and mental and physical integrity; while the Convention on the Elimination of Discrimination Against Women (Women's Convention, 1979) prohibits its signatories from discriminating against women with regard to all the established rights including access to health care, education and information, employment, freedom in marriage and reproductive decision making.

More recently, thanks to the work of women's international coalitions mentioned above, the Vienna Declaration and Programme of Action (1993), the ICPD Programme of Action (1994) and the FWCW Declaration and Platform for Action (1995) extend these basic human rights principles to specific aspects of women's reproductive and sexual freedom. Thus the international human rights vocabulary now includes not only 'the basic right of all couples and individuals to decide freely and responsibly the number, spacing and timing of their children and to have the information and means to do so' but also freedom from 'violence against women and all forms of sexual harassment and exploitation', including 'systematic rape, sexual slavery, and forced pregnancy'; freedom from genital mutilation; the 'right to make decisions concerning reproduction free of discrimination, coercion and violence'; and the right 'to have a satisfying and safe sex life' (Cook 1995; Otto 1995).

But a major problem with such formal documents is that, given the continued weakness and divisions plaguing international organizations, they depend for their enforcement on existing governments, which are often corrupt, unstable and uncommitted. Although the series of parallel NGO (nongovernmental organization) forums held during the 1990s United Nations conferences were tentative steps toward creating an 'international civil society' that might pressure governments to honour their human rights commitments, reliable enforcement mechanisms through which subordinated groups and individuals can bring claims on their own behalf are still a rarity. More important, formal statements of women's rights are not only unknown to the vast majority of women; they are also very distant from the constraints burdening poor women. [...] For most people, codified expressions of rights in national laws and international agreements are very removed from the ways they envision rights and wrongs, justice and injustice, needs and deprivations, in their daily lives – for at least two reasons.

First, the term 'rights' is commonly associated with formal arenas and mechanisms of law, whether of the state or of religious institutions. Yet many people consistently experience the authorities charged with enforcing rights (police, government officials, hospital and clinic personnel) as oppressive, corrupt and routinely ready to disregard national laws and international principles, or even common decency. As a result, they view formally constituted rights as inapplicable to them, particularly if they are poor and female. [...] In these contexts, to speak of 'reproductive and sexual rights' means little except to those who are already politicized and involved in organized struggles that presume the possibility of exacting justice.

Second, although human rights procedures do function theoretically to hold states and state agents (police, military, officials, public health and family planning personnel) accountable, perpetrators of violations against women's reproductive and sexual rights also include 'private' parties, such as parents or other kin, husbands and sexual partners. Actually, a sense of entitlement to assert one's rights or decision-making authority may be easier for many women to feel in relation to more distant authority figures – doctors, religious leaders, the mayor – than to persons with whom they are intimately involved, such as husbands. Especially for women, whose lives are still in many countries and cultures locked within domesticity, assertions of human rights must penetrate the 'private' sphere where everyday violations of their bodily integrity and personhood – marital rape, FGM, virginity codes for women, customary repudiation of birth control – occur. 'Public' actions of the state and its agents – for example, laws prohibiting or restricting abortion, or rape of civilians by soldiers and police – reinforce such daily life intrusions and, with them, form a continuum of systemic abuse (Copelon 1994; Romany 1994). Breaking down the artificial barrier between 'public' and 'private' spheres has been a principal aim of feminists organizing for women's human rights throughout the 1970s, 1980s and 1990s (Bunch 1990; Corrêa and Petchesky 1994). Yet their efforts have only begun to generate new forms of struggle and language that resonate at a local, grassroots level.

The absence of trust in formal mechanisms for securing legal rights does not, however, mean that people are passive or unwilling to stake claims and take forceful actions in order to get what they believe is right or necessary for themselves and their children. Such claims may be grounded in fundamental principles of justice or equity even if they have not yet been realized in legal terms. Moreover, effective strategies for their achievement may include not only public or institutional means, such as legal actions, lobbying or strikes, but also less formal group protests, self-help measures, and even more subtle forms of individual resistance or 'private' subversion. By viewing rights and strategies for achieving them in this inclusive way, we reached an understanding that is more politically dynamic and open with regard to the so-called private or personal realm than are conventional human rights models.

### Entitlement

Even before we arrived at this understanding of rights and possible remedies to their violation, we were aware of our need for a more flexible terminology that would take into account not only the everyday ways in which women express their sense of necessity, fairness, or self-determination in regard to their bodies but also the informal and even surreptitious ways in which they act on that sense. In order to capture our respondents' own perception of their needs and just claims (whether on husbands, parents, medical providers, or the state), beyond what may exist juridically, we adopted the concept of 'sense of entitlement'. Through this notion we hoped to illuminate the subjective component of rights (what women *feel* entitled to), and our central research question thus became: when, where, and under what circumstances does such a sense of entitlement emerge in regard to reproductive and sexual decisions and choices?

It is important to distinguish the way in which IRRRAG's framework interprets 'entitlement' from more familiar uses of the concept in public policy discourse. In the history of the European welfare state, the term 'entitlement' emerged after World War Two in recognition of the idea that every individual possesses a set of 'birthrights' and that governments have an obligation to enable marginalized or economically disadvantaged persons to enjoy such birthrights (Marshall 1975). Conceded as a way to secure social stability and mitigate the harsher effects of a capitalist economic system (such as chronic unemployment) rather than to transform that system, the welfare state also recognized that entitlements, even if based on economic and social rights, depended on statutory mandates for their legitimacy. The well-known 'entitlement approach' developed by Harvard economist Amartya Sen follows in this welfare state tradition. In order to explain the fact that famines occur, and people starve, even when plenty of food is available, Sen interprets entitlement as a lack or failure: some people get no food because they are unable to access the existing legal, political, economic and social structures of entitlement in a given country – 'the law stands between food availability and food entitlement' (Sen 1981; 1984:348). In other words, the existing system of entitlements fails to honour birthrights.

IRRRAG's subjective approach to a 'sense of entitlement' focuses more on women's moral claims, especially on partners, kin and caregivers, than on their perceptions of what the law or state owes them. Our basic hypothesis in developing this concept was that many women, including those who are poor, lacking formal education, or from cultures where rights discourse may be alien, will act consciously to secure their own or their children's needs, including in the realm of reproduction and sexuality. Sense of entitlement goes beyond the concept of 'needs' insofar as it entails a conviction of the moral rightness of one's claim, without perhaps the formal public or legal acknowledgement that 'rights' imply. It thus denotes the space in between a felt sense of need and an articulation of right. 'Entitlement' in this understanding is meant to signify those actions of speech, metaphor, or even unspoken behaviour that represent both (1) an aspiration to change one's own or one's children's situation, a hope for a better life; and (2) a sense of authority to effect these changes through one's own words or actions.

Clearly such a broad, and in many ways philosophical, research objective poses difficult analytical and methodological problems. Assuming that the terms in which people justify their own ('private') behaviour or decisions will often differ from the more 'public' forms of legitimation that activists may invoke, it becomes necessary to develop careful ways of listening to grasp the expressions, local codes and even silences that may signal a sense of entitlement. This suggests a second problem, familiar to much qualitative research but particularly urgent in research dealing with the most intimate – and often camouflaged – matters of sexual and reproductive relations: how to distinguish between the *normative* and the *behavioural*, between *what people say and think they ought to do* and *what they actually do*. [...] Thus, for purposes of analytical clarity, we need to reconfigure the concept of entitlement through several normative levels: (1) codified national and international law, that is, formal rights (both what they are and what respondents think they are); (2) custom/tradition (dominant religious or other norms that govern people's values and/or behaviour in the community); (3) practice (what people actually do in everyday life, apart from legal and normative values); and (4) vision (what respondents believe ought to be, ways they feel their sense of entitlement and aspirations are unrecognized or unfulfilled in reality).[6]

[. . .]

As this relationally grounded analysis makes clear, IRRRAG's approach to the concept of entitlement as a form of rights discourse is more complex and multi-layered than conventional Western notions of 'privacy' and 'individualism'. [. . .] Women often present themselves as acting or deciding on their own (that is, apart from husbands or in contravention of dominant community norms) out of a sense of duty to others, usually their living children. In this way, they both carry out their intentions and reconcile them normatively with centuries of patriarchal culture and socialization that define women as caretakers who ought to think of everyone else's needs before their own.

[. . .] In their everyday deliberations over matters of fertility, sexuality, work, and child care, women do not necessarily experience their own entitlement and that of their families, especially their children, as operating on different or conflicting levels of decision making. Rather, they interweave the self–other relationship in their moral calculations all the time, rooting their individual identity in family and community. For example, in the eyes of rural Nigerian women, to rest and conserve their bodies after pregnancy seems necessary for competent mothering, for the sake of their children as well as themselves. Similarly, for urban Brazilian mothers, to give their daughters greater sexual and reproductive freedom than they had as young women will enhance their (the older generation's) own dignity and self-worth. Thus 'negotiated entitlement' implies a concept of the self that 'reaches far beyond the notion of bodily integrity [to encompass] . . . the context of all significant family, cultural, social and economic relationships' (Corrêa 1994:77).

[. . .]

## Accommodation and resistance

If sense of entitlement represents women's consciousness of their rights or authority to make decisions, the cluster of strategies we have called the 'accommodation–resistance nexus' represents how entitlement gets manifested at the level of behaviour and speech. In our early deliberations, we imagined accommodation and resistance as a dichotomy, the former reflecting passive compliance with dominant norms and the latter active opposition. Implied in this model was a moral and political judgement that saw women's concessions to traditional forms of gender subordination as always one-dimensionally self-destructive. As our fieldwork progressed, however, we found that the two extremes of outright resistance and passive accommodation are much rarer than the kinds of complicated, subtle reproductive and sexual strategies that most of our respondents adopt in order to achieve some degree of autonomy and at the same time maintain their place in the family and community. We thus began to think in terms of a continuum model in which accommodative and resistant acts are linked by a large grey area in between, reflecting the specific cultural and material circumstances in which our respondents find themselves. To interpret whether a particular behaviour constitutes resistance or possibly just a resilient way of surviving or coping with necessity, we need to look carefully at the particular context in which the behaviour takes place as well as the woman's own understanding of it. An action that is accommodative in one context may be oppositional in another (for example, running away to a neighbour's house to escape domestic violence); an action that appears resistant may be in conflict with the woman's own moral judgements about it (for example, the decision to seek an abortion despite one's conviction that it is a 'sin' or forbidden). To add to the complexity, though a woman's actions and words may appear to conflict, she herself may see no contradiction whatsoever in both acting against a particular norm and speaking in deference to it. Indeed, accommodation in practice often means a nonconfrontational or conciliatory way of achieving one's wishes or sense of right.

[...]

To help navigate these difficulties, a useful analytical tool [...] [is] that of trade-offs or strategic accommodations. [...] For example, some Philippine wives comply with their husbands' desire for sex, contrary to their own wishes, in order to derive certain other strategic benefits, such as help with domestic chores or the deflection of conflict in the home. [...]

Women often *choose* to go along with traditional expectations they dislike, even ones that blatantly violate their own sense of bodily integrity or wellbeing, in order to gain other advantages under existing domestic and community power relations in which their manoeuvrability is constrained. In the end, the view of accommodations and resistances as interactive and overlapping rather than dichotomous reminds us that the strategies women adopt to express or act on their sense of entitlement almost always exist in a context of domination, subordination and limited power or resources. [...] Feminists reject most accommodative strategies, since they tend often to reinforce traditional gender relations in the long run (Corrêa 1994; Molyneux 1985). Yet this continuous process of negotiation, through the most limited and compromising circumstances, also reminds us that, for many women, success means an ability to get beyond the position of victim to that of survivor. Ultimately, however, we need to ask whether and how women's strategies within the accommodation–resistance nexus begin to change existing power relations within the household and beyond it.

[...]

To the extent that the concept of 'agency' connotes self-determination, it points to a vision of a transformed set of relations and a transformed society, in which women act as full citizens and empowered decision makers both within the home and in public life.

[. . .]

## Notes

1 In the US, the Committee for Abortion Rights and Against Sterilization Abuse (CARASA) was formed in 1977 and the Reproductive Rights National Network (R2N2) in 1978. In Europe, the International Campaign for Abortion Rights, which became the International Campaign on Abortion, Sterilization and Contraception (ICASC), was also founded in 1978. In 1984 (just prior to the World Population Conference in Mexico City), at the prodding of groups of activists from the global South, it became the Women's Global Network for Reproductive Rights (WGNRR), with a broader mandate to address all women's reproductive health issues, not only those involving fertility control. (See Petchesky and Weiner 1990; Corrêa 1994; and Garcia-Moreno and Claro 1994.)

 During the 1980s and early 1990s, national and regional networks and campaigns formed around a wide range of reproductive and sexual rights issues in Latin America and the Caribbean, South and Southeast Asia and the Pacific, and many countries in Africa and the Middle East. Among the international organizations formed during this period and embracing reproductive and sexual rights as part of their agenda were Isis International, DAWN (Development Alternatives for Women in a New Era), the Latin American and Caribbean Women's Health Network, the East and Southeast Asia–Pacific Regional Women and Health Network, Women in Law and Development and the Society for Women and AIDS in Africa, and Women Living Under Muslim Laws Network.

2 Both the ICPD Programme of Action (Para. 7.2) and the Beijing Declaration and Platform for Action (Para. 95) define 'reproductive rights' as '[resting] on the recognition of the basic right of all couples and individuals to decide freely and responsibly the number, spacing and timing of their children and to have the information and means to do so, and the right to attain the highest standard of sexual and reproductive health. It also includes their right to make decisions concerning reproduction free of discrimination, coercion and violence, as expressed in human rights documents.' For fuller discussion of women's organized efforts to impact on the conferences, see Boland 1997; Center for Women's Global Leadership 1995; Copelon and Petchesky 1995; DAWN 1995; Germain and Kyte 1995; Hodgson and Watkins 1997; and Petchesky 1997 and 2000.

3 United Nations, Fourth World Conference on Women, Beijing, September 1995, *Declaration and Platform for Action*, Para. 96, United Nations, New York.

4 See Corrêa 1994; Dixon-Mueller 1993; Ginsburg and Rapp 1995; Greenhalgh 1995; Hartmann 1995; Sen, Germain and Chen 1994; Sen and Snow 1994; *Reproductive Health Matters* 1993–97; and WGNRR 1987–97.

5 For fuller discussions of this interconnective approach to human rights, see Boland, Rao, and Zeidenstein 1994; Cook 1994 and 1995; Copelon 1994; Copelon and Petchesky 1995; Corrêa and Petchesky 1994; Freedman 1995; Fried 1994; and Schuler 1995.

6 Beth Richie of Hunter College in New York, one of our research consultants, provided this useful categorization.

# References

Akhter, F. (1994) 'Resist Reduction of "Population" Issues into Women's Issues', *People's Perspectives*, No. 8, March.

Amin, S. and S. Hossain (1995) 'Women's Reproductive Rights and the Politics of Fundamentalism: A View from Bangladesh', *American University Law Review*, Vol. 44, No. 4.

Bandarage, A. (1997) *Women, Population and Global Crisis*, Zed Books, London.

Boland, R. (1997) *Promoting Reproductive Rights: A Global Mandate*, International Program / Center for Reproductive Law and Policy, New York.

Boland, R., S. Rao and G. Zeidenstein (1994) 'Honoring Human Rights in Population Policies: From Declaration to Action', in G. Sen, A. Germain and L. Chen (eds), *Population Policies Reconsidered: Health, Empowerment and Rights*, Harvard University Press, Cambridge, MA.

Bunch, C. (1990) 'Women's Rights as Human Rights: Toward a Re-Vision of Human Rights', *Human Rights Quarterly*, Vol. 12, No. 4.

Center for Women's Global Leadership (1995) 'From Vienna to Beijing: the Cairo Hearing on Reproductive Health and Human Rights', Rutgers University, New Brunswick, NJ.

CFFC (Catholics for a Free Choice) (1995) 'The Vatican and the Fourth World Conference on Women', Washington, DC.

Cook, R. (ed.) (1994) *Human Rights of Women: National and International Perspectives*, University of Pennsylvania Press, Philadelphia.

Cook, R. (1995) 'Human Rights and Reproductive Self-determination', *American University Law Review*, Vol. 44, No. 4, April.

Copelon, R. (1994) 'Recognizing the Egregious in the Everyday: Domestic Violence as Torture', *Columbia Human Rights Law Review*, Vol. 25, No. 2, Spring.

Copelon, R. and R. Petchesky (1995) 'Toward an Interdependent Approach to Reproductive and Sexual Rights as Human Rights: Reflections on the ICPD and Beyond', in M. A. Schuler (ed.), *From Basic Needs to Basic Rights*, Women, Law & Development International, Washington, DC.

Corrêa, S. (1994) *Population and Reproductive Rights: Feminist Perspectives from the South*, Zed Books, London.

Corrêa, S. and R. Petchesky (1994) 'Reproductive and Sexual Rights: A Feminist Perspective', in G. Sen, A. Germain and L. Chen (eds), *Population Policies Reconsidered*, Harvard University Press, Cambridge, MA.

DAWN (1995) *Markers on the Way: The DAWN Debates on Alternative Development*, DAWN's Platform for the Fourth World Conference on Women, Beijing, September.

Dixon-Mueller, R. (1993) *Population Policy and Women's Rights: Transforming Reproductive Choice*, Praeger, New York.

Freedman, L. P. (1995) 'Reflections on Emerging Frameworks of Health and Human Rights', *Health and Human Rights*, Vol. 1, No. 4.

Freedman, L. P. (1996) 'The Challenge of Fundamentalisms', *Reproductive Health Matters*. No. 8, November.

Fried, S. T. (1994) *The Indivisibility of Women's Human Rights: A Continuing Dialogue*, Center for Women's Global Leadership, Rutgers University, New Brunswick, NJ.

Garcia-Moreno, C. and A. Claro (1994) 'Challenges from the Women's Health Movement: Women's Rights versus Population Control', in G. Sen, A. Germain and L. C. Chen (eds), *Population Policies Reconsidered: Health, Empowerment and Right*, Harvard University Press, Cambridge, MA.

Germain, A. and R. Kyte (1995) *The Cairo Consensus: The Right Agenda for the Right Time*, International Women's Health Coalition, New York.

Ginsburg, F. D. and R. Rapp (eds) (1995) *Conceiving the New World Order: The Global Politics of Reproduction*, University of California Press, Berkeley.

Greenhalgh, S., (ed.) (1995) *Situating Fertility: Anthropology and Demographic Inquiry*, Cambridge University Press, Cambridge.

Hartmann, B. (1994) 'The Cairo "Consensus": Women's Empowerment or Business as Usual?', *Reproductive Rights Network Newsletter*, Fall.

Hartmann, B. (1995) *Reproductive Rights and Wrongs*, South End Press, Boston, revised.

Hathi, D. (1996) 'Speaking Out on Norplant', *Political Environments*, No. 4 (Committee on Women, Population and the Environment), Summer / Fall.

Hodgson, D. and S. C. Watkins (1997) 'Feminists and Neo-Malthusians: How Sturdy Are Their Alliances?', *Population and Development Review*, Vol. 23, No. 3 (September).

Marshall, T. H. (1975) *Social Policy in the Twentieth Century*, Hutchinson, London, 4th rev. edn.

Molyneux, M. (1985) 'Mobilization without Emancipation? Women's Interests, the State, and Revolution in Nicaragua', *Feminist Studies*, Vol. 11, No. 2.

Nelson, B. J. and N. Chowdhury (eds) (1994) *Women and Politics Worldwide*, Yale University Press, New Haven.

Otto, D. (1995) 'Linking Health and Human Rights: A Critical Legal Perspective', *Health and Human Rights*, Vol. 1, No. 3.

Pateman, C. (1988) *The Sexual Contract*, Stanford University Press, Stanford, CA.

Petchesky, R. P. (1997) 'Spiralling Discourses of Reproductive Rights', in J. Tronto, K. Jones and K. Cohen (eds), *Women Transforming Politics*, New York University Press, New York.

Petchesky, R. P. (2000) 'Sexual Rights: Inventing a Concept, Mapping an International Practice', in R. G. Parker, R. M. Barbosa and P. Aggleton (eds), *Framing the Sexual Subject*, University of California Press, Berkeley.

Petchesky, R. P. and J. M. Weiner (1990), *Global Feminist Perspectives on Women's Reproductive Rights and Reproductive Health*, Reproductive Rights Education Project, Hunter College, New York.

Peters, J. and A. Wolper (eds) (1995) *Women's Rights, Human Rights: International Feminist Perspectives*, Routledge, New York / London.

*Reproductive Health Matters* (1993 97), Nos. 1–10, London.

Romany, C. (1994) 'State Responsibility Goes Private: A Feminist Critique of the Public / Private Distinction in International Human Rights Law', in R. J. Cook (ed.), *Human Rights of Women*, University of Pennsylvania Press, Philadelphia.

Schuler, M. A. (ed.) (1995) *From Basic Needs to Basic Rights: Women's Claim to Human Rights*, Women, Law and Development International, Washington, DC.

Sen, A. (1981) *Poverty and Famines*, Harvard University Press, Cambridge, MA.

Sen, A. (1984) *Resources, Values and Development*, Harvard University Press, Cambridge, MA.

Sen, G. and R. C. Snow (eds) (1994) *Power and Decision: The Social Control of Reproduction*, Harvard University Press, Cambridge, MA.

Sen, G., A. Germain and L. C. Chen (eds) (1994) *Population Policies Reconsidered: Health, Empowerment and Rights*, Harvard University Press, Cambridge, MA.

Sparr, P. (ed.) (1994) *Mortgaging Women's Lives: Feminist Critiques of Structural Adjustment*, Zed Books, London.

Srinivas, K. R. and K. Kanakamala (1992) 'Introducing Norplant: Politics of Coercion', *Economic and Political Weekly* (18 July).

Tambiah, Y. (1995) 'Sexuality and Human Rights', in M. Schuler (ed.), *From Basic Needs to Basic Rights*, Women, Law and Development International, Washington, DC.

Toubia, N. (1995) *Female Genital Mutilation: A Call for Global Action*, RAINBO (Research Action Information Network for Bodily Integrity of Women), New York.

United States Women of Color Delegation to the International Conference on Population and Development (1994) 'Statement on Poverty, Development, and Population Activities', National Black Women's Health Project, Washington, DC.

WGNRR (Women's Global Network for Reproductive Rights) (1980–97) *Newsletter*, Nos. 33–56, Amsterdam.

WGNRR (1993) 'Population and Development Policies: Report on the International Conference "Reinforcing Reproductive Rights"', *Newsletter*, No. 43 (April–June), Amsterdam.

# Part V

# Sexual Values and Life Experiments

Sexuality has itself always been an arena of moral and cultural conflict. But in contemporary societies sexuality appears to be becoming an increasingly central and explicitly debated issue in mainstream cultural conflicts and political debates over values and citizenship. Debates about who and what we are, what we need and desire, how we should live, are to a striking degree also debates about sexuality. It is not surprising therefore that debates over sexuality display anxiety and uncertainty. The fear aroused by the HIV/AIDS epidemic is more than simply concern about a new and possibly incurable disease, it also underlines our uncertainty about contemporary moral stances (Weeks 1995). The frequent waves of fear about the prevalence of the abuse of children is another example of our contemporary uncertainties. This in turn reflects uncertainty about the relations between adults and children in the contemporary world, the erosion of traditional sources of authority, and the problems of combating exploitation and protecting the vulnerable.

Advances in science serve only to compound the general air of uncertainty. How, for example, should we react to the possibilities opened up by embryological research? What are the implications for sexual values and ethics of the internet revolution? In a world where traditional sources of authority such as religion and the patriarchal family are under intense pressure, and heightened individualism is increasingly the norm, it is difficult to see how there can ever be a fixed set of values to which everyone must adhere. The challenge is to balance the recognition of individual needs and desires, mutual responsibilities, and sensitivity to difference.

For many people advances in science hold the key, and they seek a new security in the genetic revolution, asserting that differences of gender or sexuality are a result of patterns laid down in the course of human evolution. This approach, offered by the new evolutionary psychology, seems to us a false and hopeless promise. There is no reason to think that assumptions about what might have happened in the early stages of human existence can resolve contemporary dilemmas. At the same time, however, the social and historical perspective on the making of sexualities does not in itself carry any set moral or political values. The usefulness of seeing sexuality as shaped in culture is that it allows us to recognize the contingency and arbitrariness of our own social arrangements. It does not, however, tell us how we should live today.

Given these uncertainties, it is not surprising that a great deal of contemporary debate focuses on the family and intimate relationships. The so-called crisis of the family is not simply about changes in domestic patterns. It is about the relation-ships between men and women, adults and children. This leads to fundamental questions. As Giddens (1992) and Beck and Beck-Gernsheim (1995) suggest, has there been a basic shift in the relationship of men and women towards new patterns of egalitarian intimacy? To what extent does the emergence of non-heterosexual families of choice represent an augury of more egalitarian and chosen lifestyles (Weeks, Heaphy and Donovan, 2001)? To what extent are the sharp dichotomies between heterosexuality and homosexuality dissolving in a post-familial world? These questions have become the subject of heated debates.

What is clear, however, is that debates about sexualities must in the end be debates about relationships. Despite the best fantasies of prophets of the internet and of cybersex, sexuality is always ultimately about interaction with others. It is through that interaction that the meanings of sexuality are shaped, and what we know as sexuality is produced. It underlines, again, the fundamental argument of this book: that sexuality is so embedded in the social that it cannot be understood in isolation. It is through understanding societies that we can understand the meanings of sexualities, just as in understanding sexualities we begin to under-stand societies more effectively.

Much of the writing on the social shaping of sexuality which emerged in the 1970s and 1980s tended to concentrate on the role of institutional and structural forces in regulating and determining sexual life. But there has subsequently been a turn towards accepting a greater role for agency in social theory addressing sexuality. Increasingly it has been necessary to recognize the significance of sexual choice, the complex patterns of resistance, self-definition and creativity in rela-tionship to the erotic. This has led to a new emphasis on the way we shape our sense of self, the way we tell stories about sexuality and live within specific sexual narratives, particularly in the contemporary era (see Plummer 1995; Plummer's article, chapter 3). We live today in a world of apparent sexual fluidity, of an increasing degree of moral flux, with an ever-proliferating ability to talk about sex in various media. Against this cacophony, it becomes critical to distinguish between those elements which are freely chosen, and those which are determined. The battle between structure and agency in social and sexual theory therefore becomes ever more crucial in trying to understand how we construct our con-temporary sexualities. The emergence of greater reflexivity and choice for sexual subjects in late modernity, discerned by theorists such as Giddens, is a central theme of this final section.

In a world that is simultaneously globalized and challenged by emergent differences and new fundamentalisms, questions of values and ethics come to the fore. In the first contribution to this section McNay engages with the later work of Michel Foucault. In the posthumously published last two volumes of *The History of Sexuality*, Foucault tries to go beyond his preoccupation with disciplinary techniques of power in the modern world to develop an analysis of techniques of the self, the forms of ethical practice that might be appropriate in the contemporary world. Foucault explores this through studies of Greek and Roman, that is, pre-Christian practices. For Foucault the preoccupation of modern individualism with discovering the truth or essence of identity can be countered only by a process of critique and denaturalization of what seems inevitable. Looking at the pre-Christian traditions offers one such perspective. Through this critical stance Foucault develops what he terms an aesthetics of existence with the self as the object of self-creation and cultivation. McNay, in a detailed account, suggests this leads to an excessive voluntarism which ironically traps his work in an essentialist framework. Nevertheless, the challenge that Foucault makes in his later work is precisely to find values and ethical guidelines that can operate in a conceptual framework which allows for agency, without falling back on essentialized notions of sexual identity or sexual normality.

Although rejecting Foucault's position, in his contribution Anthony Giddens does attempt to take up this challenge within a broader relational framework. He sees long-term tendencies in the late modern world towards what he describes as a democratization of personal life, in which women particularly are playing a key part. The notion of personal autonomy and negotiated relationships is a key to this process of democratization. Giddens suggests that lesbians and gay men have been in the vanguard of these changes, precisely because they live their lives outside explicit heterosexual frameworks. But the process of democratization, giving rise to the notion of the 'pure relationship', based on equality and open disclosure is a key aspect of a wider process that he calls 'the transformation of intimacy'. This in turn reveals the emergence of what he describes as a 'life politics'. This does not displace traditional emancipatory politics, which challenge oppression and exploitation, but in the late modern world new forms of politics around the everyday life of emotions, the body and the erotic, are necessary.

Lynn Jamieson questions what she regards as Giddens's optimism on these developments, and explores the empirical justification for his arguments on intimacy. She suggests that there is a tendency to underplay the tenacity of conventional divisions of labour. She examines the available evidence on whether people are managing to formulate and sustain more equal ways of living, and questions whether same-sex couples are pacemakers for more egalitarian relationships, as Giddens and others have suggested. Importantly, Jamieson's analysis emphasizes the need to analyse patterns of relationships by understanding intimacy as a product not only of emotional dialogue but of ways of living, including patterns of work.

Finally, Henning Bech argues that the late modern world is witnessing the gradual disappearance of the homosexual. An example of this, ironically, is one of the triumphs of gay self-organization since the 1960s, the right to register partnerships, beginning in Denmark. Bech suggests that, far from being an affirmation of the difference between homosexuality and heterosexuality, it is a sign of the dissolution of the old categorical divisions, and hence the disappearance of the homosexual. The more there is legal equality, the less there is to justify the divide. Male–male relations continue to be fetishized, however, but as a particular sexual preference no longer signifying a defining feature of identity. Bech ends by suggesting that what we are seeing is the emancipation of men *from* masculinity *to* masculinity: as old categorical distinctions fade away in late modernity, it is possible to develop ways of being which allow the exploration of diverse needs and desires and styles of life.

# References

Beck, U. and Beck-Gernshein, E. 1995: *The Normal Chaos of Love*. Cambridge: Polity.

Giddens, A. 1992: *The Transformation of Intimacy: Sexuality, Love and Eroticism in Modern Societies*. Cambridge: Polity.

Plummer, K. 1995: *Telling Sexual Stories: Power, Change and Social Worlds*. London: Routledge.

Weeks, J. 1995: *Invented Moralities: Sexual Values in an Age of Uncertainty*. Cambridge: Polity.

Weeks, J., Heaphy, B. and Donovan, C. 2001: *Same Sex Intimacies: Families of Choice and Other Life Experiments*. London: Routledge.

# 21

# Foucault: Aesthetics as Ethics

## Lois McNay

[. . .]

### *The emergence of the self*

The notion of the self emerges in conjunction with the idea of governmentality and forms part of the self-critique conducted by Foucault on his earlier work on power and the body. Foucault concedes that the emphasis he placed there on the effects of power on the body resulted in a one-dimensional account of social agents as 'docile bodies' and a correspondingly monolithic account of power. In order to obtain a fuller understanding of the modern subject, an analysis of *techniques of domination* must be counterbalanced with an analysis of *techniques of the self.*

The idea of techniques of the self complements Foucault's earlier studies of the ways in which the subject is constituted as an object of knowledge ('objectivization') with an analysis of how individuals come to understand themselves as subjects ('subjectivization'). The notion of techniques or practices of the self is illustrated in Foucault's study of Ancient Greek and Roman morality in *The Use of Pleasure* and *The Care of the Self.* Foucault observes that, from a certain perspective, Ancient Greek and early Christian moral injunctions around sexuality appear similar. Not only did both cultures share injunctions relating to the prohibition of incest, to male domination and to the subjugation of women, but they also shared similar attitudes and anxieties about sex. Both Greek and Christian cultures expressed fear about the deleterious effects of uncontrolled sexual activity on the health of the individual.[1] Both cultures valorized fidelity within marriage as a manifestation of the virtue and inner strength of the partners involved. Although Greek culture was more tolerant of homosexual relations, it was possible to discern, nevertheless, the beginnings of 'intense negative reactions' and 'forms of stigmatization' in literary and artistic images which would extend to the Christian period.[2] Finally, both cultures privileged an ascetic ideal in which abstention from sexual activities and other pleasures was linked to a 'form of wisdom that brought them into direct contact with some superior element in human nature and gave them access to the very essence of truth'.[3]

[. . .]

Techniques or practices of the self are situated at the level of ethical practice. It is through a series of different practices or 'arts of existence', ranging from the concrete techniques used to order daily existence to the spiritual significance attached to these activities, that individuals seek to interpret their experiences. Arts of existence are, in Foucault's words, 'those intentional and voluntary actions by which men not only set themselves rules of conduct, but also seek to transform themselves, to change themselves in their singular being, and to make their life into an œuvre that carries certain aesthetic values and meets certain stylistic criteria.'[4]

*The Use of Pleasure* and *The Care of the Self* provide an extensive analysis of Ancient Greek and classical Roman arts of existence in relation to the formation of the desiring subject. The principle of self-mastery or moderation which governed the daily conduct of the Greeks was ordered around two variables: a notion of intensity of practice and a distinction between activity and passivity.[5] With regard to the first principle, what distinguished men from each other is not how they chose to live their lives or what objects they desired but the intensity with which they carried out certain practices. Immorality was associated with excessive or unrestrained behaviour: the moral individual exercised self-restraint and moderation in relation to all sensual activities. The second principle pertaining to activity and passivity arises out of this notion of moderation. For the Greeks, *aphrodisia* – loosely understood as sexual activity – was thought of as an activity involving two actors, each with a clearly defined role and function – the one who performs the activity and the one on whom it is performed. The division between activity and passivity fell mainly between adult men and women, but there was also a second division between adult free men and a category including women, boys and slaves. The ethical man not only exercised self-restraint in his sensual activities but also assumed the active role. Inversely: 'For a man, excess and passivity were the two main forms of immorality in the practice of the aphrodisia.'[6]

These two dualisms of restraint / excess and activity / passivity constituted the moral framework within which the Greek notion of the ethical self was situated and governed activity in the four main areas of daily life: dietetics (bodily regimen), economics (marriage), erotics (boys) and wisdom. [. . .]

With regard to marital relations, the principle which obligated men not to have extramarital liaisons was one not of fidelity but rather of self-mastery. Women were obliged to be faithful because of their inferior status and because they were under the control of their husbands. Men were faithful because it was a manifestation of their self-control: 'For the husband, having sexual relations only with his wife was the most elegant way of exercising control.'[7] [. . .]

The self-conscious stylization of the asymmetrical power relations in marriage was connected to the isomorphic relation that was perceived between the household and the state. The free man respects his wife in a similar fashion to the respect he accords his fellow citizens: 'The double obligation to limit sexual activities relates to the stability of the city, to its public morality, to the conditions of good procreation, and not to the reciprocal obligations that attach to a dual relation between husbands and wives.'[8] The obligation of a husband to a wife inheres not in a personal commitment but in a deliberate limitation of power which connects the sexual self to the ethical and political self. Thus, despite the potential to tyrannize one's inferiors immanent in the structures of Greek society, the ethical individual who adhered to an aesthetics of existence refrained from such behaviour.

[...]

[...] In Hellenistic Rome a new way of conceiving the relationship with the self in terms of one's status, functions and activities emerges. Classical ethics had established an isomorphic relation between power over oneself and power over others. Such issues began to assume less importance in Graeco-Roman ethics and a greater emphasis was placed on the establishment of a relation with self that relied as little as possible on external signs of respect and power over others: 'It is then a matter of forming and recognising oneself as the subject of one's own actions, not through a system of signs denoting power over others, but through a relation that depends as little as possible on status and its external forms, for this relation is fulfilled in the sovereignty that one exercises over oneself.'[9]

The intensification of the relation with the self altered the daily aesthetics of existence in the four realms of the body, marriage, erotics and truth. [...] Within marriage, there was an increased austerity in sexual relations which attempted to limit them and valorize them in relation to a 'procreative finalization'.[10] The relation between husband and wife was no longer subordinated to the needs of the *oikos* and the principle of self-mastery. Instead, there was a move towards the establishment of a more reciprocal and voluntary union between the two partners – a 'stylistics of the individual bond' – which incorporated mutual love and respect. The intensification of the concern for the self necessarily involved an increased valorization of the other.

Resulting from the privileging of the relation between men and women was a philosophical disinvestment in the love for boys.[11] [...] In short, the Roman Empire introduced the beginnings of a universal ideal of the subject. [...]

Foucault's study of the differences between Ancient Greek and Hellenic Roman practices illustrates how the relationship between codes of behaviour and forms of 'subjectivization' vary from era to era. Hellenic Roman practices are similar to subsequent Christian practices in that both are based on a morality that is oriented more towards moral codes than ethics. This is to say that the emphasis within that morality is on the individual's conformity to externally imposed codes of behaviour; subjectivization occurs basically 'in a quasi-juridical form, where the ethical subject refers his conduct to a law, or set of laws, to which he must submit at the risk of committing offences that may make him liable to punishment'.[12]

Counterposed to moralities which emphasize codes are moralities oriented towards ethics exemplified in classical Greek thought. In this second type of morality, there is a element of dynamism in so far as there exists a more flexible relation between a system of laws and an individual's actual ethical behaviour. Rather than conformity towards the law, emphasis is placed on the formation of a relationship with the self and on the methods and techniques through which this relationship is worked out: 'the will to be a moral subject and the search for an ethics of existence were, in Antiquity, mainly an attempt to affirm one's liberty and to give one's own life a certain form'.[13] In short, this second type of morality oriented towards ethics permits a greater element of freedom in individual behaviour in relation to general rules of conduct. Individuals are relatively free to interpret the norms of behaviour in their own style, rather than conform exactly to these norms.

[...]

What Foucault values most highly in the Ancient Greek ethics of existence is the degree of autonomy exercised by the individual in relation to the more general social and moral codes. In *Madness and Civilization, Discipline and Punish* and the first volume of *The History of Sexuality*, attention is drawn to the pernicious tendency in contemporary society to embed social norms and rights in what are erroneously believed to be the rational and objective structures of the law and science. This, in turn, leads to the individual being caught up within insidiously normalizing regimes of truth. Foucault rejects Christian ascetics, indeed Christianity as a whole, because it is a heteronomous system inasmuch as it requires the absolute subordination of the individual's moral conduct to an externally contrived set of principles. The pressure to conform obliterates the autonomy of the individual. In many respects, modern secular ethics are more insidious because they are no longer grounded in religion, but in the 'so-called scientific knowledge of what the self is, what desire is, what the unconscious is'. Modern power operates through the related techniques of individualization and totalization, where, as we have seen, the 'truth' of the individual is extracted through various disciplinary techniques and then is incorporated into normalizing structures of knowledge which efface idiosyncracies and limit individuality to a set of very specific patterns. This corresponds to Foucault's understanding of the subject as subject to someone else by control and dependence, and also as tied to their own identity by a conscience or self-knowledge. In this dual conception, the term subject suggests a form of power which subjugates and makes subject to.[14]

In contrast, Foucault regards Ancient Greek ethics as free from such normalizing pressures. Although they operate around certain central moral imperatives, the privileged moment within these ethics is what Foucault calls a 'certain practice of liberty', whereby the Ancient Greek was free to establish a relation with himself, to idiosyncratically stylize his existence in order to maximize the pleasure, beauty and power obtainable from life. It is this principle of an autonomous aesthetics of the self that is presented as an antidote to the normalizing tendencies of modern society.

[...]

Foucault redefines the concept of autonomy as a process in which the interrogation of the established limits of identity leads to an increased capacity for independent thought and behaviour. The aim of this autonomy is not to achieve a state of impersonal moral transcendence, but rather to refuse to submit to the 'government of individualization' by constantly interrogating what seems to be the natural and inevitable in one's own identity: an interrogation of the 'contemporary limits of the necessary'.[15] A Foucauldian ethics of the self is based not on adherence to externally imposed moral obligations, but rather on an ethic of who we are said to be, and what, therefore, it is possible for us to become. [...]

## Limit, transgression and aesthetics

The idea of an ethics rooted in an interrogation of the limits of identity recalls Foucault's early work on transgression. Foucault argues, following Bataille, that in a rationalized contemporary world it is only within the realm of sexuality that the possibility of the experience of transgression remains: 'at the root of sexuality...a singular experience is shaped: that of transgression.'[16] Modern sexuality is 'denatured' and it is only by pushing it to its limits that a transgressive or a radically challenging experience can be undergone. Ethics of the self is also primarily a 'limit experience'. Established patterns of individualization are rejected through the interrogation of what are held to be universal, necessary forms of identity in order to show the place that the contingent and the historically specific occupy within them. For the individual, freedom from normalizing forms of individuality consists in an exploration of the limits of subjectivity. By interrogating what are held to be necessary boundaries to identity or the limits of subjectivity, the possibility of transgressing these boundaries is established and, therefore, the potential of creating new types of subjective experience is opened up:

> But if the Kantian question was that of knowing what limits knowledge has to renounce transgressing, it seems to me that the critical question today has to be turned back into a positive one: in what is given to us as universal, necessary, obligatory, what place is occupied by whatever is singular, contingent, and the product of arbitrary constraints? The point, in brief, is to transform the critique conducted in the form of necessary limitation into a practical critique that takes the form of a possible transgression.[17]

As in the earlier principle of non-positive affirmation, Foucault stresses that an ethics of the self does not accede to a definitive knowledge of the self. It is not a process that involves a liberation of a true or essential inner nature; rather it confronts individuals with an obligation to endlessly reinvent themselves. 'Modern man', he says, 'is not the man who goes off to discover himself, his secrets and his hidden truth; he is the man who tries to invent himself. This modernity does not "liberate man in his own being"; it compels him to face the task of producing himself.'

[...] With the notion of ethics of the self, the aesthetic re-emerges as a central theme in the idea of a reinvention of the self that takes the form of an *aesthetics of existence*. Through a process of 'stylization', the individual takes the self as an object of 'complex and difficult elaboration', like a work of art: 'From the idea that the self is not given to us, I think that there is only one practical consequence: we have to create ourselves as a work of art.'[18] The kind of relation the individual has to himself or herself is understood as a type of 'creative activity'.

[...]

Foucault combines the utopian moment present in the idea of aesthetics with a notion of the 'everyday'. As both Charles Taylor and Henri Lefebvre have remarked, a notion of the 'everyday' has come increasingly to replace more abstract concepts as the focus of philosophical concern with morality.[19] [...]

The concept of the everyday has a paradoxical status. Lefebvre explains how, on the one hand, the intensification of capitalism since the Second World War and its extension into the smallest details of everyday life has meant that the everyday is the point at which forms of social control and exploitation are most noticeable: 'The huge multinational corporations are introduced into the economy by everyday life.'[20] On the other hand, the everyday becomes a potential site for opposition to the increasing administration of society along the lines of commodity fetishism. The very repetitiveness of everyday life gives rise to a profound dissatisfaction, an 'aspiration for something else'. It is from this malaise or second order alienation that the project of transforming everyday life arises. [...]

In a similar fashion, Foucault argues that it is at the level of the most mundane and routine experience – at the level of a microphysics of existence – that the normalizing effects of power are most insidiously deployed. Thus what Foucault calls the 'cult of the self', the preoccupation of the modern individual with discovering the truth or essence of their identity, can only be countered through a process of critique and denaturalization of phenomena that appear obvious and inevitable – an aesthetic stylization of the self.

[...]

### The ethical moment

An ethics of the self addresses itself to a critical examination of the process in which individuals come to understand themselves within the context of culturally determined notions of identity. It examines, therefore, the process of mediation through which large-scale cultural patterns manifest themselves at the level of individual identity. [...]

Having suggested such a complex relation of mediation, however, Foucault fails to sustain an analysis of this process. This failure arises in part because the reliance on an unexamined notion of aesthetics appears to block a thorough analysis of the power relations which overdetermine the interaction between the individuals' behaviour and the wider cultural context. Such a form of analysis is crucial in order to distinguish between practices of the self that merely replicate conventional patterns of behaviour, and those which have a radical force. For example, in a society in which the behaviour of individuals is often governed by an incitement to consumption, it may be necessary to determine the point at which the construction of one's life as a work of art ceases to be an act of conspicuous consumption – or in Bourdieu's terms a sign of 'distinction' – and becomes a gesture of resistance. The category of the aesthetic, as it stands in Foucault's work, also obscures necessary distinctions between practices of self-formation that may be easily stylized, and practices, such as those pertaining to gender and sexuality, that are deeply inscribed upon the body and the psyche and may not be dislodged simply through a process of self-stylization. By failing to contextualize the notion of an aesthetics of existence with regard to the social relations in which it is embedded, Foucault finishes by merely juxtaposing rather than relating the micro level of practices of the self against the macro level of the determining social horizon. As a result, his work often seems to imply an essentially voluntarist conception of the self.

[...]

## Norms and the fetishization of practice

[...]

Despite Foucault's explicit refusal of any normative grounding to his work, many commentators, most notably Habermas and Fraser, have commented on its suppressed normative content.[21] While Foucault is explicitly hostile to formulating a positive basis for critique, he nevertheless implicitly draws on forms of normative judgement he claims to have forsworn. [...]

A similar cryptonormativism operates in Foucault's work on an ethics of the self. The idea of ethics of the self revolves around a form of progressive individualism based on tolerance and respect for each other's lifestyles. Foucault states, for example, that practices of the self must be governed by 'the rules of law, the techniques of management and also the ethics ... which would allow these games of power to be played with a *minimum of domination*'.[22] Yet, by refusing to define what forms of behaviour may constitute a violation of another's autonomy, his theory seems to suggest an unregulated libertarianism. The question of how a 'minimum of domination' may be maintained remains unaddressed. Similarly, the relationship that the individual establishes with the self is determined in part by the relationship with others. This latter relation is characterized as an agonistic struggle between free individuals who try to influence each other's actions. It is 'the totality of practices, by which one can constitute, define, organize, instrumentalize the strategies which individuals in their liberty can have in regard to each other. It is free individuals who try to control, to determine, to delimit the liberty of others.'[23]

The difficulty here is that there is a multiplicity of ways in which individuals may influence the actions of another, some of which are more acceptable than others. [...]

This normative confusion has been attributed by some commentators to what is understood as the irreconcilable tension arising from Foucault's practical commitment to a radical politics and his intellectual investment in a theoretical relativism.[24] If the idea of an ethics of the self cannot be sustained in terms of an explicit commitment to a set of normative goals or through a thorough analysis of the power relations involved, then the basis of any ethical moment is undermined. The unifying moment of a Foucauldian ethics derives only from an insistence on an unproblematized notion of practice – a fetishization of aesthetic practice. It is the act of aesthetic self-assertion *per se*, regardless of its normative content, that seems to constitute the only basis for an ethics of the self.

[...]

The notion of reflexivity is central to Foucault's theory of the self, providing it with its ethical dimension.[25] The autonomy of the individual can be affirmed only through the reflexive examination of the construction of oneself – a critical hermeneutics of the self which must 'put itself to the test of reality, of contemporary reality, both to grasp the points where change is possible and desirable, and to determine the precise form this change should take'.[26] Such a reference to contemporary reality involves the critical scrutiny of the self's relationship with the self and the way in which it is implicated in larger social constructions, such as 'the problem of the relationship between sanity and insanity, or sickness and health, or crime and the law; the problem of the role of sexual relations'.[27]

Yet, having stressed the importance of a process of reflexive self-monitoring, this idea is then undercut by the argument that the establishment of analytical links between the self and the social context must be rejected: 'For centuries we have been convinced that between our ethics and other social or economic or political structures, there were analytical relations...I think we have to get rid of this idea of an analytical or necessary link between ethics and other social or economic or political structures.'[28] The injunction to rid ourselves of the idea of an analytical link between our personal ethics and other social structures arises from Foucault's concern to escape the 'regimes of truth' imposed on the body and its pleasures by the juridico-moral codification of Christianity, psychoanalysis and science. Ethics of the self should not become a form of reverse essentialism or 'scientia sexualis', hence the insistence on its contingent, local and experimental nature: 'the historical ontology of ourselves must turn away from all projects that claim to be global or radical.'[29]

By arguing against the analytical moment in an ethics of the self, however, Foucault deprives the notion of reflexivity, around which his ethics turns, of any critical force. Without examining the links between practices of the self and the way in which they are mediated through social and symbolic structures, it is unclear how individuals can acquire any insight – apart from the most parochial and intuitive – into the implications of their actions. Foucault rhetorically poses this problem but erroneously construes the dilemma in polarized terms as a choice between a 'complete and definitive' self-knowledge and a 'limited and determined' experience of our limits.[30] The possibility that remains unadmitted is that the process of reflexivity may never be fixed and complete, but may nevertheless involve a systematic interrogation of the way in which self-representation is imbricated in wider cultural dynamics at a level of awareness that transcends a purely practical consciousness. Thus, when Foucault cites the work of the feminist movement on the relation between sexes as an example of the localized transformation about which he is talking, he fails to acknowledge that the specific achievements of the feminist movement have been based, in a large part, on making analytical links between what is regarded as the private and immutable realm of sexuality and overarching structures of patriarchal domination. By precluding the analytical moment in an ethics of the self, the notion of reflexivity is deprived of any radical, critical force and is reduced to little more than a narrow process of self-introspection.

The final irony of Foucault's reliance on a problematic notion of practice as the basis of the idea of an ethics of the self is that an essentialist moment is introduced into what is intended as a radically anti-essentialist theory. [...] Far from redefining a notion of the self along anti-essentialist lines, Foucault's ethics in fact reinstalls a notion of sovereign subjectivity in which there is a short-circuited link between aesthetic self-fashioning and self-knowledge. The reflexive element in this creation of a relation with the self is little more than a hermetically enclosed process of introversion.

[...]

## Notes

1   Michel Foucault, *The Use of Pleasure*, pp. 15–17.
2   Ibid., pp. 19–20.
3   Ibid., p. 20.
4   Ibid., pp. 10–11.
5   The following description of *The Use of Pleasure* and *The Care of the Self* draws heavily on pp. 54–9 of my *Foucault and Feminism*.
6   Foucault, *The Use of Pleasure*, p. 47.
7   Ibid., p. 151.
8   Ibid., p. 170.
9   Foucault, *The Care of the Self*, p. 85.
10   Ibid., pp. 166–7.
11   Ibid., p. 192.
12   Foucault, *The Use of Pleasure*, pp. 29–30.
13   Foucault, 'An aesthetics of existence', p. 49.
14   Foucault, 'The subject and power', p. 212.

15  Foucault, 'What is Enlightenment?' p. 43.
16  Foucault, 'Preface to transgression', in *Language, Counter-memory, Practice*, ed. Bouchard, p. 33.
17  Foucault, 'What is Enlightenment', p. 42.
18  Foucault, 'On the genealogy of ethics: An overview of work in progress', in *The Foucault Reader*, ed. Rabinow, p. 351.
19  Taylor, *Sources of the Self*, p. 14; Henri Lefebvre, 'Toward a leftist cultural politics: remarks occasioned by the centenary of Marx's death', in *Marxism and the Interpretation of Culture*, ed. Nelson and Grossberg.
20  Lefebvre, 'Toward a leftist cultural politics', p. 79.
21  See Habermas, *The Philosophical Discourse of Modernity*, pp. 282–6; Nancy Fraser, 'Foucault's body-language: a post-humanist political rhetoric', *Salmagundi*, 61, pp. 55–70 (also in Fraser, *Unruly Practices*).
22  Foucault, 'The ethic of care for the self', p. 18, my italics.
23  Ibid., pp. 19–20.
24  For example, see Derek D. Nikolinakos, 'Foucault's ethical quandary', *Telos*, no. 83 (Spring 1990).
25  Foucault makes frequent reference to the notion of reflexivity; see 'Structuralism and poststructuralism: an interview with Michel Foucault', pp. 195–211.
26  Foucault, 'What is Enlightenment?', p. 46.
27  Ibid., p. 49.
28  Foucault, 'On the genealogy of ethics', p. 350.
29  Foucault, 'What is Enlightenment?', p. 46.
30  Ibid., p. 47.

# References

Foucault, M. *The Use of Pleasure*, trans. of *Histoire de la sexualité*, vol. 2: *L'Usage des plaisirs* (1984) by R. Hurley (Harmondsworth: Penguin, 1985).
——, *The Care of the Self*, trans. of *Histoire de la sexualité*, vol. 3: *Le Souci de soi* (1984) by R. Hurley (Harmondsworth: Penguin, 1986).
——, 'Preface to transgression', in *Language, Counter-memory, Practice: Selected Interviews and Essays*, ed. D. F. Bouchard (New York: Cornell University Press, 1977).
——, 'The subject and power', in H. Dreyfus and P. Rabinow, *Michel Foucault: Beyond Structuralism and Hermeneutics* (London: Harvester Wheatsheaf, 1982).
——, 'Structuralism and poststructuralism: an interview with Michel Foucault', *Telos*, 55 (1983), pp. 195–211.
——, 'On the genealogy of ethics: an overview of work in progress', 'What is Enlightenment', in *The Foucault Reader*, ed. P. Rabinow (Harmondsworth: Penguin, 1984).
——, 'The ethic of care for the self as a practice of freedom', in *The Final Foucault*, ed. J. Bernauer and D. Rasmussen (Cambridge Mass.: MIT Press, 1988).
——, 'An aesthetics of existence', in *Politics, Philosophy, Culture: Interviews and Other Writings, 1977–1984*, ed. L. Kritzman (London: Routledge, 1988).
Fraser, N., *Unruly Practices: Power, Discourse and Gender in Contemporary Social Theory* (Cambridge: Polity, 1989).
Habermas, J., *The Philosophical Discourse of Modernity* (Cambridge: Polity, 1987).
Lefebvre, H., 'Toward a leftist cultural politics: remarks occasioned by the centenary of Marx's death', in *Marxism and the Interpretation of Culture*, ed. C. Nelson and L. Grossberg (London: Macmillan, 1988).

McNay, L., *Foucault and Feminism: Power, Gender and the Self* (Cambridge: Polity, 1992).

Taylor, C., *Sources of the Self: The Making of Modern Identity* (Cambridge: Cambridge University Press, 1986).

# 22

# Intimacy as Democracy

## *Anthony Giddens*

A democratisation of the private sphere is today not only on the agenda, but is an implicit quality of all personal life that comes under the aegis of the pure relationship [based on sexual and emotional equality]. The fostering of democracy in the public domain was at first largely a male project – in which women eventually managed, mostly by dint of their own struggle, to participate. The democratisation of personal life is a less visible process, in part precisely because it does not occur in the public arena, but its implications are just as profound. It is a process in which women have thus far played the prime role, even if in the end the benefits achieved, as in the public sphere, are open to everyone.

### *The meaning of democracy*

First of all it might be worth considering what democracy means, or can mean, in its orthodox sense. There is much debate about the specifics of democratic representation and so forth, but I shall not concern myself with these issues here. If the various approaches to political democracy be compared, as David Held has shown, most have certain elements in common.[1] They are concerned to secure 'free and equal relations' between individuals in such a way as to promote certain outcomes:

1   The creation of circumstances in which people can develop their potentialities and express their diverse qualities. A key objective here is that each individual should respect others' capabilities as well as their ability to learn and enhance their aptitudes.
2   Protection from the arbitrary use of political authority and coercive power. This presumes that decisions can in some sense be negotiated by those they affect, even if they are taken on behalf of a majority by a minority.

3   The involvement of individuals in determining the conditions of their associ-
    ation. The presumption in this case is that individuals accept the authentic
    and reasoned character of others' judgements.
4   Expansion of the economic opportunity to develop available resources –
    including here the assumption that when individuals are relieved of the
    burdens of physical need they are best able to achieve their aims.

The idea of autonomy links these various aspirations. Autonomy means the
capacity of individuals to be self-reflective and self-determining: 'to deliberate,
judge, choose and act upon different possible courses of action.'[2] Clearly autonomy in this sense could not be developed while political rights and obligations were
closely tied to tradition and fixed prerogatives of property. Once these were
dissolved, however, a movement towards autonomy became both possible and
seen to be necessary. An overwhelming concern with how individuals might best
determine and regulate the conditions of their association is characteristic of
virtually all interpretations of modern democracy. The aspirations that compose
the tendency towards autonomy can be summarised as a general principle, the
'principle of autonomy':

> individuals should be free and equal in the determination of the conditions of their
> own lives; that is, they should enjoy equal rights (and, accordingly, equal obliga-
> tions) in the specification of the framework which generates and limits the oppor-
> tunities available to them, so long as they do not deploy this framework to negate
> the rights of others.[3]

Democracy hence implies not just the right to free and equal self-development,
but also the constitutional limitation of (distributive) power. The 'liberty of the
strong' must be restrained, but this is not a denial of all authority – or it only
becomes so in the case of anarchism. Authority is justifiable to the degree that it
recognises the principle of autonomy; in other words, to the extent to which
defensible reasons can be given as to why compliance enhances autonomy, either
now or in the future. Constitutional authority can be understood as an implicit
contract which has the same form as conditions of association explicitly negotiated between equals.

It is no good proposing a principle of autonomy without saying something
about the conditions of its realisation. What are those conditions? One is that
there must be equality in influencing outcomes in decision-making – in the
political sphere this is usually sought after by the 'one person one vote' rule.
The expressed preferences of each individual must have equal ranking, subject in
certain instances to qualifications made necessary by the existence of justified
authority. There must also be effective participation; the means must be provided
for individuals to make their voices heard.

A forum for open debate has to be provided. Democracy means discussion, the
chance for the 'force of the better argument' to count as against other means of
determining decisions (of which the most important are policy decisions).
A democratic order provides institutional arrangements for mediation, negotiation and the reaching of compromises where necessary. The conduct of open

discussion is itself a means of democratic education: participation in debate with others can lead to the emergence of a more enlightened citizenry. In some part such a consequence stems from a broadening of the individual's cognitive horizons. But it also derives from an acknowledgement of legitimate diversity – that is, pluralism – and from emotional education. A politically educated contributor to dialogue is able to channel her or his emotions in a positive way: to reason from conviction rather than engage in ill thought through polemics or emotional diatribes.

Public accountability is a further basic characteristic of a democratic polity. In any political system decisions must often be taken on behalf of others. Public debate is normally only possible in relation to certain issues or at particular junctures. Decisions taken, or policies forged, however, must be open to public scrutiny should the need arise. Accountability can never be continuous and therefore stands in tandem with trust. Trust, which comes from accountability and openness, and also protects them, is a thread running through the whole of democratic political order. It is a crucial component of political legitimacy.

Institutionalising the principle of autonomy means specifying rights and obligations, which have to be substantive, not just formal. Rights specify the privileges which come with membership of the polity but they also indicate the duties which individuals have *vis-à-vis* each other and the political order itself. Rights are essentially forms of empowerment; they are enabling devices. Duties specify the price that has to be paid for the rights accorded. In a democratic polity, rights and duties are negotiated and can never be simply assumed – in this respect they differ decisively from, for example, the medieval *droit de seigneur* or other rights established simply by virtue of an individual's social position. Rights and duties thus have to be made a focus of continual reflexive attention.

Democracy, it should be emphasised, does not necessitate sameness, as its critics have often asserted. It is not the enemy of pluralism. Rather, as suggested above, the principle of autonomy encourages difference – although it insists that difference should not be penalised. Democracy is an enemy of privilege, where privilege is defined as the holding of rights or possessions to which access is not fair and equal for all members of the community. A democratic order does not imply a generic process of 'levelling down', but instead provides for the elaboration of individuality.

Ideals are not reality. How far any concrete political order could develop such a framework in full is problematic. In this sense there are utopian elements in these ideas. On the other hand, it could also be argued that the characteristic trend of development of modern societies is towards their realisation. The quality of utopianism, in other words, is balanced by a clear component of realism.[4]

## The democratising of personal life

The possibility of intimacy means the promise of democracy. The structural source of this promise is the emergence of the pure relationship, not only in the area of sexuality but also in those of parent–child relations, and other forms of kinship and friendship. We can envisage the development of an ethical framework for a democratic personal order, which in sexual relationships and other personal domains conforms to a model of confluent love.

As in the public sphere, the distance between ideals and reality is considerable. In the arena of heterosexual relations in particular, there are profound sources of strain. Deep psychological, as well as economic, differences between the sexes stand in the way. Yet utopianism here can again readily be offset by realism. The changes that have helped transform personal environments of action are already well advanced, and they tend towards the realisation of democratic qualities.

The principle of autonomy provides the guiding thread and the most important substantive component of these processes. In the arena of personal life, autonomy means the successful realisation of the reflexive project of self – the condition of relating to others in an egalitarian way. The reflexive project of self must be developed in such a fashion as to permit autonomy in relation to the past, this in turn facilitating a colonising of the future. Thus conceived, self-autonomy permits that respect for others' capabilities which is intrinsic to a democratic order. The autonomous individual is able to treat others as such and to recognise that the development of their separate potentialities is not a threat. Autonomy also helps to provide the personal boundaries needed for the successful management of relationships. Such boundaries are transgressed whenever one person uses another as a means of playing out old psychological dispositions, or where a reciprocal compulsiveness, as in the case of codependence, is built up.

The second and third conditions of democracy in the public sphere noted above bear very directly upon the democratisation of personal life. Violent and abusive relationships are common in the sexual domain and between adults and children. Most such violence comes from men and is directed towards beings weaker than themselves. As an emancipatory ideal of democracy, the prohibition of violence is of basic importance. Coercive influences in relationships, however, obviously can take forms other than physical violence. Individuals may be prone, for example, to engage in emotional or verbal abuse of one another; marriage, so the saying goes, is a poor substitute for respect. Avoidance of emotional abuse is perhaps the most difficult aspect of the equalising of power in relationship; but the guiding principle is clearly respect for the independent views and personal traits of the other. [...]

'The involvement of individuals in determining the conditions of their association' – this statement exemplifies the ideals of the pure relationship. It expresses a prime difference between traditional and present-day marriage and gets to the heart of the democratising possibilities of the transformation of intimacy. It applies, of course, not just to the initiation of a relationship, but to the reflexivity inherent in its continuance – or its dissolution. Not just respect for the other, but an opening out to that person, are needed for this criterion to be met. An individual whose real intentions are hidden from a partner cannot offer the qualities needed for a cooperative determination of the conditions of the relationship. [...]

Rights and obligations: in some part these define what intimacy actually is. Intimacy should not be understood as an interactional description, but as a cluster of prerogatives and responsibilities that define agendas of practical activity. The importance of rights as means for the achievement of intimacy can easily be seen from the struggle of women to achieve equal status in marriage. The right of women to initiate divorce, to take one instance, which seems only a negative sanction, actually has a major equilibrating effect. Its balancing consequences do more than empower escape from an oppressive relationship, important though this is. They limit the capability of the husband to impose his dominion and thereby contribute to the translation of coercive power into egalitarian communication.

No rights without obligations – this elementary precept of political democracy applies also to the realm of the pure relationship. Rights help dissolve arbitrary power only in so far as they carry responsibilities towards the other which draw privileges into an equilibrium with obligations. In relationships as elsewhere, obligations have to be treated as revisable in the light of negotiations carried on within them.

What of accountability and its connection to authority? Both accountability and authority – where it exists – in pure relationships are deeply bound up with trust. Trust without accountability is likely to become one-sided, that is, to slide into dependence; accountability without trust is impossible because it would mean the continual scrutiny of the motives and actions of the other. Trust entails the trustworthiness of the other – according 'credit' that does not require continual auditing, but which can be made open to inspection periodically if necessary. Being regarded as trustworthy by a partner is a recognition of personal integrity, but in an egalitarian setting such integrity means also revealing reasons for actions if called upon to do so – and in fact having good reasons for any actions which affect the life of the other.

Authority in pure relationships between adults exists as 'specialisation' – where one person has specially developed capabilities which the other lacks. Here one cannot speak of authority over the other in the same sense as in parent–child relations, particularly where very young children are involved. Can a relationship between a parent and young child be democratic? It can, and should be, in exactly the same sense as is true of a democratic political order.[5] It is a right of the child, in other words, to be treated as a putative equal of the adult. Actions which cannot be negotiated directly with a child, because he or she is too young to grasp what is entailed, should be capable of counterfactual justification. The presumption is that agreement could be reached, and trust sustained, if the child were sufficiently autonomous to be able to deploy arguments on an equal basis to the adult.

## Mechanisms

[...]

The imperative of free and open communication is the *sine qua non* of the pure relationship; the relationship is its own forum. On this point we come round full circle. Self-autonomy, the break with compulsiveness, is the condition of open dialogue with the other. Such dialogue, in turn, is the medium of the expression of individual needs, as well as the means whereby the relationship is reflexively organised.

Democracy is dull, sex is exciting – although perhaps a few might argue the opposite way. How do democratic norms bear upon sexual experience itself? This is the essence of the question of sexual emancipation. Essentially, such norms sever sexuality from distributive power, above all from the power of the phallus. The democratisation implied in the transformation of intimacy includes, but also transcends, 'radical pluralism'. No limits are set upon sexual activity, save for those entailed by the generalising of the principle of autonomy and by the negotiated norms of the pure relationship. Sexual emancipation consists in integrating plastic sexuality with the reflexive project of self. Thus, for example, no prohibition is necessarily placed on episodic sexuality so long as the principle of autonomy, and other associated democratic norms, are sustained on all sides. On the other hand, where such sexuality is used as a mode of exploitative domination, covertly or otherwise, or where it expresses a compulsiveness, it falls short of the emancipatory ideal.

Political democracy implies that individuals have sufficient resources to participate in an autonomous way in the democratic process. The same applies in the domain of the pure relationship, although as in the political order it is important to avoid economic reductionism. Democratic aspirations do not necessarily mean equality of resources, but they clearly tend in that direction. They do involve including resources within the charter of rights reflexively negotiated as a defining part of the relationship. The importance of this precept within heterosexual relationships is very plain, given the imbalance in economic resources available to men and women and in responsibilities for child care and domestic work. The democratic model presumes equality in these areas; the aim, however, would not necessarily be complete parity so much as an equitable arrangement negotiated according to the principle of autonomy. A certain balance of tasks and rewards would be negotiated which each finds acceptable. A division of labour might be established, but not one simply inherited on the basis of pre-established criteria or imposed by unequal economic resources brought to the relationship.

There are structural conditions in the wider society which penetrate to the heart of the pure relationships; conversely, how such relationships are ordered has consequences for the wider social order. Democratisation in the public domain, not only at the level of the nation-state, supplies essential conditions for the democratising of personal relationships. But the reverse applies also. The advancement of self-autonomy in the context of pure relationships is rich with implications for democratic practice in the larger community.

[...]

## Sexuality, emancipation, life politics

[...]

In the tension between the privatising of passion and the saturation of the public domain by sexuality, as well as in some of the conflicts which today divide men and women, we can see new political agendas. Particularly in its connections with gender, sexuality gave rise to the politics of the personal, a phrase that is misunderstood if tied only to emancipation. What we should rather term life politics[6] is a politics of life-style, operating in the context of institutional reflexivity. It is concerned not to 'politicise', in a narrow sense of that term, life-style decisions but to remoralise them – more accurately put, to bring to the surface those moral and existential issues pushed away from everyday life by the sequestration of experience. They are issues which fuse abstract philosophy, ethical ideas and very practical concerns.

The province of life politics covers a number of partially distinct sets of issues. One is that of self-identity as such. In so far as it is focused upon the life-span, considered as an internally referential system, the reflexive project of self is oriented only to control. It has no morality other than authenticity, a modern version of the old maxim 'to thine own self be true'. Today, however, given the lapse of tradition, the question 'Who shall I be?' is inextricably bound up with 'How shall I live?' A host of questions present themselves here, but so far as sexuality is concerned that of sexual identity is the most obvious.

The greater the level of equality achieved between the sexes, one might think, the more pre-existing forms of masculinity and femininity are likely to converge upon an androgynous model of some sort. This may or may not be so, given the revival of difference in current sexual politics; but it is in any case devoid of meaning unless we try to specify the content of androgyny, which is a matter of deciding about values. The dilemmas thus raised were hidden as long as sexual identity appeared to be structured in terms of sexual difference. A binary code of male and female, which admits of virtually no mediating instances, attached gender to sex as though they were the same.

[. . .] A combination of imbalanced gender power and engrained psychological dispositions keeps dualistic sex divisions quite firmly in place; but in principle matters could be organised quite differently. As anatomy stops being destiny, sexual identity more and more becomes a life-style issue. Sex differences will continue for at least the near future to be linked to the mechanics of the reproduction of the species; but there is no longer good reason for them to conform to a clear break in behaviour and attitudes. Sexual identity could become formed through diverse configurations of traits connecting appearance, demeanour and behaviour. The question of androgyny would be settled in terms of what could be justified as desirable conduct – and nothing else.

[. . .]

With the development of modern societies, control of the social and natural worlds, the male domain, became focused through 'reason'. Just as reason, guided by disciplined investigation, was set off from tradition and dogma, so it was also from emotion. This presumed not so much a massive psychological process of repression as an institutional division between reason and emotion, a division that closely followed gender lines. The identifying of women with unreason, whether in serious vein (madness), or in seemingly less consequential fashion (women as the creatures of caprice), turned them into the emotional underlabourers of modernity. Along the way emotion, and forms of social relation inspired by it – hate as well as love – became seen as refractory to ethical considerations. Reason cuts away at ethics because of the difficulty of finding empirical arguments to justify moral convictions; it does so also, however, because moral judgements and emotional sentiments come to be regarded as antithetical. Madness and caprice – it needs little effort to see how alien these are to moral imperatives.

Freud rediscovered emotion – through his interpretations of female psychology – but in his thought it remained tied to the dictates of reason, however much cognition was shown to be swayed by the subterranean forces of the unconscious. 'Nothing disturbs feeling . . . so much as thinking': emotion remains the other side of reason, with its causal power increased. No connection is made between emotion and ethics; perhaps they are pushed even further apart, for the theme 'where id was there ego shall be' suggests that the sphere of the rational can be substantially expanded. If ethical imperatives exist, therefore, they are to be found in the public domain; but there it proves difficult to demonstrate their validity and they stand vulnerable to power.

Passionate love was originally one among other passions, the interpretation of which tended to be influenced by religion. Most emotional dispositions can be passions, but in modern society passion is narrowed down to the sexual realm and once there becomes more and more muted in its expression. A passion is today something admitted to only reluctantly or embarrassedly, even in respect of sexual behaviour itself, partly because its place as a 'compelling force' has been usurped by addiction.

There is no room for passion in the routinised settings which provide us with security in modern social life. Yet who can live without passion, if we see it as the motive-power of conviction? Emotion and motivation are inherently connected. Today we think of motivation as 'rational' – the driving pursuit of profit on the part of the entrepreneur, for example – but if emotion is wholly resistant to rational assessment and ethical judgement, motives can never be appraised except as means to ends, or in terms of their consequences. This is what Weber saw in interpreting the motives of the early industrialists as energised by religious conviction. However, in so doing Weber took for granted, and even elevated to the status of an epistemology, what is distinctly problematic about modernity: the impossibility of evaluating emotion.

Seen as a life-political issue, the problem of the emotions is not one of retrieving passion, but of developing ethical guidelines for the appraisal or justification of conviction. The therapist says, 'Get in touch with your feelings.' Yet in this regard therapy connives with modernity. The precept which lies beyond is 'Evaluate your feelings', and such a demand cannot be a matter of psychological rapport alone. Emotions are not judgements, but dispositional behaviour stimulated by emotional responses is; to evaluate feelings is to ask for the criteria in terms of which such judgements are made.

Emotion becomes a life-political issue in numerous ways with the latter-day development of modernity. In the realm of sexuality, emotion as a means of communication, as commitment to and cooperation with others, is especially important. The model of confluent love suggests an ethical framework for the fostering of non-destructive emotion in the conduct of individual and communal life. It provides for the possibility of a revitalising of the erotic – not as a specialist skill of impure women, but as a generic quality of sexuality in social relations formed through mutuality rather than through unequal power. Eroticism is the cultivation of feeling, expressed through bodily sensation, in a communicative context; an art of giving and receiving pleasure. Shorn of differential power, it can revive those aesthetic qualities of which Marcuse speaks.

Defined in such a fashion, the erotic stands opposed to all forms of emotional instrumentality in sexual relations. Eroticism is sexuality reintegrated within a wider range of emotional purposes, paramount among which is communication. From the point of view of utopian realism, eroticism is rescued from that triumph of the will which, from de Sade to Bataille, seems to mark out its distinctiveness. Interpreted not as diagnosis but as critique, the Sadean universe is an anti-utopia which discloses the possibility of its opposite.

Sexuality and reproduction in the past structured one another. Until it became thoroughly socialised, reproduction was external to social activity as a biological phenomenon; it organised kinship as well as being organised by it, and it connected the life of the individual to the succession of the generations. When directly bound up with reproduction, sexuality was a medium of transcendence. Sexual activity forged a tie with the finitude of the individual, and at the same time carried the promise of its irrelevance; for seen in relation to a cycle of generations the individual life was part of a more embracing symbolic order. Sexuality for us still carries an echo of the transcendent. Yet given that such is the case, it is bound to be surrounded with an aura of nostalgia and disillusion. A sexually addicted civilisation is one where death has become stripped of meaning; life politics at this point implies a renewal of spirituality. From this point of view, sexuality is not the antithesis of a civilisation dedicated to economic growth and technical control, but the embodiment of its failure.

## Notes

1  I follow closely Held's thought in the first part of this chapter. See David Held: *Models of Democracy*, Cambridge: Polity, 1986.
2  Ibid., p. 270.
3  Ibid., p. 271.
4  Anthony Giddens: *The Consequences of Modernity*, Cambridge: Polity, 1990, pp. 154–8.
5  Allison James and Alan Prout: *Constructing and Reconstructing Childhood*, Basingstoke: Falmer, 1990. The 'new paradigm' James and Prout suggest for studying childhood relates closely to the ideas developed here.
6  Anthony Giddens: *Modernity and Self-Identity*, Cambridge: Polity, 1991, ch. 7.

# 23

# The Couple: Intimate and Equal?

*Lynn Jamieson*

While for some academics, friendship is regarded as the quintessentially intimate relationship of the late twentieth century, the couple is the more popular choice. Friendship has the theoretical edge over domestic and sexual partners as a likely candidate for 'the pure relationship', a relationship based solely on mutual appreciation of each other's qualities. However, the couple is often treated as the more significant and central personal relationship both in public stories and in everyday practices. The historical shift from 'the family' to 'the good relationship' as *the* site of intimacy is the story of a growing emphasis on the couple relationship. By mid-century, the marriage relationship was hailed as the core of personal life, but by the late twentieth century the language is of partners rather than spouses. [...]

Those who are alarmed by the shift from spouses to 'partners' see high rates of divorce and single parenting as indicative of an associated demise of responsibility for children and of familial and moral obligations. More optimistic analysts see the softening in the monopoly of conventional marriage over personal life as allowing a healthy proliferation of ways of being a couple. For Anthony Giddens, a leading proponent of the optimistic position, greater instability in couple relationships is a corollary of the shift towards mutually disclosing intimacy and 'the pure relationship' of equals. Giddens refers to this instability as the structural contradiction of the pure relationship (1992). [...] This chapter uses empirical research on the details of couples' lives to examine the extent to which couples are striving for equal relationships constructed through disclosing intimacy as they live together and as they part. Are the practical arrangements necessitated by living together enhancing or detracting from the quality of the relationship? The data are examined for evidence of how important equality is to couples and how being intimate emerges and evaporates in couples' lives. Research on different types of couples, married couples, cohabiting heterosexual couples, cohabiting same-sex couples, is scrutinized for the similarities and differences predicted by the optimistic visions of change. If couples are increasingly premised on 'the pure relationship' then they should desist from seeking external validation or falling back on traditional ways of being a couple in favour of sustaining their relationship solely through intense interaction with each other. Cohabiting couples and same-sex couples are then immediately at an additional 'advantage' over married couples since they have not gone through a formal legal procedure which demands public recognition for their relationship. Homosexual couples are arguably also at an 'advantage' as temptations or pressures to adopt traditional male and female roles may not be so salient to them.

### The heterosexual couple: still she the housewife, he the earner?

Much of the research on married couples has been concerned to assess how far men and women have moved from traditional relationships in which women serve men as the accepted head of the household to a partnership of equals. Commentators of the 1960s and early 1970s talked of marriage becoming more symmetrical. Michael Young and Peter Willmott argued this symmetry could be seen in divisions of labour in the home, with the old distinction between men's and women's jobs becoming increasingly blurred, a shift to joint decision making, and increasingly shared social life (Young and Willmott, 1973). Greater intimacy was an implied effect of greater equality; Giele talked of men and women being better able to 'identify with each other' (Giele, 1974). However, even in the last decades of the twentieth century many studies have found only a modest moderation in inequalities, despite the fact that many married women are paid employees as well as wives and mothers. The most studied measures of equality are how domestic work in couples' households is divided up and how their total income is distributed. [...] Exceptional couples do exist and stand out, but heterosexual coupledom remains surprisingly organized around man-as-the-main-earner and woman-as-domestic-worker/carer despite the prevalence of dual-earner households. As cohabiting increases and becomes a subject of study, a pattern of gender inequality has been documented among cohabiting couples which is similar to marriage in many respects. Again there are exceptional couples. Clearly radical change is possible and actually happening for a minority; however, the overall picture is one of persistent inequalities. This has led some feminist authors to suggest that men's conservatism, their unwillingness to give up privileges and meet the changes that women have made in their own lives, is the cause of instability in marriage.

A number of studies of dual-worker couples in Australia, Britain, New Zealand and North America have documented a shift, albeit modest, towards redistributing domestic work between husbands and wives. Ellen Rosen (1987) interviewed 233 US working-class married women from a number of ethnic groups who were all in blue-collar jobs or had recently become unemployed. When wives were working their husbands did more domestic work; 72 per cent of working women had husbands who shared at least one 'inside' task as opposed to 35 per cent of non-working women's husbands (Rosen, 1987, p. 106). This is a finding repeated in a number of studies (Pahl, 1984) including large surveys

(Nickols and Metzen, 1982, and see the figures for routine domestic work and shopping in Gershuny, Godwin and Jones, 1994). However, the extra work done by men was relatively insignificant in comparison with the extra hours women added to their overall work time by entering paid employment. This is so even despite the fact that employed women cut the number of hours they spent on housework. Wives' employment has a more dramatic effect on the (reduced) hours women spend on housework than on the (increased) hours their husbands spend on housework (Geerken and Gove, 1983). [...] Using detailed 'time-budget' surveys in which people keep diaries of what they do in a day, Canadian analysts were among the first to argue on the basis of statistics that inequality between married men and women was increasing not decreasing (Meissner et al., 1975). Jonathan Gershuny and his colleagues (1994) have more recently taken issue with this analysis and used longitudinal data to argue that men are slowly increasing their share of housework, particularly in households in which women are in employment. They agree, however, that the shifts are not marked.

Historically, women carrying the main responsibility for housework has been regarded as the complement of the position of men as the main earner/provider for their wife and children. A man's position as the provider for the family was, and for some still is, a keystone of his sense of masculinity and power (Morris, 1987; Wilcock and Franke, 1963; Wight, 1993). Men's authority in the family household has been bound up with their position as main earner. In terms of the dynamics of husband and wife relationships, this does not necessarily mean that men have in everyday ways always used money to control and dominate their wives. Oral history shows that many working-class men have routinely handed over their entire wage packet to their wives and current research indicates that this remains the system in some low-waged households.[1] However, while it may be possible for a division of labour between he-the-earner and she-the-housewife to be lived as equal teamwork, male earners' claims to special privileges and deference from the rest of the household have long had social and cultural support. Husbands and wives have often operated on the assumption that the man's delivery of the wage entitled him to expect deference and domestic service from the woman. [...]

Extensive research on household incomes, systems of money management and who controls the money, demonstrate that patterns of management and control of money between couples have changed and are changing. In Britain, for example, there has been a clear shift towards joint bank accounts and formal pooling of income away from systems in which men give women an allowance or hand over the entire wage (Pahl, 1989; Morris, 1990; Vogler, 1994). However, despite the fact that about half of couples now pool their money, in many of these cases (estimates vary between about a third [Buck et al., 1994] and three-quarters [Vogler, 1994], one person, typically the man, exercises more control. [...]

The notion of man-as-the-main-earner persists among many heterosexual couples, despite the fact that many women are working as well as men. This is partly a reflection of the different work and promotion opportunities for men and women which result in men typically earning more. But it is also the result of associated persistent assumptions about gendered responsibilities. [...]

The tenacity of the conventional division of labour between couples is shown by the relatively small proportion of couples who institute radical reorganizations when a conventional arrangement is upset by male unemployment (Morris, 1990; Wheelock, 1990; Habgood, 1992). Men at home do not typically take on an equivalent burden of housework to that carried by most full-time housewives (Haas, 1982; Hunt, 1980; Russell, 1983), although this does happen in some households. In a study of men suffering unemployment in middle-age (in the North East of England), Jane Wheelock (1990) estimated that substantial changes were made in 20 per cent of cases. Several studies of households in which women are the main earners confirm that women do not translate their consequent financial power into the privileges conventionally assumed by male earners (Stamp, 1985; Morris, 1990).

Studies of cohabiting couples also demonstrate the strength of the woman-main-houseworker man-main-earner pattern, although, as with married couples, there are a minority who break the rule. [...] In a detailed British study Susan McRae (1993) found no significant difference between long-term cohabitees and married couples in money management, financial decision making and domestic divisions of labour. However, childless cohabitees were found to have slightly more egalitarian divisions of labour than childless married couples, although sharing tasks equally is a minority pattern among both groups (34% and 24% respectively) (Kiernan and Estaugh, 1993).

## Consequential disruption and resentment?

Has women's entry into paid employment without a matching take up by men of women's work disrupted the ease with which heterosexual couples can sustain a sense of equality, symmetry or complementarity despite inequalities? [...]

Since the 1970s, research on the practices of couples has documented both a new sensitivity to inequality and the new ways of papering over inequalities and containing resentment and disruption, such as 'talking up' and 'talking down' each other's contributions. Lillian Rubin's study of US working-class couples (detailed separate interviews with both partners in fifty white working-class marriages) found that many women complained about the 'double shift' or 'double burden'. While they had previously accepted full responsibility for housework, entering paid employment caused some reflection on the arrangements. 'When I'm not working, I think it's perfectly natural and right that I should do everything. Even now, I still feel it's my job; but it would be nice if he could help a little when I'm gone at work so much' (Rubin, 1976, p. 104). Nevertheless, these women did not generally seek to renegotiate the division of labour although tensions were visible between many couples. [...] Hochschild's study of working couples with young children led her to speak of a 'stalled revolution' in which women's entry into paid work had not been matched by changes in men's behaviour (1990). The term 'stalled' also refers to the fact that many women had expected more, that they had come to believe that marriage should be a relationship of equals and now were having to manage a gap between the beliefs and the practice. Her work provides documentation of how women kept disappointment and resentment at bay by drawing on traditional beliefs about manhood and womanhood to make sense of the inequality. [...]

Like Rubin's earlier work, Hochschild's analysis projects contradictory images, both a sense of crisis and the inevitability of change, on the one hand, and a sense of containment and business as usual, on the other. The crisis view indicates that either men shape up and do more at home or ultimately marriage-like relationships between men and women will not be sustained. However, Hochschild shows that many women work at suppressing their discontent in order to sustain their marriage. A number of British studies stress acceptance of inequality and very muted discontent rather than crisis. A study of dual-earner couples who were also coping with a new baby (a longitudinal study of 243 London-based women who returned to employment after maternity leave) found most of the women continuing to carry the responsibility for housework as well as the new responsibility for child care. But few expressed dissatisfaction with their partner (Brannen and Moss, 1991). [...]

Some of these couples sought a sense of equality and disclosing intimacy and yet re-created conventional gender inequalities. As in a number of other studies, some couples claimed to have ignored gendered notions of men-as-earners and women-as-housewives but yet, nevertheless, reproduced this division of labour in their own lives. Such couples explain their apparent conventionality by self-deceiving diversionary cover stories of gender neutral accidents of fate: 'she happens to like cooking and I'm no good at it' (rather than 'I am choosing not to learn to cook'); 'I work nearer home than him and can get back earlier to cook the tea' (rather than 'I have to organize my work so that I can do domestic chores and he has not'). [...] Closer scrutiny of 'preferences' confirmed the earlier finding of Edgell (1980) and others that men and women do not have equal rights to exercise a preference with respect to domestic work which nobody claims as enjoyable work. [...]

Other studies have shown that men and women with unequivocal beliefs in gender equality can nevertheless sustain unequal gendered arrangements. An Australian study of couples at various stages of the life cycle found a pervasive discrepancy between people's egalitarian beliefs and their practices (Bittman and Lovejoy, 1993). [...]

Studies of heterosexual couples suggest that imbalances in the degree of closeness each seeks from the other are common and gendered. After reviewing the North American research, Linda Thompson and Alexis Walker (1989) conclude: 'Overall, women tend to be more expressive and affectionate than men in marriage, and this difference bothers many wives' (Thompson and Walker, 1989, p. 846). British studies, ranging from newly married couples (Mansfield and Collard, 1988) and long-term relationships (Duncombe and Marsden, 1993, 1995a) to marriage in trouble (Brannen and Collard, 1982), find women's main complaint is men's lack of emotional participation in their marriage. [...]

Arlie Hochschild suggests that doing yet further emotional work is one of women's strategies for muting their disappointments in their relationships. 'Deep acting' (Hochschild, 1983) is the devotion of strenuous emotional effort to bringing actual feelings in line with the ideal of how a person ought to feel. Acting as if they were 'ever so happy really', while working to suppress or ignore the internal doubts closed the gap between the reality and the appropriate feeling. Duncombe and Marsden call this deep acting, to be 'ever so happy really', 'playing the couple game'. An alternative response among women in long-term relationships was to blame themselves for expecting too much and to slowly and reluctantly build an emotional life apart from their husbands, through children, part-time work and friendships with other women (1993, p. 276). Such women continue to 'play the couple game' in public but are 'shallow acting' rather than 'deep acting' (Duncombe and Marsden, 1995b; Hochschild, 1975), that is, they retain a sense of the gap between public image and private feelings. Both deep acting and shallow acting are far removed from mutually disclosing intimacy.

[...]

Not all couples contain dissatisfaction successfully, however. About a fifth of the couples in Mansfield and Collard's (1988) study were already sufficiently disappointed with their marriage to have doubts about the future. Many of the arguments cited as triggering doubts were women expressing dissatisfaction with the domestic division of labour and demanding that husbands do more. However, it seems that, while divisions of labour triggered disputes, the crux of the discontent was the lack of emotional closeness that women felt. [...]

### Heterosexual couples who did things differently

Research also identifies another group. These are heterosexual couples who claim to work out their lives without gender stereotyping and succeed in escaping the conventional divisions of labour. Among recent studies, the Australian work of Jacqueline Goodnow and Jennifer Bowes (1994) is the most optimistic about progress towards not only a more equal division of labour among heterosexual couples but a more profound equality and deeper intimacy. [...] Goodnow and Bowes recruited 50 couples among whom one or both partners took responsibility for an area of work not conventionally assigned to their gender. For 28 couples, their main style of organizing household jobs was to specialize, each with their own jobs, but men had taken responsibility for a job conventionally designated women's work: vacuuming, cooking, shopping, cleaning bathrooms, washing clothes and ironing. The other couples had much more fluid arrangements for getting the jobs done, switching responsibilities back and forth, sometimes doing jobs jointly, sometimes one or the other getting on with it alone.

These divisions of labour had been negotiated, in the case of half the couples after much talk and sometimes argument, often having started off on a different footing. In other words, things had not 'just fallen into place' [...] (Goodnow and Bowes, 1994, p. 72). [...] The process of negotiating was often a painful one. Women were more often the initiators of discussion and sometimes had to work very hard to get their partner to see the need to talk. It was difficult to renegotiate divisions of labour without bringing awareness of power issues to the surface. One woman described the difficulties she had in asking her partner to do things:

'I don't want to beg, and Don doesn't like to feel he's taking orders' (Judy, quoted in Goodnow and Bowes, 1994, p. 87).

The 'circumstances', 'competences' and 'preferences' other couples used to justify unequal divisions of labour were not, of course, irrelevant to these Australian couples. [. . .] They wanted fairness that was more real than apparent and hence, when negotiating, 'somehow, they must work their way through the use of "doesn't know how" or "doesn't see" rather than [the less self-serving honesty of] "would rather not"' (Goodnow and Bowes 1994, p. 30). Goodnow and Bowes argue that their respondents saw doing things for each other as an expression of care for each other. Their ethos was one of give and take, not of constantly watching each other to see who was doing more and, for each of them, doing more some of the time was a gift to the other person. [. . .] The couples who did things differently are not necessarily distinguished from couples in other studies by the kinds of things they wanted and valued from each other. Other couples claimed to want both the openness and honesty of mutually disclosing intimacy and more practical forms of love and care. However, the couples who did things different ultimately made a more mutual effort to match their ideal and reality. The process was often initiated by women who opted for speaking out, rather than deep or surface acting, despite the conflict that was often the initial consequence.

## Domestic violence and forced intimacy

'Domestic violence', typically men being violent towards their female partners, provides a contrasting example of couples in which women dare not speak out. Couples in which men are violent may manage an appearance of intimacy but, as violence supplants negotiation by coercion, the possibility of mutually constructed intimacy is undermined. Violent partners rarely acknowledge their violence and may claim to be intensely intimate. Janet Askham (1984), in a study of the complexities and tensions of married life, interviewed a couple in which the husband was clearly controlling and dominating his wife through threatened if not actual violence.[2] Because this study was centrally concerned with intimacy it provided insight into the extent to which a relationship was being constituted as intimate while overshadowed by the threat of violence. The husband, Alan, said he knew his wife, Anne, inside out, but, by his own testimony, he did not talk much to her and, by his wife's testimony, he was not interested in listening to her. His main confidant was his workmate of many years' standing. The couple had a conventional division of labour. He controlled the money. She did the housework. In addition, she was frightened of him. [. . .] Anne has tried to be open and Alan has responded by a variety of controlling tactics, including deliberately withholding himself and acting to generate her fear. [. . .] The dynamic between them of controlling and trying to survive being controlled is a stunted form of intimacy which involves one person wilfully not knowing another and disregarding their well-being while typically refusing to acknowledge that this is what they are doing. Domestic and sexual violence often has this character (Dobash and Dobash, 1992; Kelly, 1988; Gordon, 1988). Men who have been convicted of violence to their wives typically refuse to discuss their violent behaviour with their wives. Moreover they use a variety of strategies to reinterpret and minimize the seriousness of their violence, just as men convicted of rape often refuse to acknowledge that it was rape and minimize and rationalize their behaviour (Scully, 1990).

The fact that 'domestic violence' remains prevalent demonstrates the gap between the lives of a significant minority of heterosexual couples and the ideal of 'the pure relationship'. While there is no way of being certain, the various estimates of incidence suggest that heterosexual couples in which men intimidate women are probably more common than those who negotiate exceptional equality. A large survey of US marriages estimated that a violent assault would occur between husbands and wives in the course of over a quarter of US marriages (28 per cent; Strauss, Gelles and Steinmetz, 1980), and that attacks by husbands on wives are both more common and more dangerous to life and limb than attacks by wives on husbands. [...] Those who are optimistic about the future of intimacy and gender equality categorize such men as remnants of desperate traditionalism trying to hang on to private patriarchal power, while 'couples who do things differently' are in the forefront of social change. However, male violence seems to retain much wider roots than this analysis would suggest.

## Same-sex couples

An obvious difference between heterosexual and homosexual couples is that assumptions about differences between male and female may not play the same role in their relationship. Ideas about the gendered appropriateness of being a 'provider' or a 'housewife', notions about outside jobs as 'men's work' and inside jobs as 'women's work' cannot be unthinkingly applied to allocate tasks within a same-sex couple. [...] Kath Weston has explored the use of gender, divisions of labour and equality in gay and lesbian relationships (1991, 146–53). She found that lesbian and gay men valued equality in their relationships, although there was a considerable range of views concerning what constituted equality. A commitment to equality did not prevent some lesbians and many gay men from using gender categories. Some lesbians were strongly against any revival of butch/fem roles because they believed that contrasting roles re-created the inequalities of conventional heterosexual relationships. Others strongly denied this charge (Nestle, 1984). Most gay men use the categories 'queen' and 'butch' to place other gay men along a gendered continuum, but 'the majority agreed that within an erotic relationship they were inclined to seek congruence rather than complementarity, with a preference for the butch end of the spectrum' (Weston, 1991, p. 146).

[...] The combinations of equality, mutuality and knowing-each-other reported in literature on lesbians has led Anthony Giddens to argue that this is the group that currently most typically achieves 'the pure relationship'. However, a relatively small body of research is not a good basis for such strong generalization.

## Intimacy and relationship breakdown

Giddens's analysis of the fragility of the pure relationship (Giddens, 1992, pp. 136–40) was outlined in the opening paragraphs of this chapter. By way of supporting his case, he notes that lesbian relationships, which he identifies as exemplars of 'the pure relationship', do not typically last as long as marriage or heterosexual cohabitation. Whether or not lesbian relationships approximate to 'the pure relationship', North American authors lend support to the view that relationships founded only on mutual pleasure in an intense knowing-each-other are inevitably fragile. [...]

Some authors suggest that if a pattern of fragile serial relationships of intense disclosing intimacy is becoming the typical pattern, then such relationships must not be the core of a personal life if damage is to be minimized. A number of studies suggest that many of those who are held up as exemplars of 'the pure relationship' by Giddens – that is, lesbians, do not seek intimacy through couple relationships alone but rather through their 'family' of friends and ex-lovers. However, the public stories about the couple and the practical circumstances of men and women work against more general adoption of this pattern by the heterosexual majority. [...]

Are those relationships which are theoretically more likely to be constituted as 'pure relationships' – cohabiting relationships and same-sex relationships – un-equivocally so? Is it possible that, even if cohabiting and same-sex relationships are more fragile than married relationships, then this is for reasons that have nothing to do with 'disclosing intimacy'? The evidence on the fragility and quality of same-sex relationships is limited. Recent British work (Dunne, 1997, and the work of Jeffrey Weeks and colleagues (Weeks, Heaphy and Donovan, 2001) at South Bank University, London) reaffirms that same-sex couples themselves often believe their relationships are more intimate, more equal and less possessive than heterosexual relationships. However, it is not clear whether the quality of intimacy in their relationships is different from that of heterosexual couples who 'do things differently'. [...] The data reviewed in this chapter suggest that the majority of couples, married and cohabitees, conventional and couples-who-did-things-differently, do not found their relationships on disclosing intimacy alone. Cohabiting relationships may be less stable than marriage because they have low levels of social support from others and few binding economic and material ties. These are factors which Giddens associates with a 'pure relationship' founded on 'disclosing intimacy', but they can occur for other, more contingent, reasons in any relationship which is not a conventional marriage.

[...]

However, there is another possible direction to pursue in trying to understand the fragility of relationships and their likely future. Much of the evidence of this chapter suggests that 'disclosing intimacy' is not the dominant type of intimacy in most couple relationships. [...] For most couples, intimacy was intertwined with and expressed through practical arrangements of who did which household chores, who spent what money and the like. Men and women did not bracket off these aspects of their relationship in how they viewed each other but saw them as part of how they loved or did not love each other. Arguably, it is the persistence, not the demise of, the notion of man-main-earner and woman-main-houseworker / carer which is destabilizing, at the century's end. Failure to fully set such notions aside perverts men's and women's efforts to find a balance in practical caring and emotional work, a balance which does not simply paper over a gap between ideal and real, glued down with lurking resentment.


## Notes

1   See, for example, Blumstein and Schwartz, 1983; Luxton, 1980; Morris, 1984, 1990; Pahl, 1989.
2   Curiously, Askham does not directly address issues of gender or power in her otherwise insightful study of tensions between individual identity and the stability of the marriage.


## References

Askham, Janet, 1984. *Identity and Stability in Marriage*. Cambridge University Press, Cambridge.
Bittman, Michael and Lovejoy, Frances, 1993. Domestic power: negotiating an unequal division of labour within a framework of equality. *Australian and New Zealand Journal of Sociology*, 29, 302–21.
Blumstein, Philip and Schwartz, Pepper, 1983. *American Couples: Money, Work, Sex.* William Morrow, New York.
Brannen, Julia and Collard, Jean, 1982. *Marriages in Trouble: the Process of Seeking Help*. Tavistock, London.
Brannen, Julia and Moss, Peter, 1991. *Managing Mothers: Dual Earner Households after Maternity Leave*. Unwin Hyman, London.
Buck, N., Gershuny, J., Rose, D. and Scott, J., 1994. *Changing Households: The British Household Panel Survey 1990–1992*. ESRC Research Centre on Micro Social Change, University of Essex, Colchester.
Dobash, R. Emerson and Dobash, Russell P., 1992. *Women, Violence and Social Change*. Routledge, London.
Duncombe, Jean and Marsden, Dennis, 1993. Love and intimacy: the gender division of emotion and emotion work. *Sociology*, 27, 221–41.
Duncombe, Jean and Marsden, Dennis, 1995a. Can men love? 'Reading', 'staging' and 'resisting' the Romance. In L. Pearce and J. Stacey (eds), *Romance Revisited*. Lawrence and Wishart, London, 238–50.
Duncombe, Jean and Marsden, Dennis, 1995b. 'Workaholics' and 'whingeing women': theorising intimacy and emotion work: the last frontier of gender inequality? *Sociological Review*, 43, 150–69.
Dunne, Gillian, 1997. *Lesbian Lifestyles: Women's Work and the Politics of Sexuality*. Macmillan, London.
Edgell, Stephen, 1980. *Middle Class Couple: A Study of Segregation, Domination and Inequality in Marriage*. George Allen and Unwin, London.

Geerken, Michael and Gove, Walter, 1983. *At Home and At Work: The Family's Allocation of Labor*. Sage, Beverly Hills.

Gershuny, Jonathan, Godwin, Michael and Jones, Sally, 1994. The domestic labour revolution: a process of lagged adaptation? In Anderson, M., Bechhofer, F. and Gershuny, J. (eds), *The Social and Political Economy of the Household*. Oxford University Press, Oxford, 151–97.

Giddens, Anthony, 1992. *The Transformation of Intimacy: Sexuality, Love and Eroticism in Modern Societies*. Polity, Cambridge.

Giele, Janet Zollinger, 1974. Changes in the modern family: their impact on sex roles. In Coser, R. L. (ed.), *The Family: Its Structures and Functions* (2nd ed). Macmillan, London, 460–70.

Goodnow, J. and Bowes, J., 1994. *Men, Women and Household Work*. Oxford University Press, Melbourne.

Gordon, Linda, 1988. *Heroes of Their Own Lives: The Politics and History of Family Violence*. Virago, London.

Haas, L. L., 1982. Determinants of role sharing behaviour: a study of egalitarian couples. *Sex Roles*, 8, 747–60.

Habgood, Ruth, 1992. On his terms: gender and the politics of domestic life. In Du Plessis, R. (ed.), *Feminist Voices: Women's Studies Texts for Aotearoa/New Zealand*. Oxford University Press, Oxford, 163–79.

Hochschild, Arlie, 1975. The sociology of feelings and emotion: selected possibilities. In Milkman, R. and Kanter, (eds), *Another Voice*. Anchor, New York.

Hochschild, Arlie, 1983. *The Managed Heart: Commercialization of Human Feeling*. University of California Press, Berkeley and London.

Hochschild, Arlie, 1990. *The Second Shift: Working Parents and the Revolution at Home*. Piatkus, London.

Hunt, Pauline, 1980. *Gender and Class Consciousness*. Macmillan, London.

Kelly, Liz, 1988. *Surviving Sexual Violence*. Polity, Cambridge.

Kiernan, Kathleen and Estaugh, Valerie, 1993. *Cohabitation, Extra-Marital Childbearing and Social Policy*. Family Policy Studies Centre, London.

Luxton, M., 1980. *More Than a Labour of Love*. Women's Press, Toronto.

Mansfield, Penny and Collard, Jean, 1988. *The Beginning of the Rest of Your Life: A Portrait of Newly-Wed Marriage*. Macmillan, London.

McRae, Susan, 1993. *Cohabiting Mothers: Changing Marriage and Motherhood?* Policy Studies Institute, London.

Meissner, M., Humphries, E. W., Meis, S. M. and Scheu, W. J., 1975. No exit for wives: sexual divisions of labour and the cumulation of household demands. *Canadian Review of Sociology and Anthropology*, 12, 24–39.

Morris, Lydia, 1984. Redundancy and patterns of household finance. *Sociological Review*, 32, 492–593.

Morris, Lydia, 1987. Constraints on gender. *Work, Employment and Society*, 1, 85–106.

Morris, Lydia, 1990. *The Workings of the Household*. Polity, Cambridge.

Nestle, Joan, 1984. The fem question. In Vance, C. S. (ed.), *Pleasure and Danger: Exploring Female Sexuality*. Routledge and Kegan Paul, Boston, 232–41.

Nickols, S. Y. and Metzen, E. J., 1982. Impact of wife's employment upon husband's housework. *Journal of Family Issues*, 3, 199–217.

Pahl, Jan, 1989. *Money and Marriage*. Macmillan, London.

Rosen, Ellen Israel, 1987. *Bitter Choices: Blue-Collar Women In and Out of Work*. University of Chicago Press, Chicago.

Rubin, Lillian B., 1976. *Worlds of Pain: Life in the Working-Class Family*. Basic Books, New York.

Russell, Graeme, 1983. *The Changing Role of Fathers*. Open University Press, Milton Keynes.

Scully, Diana, 1990. *Understanding Sexual Violence: A Study of Convicted Rapists*. Unwin Hyman, Cambridge, Mass.

Stamp, P., 1985. Balance of financial power in marriage. *Sociological Review*, 33, 546–66.

Strauss, M. A., Gelles, R. and Steinmetz, S., 1980. *Behind Closed Doors: Violence in the American Family*. Doubleday, New York.

Thompson, Linda and Walker, Alexis, 1989. Gender in families: women and men in marriage, work, and parenthood. *Journal of Marriage and the Family*, 51, 845–71.

Vogler, Carolyn, 1994. Money in the household. In Anderson, M., Bechhofer, F. and Gershuny, J. (eds), *The Social and Political Economy of the Household*. Oxford University Press, Oxford, 225–66.

Weeks, J., Heaphy, B. and Donovan, C., 2001. *Same Sex Intimacies: Families of Choice and Other Life Experiments*. London, Routledge.

Weston, Kath, 1991. *Families We Choose: Lesbians, Gays, Kinship*. Columbia University Press, New York.

Wheelock, Jane, 1990. *Husbands at Home: The Domestic Economy in a Post-Industrial Society*. Routledge, London.

Wight, Daniel, 1993. *Workers Not Wasters. Masculine Respectability, Consumption and Unemployment in Central Scotland: A Community Study*. Edinburgh University Press, Edinburgh.

Wilcock, R. C. and Franke, W. H., 1963. *Unwanted Workers*. Free Press, Glencoe, New York.

Young, Michael and Willmott, Peter, 1973. *The Symmetrical Family*. Penguin, Harmondsworth.

# 24

# The Disappearance of the Modern Homosexual*

## *Henning Bech*

[. . .]

The homosexual is a kind of time bomb, encoded with its own explosion. Or perhaps rather its own discreet disappearance. The very circumstances which form the background of his existence also act towards eliminating him; at the same time, he himself helps them along. This has been the case ever since he was a boy at the end of the [nineteenth] century; but it has become all the more clear over the years.

In late modern societies there is a tendency for the particular cultural and social traits of the homosexual – his special ways of living, experiences and expressions – to spread and become universal. The conditions of modern life affect an ever-growing number of people and become increasingly more urgent, or they appeal more and more. The former buffers – above all, marriage and the family – are in a process of steady dissolution. Living in the city – in 'a world of strangers' – has become a reality for more and more people and opens up new possibilities for social life and personal development. 'The heterosexuals', too, know that the family is not an eternal institution into which they have entered once and for all: they may divorce, establish another family, live outside the family, use the world of strangers as a resource, a place where one can go and find other people to build up new kinds of relationships. They, too, experience promiscuity, broken relationships and serial monogamy, and they establish networks of friends rather than relatives. Further, urban structures as well as visual media and everyday design permeate life, suggesting such modes of

---

*EDITORS' NOTE: To contextualize Bech's use of terminology in this chapter, readers should note that, at the outset of *When Men Meet: Homosexuality and Modernity*, Bech states: 'Whenever "homosexuality" and "homosexual" are used without further specification they refer to men and relations between men' (Bech 1997, ch. 1, n. 3, p. 218).

behaviour and experience as aestheticization, sexualization, staging, camp and kitsch. For most, not much seems to be preordained or eternally secure and stable in relation to work, social intercourse and personal identity – even gender has generally grown into a role and a problem, or an opportunity. The institutions of high art, transformed, supplemented and democratized as film, video and rock music, help promote sensitivity in everyone. The theory and practice of liberal democracy increasingly become a lived reality as each identity is conceived from the outset in terms of relative oppression and the right to improvement. With changes in life space, direct social control from family and neighbours gives way to anonymous, potential supervision and control for everyone, along with the corresponding attention and awareness of the possibility of being watched. The ideologies and institutions of self-analysis are ever-expanding, leaving practically no one without some idea that they have an inner self and sexuality, precious but hidden and dangerous, always in potential need of therapy. In this way, the conditions of life which formerly belonged to homosexuals in particular are now increasingly becoming common to all. To a certain degree, these conditions are also changing; but the changes often imply a reinforcement or a further development of features and ways that were already customary for the homosexual. One example is the spread of television; with it, an urban world – a world of strangers and all that comes with it – penetrates directly into the secluded life space of the home and the family. Further, the homosexuals themselves operate a kind of socio-cultural export enterprise: by virtue of their participation in the commercial production of style and in the cultural arena, they are instrumental in spreading ways of life and forms of culture (cor)responding to the modern conditions of life.[1] In general, the processes are most advanced in societies with a certain degree and distribution of economic wealth and state-provided social welfare. Only then can individuals really use the conditions of modern life to create workable and satisfying ways of life, and only then do they achieve the necessary security to do so.[2]

Thus, what was 'specifically homosexual' tends to disappear, in that the universal becomes just like it. In this sense, a sociocultural 'homosexualization' takes place.[3]

[...]

Nothing remains of the modern homosexual, so to speak, except his special sexual preference; but that, too, in the same process loses much of its dramatic significance by way of the general sexualization (glances, signals, meetings, experiments, surfaces, etc.) and the general acknowledgement of the collapse of norms, along with the non-given of identities and ways of life. All must now decide for themselves and their given or chosen surroundings the best way to shape their lives.

[...]

No doubt this trend towards a disappearance of the modern homosexual is at work in all late modern societies of the 'west', in some cases rather prominently so. One example is the introduction in 1989 of 'registered partnerships' for homosexuals in Denmark. The public debate surrounding the introduction of the bill is indicative.[4]

[...]

The old types of justification for same-sex love and pleasure – well rehearsed in countless controversies over homosexuality and society – were largely missing. One major reason for this was no doubt that they had lost credibility. It was simply no longer convincing to refer to the essentially and naturally different personality type of the homosexuals, or to their being inherently and particularly respectable *or* alternative – when the non-homosexuals are increasingly exhibiting the same personality traits and becoming equally 'respectable' or unrespectable and 'alternative'.

[...]

The changes are further evidenced by the arguments prevailing among the supporters. Above all, these arguments centred on the principle of *equality*: homosexuals would now gain (with a few exceptions) the *right to equal freedom of choice* as had heterosexuals in relation to the privileges and obligations of forming couples. Among the gains mentioned was the opportunity for a greater emotional and financial security in relationships, as well as a higher degree of commitment and responsibility in feelings and actions. Generally, however, the various possible benefits of registered partnerships were not a main theme. The emphasis lay on the *principles* of equality, freedom and justice. The realization of these principles was often presented as a value in itself, not least in relation to the situation of minorities. Moreover, it was frequently added, legal equality implied an official, societal acknowledgement of the *equal worth* of homosexual and heterosexual relations. This would have a positive impact on the attitudes of homosexuals towards themselves, as well as on the attitudes and reactions of others in relation to them. Equality and equal worth, then, were the main arguments of the supporters of 'registered partnership', and, as it turned out, the ones that won the battle. This was in line with the views of the majority of Danes, according to opinion polls in 1988 and 1989, where questions were posed in terms of equal rights.

The background for this state of debates and events is obviously to be found in the broader equalizing of differences between the homosexuals and 'the others', as well as in the fact that this equalizing moves in a homosexual direction, so to speak. In short, any feature of the modern homosexual that you might want to emphasize as particularly characteristic or alternative is becoming increasingly – *common*. It is therefore no longer obvious why 'the homosexuals' shouldn't have precisely the same legal and social rights (and injustices) as others. This is how the matter may also appear to those homosexuals who have no desire to make use of such rights themselves, e.g. the right of 'marriage'. In fact, it seems that the majority of both gays and lesbians simply considered it an extension of their possibilities of choice and social acceptance. Therefore they saw no reason to argue against registered partnerships, even if they themselves had no plans to give up their own particular way of life in favour of it. This conclusion is further corroborated by the fact that relatively few have actually entered a registered partnership. [...]

Thus, the introduction of registered partnerships in Denmark should *not* be misinterpreted as a 'normalization' or 'bourgeoisification' or 'straightification' of the homosexual. On the contrary, 'homosexual marriage' has become possible only on the basis of the decline in prestige and importance of marriage and the family. Indeed, the decline of those institutions is a crucial aspect of the processes related to the disappearance of the modern homosexual and the basic *homo-genization* of ways of life.

Insofar as the modern homosexual is disappearing, we might speak of a *postmodernization* of same-sex love and pleasure. And in fact, it is easy to summarize the particular features of the Danish debate on registered partnership in the rhetorical terms of postmodernism: *post* Nature, *post* Respectability, *post* the Alternative – as well as *post* God, *post* the Family. Moreover, a consummate homo-genization would seem to imply yet another 'post' (although for some this may appear as the ultimate negation of postmodernity): *post difference!* Well, well. First: a disappearance of the modern homosexual does not necessarily imply that all differences will disappear (cf. below). Second: the disappearance of the modern homosexual is a phenomenon that, even in those areas where the homosexual exists, is merely a *tendency*, far from having been fully developed. To use the Danish debate on registered partnerships as an example once again: true, the old type of justification was not very pronounced. But the arguments were still made on the basis of and in relation to 'the homosexuals', i.e. explicitly or implicitly it was contended that they are of a kind that should be entitled to freedom, equality and justice. And that is also a sort of justification. Moreover, the fact that the majority of Danes did support the introduction of registered partnerships need not imply that they considered homosexuals to be of *equal worth* to heterosexuals – or even that they didn't consider them 'unnatural' or the like. All that can be safely concluded is that they thought homosexuals should be given (more of) the same *rights* that heterosexuals had. [...] The source may just as well have been a sense of pity as of respect. The fact that homosexuals were not given full marriage rights points toward this interpretation. The introduction of registered partnerships in Denmark, then, testifies to a society somewhere in the middle of the kind of transformation sketched above in relation to ways of life as well as to the end of the homosexual.[5]

In other parts of the world it is rather absurd to speak of a disappearance of the homosexual, since he doesn't even exist. In some countries he is in the process of being brought into existence, which in these contexts seems to be quite an appropriate procedure and practice. For instance, in eastern Europe where gays and lesbians are organizing and trying to manifest an identity and a lifestyle in the public sphere, it would not only be absurd but also obstructive to speak in such terms. Even where the homosexual has been well established for decades, it doesn't always make sense to speak of a trend towards his disappearance. In most (north-)western societies, the era of the 'classical' modern homosexual can be dated from the later nineteenth century and into the 1970s. What happens after this, however, takes different forms in different national socio-cultural contexts. In the US, for example, the changes do not have the character of a disappearance of the modern homosexual. They are of another sort, expressed by the phenomenon of 'queerness': the use of the word 'queer' as a self-applied label, 'queer nation', 'queer theory'. [...] The rise of the queer in the US is related to the fact that the family, with its patterns of gender and authority, is still widely considered to be the secure haven against the threats of modernity, and that modernity, for the majority of the population, is still considered threatening – convictions and feelings no doubt connected with American government politics in relation to the distribution of wealth and the level of social security. However, the recent phenomenon of the queer is not a mere continuation of the 'classical' modern homosexual. After all, it is post-1970s; and it is nourished by the sense of disbelief and anger generated by the gap between the existence of huge, openly gay worlds on the one hand, and the harshly anti-homosexual outside world on the other. Still, this situation – at least in some versions of queer ideology, and particularly in the ideas of a queer nation – gives occasion for a restating of ideas and rhetorics from the radical liberation movements of the late 1960s and early 1970s: *We're radically different from the rest of them, we're better than them, we're more liberated than them, we are besieged by them, they want to annihilate us, we are at war with them, we contain the seeds of their liberation*...[6] Even in many intellectually sophisticated versions of queer theory a certain world view is typical: the vision of a monolithically present and massively destructive 'dominant society' allowing only forms of wily resistance or oblique defiance (a vision not without some reason in the United States, to be sure). On the other hand, the diversity of queer strategies and perspectives testifies to the enormous creativity and imagination of American 'post-gay' undertakings in language, theory, art and actions. Thus, even in those countries where the overall world view does not really make sense any more, it is impossible not to be inspired by the queer – because the homosexual has in fact not fully disappeared here, either, although he is in the process of so doing; and, to the extent that he has disappeared, there is still a life to be lived and in need of fresh perspectives.

The (north-)western part of continental Europe is but a tiny part of the globe. Moreover, the world of the future will no doubt bring together increasing numbers of people of various ethnic and cultural backgrounds, and one may wonder to what extent such globalization will also bring with it a perpetuation of *radically* different values and ways of life. However, it seems very unlikely that the modern conditions of life won't become close and constant realities for more and more people. In this way, the world is no doubt becoming increasingly modernized, and modernization is becoming increasingly global. And consequently, these universally shared conditions of life will present an impetus towards a homogenization of lifestyles, i.e. towards making them share the basic traits of the modern homosexual's form of existence. Now, if differences in the amount and distribution of wealth and social welfare are severe in the future, it can be expected that many people will cling defensively to their own particular traditional values and ways of life. In that case, the homosexual may well come to be perceived, once again, as the incarnation of the threats of modernity. If, however, a high degree of equality in economic and social opportunities is realized, modernization will likely bring with it a gradual and rather relaxed homo-genization of life-styles and a concomitant *happy end* of the homo-sexual.

[...]

If the homosexual disappears, what can one imagine will come about instead? *Universal bisexuality* was the answer from parts of the Gay Liberation movement in the 1970s.[7] Yet on the face of it, there is something unseemly about this answer. If the experiences of the homosexuals give occasion for a distinct ethic, this can certainly not be one that prescribes rules for how people should find pleasure so long as they don't harm anyone. Rather, it should emphasize the right to abandon oneself to a certain preference, to make a life out of it if one wishes.

What the gay liberationists meant, though, was no doubt often precisely this: that people should do as they please, without harm, no matter if it is with a man or a woman; and they should at least recognize that they themselves have or could have erotic or sexual interests in their own sex as well. The trend already seems to be moving in this direction, in some countries at least. Whether a man wants another man is becoming a matter of preference, of *taste*, wherever it comes from, and of getting the most out of the kind of life which one taste or the other makes possible. In this way, a certain utopia is becoming real:

> In remote parts of the country, among certain groups, an explanation is still considered requisite if someone is vegetarian. In ever wider circles, explaining is no longer necessary even though the majority of people surely still eat meat. If someone came up with the idea that vegetarians are a special group, fundamentally different from the rest of humanity, with a particular life story (something about mother's nipple?) and a particular personality, that it is wrong (disgusting, sickly), a problem for themselves and for society which required the investigating and regulating intervention of medical science – no one would bother to listen. It is not being a vegetarian, but having this attitude towards vegetarians that would be considered strange, perhaps requiring an explanation.
>
> Being vegetarian is not a question of radical difference, wrongness, life history and personality type, it is a matter of preference, taste, at best perhaps of art: some vegetarians take their preference to unimaginable heights of gastronomical delight for themselves and others; at worst – for those who insist on meat for dinner every day and *refuse* to eat vegetarian – a matter of *eccentricity, foolishness, a whim*: that woman has a thing, you see, but that's her business (just as *their* perpetual demand for meat can seem ridiculous the other way around). 'Each to her own taste', 'there is no accounting for tastes'; it is possible to talk about them, i.e. *depict* their qualities, attempt to *persuade*, but it is senseless to try to *prove* that liver pâté tastes better than lentil pâté.[8]

So, too, with men's desire for men: nothing that makes radically different, wrong, radiates a particular personality or demands monitoring and explanation – but a taste; a huge *de-dramatization*. The idea of taste thus implies a complete change of attitude towards same-sex sexuality, eroticism and love. Another set of questions can be raised: not where it comes from, but what you can get out of it.

The cultivation of this taste will no doubt carve out or create its special spaces, institutions, times, ways – which will differ more or less from those developed by *aficionados* of e.g. vegetarianism, bridge or opera.[9] Socially, however, they might not be experienced very differently from these.

How large will such groups of impassioned cultivators of same-sex taste be? The question is perhaps not all that innocent. While the notion of a common bisexual praxis may seem a megalomanic projection of wishful fantasy aimed at eradicating, once and for all, any distinction between a 'homosexual minority' and a 'heterosexual majority', the idea of a community of taste may imply another latent presupposition. At least in its typical exemplifications (such as opera or bridge), it seems to proceed from the assumption that these groups would be *small*, and perhaps also vulnerable, and thus it re-establishes a form of minority–majority conception.

Obviously, one might choose other cases for comparison: aficionados of soccer, for example, or of roast veal.[10] But there remains an important and interesting dimension regarding the question of size: how do we imagine *most men* will live with respect to sexual or erotic relations with other men? Further, we can use the fear that is perhaps concealed in the size question as an incentive to ask with renewed energy: is it truly realistic to believe that a utopia of taste could come close to becoming a reality? [...] We may be certain that there is no biological or other non-historically determined aversion among men to sexuality with other men. With respect to modern societies we have furthermore been led to assume a *universal* readiness for such relations – otherwise the phenomenon of 'absent homosexuality' could not come about, i.e. the simultaneously produced rejection of *and* incitation to homosexuality, a self-reproducing and self-expanding dialectical machinery superimposing itself on all relations between men.[11] But is there perhaps a dislike which isn't merely a reflection or shadow cast from the homosexual, but rather something founded in the *modern societal conditions themselves* in which and against the background of which absent homosexuality exists? And if so, this aversion would, if anything, become more widespread with the spread of these conditions of life to ever larger groups.

Rather the opposite, I shall argue. The life spaces of most people are increasingly those of a telemediated social world of strangers – in other words, of a *telecity*.[12] This involves an emphasis on distance, gaze and surfaces which in itself implies *aestheticization* as well as *sexualization*; all the while the contrast of masculinity to femininity is accentuated – precisely, as an aestheticized and sexualized contrast. Consequently, the male body and its cultural attire become sexualized for men. It has been argued that the man or men in the picture resist sexualization by being active and averting their eyes from the viewer.[13] But this is no longer always true, not even when the pictures move: the close-ups and slow motions of the male body in porn videos or televised sports partially neutralize the activity, making the man static enough to be an object of sexualized spectation. More fundamentally, the objection contradicts itself: it presupposes that men can be sexualized only if they assume the same position in the picture as that which, in modernity, has traditionally been assigned to *women* – although, in fact, the sexualization of men as *men* would seem to require that they retain a fair amount of their culturally defined masculinity and be, for example, active and sullen (once in a while, at least).

The various forms of *aestheticized sexualization* of men for men are becoming increasingly explicit. For instance, the picture surfaces in a number of today's most popular advertisements for masculinity products are already nearly indistinguishable from the gay soft porn of the 1950s.[14] Along with the growing public debate on sexual matters, this will imply a greater general acknowledgement of the eroticism and sexuality in the attractions between men, as no shadow can fall any more from the already vanished homosexual. The result amounts to a form of sexualized or erotic relation between men which is *post* homosexualization, absent of absent homosexuality.

Conceivable, then, as one possibility, is a continuum between a comparatively small group of aficionados of same-sex tastes and a large group of part-time telemedia enjoyers. The difference, however, is not as great as it might seem, since even the impassioned cultivators of same-sex taste increasingly live in a telemediated world of sexualized, non-orgasmic relations to strangers. This is one reason why the traditional type of surveys on the prevalence of 'homosexuality' are already in danger of becoming antiquated even before they are carried out: the questions asked are partially irrelevant; sexuality is not what it used to be.

But surely there will be larger or smaller groups that, for one reason or another, have developed an aversion or estrangement regarding this taste. [ . . . ] If they aren't content with venomous comments and personal dissociation, but also wish to eradicate this taste and its impassioned cultivators in practice, they must be forced to let be. A modern rationality should not allow annihilating assaults on difference which doesn't harm anyone even though it may be alien.

In any case, however, it is difficult to imagine that a certain amount of justification would not be necessary and tempting for the impassioned practitioners of same-sex taste. In modern societies it seems altogether inconceivable that identities, ways of life or even just preferences could exist without a certain amount of legitimizing. This stems not only from the Enlightenment experience that given circumstances can be changed and that hence, there are always possibilities for creating better opportunities for particular differences and interests. It is also related to the fact that modern societies are largely argumentative in their basic structure, as is apparent in their typical institutions such as science, the judicial system and parliament.[15] What one might wish for same-sex love and sexuality is, however, that the *excess* of justification still adhering to it might be eradicated. In this connection, one could propose the rule that the more legal equality there is, the less there is to legitimize. This is supported by the fact that, shortly after the introduction of registered partnerships, the Danish debate over this right nearly subsided even among its opponents.[16]

*Utopia* might be somewhere where you wouldn't have to justify your desires for other men but could simply live them in peace with society and your neighbour. In *Negative Dialectics*, Adorno comments on an expression by Eichendorf about 'beautiful strangeness': 'The state of reconciliation would not annect the strange and alien with philosophical imperialism, but be happy that this remained, in the proximity granted, the distant and different, beyond the opposite and same.' Such a state would not imply any justification of one's little idiosyncrasies or immense joyful ecstasies. But it's utopian.[17]

[. . .]

## Notes

1  Cf. Bech 1997: pp 164–81.
2  Among the major works are Bauman 1991; 1995; Beck and Beck-Gernsheim 1990; Chambers 1986; Chaney 1990; Featherstone 1991; Fischer 1982; Fiske 1987; Gergen 1991; Giddens 1991; 1992; Lash and Urry 1994; Sennett 1990; Shields 1991; Sontag 1964, 1977; Urry 1990; Wellman et al. 1988. In relation to these changes, and put in the terminology of postmodernism, the homosexual may be said to be 'pre-postmodern', postmodern before the advent of postmodernity.
3  The notion of 'sociocultural homosexualization' is a further elaboration and specification of the concept of 'homosexualization' used by Altman in his pioneering work (Altman 1982).
4  The Danish law on 'registered partnerships' was passed on 26 May 1989 and has been in effect since 1 October 1989. In a registered partnership two people of the same sex obtain the same rights and obligations as a man and a women have in marriage, with the exception of adoption rights, rights of custody of the partner's children, and the option of church weddings. I have analysed the debate in Bech 1991b; 1992a.
5  Cf. Bech 1989; Lützen 1988; Fouchard 1994; Gaasholt and Togeby 1995: 37f.
6  For some informative introductions, overviews and discussions, see Abelove 1995; Berlant and Freeman 1992; Bérubé and Escoffier 1991; Browning 1993: ch. 2; Duggan 1992; Lauretis 1991; Penn 1995; Warner 1993.
7  Cf. e.g. Wittman 1970: 331; Altman 1971: 229, 233f, 236f; 'Guy' in FHAR 1971: 75f; Homosexuelle Aktion Westberlin 1973: 41.
8  Bech 1983: 60.
9  Plummer (1975: 171f) mentions surfing, medieval dancing and stamp collecting as other imaginable exemplifications – before voting instead for the utopia of universal bisexuality.
10  Interestingly, Kertbeny – who was probably the coiner of the term 'homosexual' – speaks of sexual preference as a taste on a par with the preference for roast lamb or roast veal. Cf. Kertbeny 1868. Obviously, the use of 'taste' to characterize same-sex sexual preference has a long history, particularly prominent in the eighteenth century.
11  Cf. the analysis in Bech 1997: 10–84.
12  Cf. Bech 1992b; 1995.
13  Cf. Dyer 1982; Steinman 1992. It has also been argued that if the man in the picture does not conform to these demands he is 'punished', e.g. by being ridiculed (Neale 1983; Poynton and Hartley 1990).
14  Cf. Mort 1988; Moore 1988; Henriksson 1989; Bech 1991a.
15  Cf. Bech 1997: 137–41, 161–4.
16  Cf. Bech 1991b.
17  Adorno 1966: 191 (I have changed the English translation).

# References

Abelove, H. 1995: 'The Queering of Lesbian / Gay History'. *Radical History Review*, 62, 44–57.

Adorno, T. 1966: *Negative Dialectics*, tr. E. Ashton. New York: Routledge, 1990.

Altman, D. 1971: *Homosexual Oppression and Liberation*. New York: Avon, 1973.

—— 1982: *The Homosexualization of America, the Americanization of the Homosexual*. New York: St Martin's Press.

Bauman, Z. 1991: *Modernity and Ambivalence*. Cambridge: Polity.

—— 1995: *Life in Fragments: Essays in Postmodern Morality*. Oxford: Blackwell.

Bech, H. 1983: 'Mellem mænd'. *Kontext*, 45, 53–67.

—— 1989: *Mellem mænd*. Copenhagen: Tiderne Skifter.

—— 1991a: 'Mandslængsel: Hankøn i moderne samfund'. *Varia* (Denmark) 1, 83–97.

—— 1991b: 'Recht fertigen: Über die Einführung "homosexueller Ehen" in Dänemark'. *Zeitschrift für Sexualforschung*, 4(3), 213–24.

—— 1992a: 'Report from a Rotten State: "Marriage" and "Homosexuality" in "Denmark"'. In: Plummer, K. (ed.), *Modern Homosexualities*. London: Routledge, 134–47.

—— 1992b: 'Living Together in the (Post)Modern World'. Paper presented at the European Sociology Conference, 26–9 August, University of Vienna.

—— 1995: 'CITYSEX: Die öffentliche Darstellung der Begierden'. *Soziale Welt*, 46(1), 5–27; revised English version in *Theory, Culture & Society*, 15(3–4), 1998, 215–42.

—— 1997: *When Men Meet: Homosexuality and Modernity*. Cambridge: Polity.

Beck, U. and Beck-Gernsheim, E. 1995: *The Normal Chaos of Love*, tr. M. Ritter and J. Wiebel. Cambridge: Polity.

Berlant, L. and Freeman, E. 1992: 'Queer Nationality'. In: Warner M. (ed.), *Fear of a Queer Planet*. Minneapolis: University of Minnesota Press, 193–229.

Bérubé, A. and Escoffier, J. 1991: 'Queer / nation'. *Out / Look*, 11.

Browning, F. 1993: *The Culture of Desire: Paradox and Perversity in Gay Lives Today*. New York: Crown.

Chambers, I. 1986: *Popular Culture: The Metropolitan Experience*. London: Routledge.

Chaney, D. 1990: 'Subtopia in Gateshead: The Metro Centre as a Cultural Form'. *Theory, Culture & Society*, 7(4), 49–68.

Duggan, L. 1992: 'Making it Perfectly Queer'. *Socialist Review*, 22(1), 11–31.

Dyer, R. 1982: 'Don't Look Now: The Male Pin-up'. *Screen*, 23(3–4), 61–73.

Featherstone, M. 1991: *Consumer Culture and Postmodernism*. London: Sage.

FHAR (Front Homosexuel d'Action Révolutionnaire) 1971: *Rapport contre la normalité*. Paris: Champ libre.

Fischer, C. 1982: *To Dwell among Friends: Personal Networks in Town and City*. Chicago: University of Chicago Press.

Fiske, J. 1987: *Television Culture*. London: Routledge, 1989.

Fouchard, J. 1994: *Seksuel adfærd med risiko for HIV-smitte – blandt mænd i Danmark, der har sex med andre mænd*. Copenhagen: Faculty of Health Sciences.

Gaasholt, Ø. and Togeby, L. 1995: *I syv sind: Danskernes holdninger til flygtninge og indvandrere*. Aarhus: Politica.

Gergen, K. 1991: *The Saturated Self: Dilemmas of Contemporary Self*. New York: Basic.

Giddens, A. 1991: *Modernity and Self-identity: Self and Society in the Late Modern Age*. Cambridge: Polity.

—— 1992: *The Transformation of Intimacy: Sexuality, Love and Eroticism in Modern Societies*. Cambridge: Polity.

Henriksson, B. 1989: 'Gossarna i reklamen'. *Lambda Nordica,* 3–4, 194–244.

Homosexuelle Aktion Westberlin 1973: *Zur Frage, warum Schwule unterdrückt werden.* West Berlin, stencilled paper.

Kertbeny, K. 1868: 'Brief an Ulrichs 6.5.1868'. In: Herzer, M. 1987: 'Ein Brief von Kertbeny an Ulrichs in Würzburg'. *Capri: Zeitschrift für schwule Geschichte,* 1, 31–5.

Lash, S. and Urry, J. 1994: *Economies of Signs and Space.* London: Sage.

Lauretis, T. 1991: 'Queer Theory: Lesbian and Gay Sexualities. An Introduction'. *Differences,* 3(2), iii–xviii.

Lützen, K 1988: *At prøve lykken: 25 lesbiske livshistorier.* Copenhagen: Tiderne Skifter.

Moore, S. 1988: 'Here's Looking at You, Kid!' In: Gamman, L. and Marshment, M. (eds), *The Female Gaze: Women as Viewers of Popular Culture.* London: The Women's Press, 44–59.

Mort, F. 1988: 'Boys Own? Masculinity, Style and Popular Culture'. In: Chapman, R. and Rutherford, J. (eds), *Male Order: Unwrapping Masculinity.* London: Lawrence & Wishart, 160–72.

Neale, S. 1983: 'Masculinity as Spectacle'. *Screen,* 24(6), 2–16.

Penn, D. 1995: 'Queer: Theorizing Politics and History'. *Radical History,* 62, 24–43.

Plummer, K. 1975: *Sexual Stigma: An Interactionist Account.* London: Routledge & Kegan Paul.

——(ed.) 1992: *Modern Homosexualities: Fragments of Lesbian and Gay Experiences.* London: Routledge.

Poynton, B. and Hartley, J. 1990: 'Male-gazing: Australian Rules Football, Gender and Television'. In: Brown, M. (ed.), *Television and Women's Culture: The Politics of the Popular.* London: Sage, 144–57.

Sennett, R. 1990: *The Conscience of the Eye: The Design and Social Life of Cities.* New York: Knopf.

Shields, R. 1991: *Places on the Margin: Alternative Geographies of Modernity.* London: Routledge.

Sontag, S. 1964: 'Notes on "Camp"'. In: Sontag, *Against Interpretation.* New York: Farrar, Straus & Giroux, 1966, 275–92.

—— 1977: *On Photography.* New York: Farrar, Straus & Giroux.

Steinman, C. 1992: 'Gaze out of Bounds: Men Watching Men on Television'. In: Craig, S. (ed.), *Men, Masculinity, and the Media.* Newbury Park, CA: Sage, 199–214.

Urry, J. 1990: *The Tourist Gaze: Leisure and Travel in Contemporary Societies.* London: Sage.

Warner, M. (ed.) 1993: *Fear of a Queer Planet: Queer Politics and Social Theory.* Minneapolis: University of Minnesota Press.

Wellman, B. et al. 1988: 'Networks as Personal Communities'. In: Wellman, B. and Berkowitz, S. (eds), *Social Structures: A Network Approach.* Cambridge: Cambridge University Press, 19–61.

Wittman, C. 1970: 'A Gay Manifesto'. In: Jay, K. and Young, A. (eds) 1972: *Out of the closets: Voices of Gay Liberation.* New York: Jove / HBJ, 1977. 330–42.

# Index

Note: The letter n after a page number means there is information in the notes on that page